To the memory of Dad and Clem,
and a better future for my children
and grandchildren

To my old friend
Stanley
Best wishes

Bernard

THE HEAT
OF THE KITCHEN

THE HEAT

OF THE KITCHEN

AN AUTOBIOGRAPHY

Bernard Donoughue

POLITICO'S

First published in Great Britain 2003 by
Politico's Publishing, an imprint of
Methuen Publishing Limited
215 Vauxhall Bridge Road
London SW1V 1EJ

3 5 7 9 10 8 6 4 2

A CIP catalogue record for this book is available from the British Library

ISBN 1 84275 051 8

Printed and bound in Great Britain by
St Edmundsbury Press

Contents

Preface   vii

Part I   PRIVATE LIVES 1934–1974

1   War Child   3
2   Family at War   23
3   Town Life   29
4   Teenage Clouds Lifting   37
5   Oxford Pleasures   54
6   American Adventures – and Seeking a Career   67
7   Academe, Politics, Finance – and Other Excitements   81

Part II   POLITICAL LIFE 1974–

8   Joining Harold Wilson   101
9   The Wilson Government in 1974   126
10   Wilson's Last Government   147
11   The Prime Minister Resigns   178
12   Harold and Marcia   193
13   Callaghan Makes his Mark   233
14   Quieter Times   251
15   Nemesis: The Winter of Discontent and Defeat   258
16   Career Turbulence: Murdoch and the City   282
17   More Turbulence: Working with Robert Maxwell   302
18   Quieter Times Again   324
19   Into Government Again: Minister of Farming and Food   336
20   Tony Blair *et al.*, Hunting and Private Pleasures   364

        Index   377

Preface

I have never thought of myself as someone of great consequence in British society, so I trust that it does not appear impertinent to produce an account of my life so far. I do so because I have been fortunate to participate on the inside of the upper levels of politics, the media, academe and the City, and to have worked with and closely observed some remarkable people. Placing these events and portraits on record may engage readers and assist future commentators. Also, in describing what it was like for one young boy to grow up in the poor working class of the 1930s, 1940s and early 1950s I have sought to recreate a picture of a colourful world rapidly slipping from collective memory.

I wish to thank for encouragement on this book my close and loyal friend Graham Greene, my wise publisher Sean Magee, and especially Sarah Berry for bringing light and joy to every day. I owe much to countless others who over the years have helped and guided me, many of whom feature in these memoirs. Amid all the excitements of public life, the private happiness which comes from loving family and true friends is to me what has always mattered most.

BD
Shurlock Row
April 2003

Part I

PRIVATE LIVES 1934–1974

One

WAR CHILD

My father in flat cap and overalls returning home from the factory, cycling over the little wooden bridge across the stream and scattering our clucking chickens.

The village postman delivering a rare letter direct to our tiny upstairs bedroom window, with my mother leaning out to collect it, her long dark hair flowing out over the window sill.

Mrs Dooley, our kindly neighbour whom I called 'Dooey', sitting at her cottage window spoiling me with 'treats'. Her son was locally spoken of with awe, being a vaudeville magician and entertainer using the impressive stage name of Benson Dulay.

And the steam expresses roaring over the brick viaduct towering above the village close to our cottage, carrying the London Midland and Scottish Railway from London Euston to the north.

The gallery of pictures in my mind has a multitude of images from later in my childhood. But those four are the only clear memories from Ashton, the south Northamptonshire village where I was born in 1934 – in a low, thatched stone cottage beside a stream, set back from the quiet country road among a group of old farm buildings.

Ashton is still an attractive small village. In 1934 it was really just a hamlet, with barely a hundred inhabitants, one pretty old pub, and a bus to Northampton every few hours. At its heart were several mixed arable and livestock farms giving employment to the village lads and men.

Its quiet rural idyll was regularly pierced by the shrieking trains, which to little me seemed to be way up in the sky. I have always liked railways. The roar of their power, the music of steam, the sense they give of escape to exciting faraway places, struck me early and stayed forever. I still prefer to take a train than travel by car.

Although my memories of Ashton are slim, the pictures of it in my mind's gallery are sunny and untroubled. My father – always 'Dad' to me – and I remained very attached to the village. For years after moving two miles from it to Roade, we often walked back there on a summer evening for a drink in the pub. One such evening, old Albert Wilson, a farm labourer who must have been over sixty, bet my father a pint that he could standing kick the (admittedly low) saloon bar ceiling. I watched with admiration as he won. Visits to country pubs in the surrounding villages of Hartwell, Hanslope, Stoke Bruerne and Alderton, as well as where we lived in Ashton and Roade, became an important part of my childhood. To me they were, and are, a very good thing. I noticed as a child that ordinary people with little to celebrate in their lives, even including my normally warring father and mother, were happy there. I am always troubled by the closure of country pubs and when in government did what little I could to defend them.

On our walks there my father told me that he had never wanted to leave Ashton and the little cottage by the stream. He was a man of simple but good taste and little ambition. It was my mother, then pregnant with my younger brother Clement, and always hankering for the brighter lights, who pressed to move to the larger village of Roade (though its lights were only modestly brighter, especially after the blackout of war descended). She was a resourceful woman and usually managed to get her way.

My father, Thomas Joseph Donoughue, met my mother Maude (often known as Molly) in the late 1920s when he was working in her mother's 'sausage and mash' shop at 17 Marefair, Northampton. He was just over thirty and she was sixteen. He was of Irish Catholic origin and told me that his family came over from County Kerry to settle with other Irish immigrants and find work in the Birmingham area. It is difficult absolutely to confirm this. He was not clear if this was shortly before or after he was born. Indeed, the factual evidence on my father's family background is thin. It broke up early and had no continuity of family knowledge.

There are no surviving documents or family relatives of him known to me; and as a child I was told virtually nothing of either parent's past. The little I know, I learned in the 1950s and 1960s when questioning my father on our Sunday jaunts to local village pubs. But he was not very forthcoming, as if his own childhood was a dark story suppressed deep within him. Most of what follows about him is based on those conversations over a pint of beer in Roade, Ashton, Hartwell or Stoke Bruerne. It may have been elaborated by him since he liked fanciful stories.

His own father died early and my dad's main recollection was of him fatally ill through an inability to pass water, sitting for hours on a chamber pot in their living room. His mother survived into the Second World War. Dad and his younger brother John – my uncle Jack – went to the funeral in Walsall but I do not think they had maintained much contact with her over many years. Dad left school and home very early and spent many years nomadically moving around England looking for jobs. He said he worked at one point as a miner in Gedling Colliery, Nottinghamshire, and also learned the factory trade of metal polisher in Rolls Royce of Derby. He tried for work in Liverpool and Sheffield, and in the late 1920s had walked and hitched his way down from the north to Northampton. There with great relief he found a vacancy as cook and washer-up in my grandmother's café. It determined the course of the rest of his life, not always happily; though for him with his background the options were never great.

He served in the First World War in the Royal Artillery and became a devoted supporter of the British Legion. On his arm was tattooed the badge of the Artillery, as well as a large red scar which he claimed was some kind of wound, but I have no idea if he saw active service. His only photograph from that time was of him, very handsome in uniform, and his 'pal' from Nottingham going off to the war.

On joining up, the two recruits visited a gypsy fortune teller and she forecast (which was not hard to guess given the casualty rates on the western front, though I have no evidence Dad went there!) that only one of them would return home alive. In 1919 they safely demobilised, but on returning to Nottingham they went swimming and his friend somehow drowned. This confirmed Dad's firm belief in the psychic side of life: in fortune tellers, in ouija boards to contact the spirits of the departed, and above all that there was no point in persisting in any endeavour if the fairies or 'the little people' were against him and it.

He was convinced that much in life is determined by fate – or usually bad luck in his case. The 'Donoughue luck', always ill, was a frequent source of comment – and I often saw the point. It may also have strengthened his delightful capacity to fantasise (which made me instinctively wary of some of his recollections in the pub).

At some point soon after the First World War, I think in Nottingham, he married a Catholic lady and they had a child. That union did not last. When I asked why he never obtained a divorce, he simply said 'because of the Catholicism', though I was not clear whether he meant his Catholicism, hers, or both of their beliefs. Consequently he and my mother could not marry, though they would have wished to.

Subsequently his experiences of the economic slump made him disenchanted with his Roman Catholic Church because he felt that it cared too little for the unemployed; in contrast he always praised the Salvation Army for feeding him soup and bread when out of work. His reactions to the slump led to a wider personal bitterness, combined with strong left-wing political prejudices. But he did not completely abandon his Church. A very tall Catholic priest, Father

Galvin, used to visit our home in Roade and say to me: 'You are a typical Irish boy' and 'You will be coming to mass with me one day.' He was a little ahead of his and my time. In fact I sometimes enjoyed attending the fine Norman Anglican church in the village, where the excellent vicar Norman Husbands earned my support by giving children books as Christmas presents. We did not have books at home. But Father Galvin was right in the long term about my ultimate spiritual destination. The church usually shrewdly takes a long view.

Most important to me was Dad's total commitment to the welfare of his children, and especially his two sons, Clem and myself, to whom he sacrificed the whole of his later life after my mother left him. He was no saint, but I was and always will be proud of him. I do not believe that any such hardworking and decent man in such a prosperous country as Britain should have had to endure such a harsh life. My politics, and my determination to improve my lot, were formed by watching him.

My mother was quite a different proposition: ebullient, raucous, dynamic, insensitive, flamboyant, funny, noisy, extrovert, melodramatic, lively company, selfish, vulgar, and often making quite an impression, good or bad, on first meeting. She was good looking in a dark gypsy way. But her most striking characteristic then was the demonic energy driving and animating her often wild personality. This latter quality probably derived from her own mother – my 'granny Andrews', the only grandparent I ever met – who was very dominating and even in her late sixties ran her Northampton 'sausage and mash' shop like a slave ship. Granny was quite an entrepreneur, founding the first autobus service in Northampton. She had driven out her husband, my grandfather, who was reputed to be intelligent and sensitive, not qualities in great demand at 17 Marefair (he apparently left home in a horse-drawn carriage, carrying with him a few items of fine furniture which he enjoyed collecting). His domestic replacement, named Walmsley, who struck me as a loathsome oaf, had been stripped of his uniform and dismissed from the Northampton police force for improper behaviour.

My mother sometimes took me into granny's café on our way back from Saturday shopping in Northampton to catch back to Roade the ancient train with a funny tall chimney which then ran forwards one way and backwards the other. The two women often exchanged sharp words, with no trace of family warmth between them. To a small child like me, standing nervously at the counter hoping, usually without success, to be offered a plate of delicious mushy peas, my mother and her mother made a ferocious pair. And to this day, when offered sausage and mash, I can smell that steamy café in Marefair and hear Granny Andrews shouting her orders. Like her daughter, she rarely showed any genuine affection to me. In time I concluded that I did not like either of them very much.

Children can of course be very cruel and unforgiving in their judgements. I realise now – looking back with hopefully more understanding – that my mother had a hard life, bearing four children by the age of twenty-eight, with little money or pleasure and living in poor housing conditions. She worked ceaselessly at home and also took outside jobs on top of that to raise more cash. But at that time, and later, I found her an uncaring and often violent mother. Although she sometimes expressed public appreciation of me, especially if I had achieved something which impressed others, I have no memory of her ever kissing me or showing affection in the privacy of our home, though surely there must have been such times which I have forgotten. I certainly have many recollections – many pictures in my mental gallery – of her berating and even beating me. (This was also one of my brother Clement's main memories.)

One afternoon when I was nine or ten, on my return from school she sent me all the way back to the Co-op at the other end of the village to buy some sugar. There were other shops nearer but the Co-op paid a 'divi', which must not be missed. I reluctantly did this shopping and on the way back joined some 'mates' playing football in the High Street, foolishly forgetting her needs and the passing of time. Suddenly my mother appeared, hair streaming, rushing down the hill past Sturgess's farmyard and screaming abuse. She dragged me up the hill, kicking and punching me on the way. It was not particularly painful, but worst was the humiliation in front of my friends. She liked to do things dramatically.

I then swore a private oath that I would get away from her as soon as possible – not realising that the opportunity would arise in sad circumstances before too many years had passed. Around that time I also began a lifetime habit during such uncomfortable experiences of focussing entirely on the brighter future, planning little treats to look forward to – holidays, visits to the cinema, football or racing, or just thinking of a warm summer ahead – so as to get through the present discomfort without noticing or being hurt. I still apply this technique and it works well for visits to the dentist, or in dark and gloomy Januarys, though the future golden horizon which I now contemplate is somewhat curtailed by advancing years.

We moved from Ashton to Roade in 1939, father and mother, my elder sister Molly, myself and baby Clem. First we lived briefly next to the church in a row of small red brick and slated-roofed houses with long gardens in the front. But we quickly moved up the hill to what was to be my home for the next fourteen years: a detached house named 'Waverley'. It was at the southern edge of the village, next to Tommy Cooper's garage on the road to Stony Stratford. Tommy's huge and untended back garden was a playground wonderland for young children, full of chickens inhabiting and laying eggs in the wrecks of ancient cars with prestigious names like Bugatti, Railton and Sunbeam Talbot, which if preserved today would be worth a fortune.

Like the Ashton cottage, our house was close to the LMS railway, so my childhood remained full of the sound of steam. I would sit for hours at my bedroom window watching the trains. At night I could hear the roar of the expresses rushing out of the deep Blisworth embankment towards Euston and – something I still now hear in my memory – the cosy huffing, chuntering and clanging of the goods engines and wagons shunting in the factory sidings. Close by in the Railway Cottages, unbeknown to me, was the baby Glenys Parry, future wife of my party leader Neil Kinnock.

Steam locomotives were to me a magnificent creation. In the holidays I sat with village friends – my 'mates' – on the nearby railway embankment and collected train numbers, excited when the signals on the fast lines indicated an express, possibly the Royal Scot, was racing towards Roade. Sometimes we travelled, sandwiches in our pockets, to Rugby or Wolverton, to train-spot on more exciting platforms. One of my earliest embankment memories is from the summer of 1940, watching the troop trains passing painfully and slowly north, packed with soldier survivors from Dunkirk, many bandaged. The sense of exhaustion and defeat exuded from the carriages. I was already following the progress of the war on the radio and in our newspaper, the *Daily Herald*. Through the rosy mist of Churchill's rhetoric, I sensed that there had been a terrible British disaster.

'Waverley' was regrettably not as impressive as its name suggested; indeed, it might more appropriately have been named 'Dodgy' or 'Rocky'. The house occupied a small plot, with a few feet of overgrown garden in the front, bordered by a rotting wooden fence which Dad refused to mend because the house wasn't ours, just rented. Beyond the road at the front was Tarpy Denton's vegetable garden and then the railway station below. At the rear, crowded in by our neighbour's garden, was a scruffy yard with lines of rabbit hutches hosting victims for special Sunday dinners and a tumbledown coal shed made of old planks with a corrugated iron roof.

Waverley had been built hurriedly after the First World War with single brick walls at the ground floor and thin asbestos sheets encasing the two upstairs bedrooms. These sheets had shrunk over time and gaps appeared between them so the wind blew through. In fact the house was a slum even before we occupied it, officially condemned as unfit for human habitation by the council on the eve of war. As such, the rent was 'controlled' and remained at seven shillings and sixpence per week during our fourteen years of occupancy.

Over time, especially after my mother departed, Waverley's condition progressively deteriorated. My father, though a passable cook, was not a great handyman. I took after him in the latter defect though not in the former virtue. Downstairs were four tiny rooms: the two at the front included the 'best', and at the back were a kitchen and living room, containing the only working fire, where we sat and ate in the evenings. The kitchen had a sink and the house's only cold water tap, together with a quaint coal-fired copper for boiling the clothes-wash on Mondays. There was no bathroom. We children had our weekly rinse in a tin bath on the kitchen floor filled with one helping of hot water between us from the copper. Beside the kitchen back door was the lavatory. To flush it required a bowl of water carried from the tap, which when small I found quite heavy. Mains water had just been introduced in 1937, but there was no mains sewage and the lavatory drained into a cesspit near the back door. This lavatory was for a time my favourite room in the house, since I could escape to it and lock the door against the surrounding clamour in general, and my mother in particular. There I usually read the *Daily Herald*, absorbing its Labour sympathies in appropriate tranquillity; when torn into square pieces the newspaper also served as the family's only toilet paper.

Later the lav became less relaxing for me. Waverley had no proper foundations and over time the damp rose from the earth below and rotted the floorboards. This happened with particular severity around the pedestal of the lavatory and a worrying gap appeared below my feet as I sat reading, opening to a terrifying darkness. In fact there was just soil beneath, but I was always petrified that I would one day fall, trousers down, into the hellish sewage void below. Consequently I sat as lightly as possible on the seat and remained there only briefly. For the rest of my adult life I have greatly appreciated lavatories which are clean, with abundant soft tissues, and above all very secure on the floor.

Our back door – for some reason I never established, the normal entry point to the house – was a piece of art. Like most of Waverley's woodwork, and especially the window frames, it had warped in the damp, finally to the point where it could no longer be locked. This did not matter from the security point, since there was little of value inside to steal. Also in those wartime and early post-war days, crime and theft were virtually unknown in the village. People had natural respect for the property of others. It was common for villagers to 'knock and drop in' to one another's households.

Homes were then open parts of the village community, not bunkers to escape to from it. The warped back door mattered not as a way in for burglars but as another of many points of entry for the cold winter winds. Waverley provided barely enough space for our growing family and was soon full to overflowing. To the five of us – and baby Sheila made six in 1942 – were added the evacuees. I remember the special buses arriving at the village in 1939 with groups of frightened London children, some crying, as if to a foreign land. Many had never set foot in the countryside or seen a farm animal before. They were decanted to the factory canteen, where the arrangements for their distribution were organised by Mr Tarry, the managing director of the Simplex factory.

I went with my mother (perhaps inspired as much by the special payments per child as by sympathy or patriotism) to pick our two. The evacuee children stood around pathetically clutching their few belongings and labelled like chickens, being inspected and fingered by village women considering their choice. Mother took almost the final two sad mites, just a little older than me. In fact they were a delightful and well brought up brother and sister, Bill and Linda Laing. As I recall, they came from 66 Kilravock Street, London W10. All five of us children slept in the upstairs front bedroom.

I quickly took to the Laings and listened with fascination to Bill's tales of life near the rough Harrow Road, where the local gangs of youths clearly made our village gang seem by comparison like a set of Etonian gents. They also had an elder brother in the navy who made a lasting impact by bringing them a native pigskin shield from Borneo. Best of all was the weekly package of comics, *Beano* and *Dandy*, which their parents sent and I shared, the first such exciting reading I had enjoyed. 'Desperate Dan' long remained a hero for me, though not necessarily a good role model.

Sadly for me, the Laings returned to London when the worst of the Blitz was over in 1941. But house space remained under pressure as they were promptly replaced by more evacuees. Mr and Mrs Greenfield were quite 'posh' by our standards; they came I think from Highgate, with a pretty daughter Jean of around my age. All three slept in the downstairs front room, previously our 'best' and so rarely used, which had now acquired a double bed and a cot, and the fire was lit in winter. So by 1942, when my sister Sheila was born, we were four adults and five children in that scruffy little house, with one lavatory, one tap, no bathroom, and no other running water. It was quite noisy and not very elegant, with frequent queues for the lavatory. It must have been an unpleasant shock for the very proper Greenfields.

This pressure on space was eased tragically when Mr Greenfield died of a brain disease, probably meningitis. He ended up in Northampton Hospital, but for many days was terribly ill in our front room. He had served in the Indian Army, with intelligence connections, and lay in bed raving loudly in some unintelligible Indian language, which I found quite disturbing as I sat in the next room. I remember his wife returning from Northampton at breakfast time and telling my mother, 'he is gone', then bursting into uncontrollable tears. It was my first contact with death and real grief. Afterwards she burned in the fireplace a pile of notebooks full of handwritten code, which she said were his secret diaries of military espionage on the Indian frontier. The Greenfields were a charming and well-mannered family and I missed them when the widow and daughter quickly left to go back to London. Only war had forced them to live – and him to die – in the front room of a grubby, noisy, condemned house full of strangers and with one water tap. Not for the first time I noticed that life can be rough and unfair regardless of people's virtues and true deserts.

The space vacated by the Greenfields was not empty for long. It was quickly and cheerfully filled by my Irish auntie Joan and then her son Bill. I had first met and liked them on a holiday visit to Ireland at the beginning of the war (the only childhood holiday I recall). My uncle and auntie, on my mother's side, lived with cousins Bill and Marjorie in Newcastle, County Wicklow, where uncle worked as some kind of engineer in the big TB hospital, having moved from County Mayo, where Marjorie was born.

Our visit to their pretty Wicklow home and garden is one of my earliest memories, giving the gallery in my mind some happy pictures. The ferry from Liverpool to Dublin was not too good, a converted cattle boat, slow and smelly, with lots of passengers being sick. We sailed in constant fear of German submarines. But our stay beside the Wicklow mountains was idyllic. Auntie Joan spoiled us with unfamiliar affection and wonderful food. I am convinced the sun shone every day.

The peak moment for me was travelling to the sea at nearby Greystones in a trap pulled by a donkey. I did not want to leave this magical place to return to the dingy clamour of Waverley. Ireland became established in my youthful mind as a very good thing, as it remains today after many happy visits. My cousin Marjorie, with her soft Irish accent, is still a lovely and treasured friend.

Cousin Bill brought a real sense of Irish fun to Waverley as well as reinforcing the general noise level. He took a job on the railway, working in the important Roade junction signal box, crucial to marshalling the flow of London rail traffic between the slow loop line via Northampton and the fast tracks to Liverpool and the west of Scotland. Bill worked very long hours and was often in the box all day on Sundays. My mother, who was very fond of him, decided he must not be deprived of his Sunday dinner (lunch). The problem of how to transport a plate of cooked meat and vegetables half a mile to the signal box was easily resolved: Bernard had to carry it. So I went, hot plate in hand, across the railway bridge and down Station Road, watching the signals, calculating when I could safely hurry across four main railway lines, two carrying expresses, and then along the clinker path beside the tracks to the high wooden steps up to the box, often with hot gravy running down my hands and wrists, and above all petrified of dropping Bill's precious dinner. I was only nine or ten years old and shall never forget (nor forgive) that hair-raising experience.

To be honest, I was also excited and grateful to get to see inside a real signal box. I listened to Bill take messages from the next box down the line, warning that an express had cleared that section and was racing towards us. I watched him pull the lever to change the signals to go or to shift the crossover tracks at the junction. From that experience I later appreciated James Callaghan's description of running 10 Downing Street as like a railway signal box: channelling Whitehall policy-making onto the right committee tracks and to the correct departmental destination. Even so, those Sunday dinner expeditions were actually very dangerous. Later I would never have dreamt of exposing my own ten-year-old children to such risks.

Fortunately not all my young life was spent inside Waverley. My fourteen years growing up in the wider village of Roade – from 1939 until I took the train from the village station to Oxford in 1953, carrying all my possessions in one old case – are burned in my memory and have shaped me as much as did experiences at home. Many snapshot recollections stem from there and most are happy.

Roade is old, mentioned in the Domesday Book of 1086 as 'Rode', meaning 'the cleared land'. There is believed to have been a settlement on the site in Roman times. It is set in rolling south Northamptonshire countryside, then made up of small family farms close to the territory of the Grafton Hunt, the beautiful spectacle of which streaming across fields ensured that I would never support a ban on hunting. (The Duke of Grafton owned land and houses in the village from 1673 and was Lord of the Manor until selling out in 1913.) I imagine that Roade had earlier been quite a pretty farming village. By 1800 a survey showed it had 'almost 370 inhabitants, chiefly agriculturist'.

But the construction of the railway cutting in 1838 brought a rapid increase in population, in houses from 100 to 150 and in alehouses from three to six. By 1900 only some 15 per cent of the men worked in agriculture. The opening of the Simplex factory in 1923 accelerated this industrial coating of the village and the spread of housing estates: the first council houses were built in 1919 and there were 250 by 1957. When we moved to Roade in 1939 the population was already 700.

However, Roade's original heart was and to me still is handsome. Lying in a deep hollow were rows of stone cottages, some thatched, some roofed in slate, around the fine Norman church of St Mary's. Through it straggled a long high street, fanning out at each end on five roads towards Northampton, Stony Stratford, Ashton, Hartwell and Blisworth. At each of the exits to these places was a farm, preserving for a little longer the village's original rural character. Several of my childhood friends left school at fourteen to work on these farms. I played on farmer Sturgess's hayricks, helped with the harvests, followed the horse-drawn threshing machines to catch rabbits for the pot, watched the horses and carts carrying sheaves to be stacked, with sunburned farmhands and 'landgirls' resting on top with their pitchforks. I also earned a paltry tuppence halfpenny an hour for picking potatoes in the cold autumn fields. The recollection of my aching back and freezing fingers deterred me from ever again growing or digging potatoes.

The centres of village activity where most of the gossip was conducted were its shops and pubs. In 1940–45, there were four general shops, two butchers, a post office, a baker (until recently three), a shoemaker, a newspaper vendor, a greengrocer, a blacksmith, a carpenter and a large Co-op, stretching along the length of the high street. Two old men cycled the village selling eggs and milk. 'Snocky' Glen, our resident mole-catcher, carried a vicious ferret in his deep overcoat pocket and used to hang a dead rabbit on the policeman's doorknocker just to show that poaching was still being practised successfully.

Our four local pubs were The George and The Swan (ale served straight from the barrel in the back room), with The Cock Inn and The White Hart at the other end of the village. In my rosy memory Roade was then abuzz with life and activity. As a child I would meet and greet dozens of villagers as I ran and played between home and school.

Today the village has changed dramatically. It has more than trebled in size to over 2,000. Its inhabitants are much more prosperous. With its fine communal facilities it won the prize as Northamptonshire's Village of the Year in 1994. But it may not be all for the better. Many of the village institutions which served my childhood have gone. Only three shops, a newsagent, a butcher and a more recent pharmacist remain. The Swan and The White Hart pubs have closed, as has the railway station. Jim Howard's magical shop – the centre of social life for us boys – has become a dismal bookmaker's. Buses are rare and often empty. Open fields such as Church Croft where we played are full of densely built private housing.

The imposing Victorian vicarage set in acres of chestnut trees, where we held the village fetes, has bowling greens but has been absorbed into the factory estate; the vicar lives in a modern detached house. The gardens of the George Inn, where our and other families sat drinking and playing on summer evenings, is an asphalt car park. Recently I walked from one end of the village to the other and saw not a soul on the street. Yet no doubt many aspects of life there have improved. Most people seem to have cars. And nobody has to live in a slum like Waverley.

The main agent of social and economic change in the village has been the factory, which originally made polish and then piano parts – polish workers such as 'Darkie' Ashby returned home with blackened faces. It went bankrupt and in 1923 was bought by Cyril Cripps, a former worker there who successfully focussed on the engineering side. The factory prospered in the war making munitions and boomed with the post-war motor car expansion. The factory buildings spread – some older villagers said 'like cancer' – to cover the fields either side of the railway line and eastwards to the Ashton road. Mr Cripps steadily bought up the local farms until he owned much of the land around the village; it came to be farmed professionally and village boys went instead to work in his factory, as did hundreds from the surrounding area. This expanding labour force needed housing and there was a dramatic expansion of council and private housing, especially to the south where we lived. The old village was steadily smothered. But as a boy I did not fully understand that process and enjoyed both the old and the new.

By the 1960s Cripps was a multi-millionaire, contributing generously to Nottingham and Cambridge Universities and the Conservative Party – which rewarded him with a knighthood. More recently the factory has suffered some of the vicissitudes afflicting the British manufacturing industry. Cripps, the classic self-made man, was shy, shrewd, almost elegant, and had a commendable sense of social responsibility. Most evenings he walked his dog around the village, like an old-fashioned squire, which indeed he effectively became. The villagers, more and more of them his employees, treated him with awe. My father, however, strongly resented him. This was partly out of envy for his success, then as now a predominant British characteristic, and partly from his left-wing political instincts, which opposed all capitalists.

He often told me bitterly that when he joined the factory around 1930 as a metal polisher, Cripps was only just setting out to establish himself. The small factory was dilapidated, with rain coming through the roof. My father was one of his earliest employees, with a low 'clocking-in' card number (later they ran into thousands). At that time Cripps mixed with his workers and told them that they were joining together in a common venture to build success. He certainly provided secure employment and paid higher wages than the local alternatives. To most villagers that is what mattered most after the terrible years of the slump. However, my father resented the whole indignity of manual labour in a dirty factory. During the war he often worked night shifts and I recall the excitement of visiting him late in the evening and seeing him dressed in rubber overalls and gloves as he dipped metal flare-cases into vats of boiling acid. The sulphuric smell was horrible, he suffered many small burns from splashing acid, and amid the heat, lights and fires against a dark background, it seemed to me like a picture from hell.

Dad also felt that the impersonal and uncaring side of capitalism was illustrated when he finally retired in the 1960s, after some thirty years of service. With Cripps a feted multi-millionaire and the factory a huge success, Dad, like others of the original employees, simply received his departure 'cards', with no acknowledgement of his contribution. I absorbed the political implications of all that, while always respecting Cripps for his remarkable business achievements and his great help with the restoration of the village church and local charities. At a key point in my later school career he generously helped me.

The village was a safe and friendly environment during the war to which I escaped to play morning, noon and night when not at school. Its communal life provided very happy times for me. Even as a child, on my own or with my mates, I loved roaming the local countryside where I knew every path, track and field. The village farmyards were our playgrounds and we always joined in harvesting, helped by the light evenings of double summertime in the war. I often walked or cycled the two miles to Stoke Bruerne to watch the working barges or to fish or swim in the Grand Union Canal or in the nearby River Tove. My elder sister Molly, recently looking back after thirty years of our separation, said that her main recollection of me as a child was of my 'never being at home; always out in the village or over the fields.' She told me that she was frequently dispatched by our irate mother 'to search the fields and fetch you home.'

Above all I grew to love any kind of sport, as I still do. Returning home from the village school, we boys would lay down our jackets as goalposts in the high street and play football with any old tennis ball. There was then little traffic to disturb us, except for the regular United Counties bus or when the factory blasted its hooter at 5.30, releasing a stream of cycling workers and summoning us all home to tea. Most villagers never dreamed of being able to afford a car, and petrol rationing meant that only a privileged few – the doctor, the headmaster, the garage owner, and of course Mr Cripps – had petrol coupons for driving. For transport, the rest of us walked, cycled or took one of the always crowded double-decker buses running between Northampton and Stony Stratford (also single-deckers to Hanslope, low enough to get under Ashton's railway bridge). I can still recite the United Counties daily bus timetable – that precious vehicle to the modest excitements of Northampton, or to friends, football and fishing in neighbouring villages.

Village life was made more exceptional then because of the unique context of a war with Nazi Germany. Indeed, together with the importance of my family, and of Roade and its school, the other great formative influence on my childhood (and hence on my manhood) was the Second World War. Growing up in it involved some deprivations but was to me in many ways a privilege. The constant sense of excitement and danger, and the daily crises threatening the whole nation's future, sharpened all our sensibilities. It forged a strong community sense in our village, as in every other.

Personally, I also enjoyed the war because it made life very interesting (at least for those of us who were not seriously at risk – nine village men were killed in the war, unusually more than in 1914–18). Vera Lynn spoke for most of us when she sang 'There'll be blue birds over the white cliffs of Dover' and 'It's a lovely day tomorrow'.

When the war finally ended in 1945, I was at first exhilarated by our success, but quickly worried because, as I asked my father, 'What will now be in the news?' I followed wartime events closely on the BBC wireless and in our *Daily Herald*. Today any book or programme on the period still fascinates me. Almost my first wireless memory is of Chamberlain's tinny voice announcing the declaration of war on Germany. We listened as a family to Churchill's famous broadcasts, though my father did not like him, recalling that 'he broke our general strike'. I pinned on the wall a map and drew on it the lines of the German advances and retreats in Russia and North Africa. I of course swallowed much of the British propaganda on our great achievements, necessary to keep up morale.

But I was aware that many events had not gone well for us: that the British army had inexplicably collapsed before the German onslaught in France in 1940 and in North Africa in 1941 and against the Japanese in 1942; and that even our famous warships like the *Hood* and the *Prince of Wales* seemed to sink easily. I had heard from several elder brothers of village mates that our tanks and field guns were not as good as the Germans' and that our army vehicles kept breaking down. The future problems of our manufacturing and engineering industries were already exposed on the battlefields.

So although I traced on my wall-maps with joy and confidence the Allied invasion of Europe in 1944–5, I sensed that not everything was proceeding perfectly and saw that America, Russia and even beaten Germany were basically more powerful than us. I was also stunned to learn the horrendous details of the concentration camps, which stamped on my mind a sense of previously unimaginable evil. It was a searing early political experience sitting watching those horrendous newsreels in the Savoy cinema. It steered me subconsciously towards the political left. It also made me for the rest of my life instinctively sympathetic towards Jewish people, even though I then knew none, and later towards the infant democracy of Israel.

When the Germans surrendered in May 1945, I went out into the village streets after school waving a little Union Jack which I had optimistically saved for such an eventuality. I felt surprised and foolish when I did not find Roade full of similar celebrations. They were reserved for the final surrender of Japan in August, by which time I was away living in Northampton.

Actually the military side of war rarely touched us directly in Roade, though I was personally made aware of its painful side when my uncle and cousin were killed in London in 1944 by one of the early flying bombs. During the 1940–41 Blitz we sometimes thought we could see a red glow in the night sky sixty miles south down the railway lines to the capital. One night a German plane, missing its railway or factory target, dropped a string of bombs in the fields facing and behind Waverley. The house rocked on its non-foundations and lost a few slates. I felt very proud of being involved in the real thing of war. Next morning I went early to inspect the bomb craters and found pieces of shrapnel which I kept for years in my special drawer of treasured possessions, together with some regimental badges and a few bullets.

The skies above Roade were constantly full of the roar of allied bombers – American Flying Fortresses very high during the day, British Lancasters lumbering through the night. On a stormy afternoon in June 1944, returning home from school, I heard a loud bang in the sky. Looking up, I saw a Wellington bomber begin to disintegrate, its wings slowly peeling off and rubber dinghies floating down with the debris. It had been struck by lightning, and all five of its crew killed. We found a body in an orchard, my first sight of death. On his flying helmet was the name 'Flight Sergeant Andrews, Royal Canadian Air Force'. Perhaps the most vivid military picture in my memory from that time was sitting one Sunday afternoon on the front step with my father drinking tea and eating with a pin a plate of winkles, when a German Focke-Wulf fighter bomber came sweeping up the railway tracks and zoomed low over us, causing Dad to spill his winkles all over the steps. I could see the pilot. It was my closest brush with the enemy.

Less threatening military fun was provided by our village Home Guard. Exercising with fireworks and blank cartridges, they had much in common with the famous television series *Dad's Army*, including the clear class distinctions between the leaders and the led. I am not sure they would ever have frightened the German panzers, but they certainly entertained us. More seriously impressive were the preparations for the invasion of Europe in 1944. I watched in awe the concentration of troops and armour, much of it Canadian, gathered in the fields and woods around the village. One day, returning to school after lunch, I made my way up the High Street through tanks and troops making a mock attack on the village with dummy shells and smoke bombs.

Equally striking and personally more instructive was one evening when a line of British army lorries parked on the verge opposite our house. I was invited into a dark cab by a friendly soldier – and followed in by Mary, a sixteen-year-old village girl I knew well. Innocently pre-pubescent, I could not quite understand what she was soon vigorously doing to him, but was seriously impressed by my first sight of a resplendent male member. After that I always viewed her with wary respect for her unsuspected worldly knowledge. The war educated and stimulated us intensely in many directions.

But the war mattered most to us in Roade not in any military fashion, but for the various ways in which it affected our daily civilian lives. Life became much more regimented (thus preparing the way for Labour's post-war planned economy and welfare state). For instance, war meant food rationing. This improved our diets, with fewer sweets and greater reliance on vegetables grown by our fathers 'digging for victory' in our gardens and allotments. But it also meant endless shopping queues, with frequent disappointments and occasional excitements – as when the first bananas of the war arrived at Tarpy Denton's greengrocery and we queued for hours for a single bunch.

My mother often sent me shopping, especially if she required something from the Co-op at the distant end of the village. I soon learned that wartime shopping required patience, stamina and inside knowledge of which particular shop momentarily stocked whichever rare treat. I clearly lacked these virtues and acquired then a distaste for shopping, selfishly trying ever afterwards to avoid it, to the understandable irritation of the women in my adult life. To my shame, there have been years when, excluding the minor purchases of newspapers and pints of beer, I have managed to do no serious shopping whatsoever. There are very long gaps between my purchase of 'good' shoes and I am usually measured at home for suits. Shirts, socks and woollens are acquired erratically as Christmas or birthday presents. Somehow the so-called consumer society passed me by.

Perhaps the greatest social impact of the war on our village was the resulting large influx of evacuees. Most, like our lovely Laings, came in the autumn of 1939. Other evacuees came later from Coventry after it was devastated in a

Luftwaffe firestorm: I heard those German bombers droning for hours over our home towards their target. One Coventry family, named Gardiner, opened a shop in a little house in Roade High Street, using remnants of their blitzed home, including their children's toys, as opening stock.

These outsiders changed the character of our village, greatly increasing the population, filling the school classrooms to bursting, and giving to Roade a more cosmopolitan and urban feel. They included the first Jew I had ever knowingly met. At first the evacuees were resented as intruders by the villagers, seeming too slick and aggressive by our slow standards. In return, they laughed at our broad accents and rough country habits. But that tension soon passed. They quickly integrated into village life and livened it up immensely, bringing a city sharpness and providing more boys (and girls) with whom to play. Many stayed on after the war, identifiable only by their fading London twang. I loved our two, Bill and Linda, and I formed a close friendship with another, Geoffrey Smurthwaite. He lived with his mother, his granny and an old village widow along the Northampton road, and his father was killed at Dunkirk in 1940. I went to play with him nearly every day. His mother was exceptionally kind to me, feeding me, taking me to the cinema in Northampton and providing some of the maternal affection which was severely rationed at Waverley. This was the first of several outside homes and families to which I attached myself over the years. It became a habit for me to drop in on these 'home-from-homes', with their alternative 'mums', at first as a child to play, later for companionship and conversation. I missed the Smurthwaites terribly when they returned to London before the war's end – though I did memorably see them once again in 1945, as will be related below.

By far the happiest centre of my village life was Roade School. I loved it from my first day's attendance and it became to me a haven of affection, interest and friendliness – and especially of physical warmth in cold weather. Unlike home, it had great hot pipes and radiators and, most importantly, books. It also had some alternative 'mums'. Physically, the school was a single-storey brick building, built as a Board School in 1876, shortly before education became compulsory. It had four classrooms, three playgrounds, and a wonderful big garden behind, and lay nearly a mile away from Waverley, at the opposite end of the village towards the exits to Ashton and Hartwell and closer to the Co-op, where my mother did most of our shopping.

The infants' class which I joined in 1939 was under the tall, beautiful and saintly Miss Dainty, a farmer's daughter from Collingtree with whom I instantly fell in love. After that, for the six- to nine-year-olds, came smart but fierce Mrs Watson. Then kindly Mrs Hobbs, with a stiff leg, prepared the next batch for the scholarship exam at eleven. The top class was full of those who failed the scholarship, kept until fourteen under the iron grip (and often the cane) of our headmaster, Mr Maxwell.

Joe Maxwell was a handsome and charismatic Scot with rich wavy hair and something of a reputation as a lothario. Mothers doted on him. Along with the vicar, the policeman and inevitably Mr Cripps, he was one of the dominant characters who took a leadership role in the village community. He was viewed as a kind of god by the children, teachers and parents alike. He was very musical and made music a feature of school life.

Such was the lack of traffic in the village, and the general social safety of those times, that from the age of six I safely walked or ran unescorted over a mile to and from school. No delivery by a 'school run' then; though for a brief period the new evacuee infants were collected and shepherded through the village, Pied Piper fashion, by lovely old Mrs Ovington, known universally as 'Mrs O'. Sometimes I joined this delightful cockney babble. But soon I had my own friends to walk with: sometimes directly up and down the High Street; sometimes taking the back paths behind the church; or even home through the noisy factory and up the Station Road. We would play games in the streets or drop in on friends' houses for tea (nobody ever came to mine, which was anyway at the far extremity of the route). My objective was to stay out playing until the last possible moment.

Some children came to Roade school from the neighbouring villages of Ashton, Hartwell and Courteenhall. If missing or unable to get on a bus ('Five only standing!' was the dreaded conductor's cry), they often walked several miles home. In bad weather this could be tough. Some winters, the local roads and even hedges were obliterated by snow. Then I enjoyed our sledging in the recreation field or frozen Church Croft – though I already suffered my life-long vulnerability to bronchial colds, often going to school sneezing and wheezing, or being kept at home in bed.

The influx of evacuees into the village meant that the school was overcrowded throughout my time there, the hundred evacuee children outnumbering the village boys and girls. For a while they were taught for half the day and we for the other half, and extra classes had to be held elsewhere in the Church Institute, in the Wesleyan and Baptist chapels, and even at the George Inn. None of us locals complained about all this, pleased to have more mates and less personal scrutiny from our dedicated but overworked teachers. When I was in Mrs Hobbs' scholarship class we had upwards of fifty children. Much of her work was unavailing, trying to teach reading, writing and 'sums' to a mixed and reluctant bunch. There were afternoon sessions when we were all, boys and girls, expected to learn sewing and knitting. Regrettably I showed little talent for either.

But I made reasonably quick progress with the more academic pursuits, inspired from the beginning by sitting on Miss Dainty's elegant lap, she stroking my long blond curls while I moved my finger from word to word, reading slowly aloud. That is a mind's picture I treasure.

By the time I reached Mrs Hobbs' packed scholarship class, I was ahead of my contemporaries on the simple basics. She would set me a week's written work on Monday and, when I quickly finished, left me to choose and read books from the cupboard in front of her desk. I loved simple history and military books, such as *With Marlborough to Malplaquet* and any Biggles. Curiously, I have no memory, then or earlier, of ever reading any of the traditional children's classics such as Arthur Ransome, Enid Blyton, Beatrix Potter or Lewis Carroll. This is probably because there were never any books at home. I do not recall my mother ever reading to me, or indeed either her or my father ever opening any book – at least until I wrote and published my own first book in 1963. Dad then ploughed through his first book, a dry and testing volume on the American War of Independence which cannot have encouraged him to take up the reading habit. I did not read wonderful *Wind in the Willows*, or the more puzzling Alices, until I was over sixty, and then saw what I had missed as a child.

By the age of ten and supposedly ready for the scholarship exam, I was moved up into Mr Maxwell's top class, no doubt to free up desk space in Mrs Hobbs's bulging classroom. He gave us an unforgettable experience, perhaps more in leadership than education. I was always treated as different by him and shielded from the whippy cane lurking behind the glowing black iron stove.

Joe left me to read in a corner while in a deep Scottish burr he addressed this bunch of rough but amiable reprobates – none with any further educational targets, just waiting impatiently to get out to work, some barely literate – on life, jobs, music, football, gardening and whatever else took his fancy that particular day. He was fascinating and captivating and in his own way did a superb job. Some days he took the lads (I was usually excused and left to read) into the expansive school gardens where they happily grew flowers and vegetables, developing useful skills for later life, from which Joe's kitchen was a major immediate beneficiary.

His pupils loved him and respected his authority. They were happy and well prepared for the working lives they soon expected to lead on the farms or mostly in the factory. None to my knowledge felt 'abused' or traumatised by his occasional physical discipline. Some, such as John 'Nipper' Coles and Walt 'Bucky' Ashby, remained good friends of mine as I grew up. (They always used my nickname 'Bubbles' even when I was quite old.) We spent many happy and some mischievous times together until I left the village. I have known cleverer people since, but none with better hearts and more generous spirits. I always believed that government and politics should be about them and their needs more than the pushy media folk in Hampstead and Islington.

I did not complete my final year in Maxwell's top class. In that last summer term, my mother intervened in my life with characteristic drama to sweep me away from the village which I loved. The domestic problems which had been simmering in the background while I spent as much time as possible out of the house playing in the village and the fields, now exploded on to front stage. I was never to enter Joe Maxwell's school again – though after a disruptive couple of years' interlude away with my mother, I did manage to return and with my father recover again the village and its fields.

Two

FAMILY AT WAR

As the war progressed, my mother grew increasingly restless and impatient with the constraints of domestic life in Roade. She wanted to move on, believing the brighter lights and greener grass were always over the other side of the hedge, or certainly down the road on her home ground of Northampton.

The relationship between her and my father grew increasingly troubled. Each was clearly still physically attracted to the other. Apart from that, the reasons why they had originally set up home together were basic and too fragile to last. The immediate reality in 1930 had been that she was pregnant with Molly and wanted to get away from her own domineering mother – the latter wish may well have led to the former condition. As for my father, after years of wandering from lodging house to lodging house seeking work, he wanted to settle down and build his own family home. The sound job at Roade factory, and the houses, however primitive, in Ashton and Roade, finally provided him with that stability.

But it was not a long-term formula. Personally, they were in many ways like chalk and cheese. My father sought a quiet and stable life. My mother was more lively and entertaining and probably appeared to him as an oasis of fun in an otherwise subdued village life. Many others found her fascinating and some men were transfixed by her sexual vitality. She often – in the house, with neighbours in the street, in shops or in the pub – performed as if on the stage, always seeking the spotlight, to my constant embarrassment. Children can be prissy and intolerant about such extravagances. But my father never lost his fascination with her, until she suddenly walked out on him in 1945; he was then shattered, his existing bitterness enhanced, and he never forgave her. On her deathbed, she told my sister Sheila that 'your father was the only man I ever really loved.'

Their emotional interaction was always volatile and sometimes explosive. Each had an impressive temper, hers quick and fiery, his dark and slow-burning. There was constant shouting and slanging between them. At times they fought, more often, on my observation, she attacking him, and more than once I saw him punch her (something I ever since cannot tolerate in men). Once he pushed her away across the living room and she fell sitting in the coal bucket. For some time she was unable to extract her ample bottom, producing one of my few smiles on such occasions.

Less amusing was when I came home from school one lunchtime and found her lying sick, having put her head in the gas oven for a while. These rumpuses could make Waverley a physically dangerous place to small persons, especially since my mother sometimes took out her frustrations on her children, or certainly on Clem and me. Molly was always closer to her and seemed protected. I deeply resented any unpredictable (and to me unwarranted) whacks. Early on I made a private resolution never to cry. Whenever possible I escaped outside into the quiet fields or the more friendly village life. Inside Waverley, my personal air raid shelters were either to sit under the table or in the lavatory with the door firmly locked – sometimes with her only feet away in the kitchen, bellowing for me to come out. I did not greatly enjoy any of this. It must have been even more terrifying for my younger brother and sister. To my shame, I did little to protect them. It was *sauve qui peut* in Waverley.

It is a reflection of the curiously fractured nature of our family life, and my separate existence, being physically and emotionally often outside it, that I have sadly so few memories of my brother and sisters while I lived in Roade, or for the two years in Northampton after the war. I adored my sister Molly. We both had the same curly fair hair and blue eyes and, perhaps self-regardingly, to me she was beautiful. I also envied the buoyant fun and laughter she shared with her village friends June Wilson and Editha Lamb (my next love after Miss Dainty). But it was all from afar; we did little together. Being older, she seemed more able to float above the warfare at Waverley, and was always more understanding of her own mother. Yet even she was not untouched, later abandoning her own three children and disappearing from view for thirty years.

Sheila, born in 1942, was still a baby and I have no pictures of her from Roade in my mind's gallery, except of once pushing her pram along the Stony Stratford road, she sleeping peacefully. After our family broke up in 1945, I lost touch with Sheila for nearly fifty years. Now that we are back in touch, she has told me that as a child she used to 'shake with fear' at the sight of Mother. She suffered from anorexia for ten years and then finally left home. On her deathbed, my mother asked Sheila to forgive her. Mother left a number of casualties in her turbulent wake.

My dear brother Clement, five years younger than me, stayed quietly in the background. It was not until his teens, both of us then living with my father and completely cut off from the rest of the family, that we became very close, a closeness which lasted for the rest of his life. He had been savagely scarred by his time with Mother after she left Dad, and never fully recovered emotionally. I tried to compensate for my earlier failures to protect him by helping financially with his adult education (he left secondary modern school at fifteen and worked as a shop assistant until going back into further education) and his career as a carpenter. But it was not enough. He was a loyal, sweet and gentle man, having most of our father's virtues without the downsides. He died cruelly early of cancer, leaving a fine wife and two young sons. His death affected me deeply and I have never recovered from it.

The other Roade branch of the Donoughue family was my father's younger brother John. He and his very fat wife Lotte lived, without any children, never more than three hundred yards from our house. But there was very little contact between us, except at the George Inn, and certainly little mutual support. Even at our hardest times after the war, when Dad was working to exhaustion to bring up two young sons, cleaning, washing and shopping after slogging away at overtime at the factory to earn a few more shillings, his brother and sister-in-law never to my recollection visited us or invited us children to their comfortable home. Working-class families were not always as warm and mutually supportive as some romantic sociologists suggest.

But it is too easy to judge harshly with hindsight. After all, I myself did too little to help. One odd occasion I remember with Uncle Jack was at a Christmas when he came to Waverley, where Dad had acquired a small keg of beer and they stood drinking together in the back yard. Dad was keeping a chicken for the Christmas table, to which I became attached, and Jack took a small axe and chopped off its head; it continued to jump and flop headless and I did not look forward to eating it. And much later, after Lotte's death, when Uncle Jack resumed his Catholic communion, he did sometimes drop in on Dad for a cheerful chat on the way home from the pub, wobbling along on his old upright bicycle. He was basically a good sort. He is buried close to my father in the village cemetery. It is sad they were not closer in life.

Indeed, our family in Roade seemed at times barely to exist at all as an emotionally supportive unit. We gathered in the house at intervals to eat and to sleep, all the children in one room. We did not play much together, possibly because we were too widely spaced in age (something corrected in my own family, having four children in four years). We did little with our parents except when mother took one of us shopping, or on precious weekend summer evenings when Dad took us to one of the local pubs. I loved that, and country pubs always figure in my mind as happy places. But home was not often a happy place.

Looking back with curiosity over nearly seven decades of a life which has shown me a fair mixture of sunshine and shade, I am keenly aware of the longstanding arguments over whether an individual's personality, behaviour, and simply what he or she make of life, are determined more by birth or by upbringing, by genes or nurture. As a lover of racehorses, where breeding so often determines speed, stamina and equine character, I am very conscious of the force of genetic inheritance. Observing the predictable peculiarities of certain hereditary families in the House of Lords has tended to reinforce this view. But in my own particular case I am less sure. I suspect that most of what is now me was shaped by the acute experiences of my childhood upbringing. Not that I wish to blame my many behavioural defects on either genes or upbringing, since I strongly reject the pathetic modern 'victim' culture. We make and lie on our own beds and should take responsibility for our own behaviour.

I am equally confident that such acceptable qualities as I possess are due mainly to my wonderful schoolteachers, to the village community in which I grew, and to friends who showed me better example. But certainly my upbringing within what might be termed an impressively dysfunctional family also played a shaping and not wholly beneficial role. It was not possible to emerge from it untouched. Even today most of my regular night dreams are based in Roade, still inhabited by my then family and village friends and neighbours. It was simply not healthy that I came to dislike my mother so unreasonably and lost contact with my sisters for decades. I clearly resented the lack of a warm and happy childhood, the absence of maternal affection, home comforts, even children's stories, since there were no books in the house. There seemed to be just too much noise and violence and general nonsense. To such a point that, although my parents' separation in 1945 was for me a shattering experience, I later actually preferred living in the quiet and supportive world of my father, despite the discomforts. Clem told me that he took the same view. And there were other compensations in life with Dad. Such challenging domestic conditions may have helped to strengthen in me a certain useful resilience and definitely a very strong determination one day to live a much better life with children who were loved. I was fortunate to have the educational opportunity, fought for by an elder generation, and the devotion of my teachers and friends, which nurtured me to that happy end. My younger sister and brother, though blessed with much kinder characters than me, were less lucky and remained casualties.

Later in the war my mother's latent business skills and moneymaking talents began to emerge. She worked for a while at Tommy Cooper's garage next door, leading to suspicions, never confirmed, of an affair. There were rows about it and my father never spoke to Tommy again. Mrs Cooper, a vivacious American lady who used to trim my curly locks, became Dad's good friend; a partnership based on mutual sympathy for each having such an awful partner.

But Mother had a grander scheme. Following in Granny Andrews' heavy footsteps, she decided to buy a café in Northampton. She and my father began to save from her garage earnings and his overtime pay. They accumulated the money in a bag kept in a disused oven in the living room. I remember watching from under the table them counting it, some £400, wealth beyond my wildest dreams, and heard them discuss her café plans. I was impressed by their discipline in saving. I was also conscious that she was the leader in this scheme, with her strong ambitions and natural feel for business. Dad appeared the reluctant, almost bemused, follower. He preferred a quieter life in the village. He may also have smelled a rat. Above all it meant that once she had financial independence, he could no longer control her. In fact the money, much of it earned by him, was her bridge to freedom from domestic constraints, from the prison of four small children in a slum house, with little money and an ageing factory worker husband.

One day in the early summer of 1945, she took the money out of the oven – perhaps with a rumoured loan from Tommy Cooper – and bought a transport café on the Marehold, in the slums of Northampton, half a mile from her mother in Marefair. This was one case where both genes and nurture certainly repeated themselves. She then left Dad and Roade – 'bolted' as the horsey set would say.

This produced a time of turbulence in my life, which I can never recall, or now describe for the first time, without some pain.

I shall never forget the day of the split and our departure from Waverley, of which I had no warning or premonition. With an open-backed lorry waiting outside, mother, looking wild and almost triumphant, divided the meagre house belongings with my father, bewilderment and tears on his face. She meticulously counted out the cutlery, one knife, or fork, or spoon for her, one of each for him, and so on. Old carpets and bedding were shared out and her half carried into the lorry.

With the asset stripping completed, she hustled us children out of the front door. My father stood there weeping, seeming to me suddenly older, bent and shrunk. As I passed him, he leaned over and kissed me, his tears wetting my face. He simply said: 'Bye bye, Bernard. I have always loved you.' It was the first time either of them had told me that, though I always sensed that he did.

Then we were gone. The mind's picture from where I crouched in the back of the lorry, looking back to a disappearing Waverley as we crossed the railway bridge, dust and petrol fumes blowing in my face, my father waving and shrinking, is seared in my memory. I felt physically full of pain, as if my whole world, the village, my mates, the fields, my school, my teachers, my father, were being wrenched out of my body. I had no idea where or to what existence we were going. That was the low point of my whole life. I was overcome with anger at my mother. She seemed, not for the last time, like a typhoon leaving a trail of human wreckage in her turbulent wake. As a child of ten I had no understanding of what unhappiness of her own may have driven her to this radical venture. I only knew that this wild woman sitting in the lorry cab, for whom I so young felt so little love or respect, had inflicted this great pain on my father and me, and presumably on my brother and sisters, though I recall no communications with them.

I then swore to myself that I would some day, somehow, get out of this pickle. Get away from her, go back to Dad, and work to climb out of that kind of world. I had seen other people, especially my teachers but also the parents of some of my friends, leading better, more affectionate lives. I decided I would get there and join them.

But for the time being I couldn't get out of anything. I was pitched straight into the slums of Northampton and a world where I knew nobody. Actually it wasn't all bad; and I learned quite a lot about life there, or at least some colourful aspects of life.

Three

TOWN LIFE

My mother had planned her escape from Roade carefully. She guided the furniture lorry to a house not far from her Marehold café, in Upper Priory Street, one of a network of streets of brick back-to-backs on a hill north of the railway station. This was then the deepest slum of Northampton, with probably not one bathroom or inside lavatory per acre. Later the whole area was rightly demolished and completely transfigured into a new street conformation; so not a trace of Upper Priory or the surrounding streets I knew now remains.

Our new home was larger than the average local house, with three rooms up and down and – encouraging to me – an outside lavatory with a solid floor. The house was entered through large brown wooden doors into a deep yard, which was used by its owner, Mr Arthur Hunt, originally from Norwich, for his activities as a dealer and general 'rag and bone' man. One of the several attractions to me of his trade was that he kept a pony and trap in the yard together with an affectionate dog named Judy. Sometimes I went out with him in the trap while he bought and sold old ovens, iron bedsteads – anything on which he thought he could make a financial turn.

Arthur was a tall, bald and weak man, twenty years older than my mother and soon completely dominated by her. But he was kind to me and helpfully gave me my first introduction to market economics. His trade in rags, bones and old iron was in fact a convenient cover for his more profitable activities on the 'black market', in which I enthusiastically participated. The role I most enjoyed was buying ration books and food and clothing coupons, and more occasionally petrol coupons. (Arthur himself disposed of them illegally to more upmarket customers – especially, he told me, to policemen.)

Our local neighbours were poor and often ran out of money before the end of the week. Thursdays and Fridays were especially busy days. Then they would come to Arthur – or very often to me, since he was frequently out in the trap – to sell the coupons which, in a better world, they might have used to feed or clothe their scruffy children. When going out, he would tell me the current price range for food or clothing coupons, gave me some flexibility, and quickly came to trust me to negotiate at the door and to keep the money safely for him. Later, as a stockbroker, I observed these same skills operating under a smoother social veneer.

Arthur also dealt in the riskier trade of petrol – the real stuff, not just the coupons. One of Mother's café drivers would park his lorry outside the house for the night. I was often recruited to suck and siphon their petrol up a tube out of the lorry's tank into cans, which Arthur sold on. To disguise the petrol loss, as if consumed *en route*, the driver jacked up his lorry so he and I could steadily and boringly 'rock' it: then the tachometer clock in the cab, which recorded when the lorry was moving to check the driver's work hours, would add extra hours of driving and justify the extra petrol 'consumed' – or actually stolen. I benefited financially from Arthur for this tedious and even risky occupation, but to this day I dislike the horrible taste of petrol in my mouth.

One particular local family (I withhold their name in case any of the girls are still hobbling the pavements) had over a dozen children and so possessed impressive coupon assets in their multiple ration books. They regularly came to our door to trade. None of them seemed to have jobs, no doubt waiting and preparing for the culture and opportunities of the new Welfare State which beckoned just ahead. Their army of boys were said to earn a steady income 'nicking and fieving', though by the excellent moral code which then (though sadly no longer) prevailed in working-class areas, they left us neighbours untroubled.

One of their daughters, then in her early teens, used to give quick and standing sex to local lads in the Arundel Street air raid shelter. Sadly just too young to participate, I watched older boys from our streets line up to 'give her one', as they said. I believe it was then done charitably on her part, though later she apparently graduated to make it a regular trade. In the mid-1950s, when I was an undergraduate at Oxford and one evening was coming home from the Welsh Pony pub, I recognised her standing on the pavement behind the Oxford Playhouse, where American servicemen then loitered.

She looked little different, just fatter and somehow squashed. We chatted.

She invited me for a drink any time in her Walton Street basement flat close to where I lodged. She didn't mention 'business'. Perhaps it was just for old times' sake. Perhaps she felt that Arundel Street veterans, even non-combatants like me, qualified for a free ticket. I didn't take up the gracious offer. Not for any questionable moral reason. I have always been obsessed with medical cleanliness and did not know what she might have picked up in Northampton air raid shelters or Oxford basements.

That first summer of 1945 in Northampton was quite eventful for me. The general atmosphere was exciting as Japan surrendered, bringing the whole world war to an end, with celebration parties in the streets and flags and bunting everywhere. It was great news, though I felt deprived of one of my main interests in life. I explored the terraced roads, usually alone, taking a tennis ball to kick and throw against walls – giving myself and similarly socially deprived contemporaries a degree of ball control which is apparently lacking in many modern footballers growing up on impressive training facilities.

At one point my mother and Arthur suddenly decided to go off to Nottingham for a week, I believe to the Goose Fair. Clearly I presented a problem. They didn't want to take me, and perhaps hesitated to leave me at home unattended aged ten. So mother decided to send me away to London to stay with my Roade evacuee friends, the Smurthwaites. 'You always seemed to prefer being with them than at home', she argued cogently, 'so go and stay with them.' The fact that she had not alerted the Smurthwaites to my impending arrival, and that although I thought I remembered their house address – 179 Bravington Road, Queen's Park, W something – I had no idea where that was, did not deter her. She probably and rightly judged it would be a useful part of my education. So she gave me a battered old suitcase as high as my waist and the money for the railway ticket and expenses. (She was always generous about money, whether hers, Dad's or Arthur's.) I went alone to Northampton Castle Station and took a train to Euston, the only London station of which I had heard. I loved the train part of the journey. From Euston I was initially stuck, having no idea where Queen's Park was, but kind people pointed me onto buses towards west London and I finally found my way. I recall feeling very hot and tired as I limped down Bravington Road and knocked on the door of number 179, a tall Victorian terraced house split up into flats.

Mrs Smurthwaite was astonished to see me. She gently asked: 'Why didn't you warn us? We might not have been in.' But she gave me a warm welcome and made me a bed on the settee in the front room. She also gave me a pair of underpants, which I had never so far experienced, to wear for decency beneath my too small short trousers. I enjoyed my stay in Bravington Road enormously, rekindling my affection for Mrs Smurthwaite. Geoffrey and I used to spend afternoons touring the Underground on one single child fare, ticking off each station in turn. When I reluctantly returned to Upper Priory Street, my mother did not enquire about my expedition. I doubt that she wrote a letter of thanks. I had not been taught that small courtesy and did not learn it until embarrassingly late in life.

Life in Upper Priory Street never seemed to acquire a proper domestic routine. My mother was out all day at the café. In the evenings some of the long-distance lorry drivers used our house for bed and breakfast lodgings, at seven shillings a time. Mum often went out to the pub with them and with her friend Connie Naylor. Connie's husband was a 'wide boy' and bookmaker, who kindly took me to help him make a book at Earls Barton greyhound track. Once on the way back he showed me the revolver he claimed always to carry; I always took him seriously after that. Connie had a stiff 'gammy' leg but was attractive, smartly dressed and very flighty. I overheard her report to my mother her flirtatious adventures with lorry drivers in doorways on the way back from the pub, assessing the men's ability or potential quite clinically. I felt that the drivers were lucky to have her company.

The two women often came home separately and accompanied. Once when my mother returned with one of her fancied drivers (she was after all unmarried) I was in my favourite bolthole, hiding under the table in the small sitting room. I could see through the table legs towards the kitchen up to waist height. From there I quietly observed my mother, though I could not see her face, apparently being 'given one' by the driver against the back door – and their panic when Connie and friends returned noisily up the yard. I stayed silently under the table until they dispersed and then slipped away to whichever bed I had for that night. Growing up with Mother was certainly educational.

My mother crammed as many drivers as possible into the house and they sometimes slept two in a bed. The downside for me on a busy evening was that if a 'regular' arrived late, and we were full, he would be sold my single bed. I would often be awakened and, as I saw it, 'slung out'.

Sometimes I moved to the hard couch at the bottom of the bed in the downstairs room where mother slept with poor Arthur – which gave me another introduction to the mechanical side of adult sex. More often I was sent across the road to the baker, where Mother had an arrangement with the Warner family. There I was put in bed with their sixteen-year-old son, who was personally deep into masturbation but did not bother me. Fortunately, I never had any experience of child abuse, on which I might, like others of the 'victim tendency', have been tempted to offload the responsibility for the later failings of my character. I find excuses boring and my father always told me to 'carry your own luggage'.

As a result of the ebb and flow of human traffic in Upper Priory Street, I never had a bedroom there, nor indeed a bed, which I could genuinely call my own. I did not mind too much, since the lorry drivers were interesting to talk to and it also meant more pocket money around the home. One kind driver from Keelings Transport in the north Midlands took me on round trips to deliver and collect loads. I enjoyed that. But I was above all sustained by the growing conviction that I would find a way out of all this mayhem at some time. And anyway I really liked old Bill Warner and his cosy little bakery, always so nice and warm. I loved watching him prepare and slap the yeasty dough into wooden vats, leaving it to ferment and rise overnight. Sometimes I rose early in the morning dark, to help him batch the dough into the greased loaf tins. The bakery had magnificent old iron ovens fired by coal and the lovely smell of baked bread freshly out of the oven has stayed with me all my life. Sunday morning was a particularly pungent time to be with him. The local houses had few cooking facilities and many wives brought their Sunday joints and potatoes to Bill Warner to cook for three pence a dish. Some – especially those who had already sold me their meat coupons – had no meat and relied on a large Yorkshire pudding smothered in gravy. Bill slid the baking tins into his ovens with a long wooden paddle, lining them up according to collection times, the earliest in the front. At dinner the women queued gossiping and then streamed away to serve what was often the only hot meal they ate all week. It was an excellent and cheerful community occasion, which had also occurred in Roade at West's bakery until the war, but is now possibly extinct.

My school education continued, though much less charmingly than in Roade. The school to which I was allocated in Northampton was Campbell Square Secondary Modern, which served a poor and deprived constituency. As a secondary modern, it was on the lowest tier of the new tripartite educational system established under R. A. Butler's great reforming Education Act of 1944, housing those who had failed the scholarship examination at eleven and so had not reached either a grammar or technical school. Actually, I have never been clear whether I did fail my scholarship, or if I simply fell between the cracks in the educational bureaucracy. I took the new exam in 1945 in Roade, from where successful 'scholarship boys' went to a charming small grammar school at Towcester (home of my favourite racecourse), six miles to the west. My village school expected me to pass. But I moved to Northampton that summer before the results were released and, with the whole system in transition from the 1944 Act, my new education authority placed me in a secondary modern, seen by many as a dustbin for failures.

Campbell Square School was a forbidding Victorian building of dirty red brick. It sat on the hill beside the new police and fire headquarters – an appropriate location since a significant percentage of my new schoolmates displayed incipient criminal and arsonist tendencies. I was told by Mr Morley, my gentle and endlessly patient form master, that a third of my class either had fathers in jail or had no traceable father at all. To get to school I had to pass through dingy terrace streets, usually running, since unpunctuality was firmly punished and a large boy named Cherry sat at the gateway taking the names of delinquents. The classrooms were grubby and the corridors smelly – the school has since been closed – making me look back on my Roade village school as a pastoral paradise.

But I didn't dislike Campbell Square. As always school was a warm oasis to which I gratefully escaped. My teachers there were dedicated and excellent. Through the high windows of my top-floor classroom I could daydream and admire the graceful spire of St Sepulchre's church; in winter the sun set right behind it. For midday 'dinner' I usually chose not to return home or to my mother's café – conveniently nearby but always a risky environment where shopping expeditions might be concocted for me – but went alone to one of the commendable British Restaurants, set up by the government in the war to provide hot and nourishing meals for those working away from home. I considered myself firmly in that category. For 5d I had hot meat, potatoes and another vegetable, usually seriously overcooked cabbage. Following that was the highlight of the meal, a magnificent steamed pudding, sodden with hot treacle or custard. Nothing with three Michelin stars today can give me more pleasure than those puddings.

I did sometimes visit my mother's café, dilapidated amid a large parking lot of lorries. There she held court with an admiring clientele, vivacious and entertaining as she served endless plates of eggs and chips and huge cracked mugs of tea. She often gave me a cake and lemonade to get me off her hands. I enjoyed listening to the chat of the drivers. But I never liked the smell of greasy fried meals and milky tea, and avoided them ever after that.

One Saturday morning during that autumn when I was there, my father suddenly arrived at the café. He went upstairs with my mother to one of the empty rooms above. I tiptoed up the stairs to listen. Through the doorway I saw him down on his knees, pathetically pleading with her to return to live with him. He looked so sad, a man without hope or dignity. Mother stood haughtily above him, eyes darting wildly, hair long and tangled, a dirty apron around her waist, her face very hard as she rejected him and told him to go away. I retreated down the stairs and ran along the street to our house, unable to cope with the deep emotions revealed to me. But that picture of my father humiliated on his knees stayed painfully with me.

Another time, and another picture which still wakes me in the middle of otherwise happy nights. I was in the café with Clem, then aged around seven. He had a doleful long face but was sweet, quiet and gentle in nature. A customer came in and commented favourably on Clem. I heard my mother say, 'Well, you can have him if you want him.' I cannot remember what or if the man replied.

Next day I was not at the café, but years later Clem told me that the man returned and asked if mother was serious about letting him have her young son. With Clem sitting there, and customers in the café, she said, 'Yes, I don't want him.' The man arranged to take Clem away. He and his kindly wife were named

Faulkener, living in a Northampton suburb without children. They looked after Clem wonderfully for some time and loved him as their own. He came to adore them, having finally found a happy family home. But one night when he was asleep there, Mother arrived noisily at the door and demanded his return. Clem said he was bundled out of bed and away. He never forgave our mother for that, and, after escaping to live with my father and me in Roade, never spoke to her again. She certainly had a way with people.

Most of my time in Northampton, when I was not at school I was 'out'. I was usually alone. I knew nobody locally except the baker and his son, who was much older than me, and they were my only 'home from home' in town. My sister Molly, showing some of my mother's vitality and enterprise, left her Catholic convent school prematurely and ran away to start a career on the stage, working at one point with a kind of magician – he cut her in half in a box, threw knives at her, and tricks like that. I once went to visit her in her theatre dressing-room. I was excited by the chorus of half-dressed girls and remember the smell of grease-paint and sweat. But I associated that kind of dramatics and irresponsibility with my mother and decided it was not for me. I have no recollection of baby Sheila in Upper Priory Street; she too may have been farmed out. We were a nomadic lot with no collective personality. I felt lonely and missed my mates and the community life of Roade. I was determined to go back to the village. The opportunity was not too far ahead.

My mother, ever mercurial and restless, soon grew bored with poor old Arthur. There were increasing rows, with her making most of the noise. He, much older and no masculine hero, cowered and visibly quivered. There were also rumours, later confirmed, of another man. So she continued to plough her destructive furrow. One day she upped sticks and again 'bolted'. This time she took us not far away, around the corner off Harding Street, to a little back-to-back lit by pretty gas mantles.

Arthur, a mild man whose life had been quietly grey until Mother exploded into it, was shattered. Like others before him, he had been captivated by her wild energy, her wit and capacity for fun, by her sexual vitality, the whole black magic of her magnetic, if selfish and destructive, personality. He could not live without her. Soon after, he swallowed a bottle of prussic acid and was found on his bed with his grossly elongated tongue lolling out. I felt for him, and worried about his dog and pony.

I had taken my bag of belongings around the corner with her. I was now firmly convinced that Mother eventually damaged everything she touched. No longer did the lavatory or the table offer secure escape from this maternal hurricane. So I began to plan my own escape. I secretly visited my father in Roade on Saturdays, also then resuming football with my old mates, enjoying regaining the taste of village life. Mother was so little interested she never enquired where I had been, though she was always generous with pocket money, which I used for the bus.

One evening after school she began to shout at me about some matter, I cannot remember what. I went upstairs and packed my few things – mainly my football boots, some items of clothing, my wartime badges and shrapnel, and a couple of old tennis balls – into a carrier bag. Returning downstairs I said: 'I am going back to Dad.'

She was sitting beside the fire darning by the light of the gas mantle. Without looking up, she said: 'OK then. Have you got the money for the bus?' I had. And I left, without a kiss of goodbye, walking along Arundel Street, past her shabby café, up Gold Street and around handsome All Saints Church to the Derngate bus station, from where I took the first bus to Roade. It was quite dark when I arrived at Waverley. Dad was sitting quietly in his chair by the fire. I had not warned him. His eyes lit up and he rose and asked, 'Have you come for good?' I said 'Yes', and he gave me a kiss, a reminder of that other devastating kiss at the front door two years before. He insisted on frying me some supper.

Waverley had deteriorated further since we left, becoming grubbier and more damp. Clem soon came to join us and he and I made a pact, deciding we would completely cut off from my mother's side and we would try to build a family out of what we had in Roade with Dad. Mother, and sadly our sisters, virtually disappeared from our lives, she entirely from Clem's. I met her occasionally and accidentally over the next few years – running another transport café in Stony Stratford, serving behind a counter in Woolworths. One meeting, not accidental, was when she fought Dad over my custody. I had to attend a court where I was asked if I wished to live with her, and replied 'No', and then if I wished to live with my father, and replied 'Yes'. But I never saw her after Oxford. Reportedly, she married a decent and docile man named Albert, had a delightful daughter, and settled down to humdrum Northampton life. But I don't imagine it was very humdrum; not always.

For the rest of Dad's life we three men tried to hold together, however inadequately, particularly inadequately on my part. Dad slaved for us. Clem, always loyal, sensitive and scarred by his maternal experiences, grew closer to me and closest to Dad. It was a scruffy and uncomfortable male household, with little money or physical warmth. I have no recollection of ever celebrating my birthdays, though Dad always cooked a goose for Christmas. I missed female company and later always sought and treasured it. But between the three males it provided a base for mutual respect and affection. Clem and I felt we at least and at last had a permanent and loving home.

Four

TEENAGE CLOUDS LIFTING

The Waverley home in Roade to which I returned in late 1946 had deteriorated visibly and over the next few years became even dirtier and shabbier, smelling of damp rot and grime. This was not really the fault of my father. He did his best to keep the house tidy and clean, in addition to his long hours of heavy factory work, receiving too little help with domestic chores from me. He shopped on Saturday mornings, often going to Northampton market. On Sundays he cleaned the house, changed the bed linen, and did the week's washing. The ironing was for Monday evening and he cooked every day on a single ring electric cooker on the table, with fish every weekend in deference to his Catholic background.

But he lacked the time to look after the house properly himself, and lacked the money to employ anyone else to do it for him. Really Waverley was a slum wreck and beyond redemption. Many years later Mr Taylor, a fellow factory worker and one of Dad's few friends, wrote to me to say: 'I pride myself in the knowledge that I was one of the privileged few who knew of the conditions which surrounded you (no longer there) in those early days, and who knows and appreciates all the more because of those conditions.' It was pretty rough. But remember that it was not unique; and that many fellow Britons had recently suffered far worse in enemy prison camps. I was in many ways lucky and free to make my own way.

My own overwhelming recollection of life inside Waverley after the war – and I got out as much as possible – is of the damp winter cold. Icy draughts came in between the gaps in the asbestos walls, and through the warped doors and window frames. In the terrible winter of 1946–7, snow filtered through the broken upstairs windows and down the staircase: in the day it half melted and at night froze again, so venturing up and down stairs was a slippery business. There was only one small fire grate in use, in the living room, the heat of which on a cold evening barely penetrated to our knees as we sat close in front of it.

The one household chore which I executed with willing enthusiasm was filling the coal bucket from the coal shed outside. During the fuel crisis after the war this involved often scraping the shovel to the bare earth floor to collect the last remnants of coal dust. Dad backed up the grate with this dust; it burned more slowly and made the fire last.

When I later did homework on winter evenings, I sat in my overcoat, with Dad sitting across the fireplace listening to the wireless, an ancient though handsome Marconi model. I learned to shut out both sound and the cold and concentrate on my books, a skill of dissociation from noise and discomfort which has been useful throughout my life. These frigid experiences also firmly convinced me that if I ever became even modestly prosperous, I would devote the maximum resources to having my central heating on full blast – a target comfortably achieved, though sometimes to the discomfort of guests. But by then my perennial bronchial weakness was established and could not be boiled away.

During these teenage years I grew closer to my father. I found him deeply sad behind his gentle smile. He had no really close friends and few interests outside his children. His main activity was work. Life had scarred him and touched him with a corrosive bitterness. But he remained kind; and happiest in his vegetable garden, or walking down country lanes with his boys, or especially in the pub. He could relax sitting in the back room of the George playing dominoes and watching the wooden skittles games; and after a few pints he might sing old music hall songs in a light Irish tenor, which I envied, being myself always off key. Pubs can provide a warmth and friendliness sometimes missing at home – though today the George is very different, full of plastic, muzak and flashing lights, with no dominoes or skittles in view.

Dad was particularly saddened by his separation from my sisters – Molly, who had always been his true favourite, and Sheila. I did occasionally see Molly over the next few years. At the age of nineteen she married Harry Poscotis, a handsome Greek salesman from Cyprus, and they had three children. I liked him and stayed with them in their flats, first in then unfashionable Notting Hill, and afterwards in a dodgy part of Brixton. Sometimes I went with Harry knocking on doors as he tried to sell brushes and toys from his case – another job I quickly decided was worth working hard to avoid.

Molly separated from him, and in the early 1960s she suddenly disappeared from our lives, inexplicably leaving her three small children at a Barnado's home. Harry bravely tried to bring them up – curiously mirroring what my father did for Clem and me. At one point he took them to live in Cyprus (I happily paid for the tickets). It didn't work and he returned, soon to die of cancer, while his son died young of a drug overdose. So his two beautiful daughters, not knowing the whereabouts of their mother, had a tough time. Thirty years later Molly resurfaced, to the delight of us all – and also produced sister Sheila, whom I had not seen for nearly fifty years. This was a great comfort to Clem, then dying of cancer. When Molly, her two daughters, Sheila's family and I attended Clem's Catholic funeral, I felt that many old wounds had been healed. After that we all kept in touch. But we were an odd family. And Dad sadly did not survive to see that ultimate reunion.

He did, however, have a new companion at Waverley – Sam Carter, who rented the small front room downstairs. Sam, who was in his seventies and had fought in the Boer War, had a long white moustache and sat and walked with military bearing, straight as a ramrod. After leaving the army he had worked at a small brickworks near Blisworth, his hands made hard as saddle leather by the hot bricks which he loaded onto horse barges on the nearby Grand Union canal. One of his jobs was to lie on top of the barges when full, with his feet on the sides and roof of the Blisworth tunnel, and walk the barges through, since horses could not pass under the tunnel. Sam always sat, quietly smoking his extremely pungent pipe, in a corner of the living room near the wireless, discreetly leaving the precious warm space in front of the fire to Dad and me. I enjoyed talking to Sam about his earlier life and felt he was a link to a more heroic age. He never complained about anything.

I happily resumed my Roade village life, though confined to evenings and weekends since I went daily on the bus to school in Northampton – where I had fortunately achieved a late transfer from Campbell Square Secondary Modern to Northampton Grammar School, having been given an IQ test, the result of which suggested that I was above secondary modern standards. There was a terrific camaraderie among the village boys, all of whom were solidly working class. There was no television then and we made our own entertainments, mainly outside. Jim Howard's friendly newspaper shop became the focal point of our young village life, where we always received a warm welcome even though usually buying nothing. Walking around the village, I often looked in through house windows and, seeing lights and people and fires, formed the impression that others were having a better time. It took a while for me to remove the impression that the grass was always greener on the other side of the fence.

Bernard 'Binny' Webster was the skilled organiser of our activities. With him were the old 'gang': Manny Abbott, whose father delivered our milk, ladled straight into our jug from a pail carried on his ancient bicycle, and who would stand on the step drenched in a cloudburst and say, 'It be a damping'; Tony and Don Curtis and Richard Johnson; Clarence Putnam and the older ones such as Bucky Ashby, Don West, Mike Connolly and my special friend John 'Nipper' Coles. I remember those people and those days with great pleasure. They were not as educated nor as sharp as many people I met later in my London worlds of politics, university and the media, but they were certainly straighter and more trustworthy.

One friend, for a time my closest, who stood apart and never joined in my village activities, was Donald 'Pip' Giddings. He lived at handsome Manor Farm at the top end of the village. Pip was with me at the grammar school, and from when I was thirteen to sixteen we travelled together to school on the bus and spent large parts of every holiday playing around the farm or in the large farmhouse. He was good looking, with black hair and dark flashing eyes, ingenious, witty, and had inherited some of his father's braggadocio. Older women around the farm fell for him and he implied he enjoyed sexual favours. His mother was kind and included me in family meals. Sometimes I slept there. Manor Farm became yet another family home-from-home to me.

Pip and I avoided physical work on the farm wherever possible. But we observed and enjoyed the seasonal routines of ploughing, harvesting and milking. So when nearly fifty years later I became British Minister for Farming, it was not alien or a total novelty to me.

Sadly, the Manor Farm idyll came to an abrupt end at the time I was entering the grammar school sixth form. Pip's father was amiable and generous, but was seen by many in the village as really a bit of a conman. He had inherited the farm from his wealthy father and just played at being a gentleman farmer, with plus fours, Purdy guns, several cars and a full social life in the county – until the money ran out and the bank foreclosed. I travelled to Southampton to wave Pip, his parents and his brother off on the boat to Rhodesia. I missed them greatly. Inevitably, Cyril Cripps bought the farm.

With the village boys, our main community activity was sport, especially football and cricket. We sold raffle tickets and collected money to buy footballs, goal posts, cricket balls and bats, and played soccer in the recreation field behind the George on rough and deeply sloping ground.

Later we graduated to better pitches along the Blisworth and Ashton roads. Sometimes I played for the village teams, which at that time attracted quite large crowds of supporters. The cricket team always broke for tea at the White Hart Inn. This was an embarrassment for me as the standard salad cost 1s. 9d., which I did not have, and I did not want to ask my often penniless father. But Freddie Blincow, our magnificent medium pace bowler and image of the great Alec Bedser, always took care of me and simply paid for two teas without ever referring to it.

When not playing myself, I took every opportunity to watch the varied sport available in Northampton. Its league football team, 'The Cobblers', was a constant source of affectionate amusement, usually around the bottom of the league. We said of them that they did a lap of honour if they won the toss; and if a spectator at the turnstiles produced a £5 note, he would be asked, 'Do you want a forward or a defender?' The local rugby team, 'The Saints', was of much higher calibre, then one of the four best teams in England and producing a string of internationals: Lewis Cannell and Don White were my heroes. I remember once seeing the Saints beaten by Cardiff in a clash of titans: the Welsh tackling by Tanner and Hayden Davies was so ferocious we could feel the concussion just watching.

I also spent many happy hours at the Northants county cricket ground, taking a bag of sandwiches and a bottle of Tizer for the day. Immediately after the war 'the County' were a poor side, under old-fashioned amateur leadership, and they had gone nearly a decade without winning a single league game. But they had fine individual players like the openers Denis Brookes and Percy Davies, and later brought in outside stars for their twilight years, such as Norman Oldfield and Albert Nutter from Lancashire, Ken Fiddling from Yorkshire, Jock Livingstone the great Australian left-hander, and Freddie Brown, the tyrant captain from Surrey who knocked them into shape as a team. When Frank Tyson arrived from Durham they began to chase the league leaders and it was very exciting to be a Northants supporter. I was lucky to be present at what I believe were Tyson's first overs in professional cricket, against the Indian touring team. I cannot really say that I saw his first overs because they were so fast that I never saw a single ball he bowled. Nor apparently did the Indians, who quickly capitulated. After his first two balls, the county wicket keeper and his slip fielders dramatically retreated another ten yards – an early example of psychological gamesmanship – and were nearer to the boundary than to the wicket. It was no surprise to those present when Tyson went on the 1954–5 Australian tour and helped England win the Ashes.

It was certainly a golden age for watching English cricket. The Australian touring team of 1948 had astonishing talents, with all-rounder Keith Miller my favourite, as he was the favourite of many willing English ladies. We boys used to gather round the wireless to hear commentaries on the Test Matches. I also saw Compton and Edrich in their glory for Middlesex, making some 200 between lunch and tea. Their approach, of using their feet and setting out to collar and totally demoralise the opposition bowling, involved risks but was usually more effective than the later fashion of grinding away slowly behind the crease. It certainly gave spectators more pleasure. Even forty years after moving away from Northamptonshire, I continue to follow the fate of their three teams, and a win for any of them gives my weekend a lift.

Horses and horse racing also began to give me pleasure, even though I never rode (an expensive middle-class pursuit in Northamptonshire.) Following the day's racing in our *Daily Herald* was one of the few interests I could share with my father. From an early age I would sit with him in a pub on a Saturday lunchtime and we went through the racecards together. He wrote out little bets, usually 3d. each way, on slips of paper which were handed to a 'bookie's runner'. These runners operated in many pubs until off-course betting was rightly legalised by Harold Macmillan. By the age of ten I was allowed to have my own bet – usually backing any mount ridden by Tommy Carey for Dorothy Paget. It introduced me not only to a lifetime's pleasure, but also to the experience of making and accepting small losses, a useful lesson in life.

Fortunately I was also able to taste the real thing. Shortly after the war racing resumed at nearby Towcester. I went, climbing over the hedge and fence at the lower Shutlanger end. The beauty of the horses in flight and the sound of their hoofbeats coming up that final testing hill caught my imagination for ever. I went often again, always climbing in. Over forty years later, the generous proprietor of Towcester, Lord Hesketh, by then an impressive House of Lords Chief Whip in John Major's government, kindly invited me to become a director (unpaid) of the racecourse. He commented to friends: 'Bernard loves Towcester and has never paid to come in, so I thought we would put it on a regular basis and give him a director's badge.' Meetings at that lovely Northamptonshire course still constitute one of my greatest pleasures.

The love of all sport then implanted in me – and cultivated even more intensively at school – has lasted all my life. I continued to play soccer until I was fifty. I still get great pleasure watching football, rugby, cricket, racing, boxing, show jumping, tennis and athletics on television; though it is hard and saddening to accept that I will never go out and physically play any of them – except tennis – again.

My political interests began to grow alongside those in sport, though as an observer rather than a participant. My father often referred to his harsh experiences in the pre-war slump and related our domestic poverty to the capitalist system and its Conservative domination. The massive Labour victory in the 1945 general election promised to alter that. The election details had been somewhat obscured in my mind by the coincidental break-up in our family, but I recall the general excitement in the air. There was an open air meeting outside the Cock Inn held by the Tory candidate Mr Reginald Manningham-Buller (later a Law Officer and known in the village as 'Bullying Manner'). A local farm labourer lobbed a soft cabbage at Buller and was promptly arrested and sentenced to three months in Bedford jail.

This confirmed Dad's conviction that everything, including the law, was still controlled in the Tory interests. My daily readings of the *Herald* left me in no doubt that Labour would win in 1945 and so right – which was politically on the left – would triumph. After that due victory I followed closely and with pride Labour's introduction of the Welfare State in the late 1940s. That government's leaders – Attlee (always known as Mr Attlee), Bevin, Morrison and Bevan – were my first political heroes. The government seemed to us in Waverley to be governing on our particular behalf. We benefited from the new full employment policies, universal secondary schooling, free health treatment and all the new social security support (though it was then the custom to turn to 'the welfare' only as a last resort and not, as later, as a way of life). I believed that Labour would surely be in power for ever. But the nation's economic situation was dire following the depredations of war; the heroes grew old and tired, Labour stumbled in 1950 and finally fell exhausted from office in 1951. In the November 1951 general election, I put a Labour poster in a Waverley window; though it helped to keep out the draughts, it could not help our easily-beaten candidate.

I was convinced, as was Dad, that the return to power of Churchill and the Tories would inevitably mean a return to the dreadful economic policies and conditions, the mass unemployment and poverty, of the inter-war years. We were wrong. The new Tories had served as one nation in the war and were committed not to go back. In fact economic conditions slowly improved under the Conservative governments. It was part of my political education to learn and accept that, however reluctantly. By the 1955 general election, Labour, still led by an ageing Attlee, was in disharmony, with little new to offer post-war Britain. The poster in our new council house window was a rare local demonstration of support for a clearly lost cause.

The domestic disturbances experienced in my early teens were for a while reflected in my own deteriorating personal behaviour, though they were no excuse for it. I took up with a small village gang which rampaged for a time. We ended up in a juvenile court following our attack on a disused – or we believed it disused – signal box on a single-track railway which wandered rusting across the countryside. I was fined 4s. 6d., which Dad paid without comment. I decided such antics were not a sensible use of my time and Dad's money. The gang quietly disbanded.

I also suffered recurrent bouts of mild ill health, bronchial colds and severe insomnia. When I was fifteen, our devoted village doctor formally concluded that I was suffering from 'undernourishment'. So he prescribed that I be sent away to Brighton for a few weeks to be fed in an approved boarding house and to enjoy the sea air, all paid for by our wonderful new Health Service. I was totally alone by the sea and spoke to no one but the landlady. While there I attended at the Dome my first concert of classical music, something I had read about in the *Observer* newspaper but had never tasted. At home, when classical music came on the BBC my parents, agreeing on this at least, would pounce on the wireless and switch it off, saying, as if somehow threatened by it, 'We don't want that rubbish.' The Dome programme is still pictured in my mind: Elgar's Serenade for Strings, some Dvorak, and Beethoven's Pastoral Symphony. I could not appreciate all that was played; but I sensed a growing entrancement and after that slowly, very slowly and privately, introduced myself to music when alone in Waverley with the wireless. But the main immediate benefits of Brighton were the food and sleep and watching the sea. I returned to Roade and the grammar school with my health much improved, though the bronchial tendency persisted for life.

My behaviour and performance at the grammar school also slumped. I neglected homework and joined in with the more mischievous and less studious types. Whereas in my first year I was usually in the top half dozen in class, by the third year, aged fourteen and fifteen, I fell to twenty-eighth out of thirty-one. The future prospectus looked gloomy: an early exodus from school like many of my contemporaries, some with good brains, and then the treadmill of boring work which I had often observed.

I was rescued, as so often, by wonderful teachers – and particularly by a great headmaster, Martin 'Stinger' Nettleton (the nickname deriving partly from the link with nettles, but also from experiences with his cane). Nettleton was six feet four inches tall and had been a distinguished flying officer in the RAF throughout the war. Public school and Oxford educated, he had firm views on the benefits of leadership in all walks of life, and he gave it in good manner to the Northampton Grammar School from 1945. Often till then known as the 'Town and County', the school was over 400 years old and until the 1944 Education Act had had its own preparatory school, taking fee-payers as well as some 'scholarship boys', though its academic record was modest and before Nettleton's tenure declining.

After the great 1944 Education Act, it became the selective school for those who passed the 'eleven plus' in Northampton and its immediately surrounding villages. It stood at the eastern edge of town, amid the private estates of Northampton's middle classes, well away from the dreary slums based on the old, declining and ill-paid boot and shoe industry. The school was blessed with vast sports fields layered down the hill into the Nene Valley below, and with glorious views to the south over it. Nettleton set out in 1945 to make the NGS an ace state school, and within seven years he succeeded. In 1952 it was one of only four grammar schools in Britain to win more than five open scholarships to Oxbridge.

It also became one of the most successful sporting schools in the Midlands. Personally, I was lucky and very proud to coincide with and benefit from that golden age.

Nettleton was an educational elitist in the best sense of the word – he enabled quality to flourish in all aspects of school life and in all types of boy, regardless of class background. He regularly lectured us at morning meetings on the need for high standards; he eased out dud teachers; attracted bright young ones from the services who shared his vision; and gave us all a sense of pride in the school's achievements. The school hummed with activity, with most teachers and many pupils staying most days until early evening for the myriad of clubs and sports engagements.

Teachers and parents were encouraged to turn out to support our rugby and cricket teams on Wednesday and Saturday afternoons – something unthinkable when my boys were at a disappointing London comprehensive a generation later. (It was always sad for me that no member of my family ever watched me play the sports I loved.)

The school in due course became the heart of my life. I owe an enormous debt to a long line of devoted teachers – Messrs Tongue, Hickling, West, Lees, Young, Stebbing, Gregor, Holloway and a host of others. Twenty to thirty years later some of Nettleton's achievement was vandalised by the egalitarian experiments and politically correct claptrap of the local Labour Party's educational prejudices. Worse occurred in London, where my own children suffered perverse educational deprivation, and never knew the school satisfactions which I had enjoyed; not surprisingly, they cannot remember the names of most of their dilatory teachers, misled by irresponsible trade union leaders, and have little attachment to their old schools. My boys certainly lacked a Nettleton, who was the driving force behind a great school.

Nettleton was also a terrifying individual for any young schoolboy to meet. At the depths of my behavioural decline, in the lower fifth form, he summoned me. I quaked in the outer waiting room, watching the red and green lights which instructed victims whether to wait or go in. He towered over me as I entered his study. I was convinced I would be lashed into submission. Instead, he gently asked me to sit down and questioned me about my home life and why I was failing to fulfil my educational talents. He stated that he had no doubt that I would go to Oxford if only I could get my act together. He promised me that it would certainly happen if I worked together with him on a programme to achieve it. He asked me to visit him each month to discuss my problems and to report progress on our programme. I had never in my life felt such rock-solid support and the inner strength which comes to any child from such support. Always before I had felt that I was truly alone in dealing with the outside world and had to plot my own rocky path through life. Now I was not alone. I promised to work with him to deliver our joint ambition. When I left him, I went straight across the playground to the lavatories, locked myself in, and wept uncontrollably – something I had not done for years since I decided never to react to my mother's aggression.

From that moment I resolved to work myself into a better world with Nettleton's immense support. We had our monthly meetings, and I was always desperate to have improved class results and reports to please him.

The following year I moved high up the class and achieved a distinction and eight credits in my School Certificate. Sport was also going well. At rugby, first as fly half then wing three-quarter, I quickly achieved my First XV colours, and played for the Midland Counties Schools XV, the East Midland Colts XV and the Northampton Saints second XV, as well as having an England Schoolboys trial. I secured my first XI cricket colours as a fast bowler and also captained the school boxing team, a skill I have occasionally been tempted to use in later life, especially when dealing with the media. Things were moving forward as we planned my future together. I felt the clouds were really lifting and I was lucky to be touched by sunshine.

Nettleton grew even more involved in my life. He visited Waverley in his 1937 open Austin Tourer to talk to my father and was shocked by the living conditions he found there. He met my brother Clem and offered to adopt him. Clem declined, not wishing to leave Dad, but spent more time with Martin Nettleton and his sturdy wife Joan, especially climbing in Wales, which was the headmaster's passion. He privately arranged for me to transfer to a local public school – I cannot remember if it was Oundle or Stowe – but I declined, saying that I too wished to stay with my father, and he respected that. He also knew Cyril Cripps and later arranged for him to pay for me to board briefly with the kindly Pearson family in a warm house near Spinney Hill, so I could prepare for my Oxford scholarship examinations in comfort. I owe Nettleton gratitude beyond expression. Tragically, shortly after I went to Oxford, he developed hereditary brain disease. He died, as he would have chosen, and may indeed have chosen, in his beloved car driving out of control down his favourite Welsh mountain.

I had many good friends at the grammar school. Closest was Gerry 'Oscar' Fowler, who lived in the north of the county in Long Buckby. I often cycled there to stay with him and his blunt but kind north country parents. He had the most powerful mind in the school and one of the best I have ever encountered. Gerry was a most curious and engaging mixture. He guided me intellectually, encouraging me with my homework and training me in methods of study; and morally, commenting with humour and tolerance on my wicked behaviour, and trying to steer me towards better ways. In return I encouraged him to play sport and to take more interest in the opposite sex. It might be said that I was the moral gainer in the exchange, though my main memory is of the fun we had together. Although he was short, fat, indeed almost as round as high – and very short-sighted – I pressed for Gerry's inclusion in the school rugby team which I captained, where he performed with great courage and enthusiasm.

At first he played as scrum half to my fly half. I would shout to warn him when the ball was coming out of the scrum our side, since without his glasses he could not always see it. Then he became a front row forward, where his short legs meant he had the advantage of barely having to bend in the scrum. Finally he found success as a wing (or flank) forward. Again I would shout to him when the ball emerged on our opponents' side, and Gerry would launch himself like a rocket at their back line. With his centre of gravity so close to the ground, he cut a destructive swathe through them, almost regardless of who actually had the ball. To this day I can see him in my picture gallery, heavy sweat on his high intellectual forehead, totally covered in mud, and a wonderfully innocent grin as he spread destruction across the field.

I made my first visit abroad with Gerry. At fifteen we went by boat and train to France, to Dijon and to Paris, on the work-exchange schemes arranged by an organisation called Concordia, devoted to bringing together the youth of post-war Europe. At Dijon we worked as gardeners at a chateau college for training French teachers of physical exercise, some of whom were disruptively nubile. This first trip across the Channel was for me a stunning experience. Dad gave me a large white £5 note, which I assumed I would be able to spend in France and would cover my expenses for the whole month. I was shocked to discover that the British pound was not legal tender throughout the world. I also found the French trains very impressive, bigger and more punctual than ours. At Dijon I was hotter than ever before in my whole life. And the food was the best I had ever eaten, with my first taste of wine. I enjoyed the smells in French shops, in the bakeries, the patisseries, the pharmacies. I began a love affair there with the country of France which has survived through many difficult periods with individual French people. Some of these latter were the most cynical and least romantic I have met; while others – such as Jacques Pomonti, Michel Albert, J-F and Eliane Leger, and the beautiful Francoise – became among my closest friends. The house I owned in the Mediterranean Pyrenees for thirty years was the completion of a dream which began in Dijon in 1949.

As Gerry matured, he devoted considerable attention to the opposite sex, not without success. He also romped through all examinations with distinctions, won an Oxford open scholarship at sixteen, took a double first in classics there and became a don, before moving into Labour politics and Parliament, being Minister of Education in Harold Wilson's final administration. One day in Number Ten in 1975, we stayed together around the cabinet table after a cabinet committee and reminisced about our long and twisting paths from Roade and Long Buckby to Downing Street.

I always loved Gerry and was devastated when he died much too young of cancer. Shortly before the end, unaware of how rapidly the disease was advancing, I arranged for him to come into the House of Lords for lunch. He had to call it off; so, alerted that little time was left, I went to visit him and his devoted wife Lorna in Camden Town. As I walked up the stairs, Gerry appeared on the landing in his dressing gown, gaunt and facially almost unrecognisable. But he beamed with warm friendship, took me into his bedroom, and was full of humour. 'Well mate,' he said, with his old grin, 'this looks like it.' He asked Lorna to bring us each a tumbler of whisky and lit himself a large cigar. 'They say that this is what has killed me,' he chuckled. 'Well, it's too late for it to do me much more bloody harm now, so we might as well enjoy it while we can.' We reminisced, and he sometimes lost track. When he suddenly became very tired, I rose to leave. But he staggered out onto the landing with me, whisky in one hand, cigar in the other. 'Thanks for coming, mate,' he said. 'Don't expect we shall meet again.' Three days later he died. Together with my brother Clem and Martin Nettleton, that death meant another precious link with my Northamptonshire childhood had gone.

By the age of sixteen my home existence with Dad was stabilised, if none too comfortable, and academic and sporting experiences at school had become exciting and satisfying. Clouds were also lifting from – and sunshine warming – other aspects of my personal emotional life. Most important, I had fallen in love with Jill Booty. She was a year older than me and a star pupil at the posh Northampton High School for Girls, studying Spanish, French and Art. (A fellow pupil there was a girl named Marcia Field, who as Marcia Williams was later to have an impact on my life in 10 Downing Street. She lived in the village next to Gerry's, and I saw her often, high heels clipping through the Derngate bus station and nose in the air, though I did not know her then.)

Jill was bright, vivacious, very slim and strikingly attractive with dark hair and beautiful eyes, quite Latin looking. She had danced in ballet and had that kind of fine posture and splayed walk which I find attractive. Together we made an odd mixture: me the scruffy and penniless country bumpkin, she a socially aware urban sophisticate. But it worked excitingly for me. I adored her and for the next four years she was at the centre of my thoughts and feelings.

Our times together were carefully structured and disciplined so as not to interfere with examination progress towards university. We sometimes met in the week, either at her house, which was near to my grammar school, or briefly in the afternoon when she came from her school, which was equally conveniently beside the Derngate bus station from which I travelled to Roade. But in term time, Saturday was our great day together. I began Saturday early, taking the bus to town before 8 a.m. and always doing homework for two hours in the excellent county library in Guildhall. Mid morning we gathered in the Derngate café, one of the few places in Northampton then serving drinkable coffee at tables – it is difficult to imagine today how dreary was life in the early 1950s for young people in any provincial Midlands town. Many of our school friends gathered there, together with our heroes from the local repertory company, and the place was abuzz with teenage chat and gossip. Jill and I usually went back for lunch at the small back-to-back home of her two formidable godmothers – the 'Nannas'. Afterwards I went off to play rugby or cricket for the school, rejoining Jill at the Nannas for late tea. (Provincial Northampton did not eat 'dinner' except at lunchtime.)

The Nannas, Maggie and Nell Knight, were two of the most remarkable characters I have ever met, authentic working-class spinsters with total integrity. Each was then in her fifties and little more than five feet tall, but fiercely combative. 'Nanna', the dominant sister, had fear of nobody. She was almost completely round and with her spectacles looked like a wary owl. She worked in a sweet factory and 'Nenna', more like a sparrow, in a clothing factory. They were strict nonconformists and Labour supporters, with very strong principles and prejudices. They saw black and white on most people and issues. Although they had left school at thirteen, they were very literate, following the arts closely, loving classical music, and strongly supporting the local repertory theatre. They stayed home nearly every evening listening to the plays and concerts broadcast on BBC radio. They had strong tastes and their heroes were the British conductors Malcolm Sargent and Adrian Boult and the composer Malcolm Arnold.

They had each lost boyfriends in the First World War and remained unattached after that, getting great pleasure from nurturing other people's children, such as Jill and myself. Nanna had a bottom drawer in which were kept precious items of female clothing, lace and silks, some of which had been there since being saved up for their own never-to-be weddings. When any one of their 'children' married, beautiful wedding presents emerged from that drawer; my eldest daughter Rachel benefited. They were particularly devoted to Jill, who had lost her own father when young and whose skittish mother, in their eyes, took too frivolous an approach to parental responsibilities. Jill returned that love throughout their lives. The Nannas took to me simply because Jill did. They also appreciated my rugby football successes, always dreaming of having one of their 'family' play for the Northampton Saints. Sadly, I only reached the second XV before retiring early, but another one of their boys made it to give them joy. I often slept in their little house at 29 Roe Road, just around the corner from the county cricket ground. They provided me with yet another home-from-home. Even after Jill and I separated, they remained my devoted friends for the next forty years until they died. They were the true salt of the old English working classes and very 'old' Labour in the best sense. Their photograph, of two tiny near-Victorian ladies in very respectable hats, still stands proudly on my mantel-piece.

Most Saturday evenings Jill and I took the bus from the Nannas to join other friends at the repertory theatre to watch the weekly play. It was an excellent company, probably second only to Birmingham in the Midlands, with beautiful sets executed by its brilliant art director Tom Osborne. Young actors such as Lionel Blair and Ronald Radd, and dear old camp Lionel Hampton – always playing the pantomime dame whatever his particular role – entertained a packed and often young audience. The theatre was just one aspect of the many ways in which Jill rubbed off some of my rough edges and introduced me to a whole new world of cultural pleasure. We went, usually by train, to see Shakespeare at Stratford-upon-Avon, other theatre, art exhibitions and modern dance in London – where we also saw my first opera, Wagner's *Tristan und Isolde* performed by the Stuttgart State Opera, which I believe was the first German company to visit Britain after the war. Wagner was quite a musical leap for me, still just coming to grips with Mozart and Beethoven. The Nannas often paid for these cultural adventures, treating me as another of their many 'adopted' children.

Jill and I read poetry and plays together in her home in Thursby Road, around the corner from beautiful Abingdon Park. Our readings included her Spanish favourites, which led me to teach myself a thin smattering of the language so I could savour the sounds of Garcia Lorca and Juan Ramon Jimenez. We discussed the authors in my English Literature syllabus for Higher School Certificate and listened to music on old vinyl records played on her massive gramophone. (Love of vinyl music has lasted until today, when I continue to collect old LP records from charity shops!) We travelled together to Spain, seeing the great paintings, especially the dramatic El Grecos, in the Prado, and visiting Aranjuez and the western provinces. Later we went on a final trip together abroad to Italy, where we studied Italian at the Universita Per Stranieri at Perugia (a preparation for her Cambridge degree and for me to take the Italian Renaissance as my special subject at Oxford under a wonderful tutor, John Hale). But life was not all highbrow culture. Each Saturday night after I had returned home on the last bus to Roade, I always switched on the wireless and listened on the BBC to *Jack Jackson's Record Round-Up*. This kept me in touch with the latest popular music and introduced me to quality singers such as Peggy Lee, Yma Sumac, Pee Wee Hunt, Spike Hughes and the jazz greats.

Jill was not always popular with everyone, not even with me, being at times snobbish and impressively self-centred. But she helped to educate me. She introduced me to cultural activities hitherto unrevealed, and which were to become central to my interests and pleasures in life. She also helped me to become at ease with a close and sophisticated female friendship. This was a good preparation for Oxford, where I found that many of my public school colleagues were painfully gauche with the opposite sex. It was nice to have an edge over some of them in something, when faced by their battery of financial, social and educational advantages.

Later Jill and I separated and did not meet for several decades. She had gone to Cambridge, I to Oxford, and we drifted apart, the slow branch rail-line via Bletchley being too slim a link. She moved quickly and easily into the dazzling Cambridge theatrical set, meeting far more classy and glittering types than me. When she cut the knot I was devastated. But never, like me, confused by sentiment or strong emotions, she was clinically right. We had enjoyed what was for me a fabulous time together. Yet we were fundamentally different. She was creative, quixotic, brittle, and apparently without any serious interests in political or social matters. I was a typical Virgo (though not *intacta*), boringly methodical and increasingly concerned with the mundane practicalities of public and private life.

Now, decades later, we occasionally meet, together with her saintly husband Robin and usually in France, where she paints successfully and where by curious chance we each had houses in Languedoc. Approaching seventy, she remains lively and strikingly attractive. She is one more person to whom my youth owed a great deal for bringing to it a certain kind of magic.

I managed to enjoy greatly my late teenage years, despite considerable financial stringency. In Roade we had not then even heard of the coming consumer society. My father, who never at his peak earned more than £14 a week before tax, gave me 2s. 6d. as weekly pocket money, less than 6d. a day, which certainly taught me how to cut out unnecessary expenditure. It did not seem to me too harsh because so much was provided free to schoolchildren in those early days of the Welfare State. I had free passes on the town and the country buses. My school lunch was free because my father's income was so low. I also earned useful extra cash from local holiday jobs of varying attraction. Stacking crates of lemonade bottles at White's factory was bad for my back and terminated for life any desire to drink the product. Working outside in a woodyard was cold, and delivering letters at Christmas even colder.

Best was my job in the Roade factory by my father's side: I was employed to knock the dents out of damaged hub caps with a hammer and upturned nail, while Dad, an experienced metal polisher, finished smoothing them off at his noisy brush machine. Around us in the factory were many of my old mates from the village. The noise and dirt was tolerable for me because I knew the tedium would end in a few weeks when I returned to school or college. For them, as it had been for my father, the same routines lay for forty years ahead. I also noticed that the lads had certain mental skills which even Joe Maxwell had left untapped. Although at school most of them had failed every arithmetic test set, when it came to working out their racing winnings they could calculate an each-way double at 6–4 and 7–1 in a flash. I realised that our education system incentivised and rewarded only the academic approach to study, and did not sufficiently take account that people need to be interested in practical aspects of a problem. I suspect it is still as deficient in this respect.

My grammar school career closed satisfactorily, with Stinger Nettleton's targets met. In my Higher School Certificate in the summer of 1952 I achieved scholarship level with distinctions in English Literature and History and an advanced level A in Economics. I won the school prizes for English Literature and for contributions to the school magazine and chose the collected poems of W. B. Yeats and W. H. Auden. These prizes were handed to me on speech day by Kenneth Pickthorne, a Cambridge don and Tory MP. Handing me the Auden book as if it were contaminated, he sneered, 'Why did you chose that fraud?' I was upset but too shy to reply. I knew I was much closer to Auden than to Pickthorne.

In the depths of the following winter I travelled to Oxford for the first time in my life, sitting English Literature exams at Lincoln College (Stinger Nettleton's old college), freezing at nights in a mediaeval room with a narrow hard bed, just a couple of blankets and a single electric fire for which I had to insert frequent shillings in a slot. There was little opportunity in the traditional exam paper to display any of the knowledge of contemporary literature instilled by my brilliant school teacher Donald Hickling, but I managed to gain an entrance to Lincoln. Since I already had won a state scholarship that was enough: my Oxford future was secure. But Stinger Nettleton encouraged me to aim higher, for an open scholarship. I went back to Lincoln, much more welcoming in the spring sunshine, and really enjoyed the History examination. A few days later I heard the glad news of my award of an open scholarship to read Politics, Philosophy and Economics. It was announced in the *Northampton Chronicle and Echo* and I don't know what my mother thought, if she read it. But to me it seemed a long way from Upper Priory Street. Without so many people, especially Dad and the teachers, I would never have made it.

Shortly afterwards we had more good news. My father was informed that we had been allocated one of the new council houses just built in the field behind Waverley, at number 11 Hoe Way – named after the Hoe family which owned the nearby Hyde Manor Farm from the seventeenth century until the nineteenth. It was a primly designed semi, with a long garden for Dad's vegetables. The house was warmed by a wonderful Rayburn stove, radiators throughout, and with a smart bathroom – the first time my family home had enjoyed such opulence. Dad and I luxuriated in it – though he commented on the rise in the rent.

Waverley, long condemned as unfit for human habitation, was promptly demolished: it took barely half a day to knock down and clear away its rotten walls and floors. One day I walked past it and it was there; the next evening it was completely gone. And part of our lives with it. It was as if it and our life there had never been. Appropriately the inevitable Mr Cripps was involved. He was the chairman of the housing committee which allocated us the council house. His daughter lived in the bungalow next door, and she acquired Waverley's small plot of land and absorbed it into her garden. Dad assumed that the Cripps did not know about the thinly covered well and cesspit. He hopefully, though fortunately fruitlessly, awaited developments.

It was a golden early autumn morning in October 1953 when I set off to take the stopping train to Oxford, changing at Bletchley. My father was already at the factory as I closed the neat front door on our new sparkling clean and wonderfully warm council house. I heaved my heavy case to the village station, past the empty space where Waverley unproudly stood until so recently. On the train I felt very strongly a sense of passing time, of moving on. I felt lucky to have survived and was conscious of the people to whom I owed so much: Dad, Joe Maxwell and Roade school, Jill and the Nannas, and above all Nettleton and his team of teachers at the grammar school.

Oxford station opened onto a bright new world. My hopes were sky high – and they were not disappointed.

Five

OXFORD PLEASURES

I staggered up from Oxford station with my heavy case, turned from the High Street between the Turl Tavern and the beautiful All Saints' Church which is now our college library, and into the Turl – opening on to the mediaeval walls lining Lincoln, Jesus and Exeter Colleges, with its old-fashioned shoemakers and traditional clothes shops on the west side, the street full of bicycles and undergraduates exuding the excitement of the first day of term. I passed through the ancient and solid gate into Lincoln main quadrangle, where the virginia creeper was just beginning to redden, and I fell in love. I adored Lincoln from my first day and my spirits still lift every time I visit. I have had close associations with other colleges, at home and abroad, but none has been able to replace that special place reserved for my own Oxford college.

Founded in 1427, Lincoln was and is one of the smallest and one of the least wealthy Oxford colleges. The advantage of its small size is that it is easy to meet and know most fellow students. So it is a friendly college. It also has a tradition of collegiate dons with less than the Oxford average level of petty bitchiness. In 1953 its remarkable Rector was Keith Murray, an old friend of Stinger Nettleton, who concentrated on strengthening the college finances with shrewd agricultural investments, and building a network of contacts with the better state schools, not just the small public schools which had been its previous staple. He was followed by a distinguished line of Rectors – Walter Oakeshott, Burke Trend, Vivian Green, Maurice Shock, Eric Anderson, Paul Langford – who recruited good teaching Fellows and strengthened the academic base.

On my first Friday I had meetings with the dons who were to teach me for Part One of my course in Politics, Philosophy and Economics. Economics had long fascinated me and I was lucky to have as my tutor a brilliant young economist, David Henderson. David rapidly exposed the limitations of my possible contribution to the academic side of the subject. My interest was really in the old-style 'applied' economics – the practical workings of a good or bad economy, or industry, or company. I suppose I wanted to know how to run the Treasury or be a successful stockbroker. But academic economics was rapidly moving away from that relevant kind of approach. A much more mathematical and theoretical approach was taking over.

David actually could do both equally well, and we later met as policy advisers in Whitehall. I passed my Part One exam comfortably enough, and continued to maintain interest in the subject, over the future years reading the more accessible parts of the literature, and concentrating on macro-economics both in Number 10 and as a stockbroker. But I knew that the more esoteric aspects of economics were not for me. Philosophy proved even less appetising, taught by an arid bachelor who had never published a word on the subject and whose main interest seemed to be in playing squash with handsome colonial boys. So I later switched to History, which has engaged me all my life.

For History my first tutor was Vivian Green, mediaeval historian and college chaplain. My weekly tutorials were held in his large book-lined study overlooking the back quad and the Radcliffe Library beyond. He was shy, seemingly very formal, unworldly, the quintessence of the English Anglican professional middle-class bachelor – everything in fact with which I had so little in common. Our first meeting was awkward as he tentatively offered me the term's reading list and the next week's essay title on something dry about the Anglo-Saxons. Yet over time I came to think the world of him. He was a dedicated teacher and scholar who was devoted to the college and its students. He was in the best tradition of Anglican tolerance and had a nice sense of humour once his shyness eased. He was also said to be the model for Smiley, the famous counter-spy in the novels of John le Carré (another Lincoln man). Clearly there was much more to Vivian than first met the eye. He helped me greatly both as a tutor and as Rector.

For more modern history I was taught by J. B. Owen. There was nothing of *Brideshead Revisited* about John, a no-nonsense New Zealander dedicated to getting his students through their examinations. He had been trained in the detailed Namier school of eighteenth-century history, which could be boring, being uninterested in the flow of ideas and mainly concerned with the impor-tance of self and group interests. He was deeply conservative, but he invested immense time and work into supporting my studies. He and Vivian were the twin pillars of my academic life in Oxford, though I enjoyed tutors from other colleges in subjects where little Lincoln did not have a specialist teacher. John Hale from Jesus lit up the Italian Renaissance for me, while lectures by A. J. P. Taylor on nineteenth-century Europe and by Hugh Trevor-Roper on the English Civil War ring in my memory. When they battled for the Oxford Regius Professorship of Modern History, I took Taylor's losing side and learned the Conservatives are so often better than Labour at arranging the advancement of their own.

I enjoyed both the academic and the social side of Oxford life. Every day seemed exciting, learning something fresh, meeting somebody new with talents I had never experienced. The centre of my pleasures were my college rooms: in the roof, up the stairs beside the chapel door. I had a sitting room with a desk and an electric fire, and a bedroom with a sink. No bathroom or lavatory – they were down three flights of stairs, across the chapel quad, and down into a basement, a long way on a cold night. But to me it was all an incredible luxury: the luxury that it was my own, quiet, with space to read and write, control of my own time, and the power to lock my outer door (known as 'sporting the oak') and protect my territory. Mrs Burgess, my elderly scout, cleaned up and made my bed. I had never had luxury like that in Roade, having shared a double bed with Clem until I was seventeen. Often in Lincoln I closed my door, stood in the middle of the room looking around and out of the windows over the rooftops and spires of Oxford, and rubbed my hands with pleasure at my luck in having this wonderful private territory, in this beautiful college, in this great university.

As an Open Scholar, I was privileged to wear a long flowing black gown and to live in my college for two years (short-gowned 'commoners' were then only allowed one year in college before moving to lodgings in town). For my third year I moved to a sitting room and bedroom in Walton Street, close enough to Lincoln and the city centre for me to walk to tutorials or lectures and to the Radcliffe Library, where I spent an increasing amount of time. With me went a close Lincoln friend, Roger Lonsdale, later Professor of English Literature at Oxford. Number 147 Walton Street was owned and managed as a boarding house by Mrs Lindstrom, a young widow who was more tolerant than the average Oxford dragon landlady, notorious for ensuring that student tenants did not enjoy anything or anybody on their premises. She was chatty, moody, emotional, and seemed genuinely to care for the welfare of her charges. In my time she also grew attached to one of her middle-aged tenants. One day there was a commotion as Roger and I went down to the basement kitchen for breakfast. The lodger's legs had been observed swinging outside the breakfast room window. He had hung himself from his upstairs window. The house was quite gloomy for several days after that.

My social life was at first mainly confined to Lincoln and I spent much of my time with Gerry Fowler, who had come up to Lincoln from our grammar school at the same time as me. He was always good fun and together we explored the mysteries of Oxford, especially its clubs and pubs.

Soon my literary interests took me into wider territories. I became literary editor of the university magazine *Isis* (for a while also serving as sports editor, demonstrating my rejection of the ancient varsity divide and hostility between 'arties' and 'hearties'). I published some very moderate poetry – much of it a pastiche of my hero, W. B. Yeats – and lots of book reviews, which enabled me to sell the pristine books to Blackwells for useful pocket money. I became President of the Oxford Poetry Society, editing a volume of Oxford Poetry, and of the Writers' Club, where a select band of university writers met to read their latest work or to meet visiting authors. Apparently I looked right for a poet, with long curly hair and a taste for wine and women. Fortunately, I quickly realised that I would only ever make a third-rate poet (at best) or a fourth-rate novelist, so I left those elevated roles to other, more optimistic colleagues.

But I really enjoyed being in the literary milieu. It gave me a wonderful social life and I became friendly with a generation of people who seriously could write – Alistair Elliot, John Gross (the cleverest and wittiest literary critic I have ever met), Anthony Thwaite. Adrian Mitchell, Alan Brownjohn, John McGrath, Francoise Eliet (a beautiful French novelist whom I both loved and neglected and who much later walked into the Seine to commit suicide), George MacBeth, Derek Wilson, Peter Levi and Gordon Snell, a hilarious author of children's stories who later married the Irish author Maeve Binchy to constitute the most entertaining partnership in current Anglo–Irish literature. I also became co-editor of an interesting literary magazine named *Departure*, which had a respectable reputation for publishing promising new writers – Philip Larkin, Elizabeth Jennings and Jennie Joseph were among our early catches. Gerry Fowler helped me with sales, energetically touring the colleges selling door-to-door, and sometimes rewarded by making fruitful contacts in the ladies' colleges. I learned a great deal about editing, printing and marketing, and especially about the hard life and low rewards of our authors. Beneath its bohemian glamour, the literary world is often harsh, shabby, lonely and full of unrewarded graft.

Apart from contact with my student contemporary writers, running the Poetry Society and the Writers' Club led me to meet various senior literary figures of the time.

The Poetry Society met weekly in college halls, with large student audiences to hear the visiting stars. Beforehand, I would meet the author, often off the train from London, and take him or her to dinner. Sometimes we were quite inebriated by the time of the meeting and I have only hazy recollections of visits by George Barker and William Empson. The latter came to my room beforehand and removed his thick woollen vest and long john underpants, saying he had 'expected Oxford to be much colder'. Empson's declamation of his own lines, 'Slowly the poison the whole bloodstream fills, the waste remains, the waste remains and kills' was quite hypnotic and for years later Gordon Snell and I would chant it to bemused fellow drinkers in London and Irish pubs. Stephen

Spender and Cecil Day-Lewis both proved much more conventional and bour-
geoisely prosperous than I expected – I had a romantic view of poets as
poverty-stricken and drunken eccentrics, reinforced by what I had heard of the
recent boozy behaviour of such visitors as Dylan Thomas and Brendan Behan.

The Writers' Club was more select, just for the 'professionals', meeting then
irregularly in my room in Walton Street to hear our own work, with occasional
visits by stars. Iris Murdoch came one evening and struck me as very earnest,
humourless and masculine. When she left I offered to escort her back across Oxford
to her college. This was not because I had any designs on her, having firmly (if
perhaps wrongly) concluded that she was of the lesbian tendency, but simply out of
some false gallantry thinking that was what officers of an Oxford club might be
expected to do for distinguished female visitors. She snapped, 'I can look after
myself perfectly well, thank you.' I concluded that she probably could.

Perhaps our most distinguished visitor was W. H. Auden, certainly the greatest
English language poet of his time. Auden had cravenly fled England to escape the
war and was then in the mid 1950s re-establishing contacts with Oxford, ahead
of his becoming the Oxford Professor of Poetry (for which I subsequently actively
campaigned, with Catherine Hoskyns painting 'Auden for Prof' in large letters
on the street outside the Radcliffe Library).

For the weeks before Auden's visit I was hot and shaking with excitement. On
the great evening, with several literary colleagues we took him to supper (I cannot
remember where, being in a haze) and afterwards we climbed in a crowded taxi
to travel to Walton Street. Auden invited me to sit on his lap. I was not entirely
naive about the world in general or his sexual proclivities in particular, but I
lacked the confidence or authority to decline an invitation from the greatest poet
I had ever met. Fortunately it was a short journey, though he had explored my
most sensitive parts by the time we reached number 147. He obviously wasn't too
disappointed since as we tumbled out of the taxi, he said in a curious half-
American drawl, 'You and I must meet again soon.' The Writers' Club gathering
went hilariously and drunkenly well. When he left, I decided not to offer to walk
him home to his college, since, unlike Iris Murdoch, I sensed he might only too
readily have accepted. It struck me as odd that he was so random in his proposi-
tions and apparently had no radar system to alert him that I was a bad bet for his
particular pleasure; perhaps he had learned that the blunderbuss approach often
paid off. It was also sad that, so famous, he was also obviously so lonely. I
remember above all, the deep lines in his leathery face, like a clay field rutted and
ploughed by time. Afterwards I bought several of his early volumes of poetry and
realised that there is often a total chasm of quality difference between a great poet
like him and mere verbal journeymen like most of the rest of us.

We had great fun in the Oxford literary set. Our pub lunches stretched into long evening parties. I regularly climbed out of Adrian Mitchell's grand rooms overlooking Christ Church Meadow and, before moving to the freedoms of Walton Street, climbed into Lincoln, over the wall covered in broken glass and barbed wire near the Rector's house, and then across the roof of the 'fleet' lavatory. Personal relationships were often intense and I found that the literary world provided access to beautiful and bohemian young ladies. As a result I became acquainted with all the ladies' colleges, especially Somerville and St Hilda's, which seemed to specialise in bright, cultured and very pretty young women. Lady Margaret Hall was the least rewarding, being snobbishly class-conscious and hence unwelcoming to wild young men from poor backgrounds with unpromising financial prospects. St Hugh's – where I found my wife Carol – smelled strongly of boiled cabbage and muddy hockey boots.

One Saturday night I delayed in Somerville until after gates were closed at seven and my lady friend decided it was better for me to stay the night and leave next day, exploiting the more relaxed rules of Sundays. Next morning at around ten, before the gates opened, I went to make coffee down the corridor and – inevitably, given 'Donoughue luck' – met the college Dean, young and severe. I decided to play it straight, said 'Good morning', boiled the kettle and offered her the boiled water first. She said 'Thank you', and to my relief moved off. I met her again years later when I was working in Number 10 for Jim Callaghan and was associated with a controversial piece of educational policy. She was by then a senior official in the Department of Education and summoned me to explain 'why Number Ten is interfering in our education policy'. She gave me a rocket – tinged, I sensed, with revenge for my earlier misdemeanour, though we did not refer to it.

Gerry Fowler had joined me on the fringe of the literary set and had fallen deeply in love with a delightful poet named Judy. One day he came to my room very disturbed. Judy was being pursued by a bohemian London author and Gerry feared he would lose out to fame in this emotional battle. The author was apparently arriving that day in Oxford, presumably to proposition Judy. Gerry – our future Minister of Education – pleaded with me, as an old friend, and partic-ularly as former captain of boxing at the grammar school, to tour Oxford with him in search of the cursed competitor and 'duff him up to discourage him'. I agreed on condition that we toured in a taxi and Gerry paid, which he agreed. We spent hours and many precious pounds in fruitless search, with the taxi driver thinking we were mad since we apparently had no destination but simply went round in circles in the dreadful Oxford traffic. Finally Gerry's money ran out and we gave up. I don't know what I would have done had we met the cursed literary suitor. I doubt if I would indeed have 'duffed him up'. Later I read excellent work by him – Christopher Logue – and discovered that he was quite puny, so I was pleased it came to nothing. Anyway, he moved on from Judy, or she from him, and Gerry himself pursued other quarry. But it was a close shave with a shameful exploit and showed me, not for the first or last time (as when Jill abandoned me), how jealousy and deep emotions can lead to very irrational behaviour.

Quite apart from the literary set, I met many distinguished young men and women at Oxford, and some became friends. The Union was then still a stable and exercise yard for budding politicians or journalists to learn their low trades. I joined but never participated in any debate, feeling that it required a particularly artificial style in which I had no background or indeed talent. Shining there at the beginning of my time were such future stars as Michael Heseltine, Anthony Howard and Jeremy Isaacs. But the Union was already beginning to wane and was taken less seriously than it had been. Someone quite unusual with whom I became unexpectedly friendly was the doomed Jeremy Wolfenden, homosexual son of the future chairman of the Royal Commission on homosexual reform. Jeremy was my coldly brilliant editor on *Isis*. He lived in what I heard – but never glimpsed – was a curious twilight world of drugs and sexual deviance. Pasty-faced and hiding behind dark shades after allegedly endless all-night parties, he padded in and out of our literary and magazine worlds and I always enjoyed talking with him. He obviously had a powerful intellect and could master any subject. I knew with him, as with Gerry, that I had met a mind much better than my own. It was assumed that he would fly to the top of any profession he chose.

But he was always tortured, even a little shifty, as if hiding something (it was not then the fashion for homosexuals to 'come out' and be treated as normal members of our society – the practice was still barbarically a criminal offence), never happy, and I was sorry but not wholly surprised when he died young, apparently of alcohol, and possibly drug abuse. He certainly had the talents to do something more serious than journalism.

My continuing political interests kept me in touch with the political clubs. Most interesting were a delightful if misled bunch of Marxists, including Ralph Samuels, Stuart Hall and Garry Pearson. All present or former members of the Communist Party, they were desperately trying to reconcile their beliefs with the horrifying news that regularly emerged from eastern Europe about the bestial realities of the communist regimes there. They were engaging and stimulating company and launched an important magazine, the *New Left Review*, which gave renewed intellectual credibility to their basically vicious and clapped-out Marxist doctrine. They were further evidence of the recurrent fact that good people can have bad thoughts, but I enjoyed their friendships immensely. Perversely, they helped me clarify and strengthen my own convictions on the right-wing social democratic side of the Labour Party.

There was over time less space for sport in my crowded literary, academic and social life. I played rugby in my first term for the Lincoln first XV, who won the league unbeaten, and having scored four tries on the wing in the university trials also played for the University Greyhounds. But my enthusiasm waned amid the welter of alternative claims on my time. I also found rugby at Oxford at that time much more puritan, less open and cavalier, than at school. On one occasion when Lincoln was twenty points in the lead, I tried an optimistic reverse pass to my centre which went astray, though without adverse consequences. Our dour Scottish captain came across to publicly rebuke me. 'I want no more of that fucking fancy stuff. Your job is to tackle and fall on the fucking ball.' I began to think that perhaps this was not my job, especially since I had never been over-keen on falling on the ball. I liked running with it, but contemporary tactics viewed that as risky and so wingers then received few passes, and most of those were accompanied by the opposing huge wing forward. The college club was also sternly professional, demanding a total commitment of one's time, energy and social life. Its members drank heavily in college 'deep hall', singing loud and bawdy songs, which was not my style; I sensed that their only experience of sex was vicariously to sing lewd songs about it.

Because of their heavy drinking, they needed regular training, something in which I had never indulged. They clearly hated 'arties', which I to some extent was. Some of them concluded openly that I was a homosexual because I had long curly hair, did not train and published poetry. Although obsessed with smutty sex, many of them were too inhibited to go near a woman and their chauvinist clanning was not my idea of how to spend a satisfying Saturday night. I preferred actual physical contact. So by the end of the season I decided to withdraw from college rugby. I continued to play in Northampton, including for the mighty Saints second XV (which contained several internationals), but that phase of my life was drawing to an end. One sunny Saturday afternoon I was playing for the East Midlands Colts against some county team on the ground of the Leicester Tigers. The pitch was bone hard, scraping my knees. I did not receive a single decent pass on the wing. Despite an acquired skill at avoiding falling on the ball, I had to go down several times and received opposing bootstuds in my ears and testicles. My girlfriend Jill was nobly watching from the terraces, seemingly offering a pretty alternative life. Afterwards we took the train back to Northampton, leaving my boots in the Leicester dressing room, and I never played rugby again. But I still watch it with great pleasure on television, and remain an avid Northampton Saints supporter from afar.

Soccer was a different proposition and I continued playing spasmodically for the college until a back injury led to temporary retirement from all sports. Lincoln's soccer team contained several literary figures and demanded none of rugby's almost religious fervour and commitment. We played for pleasure and without ambition. On that basis I enjoyed soccer at Oxford and elsewhere for another thirty years, later playing for all six LSE student teams, though not in fact a student; for Highgate Old Boys, though never having set foot in the school; and when in my forties regularly for the Houses of Parliament XI, although then not a member of either House (I have never played for them since joining the Lords). My final game in life was for them on the Tottenham Hotspur ground White Hart Lane when I was fifty and played outside the great Argentinian star, Osvaldo Ardiles. I also played on Sunday mornings on Hampstead Heath with a group of local friends and neighbours led by my LSE friend John Carrier and at times including the writers Melvyn Bragg and Martin Amis, though I think they found it excessively robust. I was a kind of soccer mercenary, turning up without affiliation and trying 'to do the business'. I have always disliked fundamentalist commitment, whether among football supporters, in Northern Ireland or on the lunatic left of the Labour Party.

I also retained a passing interest in boxing and occasionally visited the university gym to punch the bags. I did not pursue athletics at Oxford, though I had always been interested in it and had won medals for running at school. Lincoln had a distinguished middle-distance runner in Derek Johnson who had won a Blue and represented his country internationally. He was a friend and on 6 May 1954, at lunchtime in hall, he tipped me off that there was to be an attempt that evening to break the four-minute-mile barrier.

I cycled to the university running track and watched enthralled as Roger Bannister, aided by Chris Chataway and Chris Brasher, pushed, head back and gasping, to the line just inside four minutes. Of course today, with modern techniques of training, this barrier is regularly broken with little apparent effort. But then it struck me as an astonishing achievement, since four minutes had long seemed almost beyond human capability. I cycled back to college very proud to have been present on such an historic occasion and grateful to Derek for the tip.

In the long university vacations, I usually returned home to Roade to recharge my batteries; the contrast between the social and intellectual glitter of the dreaming spires and the calm of sensible village life was striking and therapeutic. Sometimes I took a vacation job to earn pocket money, including working with Dad at the factory. My university state scholarship was £312 a year, which was more than I ever enjoyed before, but had to cover my living costs in college as well as recreations, and so left little for vacation spending. Most of the time I studied quietly in our new warm council house. I always brought home with me from Oxford a trunk-load of books taken from the reading list for the following term's academic programme. This way, I comfortably kept up with the syllabus and made sure I had my lecture notes and essays clearly summarised for revision well before examination time. Each day Dad would call me as he left for the factory at 7.50 a.m. I would go downstairs for breakfast and study from nine until noon, sitting by the glowing Rayburn stove surrounded by books and files of notes. Through the windows was our vegetable garden, then the fields rolling towards Stoke Bruerne. (On those fields was soon built a new comprehensive school with which I later formed a happy association.) At midday I began the simple task of preparing lunch for Dad when he came home at 12.30, putting the vegetables to boil on the new gas stove and warming any meat – food rationing thankfully ended while I was at Oxford.

I was often lonely, especially after separating from Jill in 1954. I was also conscious of growing apart from my old village friends, many of whom were getting married and starting families in a world that I respected but was aware of leaving.

It is a feature of British higher education, where few attend local universities, that it often plucks young people out of their childhood environments and translates them into other more glamorous and yet more rootless worlds. For most of us at Oxford, our future lay in London or some other big town offering professional employment. Oxford was for me a bridge out of the village towards that metropolitan future.

I did for a time acquire another home-from-home in Roade. Along the Hartwell road, into a smart modern bungalow named Herod's Gate, arrived 'Dixie' and Annette Dean. Dixie worked at the Foreign Office radio station three miles away in Hanslope, where a nest of tall aerials monitored international radio traffic to serve the Smileys of the day. Naively, I did not appreciate Dixie's own intelligence role until twenty years later, when as a civil servant I visited one of our 'spook' operations at Gosforth near the south coast. Without prior warning, Dixie popped up smiling for lunch, like a hat out of a Christmas cracker. We often chatted about his wartime experiences. He was the first veteran to talk to me openly about the total chaos in the British army's flight to Dunkirk in 1940, when his battalion, along with many others, threw away their weapons, commandeered anything which moved, and fled before the advancing Germans to the coast. Dunkirk was clearly not a wholly heroic experience. His sumptuous wife Annette was a Czech Jewess who escaped from the Nazis to Jerusalem, where she met him. They had no children and for a while she became another surrogate mother for me, giving me tea beside the open fire when I dropped in from my afternoon walk. Herod's Gate provided another second home for me in Northamptonshire, filling the gap when Jill and the Nannas (the latter only temporarily) were cut off. I had always been something of an emotional nomad, moving from household to household, seeking warmth, affection, and female company. I was lucky in the very kind people I found.

Not all of my vacation time was spent in Roade. Once I had completed my reading lists and earned some money, I travelled: to Umbria to learn Italian with Jill; to the Atlantic coast of France with my Oxford friend Laidon Alexander; down the German Rhine with the writer Derek Wilson; and twice hilariously to Ireland with my Oxford friend Gordon Snell. The latter Irish expeditions were linked to our friendship with Sean White, then reading for a doctorate on W. B. Yeats in Oxford. Sean had trained as a priest at the famous seminary of Maynooth but withdrew at the last moment, to the fury of Dublin's notorious Archbishop McQuade.

Sean told me that when he had the final tea at the palace and told the prelate that his reason for withdrawal was that he no longer believed in the basic tenets of the faith, the worldly Archbishop replied untroubled that he could find Sean a position in the Church 'where that would not matter'. Sean withdrew to become an academic, pursued by McQuade's venom. Full of mischievous wit and Dublin scepticism, Sean was a great raconteur and drinking companion and I visited him in his fine house in Rathmines. Gordon and I attended his marathon wedding – or at least part of it. I arrived too late for the actual ceremony, but the celebrations continued over several days and we had a great time. Part of it I spent with the writer Benedict Kiely, who would occasionally pause to say, 'I must return to the office to complete that film review' – but never did.

On another visit to Dublin, I was drinking with Sean and friends in a bar near Trinity College, where he was saying goodbye to a lawyer who was flying off to Galway that evening for a big court case next morning. We cut it too fine, the lawyer missed the plane, and Sean suggested that we drive him to Galway that night. So the four of us set off westwards, pausing for relaxation in various snugs en route. At one bar we lost the lawyer, who had made a promising friendship with the widow behind the bar. We arrived in Galway in time for breakfast, after which Sean went into the court to apologise for the lawyer's absence 'on the grounds of ill health'. We had a muted drive back. Over the years I continued to see Sean, ever buzzing with wit and gossip. He died as he would have chosen, suddenly, while walking his beloved Kerry hills.

I also went with Gordon Snell on a wonderful walking holiday through Mayo, Connemara and Galway, then speckled with colourful thatched cottages, before the mass arrival of the depressing bungalow boxes. We visited our friend

Maureen Cleave in Sligo, seeing Yeats' Ben Bulben, and headed onto Achill Island, a last step before the Atlantic and America.

We meant to stay at a hotel on the far tip of the island, but never reached it. Pausing for lunch in Maloney's bar, we remained there into the following early hours, entertained by a group of local herring fishermen. They took us back at 3 a.m. to their fishing hut, full of nets, masts and rigging, and we had a huge fry-up of fresh local eggs and ham. We then tried to sleep in their rope hammocks slung from the roof – though only very fitfully, since the lights had to be kept on all night 'to deter the rats'. At six in the morning I blearily saw one of the fishermen climb out of his hammock, pull back the curtain, peer out for a moment, and quickly conclude, to the relief of his anxious colleagues, that 'it is terrible rough out there' and we all turned over to try to get more sleep. And that was long before Europe had a common fishing policy designed to deter fishermen from fishing.

Weeks later, back in London, I received an envelope from my Westminster bank enclosing my lost cheque book covered in round dried Guinness rings. The accompanying cool note simply said: 'The enclosed cheque book has apparently been returned from a bar in the west of Ireland.' I knew my chances of a future large overdraft had diminished.

But the honesty involved in bothering to return my cheque book was then typical of rural Ireland. When we were in Mayo, much of the local bar conversation was concerned with a recent visit by the notorious Dublin playwright Brendan Behan, who had allegedly stolen and not returned a local bicycle. Apart from seeing it as further evidence of the corruption of Dublin life, the main local comment was, 'Why didn't yer man ask for a bicycle if he wanted one?'

We walked and hitch-hiked along the then quiet roads from Achill to Galway, where we had booked at a youth hostel on Lettermullen. It was open, with basic provisions in the kitchen, and bunk beds made, but without sign of any management. A neighbour, from whom we bought fresh eggs, told us, 'Of course, they have gone to Moscow' – which may or may not have been true. When we departed we left the door unlocked as we found it and our payment on the kitchen table.

One Sunday afternoon in that area, Gordon and I went for a tea-time pint of Guinness at the local pub, illegally open on the Sabbath and crowded with locals. Suddenly the telephone rang and the proprietor, having taken the call, rapped loudly on the counter and shouted, 'The police are coming to raid us in five minutes. Get out as usual through the back garden and hide over the far wall. Stay there until I call you back.' So we all obediently filed out and waited noisily over the wall. I watched the two officers arrive on their bicycles, look around, and stroll into the bar. After taking refreshment they emerged and slowly rode off, clearly satisfied that no breach of the Sabbath had occurred. The publican then summoned us all back in to continue drinking. The warning call had actually come from the police station itself and was apparently part of a regular routine. This all seemed to me to be a sensible way to conduct police relations with the public in a civilised community. Today, urbanisation and the EU Agricultural Policy have destroyed some of that magic and gentle innocence of the Irish West.

Oxford Finals loomed in 1957 and I worked hard. I was greatly helped by my dear friend Stella Alexander, who during the weeks before finals had rented a cottage on the Berkshire Downs, where I converted the garden shed into a study and, surrounded by silence and idyllic views, completed my revision for the examinations.

When the dreaded days came, I put on my rented mortar board and a suit I borrowed from the saintly Roger Lonsdale, still never having owned one myself. I took a dozen examination papers and by the end of this exhausting experience had lost seven pounds in weight. A few weeks later, I gathered my diminished resources for the viva interviews and was heartened by some muttered words of encouragement, though I counted no chickens until the results and my First Class Honours were published. My father did not take on board its significance until the *Northampton Chronicle and Echo* featured mine among the grammar school successes (with a First also for Gerry Fowler). Then Dad was very proud. We both felt that Stinger Nettleton's original strategy had finally brought home the goods.

That wound up my undergraduate career, though not my association with Lincoln, where I continued the next year as a postgraduate. I have remained in close contact with the college throughout the rest of my life and was greatly honoured when made an Honorary Fellow. I visit Lincoln regularly and the food has improved immensely; when I went up in 1953, I had to take my ration book and we qualified only for a couple of shillings' worth of meat a week. Recently I attended a delicious dinner in the handsome college hall, its walls lined with many of the same old portraits on which I gazed when eating there more austerely as an undergraduate. Afterwards, looking for a toilet (never in oversupply in Lincoln), I wandered up a dark staircase and switched on a light. I found not a toilet but a door inscribed 'The Bernard Donoughue Room', recognising some past financial contribution. I felt deeply moved and proud, my mind leaping back nearly half a century. The pictures from long ago crowded into my memory and I felt that many old and dead friends, such as Gerry Fowler and John Owen, were there in College with me.

Six

AMERICAN ADVENTURES –
AND SEEKING A CAREER

Oxford did not finish for me with my finals and my First in 1957, though a very golden chapter in my life certainly closed then. Returning to Lincoln in the autumn as a postgraduate, I found college life much less exciting. Many of my best university friends had sensibly not extended the Oxford party, but had gone down to London to find jobs in publishing, at the BBC, etc., and to begin to lead adult lives.

At Lincoln I no longer had the comforting rhythm of the undergraduate terms, moving from syllabus paper to paper, from tutor to tutor. I was on my own with a project for a Doctorate of Philosophy, focussing on the British government's handling of the beginning of the American War of Independence. But Oxford was not then geared to graduate research. It was still primarily an undergraduate university. We minority of graduate students, especially in the arts and social sciences, were left isolated and lonely, expected to learn unguided how to become great scholars. So I often escaped to London. Sometimes I stayed in smart Camden Hill with Stella and Laidon Alexander, or with my old Balliol friend Gordon Snell in his bohemian flat at 48 Hogarth Road, Earls Court. Gordon was incredibly tolerant and always attracted amusing friends; there was a constant flow passing through to spend the night. For a time I borrowed a room in the flat, and opposite was the actor Peter O'Toole, a Yorkshire–Irishman then making his way to stardom on the stage and soon in films. Peter had many attractive visitors, who were observed with envy by the rest of us at all times of day and night, gliding often under-clothed down the passage. One stunning blonde passed me on the way to the bathroom in the early hours, wearing only a very small towel. Obviously feeling out of courtesy the need to at least acknowledge a fellow resident, she said primly, as my eyes gazed at her deliciously wobbling breasts, 'Peter said to make tea.' I felt it would make a good title for a certain kind of novel. Peter recently told me that Gordon named his room 'Climax County'. Number 48 Hogarth Road was for most of us a last, careless, often hungover and ultimately unsatisfying rapture of bachelordom.

After a while I grew bored with my graduate life and decided I must make a fresh leap into some new territory. However, I knew too little of the outside professional world to have any reliable feel of what the suitable territorial opportunities might be.

I then realised that the *real* disadvantage of an underprivileged upbringing is not the childhood poverty but that people from poor backgrounds usually have no knowledge of the various employment opportunities in the outside professional world. They know of physical labour, which they will probably wish to avoid. They often end up as teachers – a noble though ill-paid job – because teaching is the only profession with which they have been in regular contact. But they are usually and inevitably ignorant of the wider choice of professional jobs which might be more suited to their particular personalities and ambitions. It was only many years after Oxford that I realised that I would actually have liked to have been a barrister. Yet while I grew up I had no contact with the law and never knowingly met a single lawyer. I had no idea how lawyers were trained or what they actually did. I saw a few law students in Lincoln, but they appeared to be hidden in library corners studying dense tomes full of tedious detail on laws which seemed to have little relevance to the modern world in which I was interested. Only at the London School of Economics, through stimulating friends such as Michael Zander and Anthony Lester, and later in the House of Lords witnessing the scrutiny of legislation, did I begin to perceive what a fascinating world the law could be. But by then I was on a different escalator.

While contemplating my leap into the outer world, I shared a flat in north Oxford with my two old Lincoln friends, Gerry Fowler and Alan Russell. We three Oxford 'Firsts' lived in a total shambles, unable even to cook a meal between us. Life there was at times hilarious, with all-night parties and visiting friends sleeping on floors and settees. Finally it palled for all of us. We moved on our individual ways, though remaining friends for life. And amid all the chaos, I had identified the destination of my next great leap: across the Atlantic to the New World. My leap out of Oxford involved in the spring of 1958 winning a Henry Fellowship, one of which is given each year to Harvard University, and gaining a Fulbright Scholarship which paid for my travel to the USA. Sailing that late August out of Southampton Water in the giant *Queen Mary*, I was not clear what I wanted to get out of my year in America, but the adventure certainly worked out gloriously. Another golden chapter opened and this was to prove possibly the most exciting and fruitful single year of my life.

At Oxford, I had always enjoyed good friendships with American students – especially with Paul Sarbanes (later US Senator for Maryland), Dick Ulmann (future Professor at Princeton), Jim Griffin (now Professor of Philosophy at Oxford), Judy Davison (Russian scholar and Washington aide), and Jerry Kuehl (polymath TV producer). I had instantly liked their warmth, openness and generosity. America in 1958–9 provided those qualities in spades, and I added David Halberstam (Pulitzer Prize-winning journalist), Ed Fischer (*New Yorker* cartoonist) and Maurice Pechet from Harvard to my list of lifelong friends from across the Atlantic. But what I liked above all about the States at that time was its optimism, its sense of adventure and achievement, the overwhelming feeling there that anything was possible, that any problem was soluble, and that they would back anyone who promised to 'go for it'. That all contrasted with my experience of grey provincial England in the 1950s (or indeed later), constrained by its traditions, its personal inhibitions, its class structures, its negativism, its economic weakness; viewing adventure and success with envy and suspicion, making a virtue out of caution and 'keeping one's nose clean'. Of course these stark comparisons and contrasts are exaggerated. Not all of America was golden and not all of England was grey, as I found at Oxford. But that is very much how it struck a naive young man of twenty-four in 1958. Certainly America was to me a refreshing new world and new way of life.

Our crossing to New York was uneventful. I shared a small, smelly cabin with three others in the bowels of the giant liner – not much luxury there. One companion, a Texan returning from his first visit to Europe, never undressed and continually lay on his bunk wearing high leather riding boots day and night. The high point of the trip inevitably was the breathtaking Statue of Liberty at dawn. When the *Queen Mary* docked in the summer heat of Manhattan, I immediately enjoyed the rich variety of that great city's hospitality. In the customs shed, an officer looking at my papers said: 'You a Donoughue? I'm a Murphy. You can go straight through.' Outside, unable to find my hosts, Ed and Annie Fischer, I approached a large policeman with a revolver balanced on his huge belly. I said politely: 'Excuse me, officer, I am lost …' Before I could pose my question, he snapped: 'You are lost? I am lost. In New York, we are all lost. Now get lost!' I turned away, and there were Ed and Annie. Over the next days they showed me the noisy delights of their beloved city. I was stunned by the beauty of the skylines and the sense of energy on the pavement.

I travelled to Harvard via New Haven, staying at the home of my Oxford friend Jim Griffin. His brother collected genuine cowboy pistols from the nineteenth century American west, Colt 45s, etc. I have always been an addict of cowboy films and, seeing myself as a kind of James Stewart in *Destry Rides Again* or Gary

Cooper in *High Noon*, soft spoken but a dead shot, I lapped up the opportunity to draw from a genuine holster and fire the real guns. From less than ten yards I did not once hit a large sack hanging on a clothes line; more often than not I hit the ground in between and the kick drove me backwards. Since then I have sadly viewed the cinematic portrayal of events at the OK Corral, or Billy the Kid knocking down the sheriff's posse like skittles, or especially the infallible accuracy of Clint Eastwood, with deep scepticism.

At Harvard, I was attached to the senior common room of Lowell House. With its ivy-clad walls and grass quadrangles, it had some of the familiar atmosphere of an Oxford college, though much more comfortable. My rooms were spacious and the bathroom shower was a marvellous luxury, to which I henceforward converted from baths. Lowell was headed by Eliot (who in turn was headed by Mrs) Perkins, a magnificent Anglophile and scion of an old New England family. 'Perk' was very tall and stood in all things for 'high standards', by which he usually meant old-fashioned European standards of culture and courtesy (sadly long abandoned in Europe but preserved in Lowell). As Master, he ran Lowell on benevolently patrician lines. He had real style. As an Oxford Englishman, I had his total support. He was once clearly worried at high table dinner when I was exposed as uncertain in which direction to 'pass the port'.

But he and his colleagues, especially Maurice Pechet, the brilliant and elegant medical scientist and Dean of House, took every trouble and expense to make me comfortable. Maurice's generosity has continued to warm my life throughout the subsequent near fifty years of our friendship. That October, Maurice drove me for days in his new (now classic) Ford Thunderbird through New England to see the astonishing fall foliage, an ocean of russet and red spreading across Maine, New Hampshire and Vermont. Next summer he took myself and Carol – my girl-friend and future wife Carol Goodman, who had also just graduated from Oxford and had come out to teach in the USA – to stay in Atlantic City, a kind of transatlantic Blackpool with comfort added. Often then and after my transatlantic visit, I felt a great deal of guilt and discomfort at the realisation of how rarely do we British return this hospitality to American visitors to any degree comparable to the scale on which it is lavished on us there.

At first I joined enthusiastically in the Harvard academic life, resuming my doctoral task and visiting the Widener Library daily. But one bright autumn morning I sat there, looked around, and realised that it was very little different from the routine of my graduate student days in Oxford, and it would be a pity to spend my precious American year there, encased in characterless academe. So I collected my papers into my briefcase and left, never to return. I devoted the rest of my time to enjoying and trying to understand the real, different America.

It was a decision that I never regretted, even though it meant that any prospect of completing my doctoral thesis receded still further into the future.

Instead, I threw myself into the social life of beautiful Cambridge, Massachusetts, picnicked on my first decent hamburgers and milkshakes beside the Charles River, and visited Boston (then in drab decline) and the rest of the state. Carol and I went together on several visits to New York, walking the Avenues of Manhattan from end to end, sampling the music and theatres, and getting a feel for that uniquely exciting (though in winter dreadfully cold) city. One particularly powerful and moving play we saw was *A Raisin in the Sun* by Lorraine Hanberry, the first black playwright to win the New York Critics' Circle award. In coming to the States, Carol was perhaps making sure that I was not lost forever into the American West (which I might well have liked), or at least into the arms of some predatory American female. Actually she had little reason to fear. American women took little interest in me. And, although I fell in love with nearly every aspect of American life, the charms of American womanhood then escaped my intermittent interest. To me as an observer at that time, the American female seemed threateningly aggressive (which probably meant that they were rightly asserting an equality which today we would accept unquestioningly) and materialistic (i.e. sensible and practical). More seriously, they did seem a little two-dimensional. The dimension apparently lacking was what my Oxford friend John Gross, then at Princeton, described to me as we stood freezing on the famous bridge at Concord: 'Bernard, they lack mystery.' Even that was probably just a question of the style of late Eisenhower America. Such generalisations as mine above have a value in catching the flavour of a time, but are rarely of universal validity. America, more than any other society I have known, has a vast diversity beneath its surface uniformity. (Critics might claim conversely that it has uniformity beneath its surface diversity.) Later I made friends with fascinating American women who could have provided John with all the mystery he craved.

My closest friend at Harvard was a fascinating Australian journalist, Bruce Grant, who had been a distinguished foreign editor of the quality Melbourne newspaper, *The Age*. Bruce was handsome, charming, cultured, witty and very subtle – everything the typical Australian is said not to be. We had a terrific time together, exploring the bars of Boston and the Heights of Quebec, and I learned a great deal from him. Bruce was divorced but in a close relationship back home with a very well-known Australian musician he always referred to as 'Bambi', without an identifying surname. He missed her greatly and told me all about their relationship and his marriage ambitions. She was scheduled to visit him in the winter and his excitement grew as the time for her arrival approached. But on the eve of the great day, he came to see me looking shocked and sad.

Bambi had phoned from London, her planned stopover point, to say that she wouldn't be coming after all. Apparently, on board the aeroplane from Australia (if not before?), she had fallen for a fellow passenger and meant to marry him instead. It was quite a romantic story, if sad for Bruce. The suitor who scooped the Bambi prize was George Harewood, cousin to the Queen and a major figure in British musical life. He did marry Bambi, and Bruce continued as a friend. Years later I met the Harewoods in the royal box at a Wembley football match. I delicately revealed to her that I had been at Harvard with Bruce and had hoped to meet her then. She handled it beautifully. Such complexities can be managed by people of quality and confidence.

There were three peak experiences for me in my wonderful year in the States.

The first, boosted by the hindsight of subsequent events, was a day I spent in November 1958 campaigning with the young John F. Kennedy, while he was seeking re-election as junior Senator for Massachusetts. I joined him for breakfast at his stately apartment on Beacon Hill in the snobbish part of Boston. With great care and consideration, given that I was a young nobody without a vote in the coming election, he explained to me our programme for the day ahead and the issues which most concerned him. During this conversation, we were firmly interrupted by his wife Jackie. She struck me as very cool and determined, well polished and groomed, with a very high forehead and distractingly wide eyes, yet without warmth or 'mystery' – definitely not my type. There was a perceptible crackle of tension and not much apparent affection between them.

The other political aides arrived and we set off in a small cavalcade of large Cadillacs for his speaking tour of the sad New England towns around Boston, most of them then dependent on declining old manufacturing industries. The electronic and high-technology revolution had not yet significantly blessed Massachusetts. The most vivid picture in my mind's American gallery is of Kennedy, lean and wiry, coatless in an icy wind, standing speaking on a drab street corner as workers spilled from a nearby factory. He looked very young and vulnerable, his voice rasping in that flat and unattractive 'Borston' accent. He suddenly quoted a whole poem by Robert Frost, to half a dozen gaping men in overalls. It impressed me as a former President of the Oxford Poetry Society; and almost certainly puzzled them.

At a simple hamburger lunch in some plastic diner we discussed wider politics, including his political future and the widely mooted possibility of his running for the Presidency. He was completely open about his ambitions, in a way that no English politician would dare to be. Obviously the Presidency was firmly on his family's schedule. He spoke as if being a Kennedy was part of a political royal dynasty, with predicted roles for the sons, leaving them little personal option. I asked him directly about the implications for a White House candidate of being a Roman Catholic, and even if he regretted his religious affiliation as being an obstacle to his own supreme ambition. He thought a while and replied: 'If I had my life again and knew from the beginning that I would be running for President, I would still want to be a practising Catholic.' I was immediately impressed by his spiritual commitment. But then he went on to explain, with great psephological knowledge of the American electoral landscape, how his calculation was that his Catholicism would have 'a neutral impact' on his chances, because the anti-Catholic bigots would be balanced by a strong Catholic vote in such key constituencies as Chicago, New York, etc. Clearly he had clinically done his electoral sums and kept his spiritual dimension in political perspective. I then saw his professionalism and took his political future very seriously. I quickly wrote an article called 'Boston Stomp' in which I predicted that he could be the next President of the United States, and sent it to the *Spectator* magazine. Its editor, Ian Gilmour, wrote back with sympathetic rejection, saying he liked it but the journal's Washington correspondent had assured him there was no prospect of Kennedy being selected to run, let alone being elected. So my piece lay unpublished.

I visited Kennedy's headquarters several times and was made aware by a friend there of the candidate's sexual activities with female staff. When a journalist covering the campaign made a joke to me about this proclivity, I asked if he would publish the revelation (which would have guaranteed him headlines and money). He replied, looking astonished at my question: 'Of course not. Kennedy will make a great President of the United States and I would not wish to damage him.' There are a few if any journalists in the UK today with such commendable values.

A second unforgettable experience was my visit to the West Virginia and east Kentucky coalfields in February 1959. There was a long-running strike and an owners' lockout in these old-fashioned mines and I went to see how America handled industrial disputes. The answer there was: 'brutally'. I flew in a small shaky plane to Tri-City airport and then crossed into the mining hills by bus and hitch-hiking. It was very pretty, hillbilly country, mainly populated by descendants of the original Scottish–Irish immigrants who settled there in the late eighteenth and early nineteenth centuries. Most of their names would have been familiar in Belfast and Armagh. There had been little immigration since then because the territory was isolated, covered in beautiful wooded hills and rushing streams, and little new employment had been added to the original logging, mining and hill-farming. It was desperately poor country, with rows of simple wooden-board houses, often on low stilts against the valley floods, and many children running around barefoot on the dirt tracks. The mines were old-fashioned, under-mechanised, dangerous and paid very low wages. This was far from the American consumer dream. The atmosphere in the villages and in dreary Harlan, the capital of the mining county, was tense and menacing. Violence erupted frequently and one driver who gave me a lift told me that a miner activist had been shot the previous week by the henchmen of the bosses; he advised me to get out quick. Certainly, people viewed any stranger such as me as suspicious and I was aware I was being followed. At times, being no hero, I felt frightened. I stayed in a shabby little hotel in Harlan, visited the town's newspaper and school, and talked to locals in dingy bars. Most had never met anyone from Europe and all thought my accent was to them indistinguishable from that in New England. I was fascinated to see a part of America of which most people were unaware – nobody I knew in Harvard had ever been to that county, and Master Perkins told me that Lowell House had never had a student from there. But it was intimidating and I was glad to get away in one piece.

I wrote an article describing my experiences entitled 'Harlan County', and at least the *New Statesman* printed it – my first exposure to national journalism. But when I sent a second article, revealing that the poor miners in Harlan had been called out on strike by the giant Mineworkers' Union, led by the corrupt Labour hero John L. Lewis, and that the union itself controlled nearby mines which benefited from the closing of competitors, the *Statesman* baulked at it. Its editor Kingsley Martin, an icon of near sanctity on the British left, was happy to attack the brutal Harlan bosses, but not so keen to expose a cynical trade union leader. That was an educative introduction to British political journalism.

The final peak highlight of my American visit came at the end of my academic year. Together with Carol and Michael Rose, an English friend from the Foreign Office, we bought for two hundred dollars a second-hand car and took off on a two months' circuit of the States. We travelled south down the enchanting Blue Ridge Highway, around New Orleans (not yet a tourist theme park and full of jazz, including the astonishing Thelonius Monk), across the Confederate states to the south western deserts, acquired fifty real silver dollars in Las Vegas, toured through Yosemite to San Francisco and the lovely north-west, and then back via the less interesting northern route, where our greatest excitement was running out of petrol in the remote wilds of Wyoming.

Particularly interesting was our visit to Nashville, Tennessee. I had introductions to David Halberstam on the famous old newspaper there, the *Nashville Tennessean*. He in turn put me in the hands of a wonderful old reporter who took me on a tour of the state, and especially to the great dams built by Hoover and Roosevelt in the depression. He drove me for hours along country roads and told me endless tales sustaining his firm view that Tennessee was the greatest state in the Union, with the most beautiful landscapes, and inhabited by the greatest number of geniuses and true eccentrics. We also visited the 'Grand Ole Opry' in Nashville, then a completely authentic centre of country-and-western music. As with Harlan County, but much more comfortably, it was all a world away from the slick sophistication of Washington and New York and I understood why my journalist colleague thought it was 'the real America'.

Driving these long distances was at first quite tense for me, since I had passed my test and acquired my licence only a week before we set off on the great odyssey. On the highways, those monster lorries with their high spouting exhausts often froze me at the wheel as they hurtled towards or past us.

Our car was a comfortable 1956 blue Pontiac, christened 'Mildred'. She broke her 'rear end' in Texas (I was unclear what the rear end was – perhaps something rude, though I sensed it was serious) and we holed up sweating in a cheap hotel while it was fixed. Mildred was a wonderful partner. After her, I never again took the fashionably snooty European view that big American automobiles are vulgar and inferior. Like most American consumer products, they were cheap and worked well. Wherever we went, we found kindness and welcoming hospitality.

But the idyll had to end. Back in New York in the late summer of 1959, I took the grand old *Queen Mary* home. I have no specific memory of that trip, except that I felt that a golden chapter of irresponsible pleasure had closed. I knew that, aged twenty-five, I had to face the treadmill of adult life and above all find a career to pay my keep. The pressure to do so increased that autumn when I married Carol in the bleak Hendon Registry Office, and we moved into a comfortable flat behind Sadler's Wells in then unfashionable Finsbury for £3 12s. 6d. a week. Carol and her mother had found it, and if these two enterprising women had not made all the arrangements, I am not sure that I would have actually got round to getting married then, since I had not given it a great deal of thought amid all the welter of youthful excitements, and was no good at making such decisions and arrangements. But it turned out to be good for me and focussed me on the more important and more permanent aspects of life.

My thoughts about a career were confused. I had grown out of Oxford by 1959, and when John Owen wrote to me encouragingly about the prospect of a Fellowship in Modern History at Lincoln, I did not respond positively. I wanted to taste the real world, though did not know where or how. I was considering journalism, yet was not sure either how to enter that tricky trade nor especially how to secure a place at the 'quality' end and not amid the Fleet Street gutters. (Today the term 'qualities' has been honestly replaced by 'broadsheets'.)

I still had not written a single word of my doctoral thesis, but began to make modest progress on my three-days-a-week visits to Nuffield College in Oxford, where I had been awarded a Research Studentship which could support me while I slowly and irresolutely made up my mind to take the career plunge.

The heart of Nuffield for me lay in a triumvirate of remarkable dons: Norman Chester, the Warden; Philip Williams, its Fellow in French Politics; and David Butler, its Dean. In their day these three Nuffield dons made the college a hub of political and social activity as well as of fruitful study. More recently, since one retired and the other two died, the college has appeared more concerned with theoretical concepts and less with being at the centre of our nation's life.

Norman Chester was a cranky but shrewd Mancunian with a fine white moustache and a nonconformist belief in the superiority of provincial life over the degeneracy of metropolitan London. Aware of Oxford's snooty disapproval of the modern social sciences in which Nuffield specialised, he fought ceaselessly to have the college accepted by the university establishment.

Philip Williams was passionately interested in Labour Party politics. He quickly involved me in the Campaign for Democratic Socialism, the new Gaitskellite group just set up in late 1959 to resist the advances of what we saw as the far left, though it was pretty mild by later standards. He wrote the official biography of Hugh Gaitskell, which was excellent on the politics, though it disappointed by suppressing all Philip's own natural talent for gossip and saying nothing about his hero's mildly adventurous private life. Philip devoted endless time and energy to the interests of Nuffield students and soon became my firm friend and supporter. His room, with piles of yellowing French newspapers stacked in every corner and under his table and desk, was always my first port of call when I abandoned Finsbury domestic bliss and arrived in monastic Nuffield each Tuesday morning. He died in 1984 of a heart attack, appropriately while lunching at the Gay Hussar in Soho, then the gastronomic base of our Labour generation.

David Butler created psephology, the academic study of elections, in Britain, writing on every general election from 1945 to 2001. He chaired a famous weekly seminar in college, to which he invited to perform most of the significant political figures of his time. Apart from its academic value to his political science students, this exposure to practising politicians and civil servants gave us all the sense of being in touch with the glamorous worlds of Westminster and Whitehall. David had better contacts and could open more doors in the current London world of political affairs than anybody else I knew. Immediately on my return from America, he arranged for me to work on the BBC coverage of the 1959 general election, in which Harold Macmillan won a landslide victory against Gaitskell, thus convincing many of us of the need for radical reform in the Labour Party. This was the first time that elections were covered on television and it was very exciting for me to be involved.

I worked on a seminal computer project to analyse swings between the parties as results were declared in constituencies. We were under the tyrannical control of the formidable BBC director of political broadcasting, Grace Wyndham Goldie, who, shortly before broadcasting began, made a glowering tour of the studio to ensure that we were all at the starting blocks for the electronic revolution. Unfortunately, she trod on a cable leading to our computer and, with a flash and a bang, we lost our electronic support. Nobody dared complain. Our section did the mathematical computations by hand on paper as always before.

David also used his network to get me temporary employment at *The Economist* magazine from December 1959. *The Economist* was a marvellous place for a first job and it matched all my personal ambivalence about whether or not I actually wanted to enter the tricky world of journalism. I felt that many of its permanent staff still shared the same ambivalence after many years working there. It was itself a hybrid, taking a semi-academic view of its reporting, with its light workloads, short working week and derisory salaries (I was paid £7 10s. a week), but succeeded because the staff there were so knowledgeable and talented. Its rambling old building in Ryder Street was also much like an Oxford college, with dingy rooms and corridors, and an air of genuine intellectual enquiry. The dining room, where newcomers like myself and my friend William Plowden sat in quiet reverence, had the style of an Oxford high table, with certain distinguished writers such as John Midgely, Alastair Burnett and Andrew Boyd leading the conversation and showing a lot of real 'inside' information on British and world politics. They were in many ways more broadly knowledgeable than most Oxford dons I had met and certainly more urbane and worldly. I liked it.

One of *The Economist*'s more knowledgeable – and definitely more exotic – creatures was young Norman St John Stevas, later briefly a member of Margaret Thatcher's cabinet. Even then, Mr St John Stevas was operating on a higher social, cultural and spiritual plane than most. I recall once when he came into lunch having just covered a Papal election. He pirouetted before us mere journeymen, flourishing a rich piece of red cloth, which he claimed was from the same roll which had robed the new Pontiff. He said that he would have a new cloak made for himself from it. I sensed that this kind of dazzling show could only take place at *The Economist* and was unlikely to happen at the *Daily Express* or the unimaginative *Mail*.

The editor of *The Economist* was Donald Tyerman, a kind man who was crippled and confined to his wheelchair, from which he gave all his young staff great encouragement. My immediate editor when I quickly moved to the North American section of the journal was the famous Nancy Balfour, at the mere mention of whose name some in Ryder Street quailed. A smart, brisk, and almost pretty spinster, she frightened me a little, but I came to admire her deep knowledge of American politics and all the arts. Shortly before I joined her, I had married Carol, but I did not want to jeopardise my reputation for professionalism by taking a week off for a honeymoon. When Nancy heard of this ungallant behaviour, she took me out to lunch in St James and, herself unmarried, gave me a deserved roasting, saying that marriage is 'the most important event in life', that I should not treat it as less important than one's work. I sat silently and meekly but warmed to her then. Nancy actually required me to do little, just to write one 500-word note a week. For the other journalists who knew their subjects inside out, *The Economist*'s work burden was light. I did not have their degree of knowledge or confidence and I agonised over every word, seeking some profound comment. Only later did I realise that the ready facility which comes from superficiality is the key to journalistic success.

When my apprenticeship at *The Economist* came to its prearranged end in the summer of 1960, Donald Tyerman kindly arranged for me to move to the *Sunday Times*, then owned by Viscount Kemsley (father-in-law of my present partner, Sarah Berry). It occupied the old building in Gray's Inn Road, reeking with the smells of oil and print. I was allocated as a junior member of the paper's amiable gossip column, Atticus. In those days it was not thought necessary to be snide and malicious in order to write a readable and entertaining column. Our team of virtuosi was led by Godfrey Smith, one of the most charming, tolerant, and cultured men with whom I have ever been privileged to work. I could not have enjoyed a friendlier introduction to the (marginally) rackety side of journalism. Also keeping an eye on me was Michael Cudlipp, the news editor and descendant of an incredibly successful family of journalists, who was to become a good friend.

Working there gave me an insight into the side of journalism which matters most to many journalists – the claiming of expenses. On a visit to Liverpool covering a dock strike, I had been careful to restrain my expenditure to the minimum, keeping receipts or records for each few pence I spent on the bus or for sandwiches for lunch. I hoped this would impress my newspaper masters with my great responsibility.

But it turned out quite the reverse. Godfrey summoned me to his office, his normally jolly round face looking deeply perturbed. He handed me back my expenses claim form. 'I am sorry, Bernard. But this won't do. It cannot go forward.' I flushed with shame and protested that it was completely honest and that I had a receipt or record for every penny claimed. 'That is not the point,' he said patiently. 'And I personally have no objection. But you simply cannot submit a claim as low as that for a trip of several days. The accounts department will be uncomfortable and your fellow journalists will be furious. You see, it will raise questions against their own claims. If it is possible to go on a big trip like that spending so little, then what about everybody else? Many of them claim more for just a lunch around the corner.' He handed the form back to me and I soon submitted one three times as large. I said that I was embarrassed to do so because I had not spent all that money and had no receipts for some of it. Godfrey, himself a very honest man and clearly speaking only for the trade in general, said: 'Nobody worries about receipts – until they want to sack you. Then they use unsubstantiated claims as an excuse.' He was right, as I later learned when I was sacked by Murdoch in 1982 and his craven managers did a trawl through my expense claims to find something against me. Fortunately, I had slipped back into my original puritanical habits and they were deprived of at least that line of attack.

At the *Sunday Times* I soon realised that I lacked the necessary hard aptitude for the 'rackety end' of journalism – though I was to continue dabbling in it on and off for the next twenty-three years. Pat Murphy, the huge Irish manager of the paper, who anyway had little time for so-called intellectuals, readily agreed with me. So I slipped away to the semi-real world of research into current affairs, which suited me better. I was appointed, at £1,200 per annum, as a Research Officer at Political and Economic Planning, an institute set up (by Harold Macmillan among others) during the pre-war slump to examine the problems afflicting contemporary society. PEP was based in a beautiful Georgian house in elegant Queen Anne's Gate, from whose windows we could gaze across St James's Park to The Mall. Together with Keith Hindell, a loyal colleague with a very sharp mind, we managed a study on 'Trade Unions in a Changing Society'. The subject was prescient, focussing on the early manifestations of the malaise which was to afflict our trade union movement and blight the British economy over the next quarter of a century.

Our progress was slow, interrupted by a staff coup to remove the Director. I was also distracted by the daily calls to our receptionist from a famous national jockey, giving her the inside information with which to bet (contrary to Jockey Club rules) on his behalf. I followed them for a while but soon learned that tips from jockeys are just as bad as any others. Eventually, Keith and I published a detailed analysis of the growth of the white-collar and the decline of the blue-collar work force, with its implications for the trade union movement. We followed this with a general survey of the reforms necessary if the trade unions were to adapt successfully to our changing society. Our recommendations predictably passed unheard, by the dinosaur unions at least.

But the main benefit from my time at PEP was the valuable experience of working with the study's managing committee, composed of some remarkable individuals, including Lord Heyworth, chairman of Unilever, Professor Ben Roberts from the LSE and Jack Cooper, Gaitskellite boss of the mighty General, Municipal and Boilermakers Union (which I joined and of which I remain a member).

Jack and I became close and he wanted me to become a Labour MP to 'fight the left'. In 1962 he 'offered' me a safe seat in the north-east, a constituency which his union then controlled (and which has remained safe Labour ever since). I was tempted, reluctant to snub such generosity and impressive political power. But I talked to Carol about our plans for an imminent family and turned the offer down, a decision I have never regretted. Parliament and families do not usually mix.

Although I enjoyed PEP from 1960 to 1963, I was personally incapable of sticking to my last, and my dalliance with Fleet Street journalism was soon resumed. I was approached in 1960 to join, on a part-time basis, the launch of a new Sunday newspaper, the *Sunday Telegraph*. The first editor, a quiet Scot named Donald Maclachlan, asked me to work with Peregrine Worsthorne on the leader column. He felt that most newspaper editorials were too verbose, and go unread by the majority of readers. So he introduced the 'To The Point' column, containing editorial pieces running to no more than 100 words, and preferably less. I was paid three pounds a 'point', not over-generous since a point might take several hours to phrase and refine – it is always harder to write short than long. But I found the launch of a new newspaper fascinating. Its young team was selected presciently – including two future Chancellors of the Exchequer, Nigel Lawson and Geoffrey Howe, and the engagingly eccentric Alfred Sherman, future adviser to Mrs Thatcher.

My immediate boss, elegant Perry Worsthorne, was liberal and tolerant and great fun to work with. I admired his capacity to take a quite original (if usually right-wing) approach to any subject. I enjoyed it all and was sorry when after a couple of years I felt it necessary to leave due to the pressure of my work at PEP and finally completing my Oxford doctorate. Hopefully, I had learned how to get quickly to the sharp point of an issue.

With my doctorate accepted by Oxford and the PEP assignment winding to a close, I once again had to take a decision about my career. At exactly that time, a vacancy occurred for a lecturer in the Government Department of the London School of Economics. Ben Roberts, now a personal friend, supported me and I secured it. I started in the autumn term of 1963 at the princely pay of £1,250 a year, with £60 increments *per annum*. At last, aged twenty-nine, I was able to settle down with a proper job.

Seven

ACADEME, POLITICS, FINANCE –
AND OTHER EXCITEMENTS

Securing a lectureship at the London School of Economics introduced a welcome stability into my life and I stayed there, relatively happy, from 1963 until 1974 – the longest period spent in one job in my career. Of course, I have never been able to concentrate all my time on one occupation and I soon diversified into other political, financial, business and sporting activities. One of the many advantages of being an academic at that time was that it allowed ample spare time to spend on such outside interests. But most important of all to me was the inside interest of my family. Having finally settled my central career as a university teacher, Carol and I decided it was the time to have a family and buy a proper home to house them.

Our flat in Finsbury where we had cheerfully lived since marriage in 1959 was not big enough for the size of family we had in mind. For a while we searched Islington, which I sensed one day might become more fashionable, with its handsome Victorian squares and terraces close to the City. It was very cheap, with plenty of houses below £5,000; but was visually bleak with an inefficient council and very poor schools. Instead, I played safe and fell in love with a house in Parliament Hill Fields, close by Hampstead Heath, and bought it in 1965 for £11,000. That was a lot of money for me (earning £1,250 a year at the LSE). A friend, the LSE sociologist Julius Gould, saw it and, with his professional knowledge of the English class system, commented, 'That is not a lecturer's house, that is a professor's house.' More important, it was a real family house. Within five years Carol and I had four children living there: two girls, Rachel and Kate, and twin boys, Paul and Stephen. Number 7 Brookfield Park was every-thing that Waverley had not been. It was an Edwardian semi, spacious and light, with plenty of rooms for the family and a sunny garden, in which the children played and I read.

The huge sitting room, which I opened up to run the depth of the house, was later excellent for my quality Linn Sondek/Quad/Naim all-British hi-fi system.

I slowly filled the walls with paintings bought cheaply at auctions – including Paul Nash, Mathew Smith and Laura Knight from my favourite British moderns, and David Cox and Alfred Vickers from earlier times. At school in Northampton, I had been able neither to sing nor to paint and was rapidly removed from both art and music classes. But music and painting give me enormous pleasure and number 7 became full of both.

Carol worked for the BBC in the very beginning of educational TV. She took off several years from work to look after the children full time, which I am convinced is essential for a healthy family (though it matters not from the children's point of view whether the career sacrifice is by husband or wife). Later she returned to work as a successful inspector of education, an important role in an educational system where standards were patently falling. She provided the domestic stability and devoted motherhood to our children which I had lacked as a child. I remained inexcusably useless around the house; but until entering Downing Street in 1974 I was able to spend a good deal of time with the children, a privilege which few modern professional men and women enjoy.

Our home life throughout my thirties was happy and we were fortunate to live in a pretty and friendly neighbourhood. Within that small locality of Parliament Hill Fields were many other young families and friends. We created there a kind of village life with echoes of Roade. We dropped in on one another's houses, exchanged babysitters, used the local schools, often dined together and walked our families over the nearby Hampstead Heath. Within a couple of hundred yards were my special friends Nori and Philip Graham; also Alan Russell, who like Nori was with me at Oxford; the delightful Celia and Tom Reed; Helene Hayman, who became my impressive successor as Minister of Farming and Food; my LSE colleague John Carrier, with whom I regularly played football on Sundays and ran on the Heath each morning at dawn; and my longstanding friend Harry Evans, Britain's greatest post-war newspaper editor and my future boss at *The Times* and *Sunday Times*. It was a remarkable community. Each evening, returning from work, I looked forward to escaping from the appalling shambles of the Northern Line tube, to breathing the fresh air of Hampstead, and seeing our local friends.

Later in the 1970s I bought first a cottage in rural Suffolk and then a house on the edge of the French Pyrenees to give us and the children a chance to escape from London and recharge batteries in real countryside. But Hampstead remained our core base. When I divorced and moved to Belgravia in 1986, I certainly appreciated never having to use the appalling Northern Line ever again in my life, but I missed the community and friendship of that particular era in Parliament Hill Fields.

Workwise, teaching and writing at the LSE constituted the central core of my life through the rest of the exciting 1960s and the more drab early 1970s.

The School suited me perfectly. Bustling, crowded, vibrant, shabby, in the centre of London at the Aldwych, within close reach of Westminster, Whitehall, Fleet Street and the City, with bright staff and students interested in the current political, economic and social world, it met my desire to be both academic and yet involved with relevant national policy issues. It was more international than any other British university. It especially benefited from the influx in the 1930s of such brilliant Jewish refugees escaping from Hitler as Karl Popper, Claus Moser, Hilde Himmelweit, Ann Bohm and many others. They brought an intellectual vitality, a cosmopolitan vision and a warm humanity which made the School very special. Some, such as Claus Moser, the distinguished statistician and musician, and beautiful Hilde Himmelweit, the social psychologist, became close friends for life.

My own Government Department was interesting in many ways, though perhaps was not the most exciting among the many fine specialisms in the School. There were stronger candidates for that honour. The large Economics Department harboured such world-class economists as Amartya Sen, Michio Morishima and Frank Hahn, together with Harry Johnson and Alan Walters from the monetarist school who were to influence Margaret Thatcher, and my good friends Basil Yamey, Maurice Peston, Robert Cassen and Meghnad Desai, who were more of the traditionalist school. The vibrant Law Department had Otto Kahn Freund, Jim Gower, Derry Irvine (future Lord Chancellor), Bill Wedderburn and my old friend Michael Zander setting the pace in radically applying a legal approach to current national problems. There were also the various new 'social' disciplines, led by the saintly Richard Titmuss in Social Administration, supported by David Donnison, and Tessa Blackstone and David Piachaud who were to work with me in the Labour government after 1974.

These latter social sciences were outside anything taught me at Oxford – and indeed were often deplored as not 'respectable' in the more traditional vales of Oxbridge academe. To me they were novel and exciting, though sometimes lacking in intellectual rigour, and I took great interest in the work of these colleagues in other disciplines. Those early years at the LSE were perhaps the most stimulating of my whole working life.

The Government Department, while still carrying the radical aura – or stigma, according to taste – of the late Harold Laski, was when I joined led from the right by its remarkable convenor, Michael Oakeshott, a distinguished Cambridge philosopher who shared my enthusiasm for horse racing and who welcomed and helped me from the start. Physically and spiritually like an Irish leprechaun, Michael was a complete one-off who brought style, grace and generosity to everything I saw him do. Politically, I disagreed with him on many issues, and thought some of his disciples not worthy of his league. But I count him among the most delightful academic colleagues I have known. Our department was deeply divided along broad political lines. Supporting Michael's far right wing were most of the philosophers – Kenneth Minogue, Oliver Letwin and Robert Orr, together with Alan Beattie and John Barnes from the younger institutional side and the orientalist Elie Kedourie.

The opposing left contained old-fashioned Marxists such as Ralph Miliband and more moderate Labour figures such as Peter Self, Bill Pickles, Bernard Crick, my friends George Jones, Wiliam Plowden and Vincent Wright, and myself.

The old liberals in the department, led with international distinction by our Russian expert Leonard Schapiro, usually aligned with Oakeshott's right in order to block the depredations of the non-democratic left, then quite vocal in the School. Such ceaseless divisions were often petty, though familiar in academic life. I enjoyed watching the surrounding Byzantine intrigues, which occupied a disproportionate amount of some colleagues' time.

My working week at the LSE was far from testing. I gave a big lecture on the 'Introduction to British Government and Politics' course and also held a couple of politics classes and a postgraduate seminar, and looked after several students as their personal 'moral' tutor. In the early years I read hard to prepare for these engagements, since I had never before actually studied modern government academically. At times I was barely ahead of the students on the course. But once I had read myself on top of the syllabus, I found time on my hands and began to think about writing more books.

My doctoral study of 'British Politics and the American War of Independence' was adapted as a book and published by Macmillan in 1964, a fine example of the responsible attitude of that generation of publishers, since there was little chance of much profit in it for them. It brought me a wonderful lunch at their headquarters with their chairman, only recently retired as Prime Minister.

Harold Macmillan was extremely gracious to a young author unknown except for being a supporter of his political opponents. He also told a lovely story from the war, when he was Minister for North African Affairs after we invaded Tunisia and Algeria. He said he took a very cold flight there in a Liberator bomber. The Women's Auxiliary Air Force officer looking after him explained that they would be flying over enemy waters and might crash in the ocean. She showed him the inflatable life belt, and a torch and a whistle to assist his rescuers. He claimed that he declined them, saying: 'Young lady, I am a middle-aged member of Her Majesty's

Government, who has had a good life and still has some dignity. I simply refuse to go swimming around in the Atlantic, shining a torch and blowing a whistle.' He performed exactly like the then current political satires of himself, rather as if out of Edwardian vaudeville. But I sensed the political genius that lay behind the carefully constructed façade and was grateful for his charming hospitality.

The book was well received as a scholarly work, but I felt it was time to write something more in the contemporary area which I taught. So I joined with Bill Rodgers, a young MP with whom I was closely allied in Labour politics, to write *The People Into Parliament*, an illustrated history of the Labour movement, published by Thames and Hudson in 1966. It was not profoundly original, but it presented the story from our position on the radical right, sold quite well, and brought in some useful cash to support the babies currently arriving regularly in Brookfield Park. Shortly after, I contracted to co-author, with George Jones, the official biography of Herbert Morrison, a much more weighty exercise, which was not to be published until 1973.

The cosy atmosphere which I enjoyed at the LSE was suddenly disrupted by the violent student protests of 1967–8, which mirrored a current pattern of rebellions on campuses across America and Europe. They were usually led by a hard core of left-wing agitators from various Marxist sects, but with varying views on the legitimacy of violence and some fringing on anarchic fascism.

Most of the leaders believed that capitalism and liberal democracy were doomed and the coming Marxist revolution would be advanced if they could control any 'capitalist establishment' institutions and convert them into 'red bases'. Universities, with their traditions of tolerance, their absence of discipline, and packed with students anxious for political excitement and to create media headlines, were an obvious target to be 'politicised', and the LSE was an obvious prime target in the United Kingdom. It was situated on the doorstep of Parliament and around the corner from hordes of newspaper and TV journalists desperate for a story. It had a long radical tradition – and also then played host to a number of American campus agitators who already had experience of manipulating student audiences across the Atlantic.

Given the total collapse of communism and Marxist ideology some twenty years later, it may now seem odd that those student protests in the 1960s were taken so seriously by the media and the authorities in Britain. But in the 'Swinging Sixties', with its questioning of all established values, they grabbed the front-page headlines and totally absorbed the time and energies of university authorities. The Beatles and the LSE rebels seemed somehow entwined and feeding off similar instincts, as if they were showing us the future. The Marxist agitators were also encouraged by often-ageing museum pieces on the left of the parliamentary Labour Party, who saw in the student marchers a potential mass support which they themselves had hitherto signally failed to attract among the ranks of adult Labour voters.

I was personally involved very closely in the handling and mishandling of the LSE student riots. I had been elected as the youngest staff representative on the Standing Committee of the Court of Governors, which was effectively the governing body of the School. That committee found itself in constant emergency session as we faced continuing disruptions. The administrative building was occupied, lectures interrupted, visiting outside speakers were intimidated, companies coming to offer 'capitalist jobs' (which meant any kind of serious employment) to graduating students were threatened and driven away, and a popular porter died of a heart attack amid the rabble. The Director, Walter Adams, a benign liberal who had worked for many years in Africa to oppose racism and apartheid there, was besieged, physically threatened and denounced as a 'fascist racist'. Staff and students who criticised the agitators were threatened with physical violence – I was amused to be pictured on the front page of the Trotskyite students' newspaper with a noose around my neck. It was lively stuff and I enjoyed much of the game immensely.

But I did deeply resent the waste of our time and especially the attempts by leading agitators to persuade fellow students, as a gesture of dissent, not to take their examinations. Many of these boys and girls were from working-class families whose parents had worked and sacrificed to get their children the reward and privilege of an LSE education and degree. It would have been tragic to throw that away solely to satisfy the political ego trips of some left-wing self-publicists, most of whom came from the privileged prosperous classes. When, following parliamentary pressure to withdraw financial grants from the riot leaders (since they were clearly not doing any academic work and were stopping others from doing any), we pursued this question with the various grant authorities. We discovered that virtually none of the leaders were actually receiving any public grant money: they or their parents were too wealthy to qualify for financial payment.

At times it did seem that the School structure might collapse. We had few rules to impose discipline. As in any democracy, we had to work slowly to find a consensus which would bridge the majority of staff and students. But early on we had to make clear that the School authorities would not tolerate continual disruption of its basic educational functions. Academics as a breed are not usually suited to effective executive action, so it required the concentrated efforts of a few sturdy individuals with some understanding of the real world. Prominent among these were my old friends Ben Roberts and George Jones, with their practical experience of dealing with the militant left in the Labour movement. Crucial was our remarkable Chairman, Lionel (Lord) Robbins. Lionel was a distinguished economist with long experience of public life, having served Churchill's war cabinet. Tall, with the heart of a lion, Lionel Robbins loved the School and brought to it a strong sense of the necessary authority to save it. More than anybody, he maintained stability of leadership, while many fellow academics, unaccustomed to the rough practicalities of political life, lost their nerves and simply hid in corners rubbing their hands in despair. Some left-wing staff foolishly encouraged the students in trying to destroy the academic principles of free speech which the teachers were supposed professionally to uphold, while on the Conservative right were many who had been loud in denunciation of the student agitators but showed little appetite for the hard graft of organising their defeat. That task fell, as so often, to the tough men of the Labour right, accustomed to facing this kind of nonsense in their own party. But liberal Lionel Robbins was the rock on which this minor revolution was crushed.

Ultimately, of course, we won because the Marxist revolutionaries were only a small minority, however loud. The majority of students went along briefly for the excitement of the ride, while also rightly demanding and securing greater student representation in the governance of the School. Once we showed both the steel of authority to the agitators (we sacked three staff and seven students for inciting violence and disrupting the School's activities), and that we would also listen and respond to the legitimate requests for reform of the sensible student majority, then the battle was won. Once it was clear that we would not tolerate extreme and violent disruption, but would equally respond to legitimate protest within the rules of our society, which is the right of all members, life at the School calmed down.

But the conflicts had damaged some personal relations at the School. I certainly felt less contented there, as if the previous idyll of my happy relations with my students had been broken. It was a first nudge towards my eventual departure from academe. I focussed more on finishing the biography I was writing on Herbert Morrison. Certainly handling the riots accelerated my own personal politicisation.

The Morrison book had originated with Norman Chester, my old warden at Nuffield College, who was an executor of Morrison's literary estate and the few interesting papers he left behind and who asked me and George Jones to write the official biography. George was an ideal partner in such an enterprise. He was loyal, straight and hard-working, with practical political experience – qualities not always then in over-supply in academe. He promptly delivered his first half of the book on Morrison's early life, brilliantly catching the political and social environment of the early days of the Labour Party. Together, we interviewed Morrison's surviving political, governmental, and personal colleagues. Our book was one of the first to use extensive interview techniques in this way as a basis for biography. It was published in 1973, rightly dedicated to our wives who had suffered neglect while we worked on it, and was widely and generously reviewed. Among my voluminous archives is a typically over-generous letter from Michael Foot, dated 25 September 1973:

> I cannot refrain from writing to you again, since I have sat up, utterly absorbed, reading your book for half the night. I have not quite finished it yet, and I must confess I have not read consecutively, since I wanted to look at some special incidents – about which I disagree. However, the book itself is marvellous. I do congratulate you and George Jones. Apart from setting a new standard for research in Labour biography, it is really ... as fine a portrait of a modern politician as anything I have read. So I send you my envious congratulations.

From the great biographer of Nye Bevan and someone on the opposite side of the party from me, that was praise which I treasured. It also carried the generosity of spirit of a lovely man. Of the half a dozen books in which I have been involved, *Herbert Morrison: Portrait of a Politician* is the one of which I am most proud. Morrison had of course been a great political figure during my childhood, one of my earliest heroes. (In Waverley, we possessed a 'Morrison air raid shelter', though it was never used.) Morrison's record as one of the great 'achievers', as opposed to 'talkers', of British twentieth-century history was remarkable. Over a political career spanning fifty years, he was a key figure in building the early Labour Party, in establishing good municipal government at the London County Council between the wars, and in Churchill's and Attlee's cabinets enacting the social and welfare revolution during and after the Second World War. But he was not a wholly attractive personality and his reputation dimmed after his death in 1965. Fortunately, interest in him revived somewhat in the early glow of achievement of his grandson Peter Mandelson, and the book achieved a reprint in 2001 with a fascinating foreword by Peter. But its sales were never great. Since it contains little 'psychobabble' or speculation about Morrison's (undoubtedly thin) sex life, it might anyway be unsuited to the modern literary market.

My non-academic activities at this time inevitably took me towards sport. Apart from playing soccer regularly for the LSE students' teams, and on Sunday mornings on the Heath, I was also drawn towards the governance of sport. My friend Denis Howell, the first designated Minister of Sport in the 1964 Labour administration, appointed me to the new national Sports Council in 1965. Denis, himself our dynamic chairman, overcame all the obstacles placed in his way by the Whitehall machine and we made some progress towards modernising amateur sport in Britain. Denis was impatient with grey men and had chosen some striking personalities for the Council. Roger Bannister still carried charisma from his four-minute mile and ran our committee on promoting research into sports medicine, then a neglected field. Lord Porchester (later the Earl of Carnavon), who became one of my closest friends, brought an immense fund of wisdom and knowledge of local government, which was the key provider of sports facilities across the country. David Bacon's shrewd financial brain was welcome in the sports world, where financial and administrative competence were in short supply. Walter Winterbottom, the former England football manager, was overall Director.

We were a happy team and made modest progress in many areas, especially in promoting dual use of sports facilities, in advancing research into sports medicine, and in trying to encourage some degree of efficiency and accountability among the multitude of sports governing bodies.

I also enjoyed another experience of viewing and analysing the government of sport. Having got his Sports Council off the ground, Denis Howell decided to investigate the present state and future prospects of Britain's most popular sport, football. He set up in 1966 a committee of enquiry, chaired skilfully by our old friend Norman Chester, which reported in 1968. We visited many clubs, including Manchester United, where the famous manager Matt Busby told me presciently that the then young George Best 'could be the best footballer I have ever managed – providing his character holds up.' My particular pleasure there was to be allowed on the sacred turf of Old Trafford and smash the ball into the net from the penalty spot – assisted by the absence of any goalkeeper to hinder it.

We also interviewed the game's then top administrators. They were mostly a woeful lot with little real understanding of their sport or any vision of its future as a great leisure industry. Denis Follows, then Secretary of the Football Association, was scornful of me for suggesting that one day football grounds might be all-seater or that women would play team football. Prejudice wrapped up as experienced wisdom is a common feature of British life. Our report stands the test of time quite well, pointing to a future where football would be a major leisure industry, without the slave transfer system, with a small top elite of successful clubs and having comfortable stadia with seating and facilities for family entertainment. I wrote the main part of the report's chapter 3 on the professional game, working closely with Clifford Barclay, a brilliant accountant who carried out the first ever audit treating professional league football as a company with subsidiaries, thus identifying its sources of revenues and profits and losses. Clifford had one of the best 'lateral' minds I have encountered and became a friend and mentor.

When the committee's labours were nearly concluded in 1967, Clifford took me out to lunch in Park Lane. He said he thought I would do well in finance, and especially on the Stock Exchange. The thought had never occurred to me and I had then never knowingly met a stockbroker. I told him that I knew nothing of investment finance, as opposed to academic economics, and had had no opportunity to practise, having little money. 'We must put that right,' he said. 'I want you to help run the finance of my family business.' I was stunned. But I liked him, needed the money, and accepted.

He then, together with his energetic son Stephen who became the dynamic core of the business, set up two companies in which I was allocated generous share holdings. Through these we handled the family's financial investments along with the private portfolios of rich individuals, with several stars from the film industry. My earnings there were far greater than my paltry LSE salary and that eased the pressures from our growing family in Brookfield Park. I also learned a good deal about the wider financial world, making contacts with my future employers and partners at the top stockbrokers Grieveson Grant. Among our business ventures was setting up a graphics art studio based on the work of the brilliant 'pop artist' Alan Aldridge. This took me into a very 'swinging' world. We produced colourful covers for books and also for hit records – Alan once took me to visit the young Paul McCartney concerning our sleeve for the Beatles' latest record. We also produced our own beautifully illustrated books, such as *The Butterfly Ball*, which was made into a cartoon film. Alan was a graphics genius and also an effective footballer in our Sunday morning games.

Clifford, Stephen and I strongly believed that leading football clubs could one day become valuable leisure assets. We bought into Arsenal and Aston Villa, hoping to convert them into modern leisure centres. But we were unable to gain influence. (Arsenal has anyway done quite well without us and their shares, which I bought at around £20–25 each, are now over £2,000.) We also bid £8 million to convert Wembley Stadium into a modern leisure centre, but the existing management did not wish to share our vision.

This was heady stuff for a young LSE lecturer. One important success I did enjoy was in forecasting the start of the long bear market in 1972. That year London's equity index had risen to an historic high over 500. I woke one night convinced it was about to fall. I went to tell Clifford and he replied, 'Well, what are you going to do about it?' I answered with cowardice that I was thinking of moving to 10–15 per cent in cash. He said, 'Why 15 per cent? That is ducking and hedging it. If you are right we should be out of the equity market altogether.' We immediately began to liquidate many of his assets and he was soon well placed to ride out the long financial storm ahead.

Clifford was wise about many aspects of life beyond finance. He once gave me a piece of advice which would have benefited many modern politicians whose careers have been excessively blighted by journalists' obsessions with so-called 'sleaze' (which is often just normal human behaviour). Clifford said: 'Bernard, you like the opposite sex. Be careful to attach only to ladies socially equal to or above you. Those below have a temptation to boast of you as a partner and an incentive to sell the story to some nasty newspaper. Those above don't want the publicity or need the money.'

The abundance of spare time at the LSE also gave me space to get more directly involved in politics – real politics, that is, not just the political games at the LSE. My own political position had long been firmly on Labour's radical right wing. By the 1960s I had become convinced that the Labour left was wrong in many of its extreme statist policies – and especially in its often blind attachment to the appalling communist regime in the Soviet Union. I was sure that the broad British public, including the majority of the working class, would never support those positions. The left also seemed to me far too conservative, too attached to the antique dogmas of long ago. Therefore in order to win electoral power to pursue social democratic reform, it was necessary to defeat the left within the party. In early 1960, shortly after returning from the United States, I joined my local constituency party in Finsbury. I became ward treasurer and in 1964 worked intensely, with the sturdy help of John Burrows and the Post Office Workers Union, to prevent the left-wing trade unionist Clive Jenkins from becoming candidate in our safe seat at the coming general election. Our candidate Ron Brown (brother of George) won comfortably, with Jenkins polling fewer votes on selection day than he claimed to have to start with. It was all part of my political education. This was soon sharpened by my work in the early 1960s with a radical right wing pressure group called the Campaign for Democratic Socialism (CDS). It was a new grouping formed after Labour's 1959 electoral defeat to try to modernise the party and in particular to resist the advance of the left. Its initial inspirers were Tony Crosland in London and my friend Philip Williams at Nuffield College, Oxford. At the 1960 Scarborough conference the left had secured a crucial party commitment to Britain's unilateral nuclear disarmament, something naive which would certainly have guaranteed Labour's defeat at the following 1964 election. Labour's leader, Hugh Gaitskell, then announced his crusade 'to fight and fight again' to save the Labour Party from left-wing nonsense. In the wake of that clarion call, CDS was launched at a great rally which I attended in Caxton Hall on 9 October 1960. CDS fought to help overturn the unilateralist resolution (reversing a previous 3–1 majority) and in its organisational support for Hugh Gaitskell's leadership of the party proved to be one of the more effective political operations in which I have participated. It was brilliantly organised by its Secretary Bill Rodgers (later a Labour cabinet minister and co-founder of the Social Democratic Party) with Denis Howell (who was to become my closest political friend) and Tom Bradley whipping in the trade unions, and Frank Pickstock from Oxford local government acting as a grass roots chairman.

Through CDS I met Gaitskell himself and Hugh Dalton from the earlier political generation, and such rising stars of Labour's political right as Roy Jenkins and Tony Crosland. (Brian Walden, Dick Taverne, George Jones, David Marquand and Anthony King were among many other young Turks also heavily involved.) Hugh Gaitskell was to me a charismatic leader of blazing integrity and courage. He was also shy, and could sometimes be prissy, inflexible and intolerant. He seemed very middle-class and often infuriatingly stubborn. But none of those irritating faults mattered to me on the outer fringe of the political battlefield. He was a man of great honour and principle, and again and again displayed bravery in support of what he believed was right. He was as passionate in his emotional defence of his democratic socialist beliefs as was any left-winger's attachment to Marxist socialism. Gaitskell gave us supporters of CDS some hope that, with such a sympathetic leadership, the Labour Party could be modernised and reformed in our social democratic direction, and so might once again both recover and deserve political power. In CDS, we were above all loyal to his leadership – almost to the dangerous point of 'our leader, right or wrong'. I was devastated when he died suddenly in 1963, and he remains one of my heroes, one of the 'lost leaders' of British history.

Despite this emphasis on supporting Gaitskell's leadership, probably the most effective impact of CDS lay at constituency and trade union level, influencing grass roots votes on Conference resolutions and on the selection of candidates. To some extent we adopted the same tough organisational practices by which the left had previously gained control of parts of the Labour movement. It was my apprenticeship in real politics, sharpened when I succeeded Bill Rodgers as the Secretary of CDS in 1962. I was of course very much a junior in a distinguished team. At the beginning, from our office in Red Lion Street, my first task was to assist with writing and editing the monthly newsletter, *Campaign*. In this publication we advocated the reforms in the party which most of us saw as necessary if Labour was to succeed in elections and in government. (Some of this proposed modernisation had to await Tony Blair's leadership for implementation.) Our main thrust, set out in CDS's 1960 manifesto, was towards modernisation and away from outdated Marxist ideology and class war prejudice. CDS's 'democratic socialism' actually meant 'social democracy'. From that time onwards, I never knowingly referred to myself as a 'socialist' but always as 'Labour'; that became aggressively more true when the party was taken over by left-wing zealots in the 1980s.

CDS never progressed so far as to contemplate Tony Blair's overt abandonment of nationalisation and distancing from the trade unions. We did, however, state that nationalisation should no longer be supported on principle but be judged on its economic merit, and we did contemplate a looser link with the unions. Much of what we argued in CDS was pointing broadly towards the position and image which New Labour was to adopt thirty-five years later – which is why I personally found it so easy to agree with and accept the new approach in the 1990s.

The last time that I saw Hugh Gaitskell was at a meeting at the home of Bill Rodgers in Kentish Town in the autumn of 1962. He came to explain to some of his most loyal supporters why he had taken such a hostile stand against Britain's membership of Europe at the recent Brighton party conference. He seemed inflexible, confessed he was 'bored' by the European issue, and, to our dismay, seemed almost willing to break with CDS over it. He visibly tired and seemed a little irritable towards the end of the meeting. We had no idea that he was already suffering from the rare and incurable Lupus disease of the tissues. He died three months later on 18 January 1963, aged only fifty-six.

The contest for his succession as leader of the party, between Harold Wilson from the opportunist left, and George Brown from the conservative right, created depression and dissent within the ranks of CDS.

Neither candidate stood for our new politics. We saw Wilson as a tricky and unprincipled man who had risen with the support of our enemies on the left and so was likely to remain always in hock to them. Brown was full of vitality and certainly 'anti-left'. But his was a flawed personality and he had never shared Gaitskell's conceptual grasp of the way in which Labour's philosophy, attitudes and policies must change. Wilson was seen by us as 'Old Left' and Brown as 'Old Right'. We had used the support of the Old Right in our battles, but I certainly was never of it, seeing it as insufficiently radical. To me, we were 'New Right', and so neither candidate was really one of us. Some in CDS reluctantly concluded in my hearing that for the leadership it was 'better George drunk than Harold sober'. I was not convinced by that, sensing pragmatically that Wilson was a skilful opportunist and campaigner who would help Labour at least to win the coming general election, whereas Brown seemed fated to blow his and our chance. The choice gave little pleasure or reason for enthusiasm on our side of the party.

Wilson deservedly won the leadership battle, but did not win our right wing's loyalty or affection. We felt bereaved. Having lost our leadership, CDS also lost momentum, and in the summer of 1964, with an election due any moment, I as general secretary together with our chairman Frank Pickstock issued the press release announcing that our organisation would dissolve and we would unite with Harold Wilson to create the party unity essential to election victory.

Wilson did indeed win the 1964 election, but only by a majority of thirteen over the Conservatives and overall of only four. I had canvassed locally in Hampstead and Kentish Town, and also followed the campaign every day in a London constituency in order to write a chapter of the Nuffield College study *The British General Election of 1964*, edited by my friends David Butler and Anthony King. The constituency which David and I choose was Finchley, mainly because it was a favourite for the predicted Liberal advance in the Tory suburbs, but also because it had two attractive candidates who we both felt might have a future in British politics. For the Liberals was John Pardoe, an energetic and intelligent campaigner who later became a leading Liberal MP from the south west – and also a personal friend of mine who gave Harold Wilson assistance when taking power again in 1974, as will be described below.

The Conservative candidate defending her seat for the first time was described in my chapter: 'An attractive mother of twins, trained first as a chemist and then a barrister, and now serving as a junior minister in the Government, [Mrs Thatcher] was a formidable sitting member. In our pre-campaign survey of electors, almost half were able to name Mrs Thatcher as the Conservative member, compared to only one in fourteen who could name the Liberal candidate and one in thirty who could name the socialist.'

My first sight of Mrs Thatcher was at an evening meeting in a Finchley school. Outside it was raining heavily. The door swung violently open and she marched in. Taking off her wet raincoat as she moved to the rostrum, she threw her coat over her shoulder without a glance behind. In her wake were two or three hurrying aides, one of whom caught the coat cleanly as if very experienced at doing it. I asked a neighbour who was the man who caught it? 'That is Denis.' I grew more impressed by her as the campaign progressed, and a few years later pressed success-fully for her to be invited on to the LSE Court of Governors. After one Court meeting I took her to the nearby Waldorf Hotel for tea. She was engagingly flirta-tious but quite hard on educational policy. She told me she had 'never known any parent who had willingly sent their children to a comprehensive school.' I saw then the attractive glint of steel and the more worryingly rigid mindset which was later to make such an impact on British politics – on balance probably for the good. Her majority in Finchley in 1964 halved but was still a comfortable 9,000.

However small was Wilson's Commons majority in October 1964, it was very exciting finally to have a Labour government again. I was now aged thirty and this was the first time as an adult that I had lived under a Labour government – the last one fell when I was seventeen years old and still at the grammar school.

Many in the media predicted that Wilson would not be able to hang on for long, but our side was optimistic. Anthony Wedgwood Benn – with whom I then had much more friendly relations than later in his apparition as plain proletarian Tony Benn – wrote to me a week after the election: 'The result really is wonderful. I think that Harold Wilson will be able to hang on for much longer than most of the experts expect and I think there will be a swing toward Labour when people see that we don't have horns and a tail.' The question of the horns and tail actually grew worse rather than better for Tony personally, but he was right about the coming swing to Labour. Wilson proved remarkably skilful at governing with a small majority – a real survivor. When Benn's predicted swing occurred, the Labour prime minister called a second election early in 1966, securing a majority of over 100, and remained in office until 1970.

But soon the old left–right fissures reappeared in the Labour administration. The battle for control of the party continued in government as previously (and subsequently) out of it. CDS's supporters continued to meet regularly and plot together. The 1963 Dining Club was formed in Gaitskell's memory and held dinners regularly at the Commons, and I attended either as the guest of Denis Howell or Bill Rodgers. We had heated discussions of how to stop any lurch to the left by Wilson, and much carping about 'Harold's lack of leadership'. Jenkins, Crosland, Rodgers, Howell, Diamond, Taverne, Owen, all ministers or about to be ministers, together with such aspirants as David Marquand and Brian Walden, were often present. Bill Rodgers' house in Patshull Road, Kentish Town, conveniently down the road from Brookfield Park, was also a base for frequent lively parties where our ministers, MPs and activists gathered. Ministers impressively tried to balance their instinctive loyal defence of the government with sectarian criticisms of Wilson's leadership failings. It was heady political stuff and I felt privileged to be involved.

I was further involved after Labour's unexpected election defeat in 1970. I was invited to be special adviser to Harold Lever, who had served as a minister in the Treasury in the recent administration and was a member of the elected Shadow Cabinet in opposition. Harold, son of a former Lord Mayor of Manchester, was a successful financial investor who had made millions on the markets, mainly in gilts and property. His wealth and financial expertise were rare in the Labour party. Wilson (as did Callaghan later) greatly appreciated his originality and liked to use him as an alternative advice to the staid conventional wisdom emanating from the official Treasury. Personally, Harold was engaging, funny, full of Jewish humour, and enjoyed a grand social life. His wife Diane added to the quality of his life: he told me that one reason he married her (she was also delightful, bright and beautiful) was that she was 'the only lady I knew who was richer than me.' His apartment, covering two floors across two great houses in Eaton Square, was astonishingly elegant and comfortable. I went to 86 Eaton Square two or three days a week, often staying for delicious lunches (as I still do with Diane today). Sometimes we worked on serious speeches in his special areas of international finance, later greatly helped by Ray Richardson from the LSE, whom I brought in for the technical theory beyond my current grasp. Sometimes we just gossiped for hours about the terrible state of politics in the current Labour Party, which was tearing itself apart over whether to support joining the Common Market, of which Harold was a strong advocate. These tensions may have contributed to the severe stroke which Harold suffered in 1972, which paralysed his arm and leg. I was one of the first to see him after the stroke and was shocked to see the devastating change in his appearance. But his mind remained clear and he fought back to participate in the next Labour government, when Wilson appointed him as Chancellor of the Duchy of Lancaster, which really meant the prime minister's special economic adviser.

For me those four years with Harold Lever were a crucial part of my political apprenticeship, preparing me for the leap into Downing Street which lay just ahead. At times, starting with Jack Cooper's offer of a safe Labour seat in the north east in 1962, I was approached with suggestions that I fight a constituency and hope to become an MP, like so many of my CDS colleagues. But over time I grew less and less tempted. I was content working at the LSE. Above all I was happy at home with Carol watching our four children grow up.

Two family blows in the early 1970s were the deaths of my father and then of Carol's father 'Goodie' Goodman – a fine man with whom I enjoyed an especially warm friendship.

Dad was buried with Catholic rites in Roade in 1971. After the funeral, Clem and I cleared out his few belongings from the council house, burning much of the furniture and keeping a few nostalgic photographs. But he had nothing of value and not even the money to cover the costs of his funeral, which I paid. His gold fob watch which he had treasured for forty years had disappeared on his final stay in hospital.

In 1970 I bought a pretty thatched cottage in Suffolk (costing £7,000) for weekends and holidays. By then twin baby boys, Paul and Stephen, had joined Rachel and Kate – four in four years, which was good scoring, and fun for them, but hard on their parents' sleep and pockets. It was a squash with the six of us in our Ford Cortina heading for Suffolk on a Friday night, but I enjoyed the quiet there, the wonderful big skies and rolling fields of corn. Domestic life was good, stable and comfortable, happy, in a warm house – all the things I wanted but lacked as a child. I loved my friends in Parliament Hill Fields and valued having time to spend with them. And I knew that becoming an MP would threaten and even possibly destroy all of that. The frequent and usually unavoidable neglect of their families and friends by MPs is sad to witness. I did not wish to risk that damage. I was lucky to enjoy what I felt were the best of all worlds in life: a happy family, an interesting job and time on my hands for an enjoyable social life – that is until 1974, when the politics of Number 10 Downing Street took me over, and my world totally changed.

Part II

POLITICAL LIFE 1974 –

Eight

JOINING HAROLD WILSON

I had met Harold Wilson only twice before joining his staff for the run-up to the 1974 general election. The first time was when interviewing him in his room at the House of Commons in 1971 for my biography of Herbert Morrison. He struck me as a very small man with little to say of political interest about his former cabinet colleague. Later, in 1973, we talked at a City lunch, specifically arranged by Harry Kissin (later Lord Kissin), a very intelligent tycoon who claimed to have known Wilson well since the politician's days as the President of the Board of Trade in the late 1940s. They shared an interest in trade with eastern Europe. Kissin later told me that his motive in arranging the lunch was to insert me into Wilson's team as a counter to, and possibly a replacement for, Marcia Williams, whose influence he had often observed and disliked. (Later Wilson told me that Marcia accepted me because she hoped to use me as a counter to, and possibly a replacement for, Joe Haines, whose influence *she* disliked.)

Harry was a subtle operator with far greater political understanding than most successful businessmen, and his intrigue worked. In the autumn of 1973 I was approached at the LSE by Peter Davies (later Lord Lovell-Davies), a close friend of Marcia's. Peter invited me to join a small team to supervise some opinion polls to be conducted for Wilson monthly through to the next general election, due at the latest by the summer of 1975. I understood sampling techniques and Wilson wanted me to help shape the questions from the viewpoint of Labour's electoral interests. Naturally I was flattered to get the opportunity to work close to a distinguished politician and former Prime Minister. I was also intrigued that Wilson should look to me since, although always a Labour loyalist, I had never been identified with his brand of Labour politics. Indeed, as described earlier, I had worked closely with the supporters of Hugh Gaitskell in their battles against Wilson and the left in the 1960s and supported most of their policy views, and I frequently dissented from Wilson's 'fudge' style of leadership. Wilson was fully aware of all this and, after I joined his team, often referred with a grin to

'Bernard's suspicious track record'. I did not change my policy positions when working for him – though I came to understand better the bases of his leadership style – and he, being above all tolerant, clearly did not mind.

Joining Wilson's opinion polling team in late 1973 plunged me straight into some of the typically dark and complex aspects of political life in the then Labour Party. The polling situation I found reflected the party's divisions and also Wilson's typically oblique ways of dealing with them. For a start, there were now two committees advising on opinion polls, an official one run by the party organisation, and now our new and secret one, privately financed and reporting directly to the party leader. The former met rarely and did little, which was what the headquarters in Transport House wanted. In fact, the General Secretary Ron Hayward (a man of infinite vanity) and the left-wing majority on the national executive committee fundamentally disapproved of the whole business of opinion polling. This dislike derived partly from a belief that their own old-fashioned approach to elections was best: that small groups of dogmatic activists calling meetings of the like-minded in draughty halls was the best way to elicit views and influence the mass of public opinion.

Their more deep-rooted hostility to opinion polling was because, since the 1960s, the polls had increasingly demonstrated that the public in general, and Labour voters in particular, disliked the left-wing policies which the party activists were proposing. The activists were disenchanted with the polls because the polls showed that the electorate was disenchanted with them. The left preferred to believe that they alone knew what the electorate wanted, and certainly what was good for the public – which they saw as a strengthened diet of state nationalisation, intervention and controls over industry and the lives of ordinary people, together with fiscal punishment for anyone who had the impertinence to pursue success in the private sector. When the polls – and the reactions to our political broadcasts – repeatedly showed that in reality voters, and especially younger voters, did not want left-wing socialism, the reaction of the party activists and apparatchiks was to denigrate or suppress the polls. This typified that damaging process familiar in the years ahead, whereby the Labour Party was increasingly run by people who represented a diminishing sectarian minority, more and more out of touch with the wider and younger electorate. That process, which reached its near-fatal culmination during the dominance of Tony Benn and the 'loony left' in the early 1980s, had, as I then witnessed, already begun a decade before. Wilson was fully aware and respectful of modern sampling techniques. He wanted to use polls to his own and Labour's advantages. So he set up his own polling group. Himself a true professional, he wanted it to do a professional job of helping him to win the next election.

Our group contained just four people: Robert Worcester, American chairman of the polling firm MORI, with whom I established a lasting rapport; Percy Clarke, the party's beleaguered but helpful Press Secretary; Peter Davies; and myself. We were to report directly to Wilson and not to the party, which was supposed not to know of our activities. At our first meeting, just before Christmas 1973, we drew up the politically sensitive questions for the first poll in the New Year. When Bob Worcester's team had processed the responses (which were not particularly encouraging to Labour), we arranged to meet Wilson for lunch on 7 February 1974 to discuss the political implications of the poll findings. By the time of that meeting on 7 February, the Westminster political world was in turmoil.

When I arrived at the Commons at 12.45 to see Wilson, walking up the echoing steps and corridor to the Central Lobby, the atmosphere was buzzing with excitement. Prime Minister Edward Heath had just dissolved Parliament and called a general election for 28 February. I had walked into the middle of a political crisis which was dramatically to change my life.

Such an early dissolution of Parliament had in no way been anticipated at the previous autumn's party conferences. It also seemed to me as a teacher of political science very curious. Mr Heath's justification for this early dissolution was the extremity of the multiple crises facing the nation over the recent months: an energy crisis, an industrial relations crisis, a financial trade crisis, an inflationary price and wage crisis, an apparent social crisis, and an alleged constitutional crisis. There were certainly enough facts to support Heath's view that the national situation was grave – and looking back from a quarter of a century later it is clear that such modern Prime Ministers as Tony Blair happily have no idea what it is like to face economic crises of such gravity.

On the energy front, the OPEC oil producers on whom the British economy then depended had cut supplies and raised prices fourfold, with devastating implications for Britain's trade balance and inflation prospects. The miners, having enjoyed humiliating Heath's government in 1972, now saw a further opportunity to exploit their position as the suppliers of the key energy alternative to oil. So in October 1973 they had refused to accept Phase B of Heath's staged incomes policy (with its generous offer to them of a 16 per cent increase against a national norm of 7 per cent), on which the success of his whole economic policy and the credibility of his government rested. The miners launched an overtime ban in November and Heath responded in December by declaring a State of Emergency, with a three-day working week to conserve energy, starting in the New Year.

At the same time Chancellor of the Exchequer Anthony Barber announced savage public expenditure cuts, describing the national situation as 'the gravest since the war'. On 24 January 1974, while I was working on the opinion poll results, the miners' leaders called for a strike ballot. On 4 February, the Monday before I went to see Wilson, their members voted 81 per cent for a strike to start the following weekend. The spiral of confrontation led quickly to a crisis of such immensity that Heath believed it had become fundamentally constitutional, raising the basic issue on which he tried to fight the election, of 'Who Governs Britain?' – the elected government or an over-mighty and unaccountable trade union. The gravity of the situation could not be questioned. But to me it was not then and still is not clear how holding a divisive election in the middle of the miners' strike would have solved all, or indeed any of these problems. But the Conservatives – less Heath than some of his cabinet colleagues – saw political advantage in holding the election promptly, and clear disadvantages in waiting while the economic situation inevitably deteriorated.

Wilson was not pleased with the prospect of an election. The polls had recently moved into a Tory lead for the first time in over two years as association with union strikes damaged Labour. Our first Worcester poll showed sympathy to Heath's incomes policy and hostility to union militancy – and Labour behind the Tories. Labour's party machine was not yet geared up (if it ever was). The campaign was bound to be an uphill struggle, with all media attention on the miners' dispute which, with its implications of 'reds under the bed' and trade union irresponsibility, was safe Tory ground on which Labour would prefer not to fight.

At the House of Commons, Wilson's amiable aide Albert Murray came to collect Bob Worcester and me from the central lobby. Albert had been a Labour MP and minister until his defeat in 1970. Ruddy-faced, sandy-haired, round and with a rolling walk like a sailor, Albert had an irrepressible cockney humour and the innate masochism of a Millwall football club supporter. I came to love him and was shocked at his early death only six years after our meeting in the central lobby. He guided us through the dark Commons corridors, littered with groups of MPs discussing the coming election, to the room of the Leader of the Opposition. There Harold Wilson shook hands, apologised profusely and said he could not now have lunch to discuss our poll since he had to go to a party meeting to discuss the organisation of the election campaign. So we ate in the Commons restaurant with Albert and others from the Leader's office.

I naturally wondered whether this was both the beginning and the end of my brief assignment as Wilson's adviser. Certainly there would not now be time for any more monthly opinion polls. However, immediately after lunch I was summoned back to the Leader's crowded office. Present was the heart of Wilson's notorious 'kitchen cabinet', maligned for years throughout the press: Marcia

Matilda Williams (soon to be Baroness Falkender), his Personal and Political Secretary since 1956, long before he became Leader in 1963; and Joe Haines, Press Secretary since 1969. Joe already had behind him thirty successful years in political journalism and was later to become the *Daily Mirror*'s outstanding Political Editor and columnist. He was then in his mid forties, wiry in build, springy in stance, with dark bristly hair, an impassive face, and sharp eyes behind menacing rimless spectacles. I felt he had the tension of a coiled spring and he reminded me of Humphrey Bogart about to flatten some Chicago hood.

I was aware of 'Vinegar Joe's' reputation as a truly hard man, toughened by his childhood in Rotherhithe poverty and a working lifetime at the rough end of newspapers and the grass roots of the Labour Party. Many acquaintances had warned me to be wary of him and some journalists spoke of him with fear and loathing (and above all jealousy). I could quickly see that he was short of temper, fiercely competitive, and certainly not somebody lightly to be crossed. But the fact that so many journalists criticised him made me instinctively suspect that he must have seriously good qualities. This view was to be massively confirmed as over many years of close friendship I found that he was very able, of high self-educated intelligence and with remarkable political judgement. He proved to be a warm and loyal friend and a man of complete integrity. But I then viewed Joe with some immediate apprehension, sensing he would have little patience if I proved to be not up to the job.

I viewed Marcia Williams with even more caution. I recalled as a teenager seeing her, then Marcia Field, walk briskly into the Northampton Derngate bus station after her day at the 'posh' Northampton High School for Girls to travel home to East Haddon. My close school friend Gerry Fowler lived in a neigh-bouring village and knew her, and my then girlfriend Jill Booty was at school with her, so I was aware of her. But we had never met. Her reputation from Gerry and Jill was one of unapproachability.

That afternoon in the Leader's office, Marcia dominated our proceedings. She exuded authority. We were all made aware that she was the closest and longest adviser to Harold Wilson. He clearly deferred to her. She sliced through our election arguments like a knife. Then, in mid-afternoon, she suddenly rose from her chair and announced that since there was nothing more which any of us could usefully say or do, we should all go home. Everybody, including the party leader, who had already revealed his pessimism about the outcome of the coming election, mutely obeyed. I felt dismissed by the real centre of power.

As we dutifully dispersed, Harold Wilson leaned towards me and whispered almost nervously to me that we would all reassemble to discuss campaign strategy at his house in Westminster on the following Sunday, 10 February. With those few words I was in effect recruited to the Labour leader's election team and campaign. I was never afterwards formally asked if I wanted to join, or ever told that my invitation was for the whole three weeks of the campaign. All that happened was that each night, as I said goodbye, Harold would say, 'See you in the morning, Bernard.' It was typical of him to be oblique and never explicit. It reflected his short timescale, his habit of living politically from day to day, and his desire always to keep his options open. But it probably also reflected his long experience of Marcia's wilful temperament. He was aware that she might at any time withdraw approval of me. Then he might not again feel able to say, 'See you in the morning.'

During this first meeting with Joe and Marcia I recalled that for many years the newspapers had referred to Wilson's 'kitchen cabinet' as full of 'lackeys'. It was quickly clear to me – and over the next two years became even clearer – that this was familiar media trash. Joe Haines and Marcia were fiercely independent and very ready to express firm disagreement with Harold Wilson, she sometimes with a humiliating directness that visibly terrified him. Joe was physically and psychologically incapable of being a lackey to anyone, and he specialised in barbed dissent. Both said to Wilson exactly what they thought and believed, however critical. Wilson in turn was almost masochistic in inviting contradiction and in accepting dissent from those who worked for him.

I turned up on that first Sunday evening of the campaign at 5 Lord North Street, an elegant Georgian house, which had the atmosphere not so much of a family home as a base of political operations conveniently close to Parliament and the party headquarters in Smith Square. Mary Wilson flitted uninvolved in the background as if she would rather not have been there. I was at first very anxious, not yet clear what was to be my role. But I was put at ease by the relaxed and democratic manner in which Wilson conducted our discussions, asking each of us for our views on the priority to be given to various election issues and on points of political tactics.

As on many future occasions, I was struck by his openness and lack of side. Here was Britain's most experienced and successful political tactician, yet he treated my youthful and amateurish opinions as equal to his own. He was clear and decisive when we came to the summing up and he eloquently outlined his broad strategy for the coming campaign. It would, he said, be similar to the English Civil War battle of Marston Moor. We would have to spend the first week of the campaign on the defensive, absorbing the opening attacks by the Tory cavalry on the issue of the miners' strike. We would fight to undermine Heath's claim that the election was only about 'Who Governs Britain?' Then in the second week we would counter-attack on our own chosen themes, especially rising prices and pensions. In the final week we would skirmish on the flanks over Heath's addiction to Britain's membership of the European Common Market regardless of the terms. Wilson would also then float the case for Labour's proposed 'social contract' with the trade unions – although that was only in its early stages of formulation. Despite the hindrance of a persistent cold, he was perceptive, witty and punchy. I was impressed by his detailed knowledge of the Civil War, though sensing that he was a firm Puritan while I was a longstanding Cavalier.

For the first time, listening to him in his sitting room, it even fleetingly crossed my mind that, despite the adverse polls, we might just have a chance of winning the election. But I sensed that Wilson was himself less convinced by his own arguments than I was. Certainly he didn't seem hungry or even enthusiastic for victory. He spoke in a detached way, as if the election was some game and he was demonstrating how it might be won. His concern was only for the winning political moves, not for the fruits of victory. That was I suppose understandable since the fruits were bound to be sour. The industrial and economic prospects of Great Britain were worse than at any time since Attlee and Cripps faced the post-war reconstruction crisis. Injudicial Conservative financial management after 1970 pushed the economy booming out of control in 1972, with output rising at an unsustainable 7 per cent and inflation rocketing into double figures in 1973. The OPEC oil crisis moved the external economic environment dangerously against Britain. The number of strikes rose dramatically. Barber's pre-Christmas mini-budget showed the painful squeeze which faced the economy. Harold Wilson in February 1974 cannot have felt that the fruits of victory would be much better than his present thin prospects of winning the election.

Our daily schedule in the campaign proved repetitive and exhausting. Each morning I drove to Lord North Street from Kentish Town at around 8 a.m., by which time Wilson had read our draft for that day's speech which we had left with him overnight. Mary Wilson produced tea and biscuits for the team and we discussed any amendments which he wished to make, any overnight electoral developments with our tactics towards them, and which issue he should highlight at that morning's press conference. At 9 a.m. I accompanied Wilson down the street to Smith Square to attend the campaign committee at Transport House, the main purpose of which was to give party stalwarts a sense, however misplaced, of involvement in the campaign. While he was in there, I worked with Joe to complete Wilson's formal statement to the daily press conference. He would join us at around ten to help that and to finalise that day's speech, either in his office in Transport House or back in Lord North Street. We also then agreed the main theme for the following day's speech. I usually accompanied Wilson into the press conference at 11.45 and would sometimes take revised drafts and suggested replies to journalists' questions up to him on the stage – Marcia having refused, saying that 'I never service Harold on a public stage.'

At around lunchtime Wilson would leave us and set off to campaign and address rallies in the regions, accompanied by Albert Murray, Terry Boston (later Lord Boston) in charge of his baggage, and secretaries. Once he had gone, Joe, Marcia and I would go to our office in Transport House to work on his next day's speech. In the first few days Wilson tried to dictate his own speeches on the morning of delivery. But he lacked the time and this produced disruption in the office, with delayed departures and some pretty awful speeches. Under pressure from us, he reluctantly agreed that we should produce the draft the evening before – which in practice meant Joe writing the central text, with Marcia and myself contributing sections which particularly interested us (or did not interest Joe). This released Wilson to focus on tactics and presentation, although he never emotionally accepted having someone else to write his speeches. Joe, Marcia and I sat closely packed together in a high gloomy office. It was often chaotic, with research assistants and secretaries running in and out, an endless flow of documents and messages, and the telephone ringing constantly. In the outside office were a jam of assistants, hangers-on, a brace of secretaries, and Marcia's sister Peggy, ever ready to make tea and execute her younger sibling's orders. It was like Euston station in rush hour.

Inevitably our team atmosphere sometimes grew tense, with Joe long on courage but short on temper, and Marcia very febrile, tall and rangy, with eyes like a hawk. Throughout much of the campaign, I found her contributions shrewd and sensible, based on long political experience, and I could see why Wilson relied on her. Working together, Joe and Marcia were an impressive and intimidating pair, though slipping easily into edgy hostility. I tried to oil the wheels. I also had to fit in my weekly routine of lectures and classes at the LSE, where nobody knew of my moonlighting with the Labour leader.

Matters were not eased by the notorious inefficiencies of the party headquarters at Transport House. Their arrangements for Wilson's meetings and media coverage were appallingly lackadaisical and confused. Campaign documents were often muddled, photocopiers out of action and typing painfully slow, holding up the Leader's departures to crucial appointments. On one occasion the whole operation ran out of paper because the officers had not anticipated that an election would dramatically increase consumption; at the press conference there were no press releases because we had no paper. The distribution of campaign posters was erratic, with the ones printed in Urdu for a West Midlands constituency sent to the Highlands of Scotland. (Frank McElhone, our MP for the Glasgow Gorbals, also told me that our national campaign poster, with the slogan 'Back to Work with Labour', was seen there 'more as a threat than a promise' to a community where many had lost sight of the work ethic.)

When we flew back from Liverpool after the election and I telephoned Transport House for the latest situation, nobody there seemed to be monitoring the final results, in which they might be thought to have a passing interest. The organisation was riven with jealousies and internal hostilities, more energy seeming to be devoted against colleagues than against the Tories. There was too little pursuit of the internal unity necessary to win any battle or election. There were terrible rows between the ambitious General Secretary, Ron Hayward, and the gentle and loyal (though tetchy) Press Secretary, Percy Clarke. During one spat between them, Clarke walked out in fury – and in his socks, having removed his shoes to ease the tension. Percy then burst into tears before visiting Marcia for some of the tranquillisers which she would take to calm her own frayed nerves. Had this not been an important election but a vaudeville entertainment, the whole circus which surrounded us in Transport House would have been hilarious. And those who today foolishly criticise the superbly efficient New Labour election machine as 'heartless' or 'too mechanistic' show little under-standing of how necessary it was to replace the previous shambolic incompetence.

At the end of each day, by the time Wilson returned at around midnight from Glasgow, Bristol, Manchester or some other distant mass meeting, we had the next day's speech in draft and were waiting at Lord North Street to give it to him to read overnight, ready to begin the daily cycle again with his comments next morning. These occasions were also an opportunity for us to relax with him over a huge glass of whisky and analyse the day's events, drawing conclusions for our tactics in the days ahead. I usually returned home to Brookfield Park between midnight and 2 a.m. – and was heading back again to Lord North Street by 8 a.m. It was a relentless treadmill. I lost ten pounds in weight in three weeks, having started off fairly slim. But I personally loved every exhausting moment of it.

Through Wilson's speeches we tried to point the media towards our preferred policy priorities, but in the first week of the campaign, as Wilson feared, we failed in this endeavour. The newspapers, mainly Tory owned and edited, focussed only on the issue of the miners' strike, which they unanimously presented in the context of 'reds under the bed' (and, by implication, reds in Labour headquar-ters, which wasn't always wrong). But we kept hammering away, timing Wilson's speech deliveries to coincide with the deadlines of the television news. It was therefore possible to project our main arguments into most homes each evening, regardless of the worst efforts of the *Daily Mail*, *Telegraph*, and *Express*. We welcomed and used the growth of television to give some political balance in the media.

Edward Heath defined what he saw as the central issue of the February 1974 election in his broadcast on the 7th when he announced the dissolution of Parliament. He told the electorate that the time had come to tell 'the extremists, the militants ... we've had enough.' So for the Conservatives it was only about the miners' strike and 'Who Governs Britain?' Wilson tried to refute that in his broadcast reply next day. 'This election', he said, 'is not about the miners ... not about the power of the unions.' The real issues were 'the government's record on prices ... on housing ... on the Common Market.' So the battle lines were drawn.

The Tory strategy was to keep the spotlight on the irresponsibility of the miners. In fact it proved impossible to maintain that narrow focus over the whole three weeks of the campaign. Wilson's counter, in the framework of Marston Moor, was to move attention away from the miners, on which Labour could never win, and towards the other issues which he outlined to us in Lord North Street and to the country in his broadcast. In this strategy, Wilson's own persistence, assisted by fortuitous events, prevailed.

But neither side, including myself, really understood the deeper economic and political trends then emerging, which would ultimately lead Britain to move towards a more liberal free market economy, while at the same time forcing the Labour Party to abandon much of its Marxist language and statist policies. But that was some way ahead of this campaign as it moved into its electoral rhythms.

At the end of the bad first week, during which we had been as much as 12 per cent behind in our own polls, the *Financial Times* commented that 'the present one-sided picture of a relaxed "statesmanlike" Prime Minister [Heath] chastising the militants on behalf of the nation, and a rather tired and rattled Labour party leader swinging wildly, can produce only one result.' But in the second week matters moved a little more favourably for us as record price rises led the press for the first time to write about a Labour issue and not just the miners' strike. In the Gallup poll, prices rose as 'the most urgent issue' from 35 per cent to 49 per cent. Actually it was never clear to me why price rises were a good issue for us, since we did not really have any policy to deal with inflation, whereas Heath did. But politics is not logical. The public blamed the government in office – and we were able to talk about our 'social contract' with the unions as a more consensual approach to pay policy than Heath's combination of confrontation and statutory controls.

Wilson still had a persistent throat and eye infection, but by the second weekend I observed an improvement in his morale. He looked brighter, less hunched, and told me he was greatly lifted by the enthusiasm shown at Labour rallies. Late on the night of Monday 18 February I walked with him from Transport House to his home. He said: 'It is a funny election. I don't know how it is going. But it is better organised than ever before, especially with Joe doing my speeches.' And he added that 'the spirit of the office is so good. I don't know if I shall win or lose, but this is my happiest election.'

But it still looked as if we would lose. Over the last weekend our private polls showed our deficit in the range of 7 to 8 per cent. But a number of helpful events occurred. The enquiry into miners' wages concluded that Heath's tough line was based on exaggerated miners' earnings. Joe and I immediately wrote into Wilson's speeches that it proved the whole crisis had been unnecessary. In Gallup, strikes declined as 'the most important issue' from 34 per cent to 23 per cent. Television commentators began to ask Tories whether the whole election was not called on a false prospectus. The campaign suddenly took fire.

Over the final weekend Enoch Powell, then a charismatic right-wing politician, intervened on the Common Market issue which obsessed him, concluding with an appeal to the electorate to vote Labour because we at least offered a referendum. His speeches on 23 and 25 February had been signalled to us in advance, with the journalist Andrew Alexander acting as intermediary to Joe. He said that the first speech on Saturday would be 'deliberately cool' but the second on Monday would be 'hotter', and assured us that Wilson would be 'pleased'. The latter handled the Powell sensation gingerly while making it clear that he welcomed Powell's support for Labour's position on renegotiating the terms of our Common Market membership. He was aware that the Common Market in itself was not an election winner. But it further diverted comment away from the miners' strike – and in Powell's home territory of the West Midlands the voters responded to Powell's clarion call and the swing to Labour there was to be 5 per cent above the national average. Over the final days the polls still showed Labour well behind, though with the Liberals making ground, especially in Tory marginal seats. More encouraging to me was that in our private polls our 'issues' – prices, housing, pensions and the Common Market – began to move to the top of the electorate's priorities. In that sense our campaign strategy was finally working.

But the mood in Wilson's team deteriorated. Marcia, who until then had greatly impressed me, told me on the final weekend that she did not want us to win and did not expect us to win. 'I do not want to go through all that again,' she said. 'I just want to live my private life.' Joe and I had lunch with her at a hotel in St James's on the Sunday before polling. Her earlier bright friendliness had changed to hostility, and she became very upset when Joe referred to her jokingly as 'our Lucretia Borgia'. As the day progressed she became ever more edgy. Next day, Monday 25 February, the explanation for her nerves emerged. The *Daily Mail* was typically about to print a story smearing Marcia about an alleged involvement in land deals, apparently held back for some time until it could be used with most damage to Harold Wilson on the eve of the election. In Lord North Street, Marcia became very agitated. She put on her coat and announced that 'I am leaving to catch a train and will not return.' That night the atmosphere was very bad. Powell's helpful speech was ignored. Wilson sat slumped, tired, sour, scowling, his eyes dead like a fish. He snarled at Joe about his speeches being 'too sophisticated'. He drank brandy heavily.

The smear never appeared. Albert had arranged for his friends in the print unions to disrupt the publication of the newspaper should the *Mail* try to print the story. Next day we resumed our final hours of campaigning as if nothing had ever arisen. But I had glimpsed the more difficult side of Marcia, the darker side of Wilson and his unhealthy obsession with the press. It was the kind of diversion away from the central political issues which was to become sadly too familiar in the two years ahead.

With campaigning in London effectively over on Wednesday 27 February, Wilson flew off to Liverpool to spend the final twenty-four hours campaigning in his constituency of Huyton, a very safe Labour seat. I joined him there on polling day, together with Mary Wilson, Marcia, Joe, Albert and Terry Boston, who efficiently supervised our luggage. Terry had endless patience and, due to his predictably calm reaction to all crises, however severe, was known in the team as 'Bless My Soul Boston'. Our mood was fairly sombre since every election-day opinion poll showed us behind, with the Tory lead ranging from 2 to 5 per cent. Our own Worcester poll, more recent than the national ones, showed us only one per cent behind the Tories (in fact close to the final result in votes), and gave me encouragement because it showed our issues coming to the top of the electorate's concerns. Every newspaper that morning forecast a clear victory for Mr Heath.

That afternoon, while Wilson went off canvassing in Huyton, I took a long walk with Marcia along the misty Merseyside waterfront. She again said that she did not want to win and wanted Harold Wilson out of the whole political jungle. From all the media reports it seemed that she would get her way. By the time we returned to the Adelphi Hotel it was snowing. Back in the hotel, Wilson astonished me by revealing his complicated plans for returning south after his Huyton result was declared. He proposed first to switch secretly from the Adelphi to a smaller hotel, the Golden Cross, then to slip away unseen in our plane, indicating to the air traffic controllers that he was going to London, but during the flight to divert to a small airfield in Bedfordshire. Wilson would then race away by car to some secret hideaway in the country. He had an old road map on his lap. Albert tried to break the silence which greeted this bizarre scenario by jokingly suggesting that on take-off we should blindfold the pilot so that not even he knew where he was going. Wilson did not even flicker in response. I suddenly realised what was behind this crazy fantasy. Wilson was assuming that he would lose the election and was preparing his getaway, to escape the triumphalist press exalting in his humiliation and wanting to jump on his political grave.

It revealed the deep bruising which persisted from his 1970 defeat and the relentless hail of press criticism on his thinning skin in recent years. It was also a pathetic fantasy in a major politician and former Prime Minister of Great Britain. At dinner, Wilson further developed his escape plans, with mentions of false trails, diversionary cars and trains, as well as more plans for the fleeing invisible aeroplane. So many complications were introduced, so many bluffs and covers, that I could not work out how or when I was supposed to travel back to London, if ever at all. Was I to be a bluff, a cover, part of the media deception, or to be a refugee? I tentatively asked the hitherto silent Marcia. She dismissed all 'this schoolboy behaviour' and simply said: 'You will be on the plane to London, like everybody else, including him.'

For two hours that evening I toured the Huyton constituency with Harold Wilson. It was eerily dark in the wind, rain and sleet. I often felt lost among miles of bleak council estates, with few people to escort or show an interest in us. I still have a clear picture of Harold that night, lonely and desolate, a small windswept figure, apparently yesterday's man, heading for political oblivion, ignored by press and security alike. A few policemen followed at a distance, treating Wilson in a very offhand way, clearly assuming he was the loser in the national battle and would not again be of special responsibility to them. We occasionally escaped from the rain to call in on local party offices or clubs, which were gloomily empty, everyone, it was alleged, being out canvassing – though we saw few if any of them on the streets. At one point I asked Wilson what he thought the election result would be. He declined to answer, obviously puzzled, and asked what I thought. I said: 'I suspect it is like 1964 when we just scraped home.' He cheered up at that and suddenly began to reveal how he would run his next government, using his later familiar football image of how, having now such experienced players, he would play 'as a sweeper at the back and not as a centre forward.' He told me that there would be 'no presidential stuff, no first hundred days', and also 'no beer and sandwiches in Number 10.' In the car back to the Adelphi he repeated how happy he was with his campaign team – 'my best ever'.

In his Adelphi suite we settled down with large whiskies to watch the results on television. Wilson was calm and professional, showing total command of the electoral statistics in each constituency, correctly forecasting which Lancashire seats would fall to Labour on the current, but fluctuating, swing.

The first two results were from Guildford and from Cheltenham, with Labour pushed humiliatingly into third place but the Tory vote slumping before the Liberal surge. Our spirits quickly lifted when Salford and Wolverhampton (Powell country) showed very strong swings to Labour. But by the time we set off for his Huyton count, the situation was gridlocked and unclear.

After the declaration of his predictable victory in Huyton, the atmosphere in his packed Labour club was different from anything I had ever experienced in the cool south of England. His supporters gave Wilson a tumultuous reception. A woman standing next to me, tears streaming down her face, shouted, 'I love him, I love him!' Harold himself came warmly alive, relaxed and joking with the party members, and they clearly thought the world of him. It was a long way from the hostile horrors on the party's National Executive Committee, who claimed that he was out of touch with the party and that they alone represented 'our people'. No one who had not seen that spontaneous display of affection, and certainly no cynical Westminster journalist, could hope to understand the northern roots of Harold Wilson's political strength.

But soon we also saw his psychological weakness as he left the club. He now began to implement his strange escape plans. He was still pursuing his 'loser' strategy, even though it seemed he might well be winning. Our cavalcade dashed, optimistically hoping not to be noticed, across town to switch to the dreary Golden Cross Hotel. I went to bed at 4.30 a.m. but could not sleep. I talked to Marcia on the phone and we agreed how crazy it all was. She phoned Wilson, and then summoned Albert, who arrived with the early morning newspapers all exulting in Heath's assumed victory. (The *Telegraph* announced that 'The Tories have won, but not by as many as we would have wished.') We decided to get up and go back to the Adelphi to hold a press conference, and Joe and I blearily helped Wilson prepare his statement. Then we drove sheepishly back to the Adelphi. The mad escape plan was quietly binned.

The team flew back to London in the sleet and rain of that Friday morning, frustratingly cut off from the decisive constituency results declared while we were airborne. At Heathrow I tried to get the results from party headquarters, but nobody there seemed to know, or was particularly interested to help their party leader find out. To the end, Transport House seemed to be fighting a different battle. So I telephoned the *Daily Mirror*, who told me that Labour had won three more seats while we were in the air, and an overall majority was still just possible if the remaining results went our way. We drove into Westminster, exhausted and incapable of any emotions or victory celebrations. It was not until later that day, when Labour won Carmarthen by three votes after five recounts, and Saturday morning when the Tories lost Argyle to the Scottish Nationalists, that it was finally clear: not that Labour had won, but that Edward Heath had lost.

The final figures showed that Labour had made a net gain of only three seats since 1970, winning 301, a lead of five over the Tories (with 296). But we were twenty-nine short of an overall majority, the first such deficit since 1929. The Liberals, although getting 22 per cent of the vote, had only fourteen seats (with the other small parties getting another twenty, of which the Scottish Nationalists had seven). So neither Labour nor the Conservatives could produce an overall majority, even if in coalition with the Liberals. In terms of votes there had been a small swing to Labour, but we ended up with only 37.1 per cent, 0.8 per cent less than the Tories, and the lowest winning share of the vote for over forty years. But Worcester's final private poll, showing us 1 per cent behind, had been spot on. We had more seats than the Tories because the Liberals late surge did, as Wilson had forecast, damage the Tories more than us.

The outcome was in fact quite a pickle. It was simply not clear what the electorate had voted for. There was no clear mandate for either our or the Tory policies. My personal interpretation was that the electorate realised that Heath was right and one day there had to be a battle with the unions to curb their irresponsibilities. But the public was not quite ready for it yet. They were tempted by Wilson's Labour as the fudge to put off the evil day of battle. They hoped that Wilson's explicit appeal to 'a quiet life' under him might work and find a consensual solution within the Labour movement by some device such as the promised 'social contract'. Only when the 1979 Winter of Discontent demonstrated that the left-wing trade union leaders were in their own sectional interests, prepared to destroy even a Labour Government did the electorate agree to grasp the nettle with Mrs Thatcher – and even then not by a clear majority of votes. People don't readily grasp nettles.

Wilson's own contribution to our marginal victory was significant. His campaign style was much less glitzy than in 1964 and less complacent than in 1970. He was now clearly an older man, subdued, streetwise, and certainly no longer hungry for office. He often looked exhausted by the relentless treadmill of the campaign, his voice croaking and his eyes puffy and red-rimmed. He was certainly no rhetorician. He had no feel for words, being more at home with dates and statistics. In fact he could not rely on remembering even the shortest phrases, which is why he had to read every word of every speech from the text in front of him and told me he was afraid of having to ad lib in case his mind went blank. (Later, at a small Downing Street lunch, I wrote out for him a single sentence saying what a pleasure it was to welcome these guests and he hoped they enjoyed their meal.) He deliberately reversed much of the presidential style (advised by

Marcia) which lost in 1970. He abandoned 'walkabouts' and used only structured meetings which could not get out of control. He was more 'collegiate' at his press conferences, deliberately bringing in James Callaghan, Denis Healey, Roy Jenkins and other colleagues to answer questions. He tried his best to work with the party machine, despite its bickering and inefficiencies. He was pragmatic and undogmatic, consistently playing down socialist and sectarian themes. He recognised that British society was changing, with fewer class divisions, and that the general public did not want socialist dogma.

It was Harold Wilson's fourth general election campaign as leader of the Labour Party, so it contained no exciting novelties for him. He was widely expected to lose, including by every Labour Party colleague of his to whom I spoke, whether from the right or left. He himself shared that view, seeing Labour behind in every single public or private opinion poll. He was derided in the media, and written off as a finished loser by journalists unfit to shine his shoes. The Oxford historians of the February 1974 election concluded that British newspapers expressed a 'full-blooded campaigning partisanship greater than in any election since the 1950s.' Most papers simply echoed and trumpeted the Tory campaign. On polling day the ever biased and so hated *Daily Mail* to our glee ran the headline 'A Handsome Win for Heath'. I began to feel that Wilson's notorious paranoia about the press might have a rational basis, since they were clearly out to destroy him.

His public appeal was much dimmed compared with the glamorous bright mornings and great promise of 1964. Yet he kept doggedly plugging on, playing a consensual and even humble line. Basically he asked the public to trust him to heal the social wounds, not to widen them further as he genuinely feared Heath's confrontational approach would do. As he perceptively admitted to me in the campaign, 'Really, Bernard, I am just offering them a quiet life.' And yet he was still fairly quick on his feet, exploiting each of the tactical opportunities which arose. He proved himself in this campaign a better electoral strategist and tactician than Edward Heath. He did not have very good cards in his hand, but he did not miss a trick. He held the core Labour vote together and made it possible to slip into power.

However, he was not able to get into power yet. Heath refused to resign. The Tory leader clung to office for three more days, hoping to form a minority coalition with the Liberals. On that Friday afternoon Harold Wilson, after long discussion with us, issued a statement saying he was prepared to form a minority government but not to enter a coalition.

I went with him to Transport House for the shadow cabinet meeting and back to Lord North Street, where we constantly chewed over the tactics of the deadlock. The house was full of family and children and it was impossible to hold a sustained tactical discussion. We all grew tetchy. I was absolutely whacked. Harold dispatched Mary and the children off to Grange Farm, his country house at Great Missenden. Marcia was tired and emotional and wanted Harold to issue a savage denunciation of Heath for hanging on and 'cheating the British people'. I was more cautious, advising him to go to the farm and 'play it with dignity like a Prime Minister in waiting'. He dithered and then compromised between our advices, phoning Jim Callaghan and asking him to issue a statement denouncing Heath for 'cheating'. Jim was too shrewd for that and bluntly refused.

We received intriguing phone calls from Number 10, at first suggesting that Heath was about to resign, and then saying there would be a delay while he tried to get the Liberals into coalition. I contacted my Liberal MP friend John Pardoe, who was in his constituency in Cornwall. He said that his leader, Jeremy Thorpe, was 'keen to get his knees under any top table.' But he assured me – and I told Wilson – that the younger radical Liberals would not allow it. We were relieved at that but otherwise grew more tired and irritable. Our tactical judgement grew less reliable. In the end, close to utter exhaustion, we left for our homes, Wilson to his farmhouse, as I had been pressing him to do for some hours. I collapsed into bed in Brookfield Park and slept straight through until 9.30 next morning.

But I had little chance to relax over the weekend as Heath went through the process of trying to form his coalition, seeing Thorpe on Saturday, the Ulster Unionists on Sunday, and waiting for the final rejection by a meeting of Liberal MPs on Monday. I spent much of the Saturday and Sunday on the phone to Wilson and Marcia, both out in the sunshine at Great Missenden. To the media Wilson appeared impressively relaxed, walking his dog and confidently playing the role of Prime Minister in waiting. But over the phone he was jumpy and worried about the Liberals. We also had long telephone discussions about his coming cabinet. I suggested that James Callaghan, Roy Jenkins and Michael Foot might have positions different from the ones they held in the current shadow cabinet, but he didn't want to upset the party equilibrium and would not divert from the existing dispositions.

That Sunday evening Harold Wilson summoned me to Lord North Street and explained the job he wanted me to do in Number 10 running his new Policy Unit. He said he wanted it to act as his 'eyes and ears in Whitehall'. He was very clear about its tasks and objectives and how it must have full access to committees and papers. He was very supportive, stating that we four in the team (Marcia, Joe, himself and myself) 'must stick together' and if there were any problems with the Civil Service machine we must 'all walk out of the door together'. He also intriguingly mentioned to me the opportunities the job would give me later to write about his government from the inside, referring to the role of Professor Arthur Schlesinger at the court of President Kennedy.

More worrying was when that day he explained to me why he could not put Roy Jenkins into Healey's place at the Treasury so soon after Roy's 1972 rebellion and resignation as Deputy Leader over joining the Common Market. He said he wanted me personally to explain this to Roy. Wilson himself seemed nervous of talking directly to Roy and suggested that the bad news might be less unwelcome coming from me as a longstanding admirer of Roy. I shared Wilson's lack of heroism in this situation and pressed the arguments why it was more appropriate that he as Prime Minister should talk directly to a senior cabinet colleague. But it was clear he was not convinced. Wilson did not like face-to-face confrontation. In this case it verged on the cowardly to nominate a novice to face Roy's ire; though he may genuinely have believed – or convinced himself – that it might be politically more acceptable to use an old Gaitskellite hand as a messenger. He did not convince me and I was certain it would not convince Jenkins.

On Monday 4 March, Edward Heath's desperate attempt to keep a grip on power came to its doomed conclusion. The fourteen Liberal MPs unanimously rejected his coalition offer (and Wilson congratulated me on my inside information). Heath finally went to Buckingham Palace to resign at 6.30 p.m. and the Queen then summoned Harold Wilson to form his third administration.

In the team we had spent the day waiting and confidently preparing to take power. But for me the day had its unpleasant side. Wilson again raised the Jenkins issue. He explained why Roy had to go to the Home Office in the short term, say for eighteen months. He said I was to tell Jenkins that he would then retire and Roy, he hoped, would succeed him. But he felt that Jenkins would only be in a strong enough party position to win the leadership ballot if he had done a solid job in another ministerial office; this would make up for his misdemeanours over the 1972 Common Market vote. He said it was not possible, in party political terms, to give him Healey's place at the Treasury or Callaghan's at the Foreign Office immediately. Wilson's concern, as ever, was internal party balance. He suggested that I telephone Jenkins and explain all this.

I again resisted, arguing that whoever conveyed the bad news must out of courtesy do it directly to Roy's face and that details of a top cabinet appointment should be given to a senior minister by the Prime Minister, not a junior aide such as me. But he insisted. So I arranged to see Roy personally after lunch and conveyed the unhappy message directly to his face. Basically I concluded that it was not for me to instruct an experienced Prime Minister how to conduct his relations with his ministerial colleagues – though with more experience I would have taken a different view.

I met Roy Jenkins in the corridor of the Commons and simply conveyed the information from Wilson. He was understandably unhappy with both the message and the messenger. He thanked me with cool politeness and abruptly walked away. I reported back to Wilson and restated my view that now he must talk directly to his colleague. He finally agreed, though asking me to go back to invite Roy to come and see him. When I did, Roy finally did explode at me with pent-up anger, which I understood, shouting, perhaps rather grandly, 'You tell Harold Wilson he must bloody well come to see me, and if he doesn't watch out, I won't join his bloody government!' He repeated this on a public staircase, with others around, concluding that 'this is typical of the bloody awful way that Harold Wilson does things.' I wrote a record of the exchange.

By now I was quite fed up with this whole business and my own miserable role in it. I went back and told Wilson that he really must go to see Roy in order 'to mend bridges' for the new government. He readily agreed and trotted off for the meeting. He looked very gloomy on return and clearly had not enjoyed the experience. He reported that Roy had accepted the arguments for his own downgrading to the Home Office, but stated categorically that he would not join the government if Peter Shore, an obsessive anti-European, was appointed to his shadow position at the Board of Trade. Both Marcia and I expressed sympathy for the Jenkins position on this, saying it was excessive both to demote him ministerially and to humiliate him on Europe. Wilson again insisted that he had virtually no flexibility on cabinet appointments but must stick to the existing shadow cabinet composition (as he did).

I apologise for devoting a disproportionate space to the minor Jenkins episode. But apart from exposing my own inexperience, it was revealing in a number of ways. It showed two big beasts of the Labour jungle in uncomfortable confrontation. It showed Wilson's belief that even after eleven years as leader he had no scope to make his own appointments to his initial cabinet. It revealed his personal weakness and his discomfort in dealing with Jenkins.

It also led him to reveal to me his own personal intentions to retire within a couple of years (at the time I was not sure how seriously to take that, but it was proved true), and his own then apparent preference for Jenkins as his successor – though that had changed to Callaghan by the time of his resignation two years later. It also taught me that in politics and government one has to carry out some uncomfortable tasks. And if you don't like the heat, you should get out of the kitchen cabinet.

Immediately after we settled in office, I took steps to try to repair relations with Roy Jenkins. I invited John Harris, his great supporter and now junior minister, into Number 10 and we agreed that the situation between our two bosses needed to be improved and we would arrange for them to meet and have a reconciliatory chat. That meeting took place on that first Friday, 8 March. Harold Wilson told me afterwards that Roy had complained that although they were 'the two most important men in the government', their relations were damagingly poor, and he outlined their past disputes. Wilson pointed out that he had generously made John Harris a peer and Minister of State at Roy's Home Office, although he did not like him and despite 'John's constant attacks on me.'

But Harold felt better after the meeting – now 'we have got it all off our chests'. I also repaired my own relations with Jenkins in September over large gin and tonics in his grand room in the Home Office, once occupied by Herbert Morrison. I pressed him to take more active participation in the Government and give more active leadership to the right wing, feeling he was too semi-detached, as if not wishing to be contaminated by events there. I believed he could not win the party leadership from outside the centre of action. He laughingly promised he would 'try to love Harold Wilson more.'

At 7.30 on the Monday evening, Harold and Mary Wilson were driven to the Palace by his long-standing chauffeur Bill Housden in Wilson's own old car. We – Marcia, Joe and Albert, together with Marcia's devoted servant Gerald Kaufman (a former Wilson aide and later MP) – followed in a rented and stately Daimler. I could hardly suppress my excitement, driving through the gates of Buckingham Palace past mildly cheering crowds and flashing cameras. We sat waiting nearly an hour while Harold received his commission from the Queen. We discussed how to run Number 10, with Marcia insisting we must sack the Principal Private Secretary, Robert Armstrong, and in general have no relations whatsoever – not even bad ones – with the civil servants. When the new Prime Minister emerged from his audience, he was quickly grabbed by Armstrong and steered towards the Number 10 official Rover 3.5, the public symbol that he was now indeed Prime Minister.

But Joe decided to make the equally symbolic point that the civil servants should not assume that they now completely controlled Wilson and could shut out his personal team – as had, according to Marcia, happened in his previous administrations. So Joe nipped across the courtyard to the Rover, sharply eased Robert aside, and slipped into the back seat beside the new Prime Minister. I could see Harold grinning with impish approval at Joe's cheek – he never had the courage to fight the machine himself, but he liked his personal team to fight their territorial battles hard. Robert Armstrong simply nodded with acceptance and mandarin professionalism and hurried to the second official car, speeding off to make sure that he reached Number 10 before the new Prime Minister. He knew he would have many more opportunities to assert his official supremacy. The rest of us in the team travelled behind in the Daimler to Downing Street.

In those days, before the security blight imposed by IRA terrorists, Downing Street was completely open to the public, a small but invaluable symbol of open democracy. Citizens could saunter along and watch their Prime Minister emerge and wave, accompanied by his advisers – the publicity-seekers among these making sure they were in camera shot, the prudent ones hiding in the shadows of the doorway. That evening Joe, Albert and I loitered in the shade, advised by Joe that if we were to be photographed twice sharing the Prime Minister's fame, then Marcia would exact revenge. As we crossed the pavement some spectators cheered, others booed. It was not an ecstatic public acclamation and Harold Wilson slipped through the door almost guiltily. I was tingling with excitement. I could simply not believe that I was going into Downing Street to work with a Labour Prime Minister. I felt almost detached from my body, floating on air above the scene, watching myself get out of the car and move nervously towards the big black door which has no working handle on the outside so that it can only be opened from the inside. Beside it was the brass plate reading 'First Lord of the Treasury'. The benign pantomime policeman, who had already by then become more a tourist icon that an instrument of law and order, ushered us inside. It was as if it was happening to someone else, not me. Certainly it was a long way from Ashton and from Roade.

The big door closed behind us, shutting out the cheers and boos, the media circus and the lingering echoes of the recent election campaign. Inside it was eerily quiet. Ahead of us lay the lobby and the hallway, with corridors branching off left to the Chancellor's residence and right to the press office. Beyond was the long corridor to the back of the house, to the cabinet room, the private secretaries' offices where Armstrong presided, and the staircase to the study and the state reception and dining rooms above. Filling the hallway were several dozen of the Number 10 staff: high-flying policy and press advisers; administrative secretaries who had served many Prime Ministers, some back to Churchill; messengers, police and security officers. They were totally silent and appeared apprehensive, as if we were a threatening force of alien occupation. The tension was tangible. This was, after all, the operations centre from which Edward Heath had campaigned on the theme that Wilson's trade union friends had rendered Britain ungovernable. Heath's confrontational speeches, in which he had for the past three weeks declared that it would be a national disaster if Wilson and his team took over government, were crafted here. Some of the staff before us were still visibly weepy from standing here only a short time before and waving a tearful goodbye to Mr Heath.

I hung back shyly, almost wondering if I should be there at all. But then the silence was suddenly broken in true mandarin style by Robert Armstrong. He had been particularly close to Edward Heath, sharing his love of music and his management style. Knowing this, Marcia had earlier pronounced his death warrant. The cold glint in her eyes as she clipped briskly across the lobby behind Wilson suggested that Armstrong's immediate execution might be only the start of a full official purge: her dislike of Number 10 private secretaries and administrative secretaries (especially the pretty young ones in the Garden Room) was well known. Robert knew he had a sticky time ahead and the girls would need their tin helmets. Whether as a last-minute attempt at self-preservation, or, more likely, out of traditional Whitehall courtesy, Robert somewhat self-consciously led the applause and even aroused some desultory cheers. It worked. Harold Wilson moved warmly forward, arms stretched to shake hands with his new staff. The atmosphere melted.

We had witnessed a unique and civilised British convention, smoothing the transition of power and symbolising the continuity of government across parties. It reflected the tradition that British civil servants serve all their Prime Ministers with equal loyalty (in my observation certainly true of Number 10, but less guaranteed with ministers in some departments). Anyway, Robert Armstrong was safe in the hands of a Prime Minister always concerned not to upset Whitehall.

While Wilson went off to be briefed on some urgent policy issues, we went to Marcia's room, strategically situated beside the entrance to the cabinet room. From there she could operate as the tigress at the Prime Minister's gate. After a drink and a quick gossip, Robert Armstrong came to invite us on a quick tour of Number 10, which Marcia declined. I took part with fascination, since understanding the geography of the house was important to my operating successfully there.

Actually Number 10 is part of an unlikely jumble of mainly nineteenth-century offices and older houses which contains the central capability of British government. The Downing Street and Cabinet Office complex is networked together by rambling corridors and stairs, and often-locked doors.

It encompasses the north side of the street and a whole block on lower Whitehall. The street was built by Sir George Downing in 1681. Many of its splendid town houses, and their coach houses and stables, were knocked down in the nineteenth century, together with a famous corner pub, the Cat and Pipes.

Other than Number 10, only two original buildings remain: numbers 11 and 12, then inhabited respectively by the Chancellor of the Exchequer and the Chief Whip. (Tony Blair's hugely expanded media team has recently ejected and replaced the Whips from Number 12.) During the eighteenth century the house

– really two town houses joined back-to back like Siamese twins – was offered by George I to Robert Walpole as Prime Minister. Walpole accepted, with the honourable pre-condition that, it was not given to him personally, but attached to his official position as First Lord of the Treasury. In this way it became the base for all subsequent Prime Ministers. Most have lived there; some have used it only as an office and a location for cabinet meetings. The house contains a typing area in the basement, the state reception rooms, dining rooms and study on the first floor, corridors of offices on the second floor, and then had at the top a long and narrow apartment providing the Prime Minister's modest living quarters. (After March 1974 the Wilsons preferred not to occupy them, choosing to live at home in nearby Lord North Street, and Tony Blair has moved to occupy some of Number 11.) In all there were some hundred employees there – no other head of a major state was served by so few. In fact Number 10 still has most of the rambling features and all the intimacy of a Westminster family residence.

This cosiness was a great advantage to me and others in the Prime Minister's personal team. It meant we could get to know everyone in the house very quickly. There was little scope for hierarchy and standing on ceremony and all of us had the common task of serving the Prime Minister.

Having noted the geography and absorbed the atmosphere, I decided that my number one priority was to secure good offices for myself and the new Policy Unit. In government one of the most important ingredients of power is access – access to decision-makers and access to information revealing what is going on in Whitehall. Within Number 10, that meant claiming a room close to the Prime Minister, for quick briefings, close to the private secretaries who receive all policy papers and telephone information, and close to both the cabinet room and the Prime Minister's study where most important meetings took place.

Joe had earlier advised me to take a suite of rooms known as the 'Wiggery', named after the Labour politician George Wigg, who had occupied it during Wilson's 1960s government and had succumbed in a power struggle with Marcia. The precedent may not have been encouraging, nor was the likelihood that Wigg had left it 'bugged' by his beloved security services.

But the location was perfect. It occupied a bridge linking Number 10 with the key Cabinet Office. It gave me quick access to the action points of the house, to where the Prime Minister and his officials worked and met, and especially to the Downing Street cockpit and gossip centre, the cabinet room lobby where ministers and officials gather for meetings with the Prime Minister. My target suite had only two rooms. The grander of them, which I proposed to occupy, had a wonderful high ceiling, wooden panelled walls in light green with white skirtings, colours complemented by a deep sofa and armchairs upholstered in lemon yellow. Its high windows looked over a yard towards Downing Street and the Foreign Office beyond. A number of excellent eighteenth-century portraits included a Reynolds above the huge open fireplace. It suited me fine.

Unfortunately my occupation plan soon hit a rock. When I opened the door, I found a sad figure still at his desk, apparently writing formal letters of farewell and making final telephone calls, a half empty bottle of whisky at his elbow. It was like finding a member of the Czar's family after the Bolsheviks stormed the Winter Palace. It was Robin Hayden, a Foreign Office regular who had joined Heath's personal staff and as a superior civil servant seemed to feel that the change of government need not touch his convenience. I froze in the doorway as he offered me a drink. Joe had urged me earlier to throw out ruthlessly any human leftovers from the defeated Heath regime, saying it was important to impose one's will and show them who was now boss. Unfortunately, I am incorrigibly soft-hearted and not really a toughie – never really tough enough to operate successfully in the political jungle. Hayden looked pathetic and I apologised, saying I would delay my occupation until tomorrow. (To my astonishment, he was still there next morning, so I then did throw him out.)

I returned to face the uncomprehending scorn of Marcia and Joe. Marcia immediately appointed me in charge of 'dining' – a role which was to contain more political dynamite than I then realised – and I went upstairs to explore the inadequate cooking facilities. Given my lifetime's failure to contribute anything in this area at home, I was not optimistic. I was also asked to secure a cook, not an area in which I had much of a network apart from Carol. Fortunately Robert Armstrong produced a friend, Paddy, who later became his second wife – no doubt a tribute to her culinary skills.

More important steps were then in progress towards the formation of the new government. The TUC was summoned to Number 10 for the following day to discuss Wilson's proposals to end the miners' strike and the three-day week. The Prime Minister himself started late at night seeing his first cabinet appointments, starting with an ebullient Elwyn Jones as Lord Chancellor. Other ministers streamed in, accepted what was offered and left smiling. Michael Foot was the most nervous, taking his first ministerial job at the age of sixty and facing the trade union troubles at the Department of Employment. Wilson was still negotiating with Jenkins about Peter Shore – and remained sympathetic but unyielding.

He finished at midnight and we went back to Lord North Street for a final farewell drink to our election campaign. We were none of us triumphal. Ahead lay the harsh realities and the insoluble problems of government. It would now be not a question of words and speeches but of policies and action. As I drove home to Brookfield Park, I could hardly believe that only a few weeks after starting the

MORI opinion poll, I was now to find myself at the centre of government. Responsible for that great opportunity were two of the most important factors in all life careers – chance and availability. My mind was full of the challenges of recruiting and running the Policy Unit, a new institution in central government. I also knew that my relations with Marcia, Wilson's closest aide, would be critical, many of my predecessors in Wilson's entourage not having survived in that enterprise. I sensed that our relationship would be like walking on glass. I was both excited and daunted. Number 10 Downing Street was to dominate my everyday life over the next five years, and to haunt it long after.

Nine

THE WILSON GOVERNMENT IN 1974

T he multiple economic and industrial problems which Harold Wilson's new government faced without a parliamentary majority in March 1974 were the gravest since the Attlee government. He decided to proceed as if he had a full majority, and immediately moved to end the miners' strike, where both sides were ready to make peace, and terminated the three-day week and the State of Emergency. Wilson jauntily said to me after the settlement that 'normalcy has been restored'. But it was really a capitulation on the miners' terms and solved little in the longer term. Final confrontation between the miners and the elected government was merely delayed a decade.

We pushed ahead with our legislative programme, rapidly announced in the Queen's Speech. It was worthy and cautious, promising Bills to control prices, freeze rents, increase pensions and food subsidies, and to repeal Heath's Industrial Relations Act. All these reflected our election manifesto commitments. Healey's first budget, hurriedly cobbled together within two weeks of taking office, slightly raised the cost of living but was nowhere near as deflationary as the Treasury felt was required. However, the tough language of Healey's speeches, with their implication that the rich would be firmly squeezed, created uncertainty and even panic in the City, where many of the rich operated. In fact the Chancellor's language was too tough and his measures too modest, when we really needed it the other way round. The central problems after the election remained the same as before – the energy crisis; relations with the EEC; Ulster; and above all the fatal nexus of bad industrial relations, strikes, and rocketing price and wage inflation. Nothing in the change of government had changed that.

In confronting these daunting problems, Wilson was fortunate in March 1974 to lead a formidable cabinet. At its heart were eight politicians – Wilson, Callaghan, Jenkins, Healey, Crosland, Castle, Benn and Foot – of great individual and collective political weight, experience and skill. Four of those eight became leader of their party and the other four could easily have done so. It is not clear to me that any subsequent cabinet of either party, so far, has contained at the same time eight members of such political, governmental and parliamentary status.

James Callaghan at the Foreign Office had been in Parliament since 1945 and was Chancellor of the Exchequer and Home Secretary in 1964–70, and Harold Wilson saw alliance with Callaghan as essential to the political stability of the 1974 administration. There had earlier been jealousies and competitive tensions between them, but Wilson was determined that this should not be repeated, and consulted Callaghan on all important issues. Callaghan, an older man, believed that his leadership chances had now passed and he proved very supportive of his Prime Minister. Together they formed a formidable partnership.

As Chancellor of the Exchequer, Denis Healey was a man of considerable intellect and incredible physical stamina, who would probably have made an even better Foreign Secretary than Chancellor. He was not blessed with great subtlety or the deft touch, but the burden of permanent economic crisis which he carried on his broad shoulders was immense.

Roy Jenkins had in 1974 greater national political influence than Healey, being the leader of the party's right wing and appealing to England's middle ground, and was still seen by many, including briefly by Wilson himself, as the heir-apparent to Downing Street. Roy was a senior baron at Harold Wilson's court – though increasingly semi-detached from his party.

There were three other ministers of major governmental stature. Debonair Anthony Crosland, at Environment, was the most celebrated intellectual in the post-war Labour Party, able to put discussion of policy issues within the philosophical structure of a democratic socialist movement, though his political judgement – as with his opposition to our proposed sale of council houses – could be questioned. Barbara Castle, at Health and Social Security, was a leading party and ministerial figure, aggressive, politically shrewd, skilled in self-publicity, and a long-standing associate of the Prime Minister – though by 1974 Wilson seemed bored by her increasing shrillness and almost frightened of her. Last of these three major players was Tony Benn at the Department of Industry, a skilful political operator and brilliant speaker who presented his sometimes dubious arguments with great clarity. Most impressive was the way Benn was never distracted by hostility from cabinet colleagues, parliamentary opponents or ill-mannered media interviewers. At all times he remained polite and almost clinically cool, simply restating his own case over and over again. He appeared to me much more interested in leading the far left to power than in contributing to that Labour government's success in Whitehall and Westminster. Indeed, he cleverly managed to give the impression of being a member but not a supporter of the Labour government. Together with his left-wing allies, he was able to push the Labour Party virtually into electoral annihilation in the early 1980s. I was not surprised when recently he became a 'pop' celebrity performer, nor when he arranged to visit Iraq, giving comfort to the murderous Saddam Hussein. He has always been an impressive self-publicist – and has also been wrong on every major policy issue in our lifetime.

Standing in a different political dimension from the other seven colleagues was Michael Foot, of whom I grew increasingly fond with every contact. He then had no governmental experience, was not a successful operator in the jungle of power – and certainly should never have been elected as leader of the Labour Party. But Michael was a man of great integrity, warmth, humour and culture, as well as being a feted parliamentarian and probably (with Enoch Powell) the best rhetorician of his generation. He also served as a beacon to the non-Stalinist left and could carry their support on difficult issues. He gave unwavering loyalty to Harold Wilson and especially to James Callaghan throughout their administrations in 1974–9.

Wilson seemed less interested in his junior ministers. Some he left to departmental ministers, such as Jenkins, to choose for themselves. Others were decided over tea in Marcia's room on the second day of the Government. There I pressed hard for the inclusion of my friends Gerry Fowler, Bill Rodgers and David Owen. He was sympathetic to David, but at first resisted Gerry and Bill, especially wishing to punish the latter for his 1972 rebellion over the Common Market, but he finally conceded.

Such a great collective ability in cabinet should in theory have produced a successful government for Harold Wilson. But it did not succeed. The reasons for its failure lay beyond the collective ability of any cabinet – in the overwhelming external factors outside its control: the intractability of the economic problems facing ministers, the chronic weaknesses in British industry, and the divisions in British society as reflected in its industrial relations. Above all, ministers were inhibited by Labour's antique ideological commitments and the resulting divisions within the Labour Party and movement. These factors, rather than any deficiencies of talent in the cabinet, prevented the Government from functioning with the necessary decisiveness. They were to restrain Harold Wilson in the final two years of government which faced him in March 1974.

While Prime Minister Wilson launched his government into an optimistic 'return to normalcy', I was personally totally absorbed in creating my new job in Number 10. First of all, I had to get leave from my position as Reader in Politics at the LSE. Wilson told me specifically to 'get two years till Easter 1976, because I will retire then.' So I arranged it. When Wilson did indeed retire in the spring of 1976, the Tories and most of the media snidely insinuated that it was a sudden decision precipitated by impending scandal – but I had the evidence that it was a long pre-meditated decision (described in more detail below). When I told this to journalists they simply refused to believe it; presumably the facts spoiled a good story.

I had a particularly delicate task for a new boy in Whitehall. I was urgently required to create and run a new institution in central government, the Number 10 Policy Unit, against the scepticism and occasional hostility of some of the regular civil servants (though not those in Number 10). The Prime Minister simply left me to get on with it and assumed it would happen.

In fact it was a daunting task. First it involved defining the actual functions and recruiting the staff of the Unit. The functions were clear in my mind. Until Wilson created the Policy Unit there had been in Whitehall no systematic policy analysis separate from the Civil Service machine and working solely for the Prime Minister. That was the main function I now had to establish. The Prime Minister's chief role is to be head of the executive side of government, coordinating its policies through cabinet and the Whitehall administrative machine. The Policy Unit would be chiefly concerned with servicing that role. I set out those executive policy functions formally in a memo, approved by the Prime Minister, stating that the Unit 'must ensure that the Prime Minister is aware of what is coming from departments to cabinet' – what Wilson described to me as being his 'eyes and ears'. It must 'scrutinise papers, contact departments, know the background to policy decisions, disputes and compromises, and act as an early warning system.' It should 'feed in new policy ideas', including minority reforms which departments may overlook.' The Unit was also to service the Prime Minister's key political roles, deriving from his leadership of the dominant party in Parliament and in the country. We had to be aware of 'the political dimension' in policies and to support the Prime Minister's 'responsibility as custodian of the Labour manifesto'. The press release which I drafted for issue by Number 10 stated in more general terms that the Unit would 'assist in the development of the whole range of policies contained in the Government's programme.'

With our functions defined, it was now time to recruit staff and establish our credibility in the Whitehall jungle. Recruiting staff at such short notice proved a very stressful experience. The success of the new Unit would ultimately depend wholly on the quality of its members. If I failed in recruitment, the whole enterprise would fail. I needed advisers in the main policy fields who would carry weight as experts and at the same time would both sympathise with the Labour Government's philosophical approach and be able to work with the Whitehall machine. Quite a tall order – especially as I wanted them in place within weeks or we would miss the chance of shaping policies from the beginning. I spent hours telephoning my whole network of university, city and media friends to get recommendations. What I had to offer was the unique opportunity to work at the centre of government directly advising the Prime Minister. Most would be excited by that prospect, as I was. But the downside was that I could offer no job security. A special adviser's appointment terminates with the government which appoints it – and our government lacked a stable majority and faced an early election (my own appointment was terminated twice in the coming two years).

The pay was poor. My salary in 1974 was around £9,000 a year – today my current equivalent successor gets around ten times that. Prospective candidates were also aware how badly previous generations of special advisers had been treated by the Whitehall machine. But fortunately people of the highest quality and sense of public service are rarely deterred by insecurity and low pay. I was lucky to find a team of gifted advisers who were prepared to take the plunge.

The bedrock of the Unit from the beginning was Andrew Graham, Fellow in Economics and later Master of Balliol College, Oxford. He had advised the previous Labour government, had Wilson's confidence, knew the tricky ways of Whitehall, and was a totally supportive colleague. He was the source of many of our best economic policy papers to Wilson until 1976, when he returned to Balliol, though remaining with us as a consultant. He also brought in as his brilliant assistant Gavyn Davies, then a young graduate, who succeeded Andrew as my chief economic adviser after 1976 and was later to enjoy a phenomenally successful City career and become Chairman of the BBC. Richard Smethurst, later Provost of Worcester College, Oxford, and David Gowland, future professor at York University, in time reinforced the strong economics team.

Social policy was of prime importance to the Labour movement. Here I was fortunate to attract David Piachaud, a future professor from the LSE, who had previously worked with Richard Crossman when minister and the guru Richard Titmuss. Short, balding, gentle and entirely lovable, David had detailed knowledge of the whole range of social policies, where I was often weak. He had a strong sense of what Labour party activists (with whom at that time I often had little sympathy) would and would not accept. He was 'soft' on welfare, where I was instinctively 'tough'. I believed that people should 'carry their own luggage' and not always look to the state to bail them out. Between us we usually reached a happy compromise with which the Prime Minister was content. When he returned to LSE in 1976, remaining only part-time with us, I supplemented him with Liz Arnott, a clever young lady from party headquarters who grew in stature later when Jim Callaghan took up the banner of better standards in education, with which I was deeply in sympathy. To monitor Tony Benn's alarming industrial policies, I wooed Richard Graham from British Airways, and later Jim Corr from the World Bank to track Benn's energy policies. After Tony Crosland died in early 1977, his special adviser David Lipsey (later a fellow Labour peer) joined us and brought a sharp mind, a facile pen and a sweeping knowledge. Kay Carmichael came from Glasgow University with a strong Labour pedigree to act as adviser in the tricky area of Scottish devolution, where local expectations were higher than our capacity or will to deliver. Finally the whole team was whipped into line by our stern administrative secretary, Brenda Phipps, who a decade later moved to work with my close friend Harry Evans at *The Times* and then in New York. Without that distinguished team I would have achieved little.

While waiting for them to arrive, I had to deal with the final issue which would determine the success or failure of the Unit – ensuring that it functioned as part of, and was accepted by, the whole Whitehall machine. It must have continuing access to and cooperation with all branches of the central administration (and especially with the Cabinet Office as the engine room of government). Under the previous Wilson government Whitehall had viewed special advisers with suspicion and had used a battery of petty bureaucratic tactics to render them impotent. Some advisers, such as Thomas Balogh, had tried fighting the machine on every front and were inevitably defeated. Unless I overcame the innate hostility of the bureaucracy to outsiders, then I would suffer the same fate and the Unit would fail. My greatest challenge so far was to set up this new institution in government and to make sure it succeeded under me – and hopefully would survive after me. I persuaded the machine to accept the Unit, to service it and integrate it into its own policy processes; yet without allowing the bureaucracy to smother and blunt it. I particularly had to negotiate guaranteed access to confidential papers and to ministerial and official committees, since in Whitehall access and information are the sinews of power. Without them we would be neutered from the outset. It was overall a complex and difficult balance which I sought – and I knew that I had to achieve it speedily at the very beginning or I would not achieve it at all. The only way was to go directly to the top of the Civil Service machine, the personification of the machine, to the Cabinet Secretary, Sir John Hunt.

In the later television series *Yes Minister* and *Yes Prime Minister* (on which I acted as a regular chief adviser to the authors Jonathan Lynn and Anthony Jay, and where the Prime Minister's personal adviser is named Bernard), the classic Cabinet Secretary is believed to have been portrayed in the historic figure of Sir Humphrey Appleby. Some of Sir Humphrey's silky and Jesuitical skills were indeed present in Sir John. But he was in no sense a comic figure. He was impressively efficient and tough – 'the iron fist in the iron glove', as one of his deputy secretaries commented to me in 1976. He managed and manipulated the machine with ability and inexhaustible energy. He had the essential talent of making the Whitehall machine deliver. If a Prime Minister knew what he wanted, then Sir John knew how to deliver it. At times I was personally unsure whether the smile which occasionally flickered at the corner of his lips was entirely friendly, and I was always conscious of his sensitivity and insecurities over what he rightly saw as his own territory. But, his cooperation was a most important factor in the success of the Policy Unit. As his deputy secretary told me, 'At first John wanted to control you, but you handled that cleverly.'

Under the written 'Concordat' which we agreed, I received copies of all the confidential letters which went to the Prime Minister, except those concerning secret defence and intelligence matters. I could attend all the cabinet committees chaired by the Prime Minister (which were the most important ones) and could attend others on request. I did not normally attend cabinet in Downing Street, but did not mind since the deepest discussion of policy options, and the real opportunity to influence them, occurred earlier in committee where I attended. In practice, the Prime Minister sometimes did ask me to attend cabinet, and I went to all special cabinets at Chequers. I or my staff attended many mixed or official committees when it was felt by us that the Prime Minister and the Unit had an interest. I also attended the weekly Cabinet Office meetings of deputy secretaries to determine the Government's future policy programme and the Friday morning 'prayers' meeting with the Prime Minister, the Chief Whip and senior ministers to discuss the following week's parliamentary business. In fact the main constraint on my participation in government became not the right of access, which I had won, but simply not having enough time to attend everything.

In return for granting his blessing, Sir John wanted assurances that advisers in the Unit would not attempt to replace the normal channels of communication between Number 10 and ministers and their departments – and especially that we would not attempt to replace the normal channels between the Cabinet Office and the Prime Minister.

I was particularly required to promise formally 'not to show papers of official committees to the Prime Minister or report the views of individual officials to him.' I agreed all this at long sessions sitting in Sir John's stately panelled room in the Cabinet Office, with cases of fine china and porcelain around the walls. It was drafted into a formal list of 'General Rules' which met the concerns of both sides. These were circulated to senior Whitehall officials in late April 1974, together with a request that they assist the Policy Unit 'with advice and information to the maximum extent possible.' If I or my staff wished to attend official committees or receive papers, 'there should be a disposition to say yes' (wonderful 'Whitehallese'!). In terms of access these were a great advance on anything achieved by special advisers before. They basically gave the Policy Unit everything it needed in order to function at the centre of government. I had established where Unit members could go and what they could see, on a basis generous enough to ensure that the Unit could succeed if it were good enough. Most important was the blessing from the top indicating that the Unit was legitimate and now had its Whitehall passport. Subsequently there were occasional tensions between my Unit and the Cabinet Office, but our concordat had launched us on a sound and potentially lasting basis.

Having secured the Papal blessing of the Cabinet Secretary, my next most urgent task was to get the active daily support of the Prime Minister's private secretaries (now called 'advisers'). The Private Office (merged with the Policy Unit in 2001) is the communications centre of Downing Street and is in contact with all ministerial private offices. Virtually all official communications to or from the Prime Minister are channelled through Private Office. The half a dozen or so high-fliers working there sift all messages and papers and decide what to put to the Prime Minister for decision and what to deal with themselves. They fill his 'red boxes' for nightly or weekend reading. Usually a close bond of trust builds up between a Prime Minister and his Private Office. There is always a danger that this may become a dependence on the Prime Minister's side and that officials gain an unhealthy control. Marcia believed that had happened with Wilson in 1964–70 and she appeared to mistrust most private secretaries in principle. I quickly decided to avoid any such sterile trench warfare. The Policy Unit could succeed only if it received the cooperation of all the key players inside Number 10, so I decided to be completely open with Private Office and share with them our policy ideas and intentions. Such a collegiate approach is anyway closer to my personal instincts and preference, and I believe that it worked.

The Principal Private Secretary, Robert Armstrong, gave me crucial support in some testing crises. Robert's wonderful successor Kenneth Stowe treated us completely as equal parts of the Number 10 family. Robin Butler (later to succeed Robert Armstrong as Cabinet Secretary), on the economic desk, was immediately warm to me. Straight, wickedly humorous, and a real team man, he became one of my most valued personal friends. His successor, Nigel Wicks, was more of a Treasury man, but was equally cooperative and helpful. On the foreign desk, Patrick Wright, later Head of the Foreign Office, tolerated my occasional intrusions into his affairs with a patient smile and was immense fun to work with.

For me, working with the Number 10 Private Office was an education and a pleasure. Once I had their trust, backed by Sir John's blessing, and supported by Joe Haines' total loyalty, I felt that I and the Unit had a fair chance of survival, and even possibly of success in the Whitehall jungle. My friendships with the private secretaries were summed up in a warm letter written to me by Robert Armstrong when he moved away shortly to become Permanent Secretary at the Home Office in April 1975: 'One of the happinesses of this last year for me has been how you and I have been able to build on the mutual respect with which we started, not just an ability to work together, but much more a personal friendship of great warmth and understanding.' That made life in the steamy Whitehall jungle worth while.

We had created a Policy Unit which, against all the odds, and under five successive Prime Ministers from both main parties and a medley of directors, has survived to this day. By late April 1974, most of the Unit's team were in place, the concordat was agreed with the Cabinet Secretary, and good relations had been established with Private Office in Number 10. I was personally into my regular work routine, processing the relentless flood of paper flowing onto my desk, which I calculated was equivalent to reading a 250-page book every day. I distributed papers to the individual staff specialising in the relevant policy areas and they in turn returned them to me with accompanying comments. I then decided on which ones to write a brief to the Prime Minister on our distinctive green paper (which he had suggested to me so that he could find them quickly among the mass of documents in his box).

I in fact had three distinct jobs, each of which was virtually full time. First was running the Unit, reading and writing briefs. Second was attending the endless treadmill of committees covering a whole range of government policies. Third, and most fascinating if most stressful, was being one of the Prime Minister's 'kitchen cabinet'. This involved helping to write some of Wilson's speeches (mainly done by Joe) and attending all briefing sessions before his Commons Questions, then on Tuesday and Thursday afternoons. There we tried to spot possible trick questions from the Tories and suggested ripostes. I also sat in his box for all his Commons performances.

But the most time-consuming, though least easily definable task, was that of simply being available to him in his study at all times of day and night. The moment an interview or committee was over, Wilson would send for Joe Haines, Albert Murray and me to come up to the study, pour us a drink and banter cheerfully about politics, football, gossip or whatever interested him that day, however trivial. This was fun and gave us useful insights into the character of this very complex man. It also helpfully gave me constant access to the Prime Minister to raise serious policy issues.

Less fun, and a more exhausting and depressing side of membership of the kitchen cabinet, was having to fend off the competition from Marcia, which threatened to impede my capacity to do the tasks outlined above. Altogether this personal role consumed many valuable hours a day and kept me in Number 10 until late in the evening, leaving little time to see my family in Brookfield Park.

Harold Wilson's top priority after taking office in March 1974 – and therefore the Policy Unit's top priority – was to prepare to win the inevitable early general election. He approached all issues at this time with that perspective in mind. But we were also drawn into a range of problems which had to be treated on their merits.

During the six months before the dissolution of Parliament in September, I sent fifty memos to the Prime Minister. Over a third related to the looming economic crisis. Industry, energy and social policies covered another dozen briefs. There were a smattering on transport, land, housing and local government, Ireland, and just one on education (which rarely troubled Wilson's cabinet). The Prime Minister was particularly taken by a Unit paper I wrote with Joe Haines entitled 'Little Things Mean a Lot'. This suggested sixteen minor policy reforms which would give disproportionate pleasure to a significant number of people. Wilson scribbled enthusiastic comments next to most of them.

Those most popular with him were:

- preserving the pint beer measure from Brussels ambitions to convert to litres;
- protecting local breweries from takeover by the giants;
- concessionary fares and free television licences to all old-age pensioners;
- protecting the rights of caravan dwellers;
- giving vehicles to the disabled;
- controlling juggernaut lorries;
- better funeral grants;
- extending the scope of the Open University;
- expanding local Gaelic radio in Scotland;
- better access to waterways;
- having May Day as a public holiday.

It is satisfying to note that most of these were enacted by Labour or successor governments in future years.

Apart from frolicking among these minor matters, I personally was particularly involved in three major policy areas over the summer of 1974: Ireland, economic strategy and industrial development. I had long been interested in the whole complex Irish question, having often visited the Republic and enjoying lasting friendships there. By 1974 I was convinced that the sullen constitutional settlement hurriedly established under pressure of civil war half a century earlier could not survive peacefully much longer.

The civil rights riots of the late 1960s and recently revived IRA terrorism underlined the instability on the Catholic nationalist side. The loyalist hostility to Heath's honourable Sunningdale power-sharing agreement, and the massive swing to the hardline Ulster Unionists in the February election showed that the Protestant majority was becoming militant in defence of its historic political dominance in the province. My personal position was then emotionally on the 'green' and Catholic side. I felt too little empathy towards the dour Orangemen, and this led me to miscalculate the realities of political power in Ulster.

Harold Wilson was particularly interested in the Irish question, and in March 1974 he summoned Joe and me for private discussions on a new initiative for Northern Ireland. He asked me to put up my ideas to him and I drafted a paper, marked 'Top Secret', in which I set out proposals for granting Northern Ireland 'Dominion Status', similar to the earlier constitutional position of Canada. Final sovereignty, together with certain key aspects of government, such as defence and foreign affairs, would remain with Britain, and Ulster citizens would remain subjects of the Crown. But much of the government of the North would be effectively independent. I suggested a Bill of Rights and elections by proportional representation to protect minority Catholic rights. I believed strongly that it was crucial to widen the context within which the Northern Ireland problem was considered, and so proposed that the USA, the EEC and especially the Republic of Ireland, be jointly involved to form a tripartite agreement guaranteeing the new constitution, as well as to join with Britain to provide huge financial assistance to help end the mass unemployment in which sectarian violence thrived.

It seemed to me that the Northern Ireland question could never be resolved when confined within the historic and parochial context of the United Kingdom, since its ancient sectarian instincts and tribal divides would there prove intractable. I was particularly concerned to involve the Republic of Ireland, having quickly observed that the British government then rarely worked with it, and yet I could not see how any solution could ever emerge without the direct cooperation of the country to the south, to which a large minority in the north looked as their national, spiritual and cultural home. Much troubled water has flowed under the bridges of Ireland since I wrote that memorandum and some of my ideas now look archaic after the progress recently made under John Major and Tony Blair. But several of its approaches have featured in these future and more successful moves towards a Northern Ireland settlement.

Wilson was both excited by my 'Dominion' scheme and frightened by its implications. He established a secret committee in the Cabinet Office, with myself on it as his personal representative. But before we could make serious progress, the Protestant Workers' Strike exploded in Ulster on 15 May, bringing the whole province to a standstill for two weeks. Concurrently, loyalist terrorists launched a bombing campaign in Dublin and elsewhere, killing and injuring 130 civilians. At first Wilson decided to stand firm against Protestant terrorism, as we had against that from the nationalist side. But when the military top brass came into Number 10 on 23 May, the discussion was pessimistic, questioning if we could in fact restore order and authority in Ulster by force. The military claimed that they could not run the key electricity generating plant. I was shocked by the sudden defeatism in Whitehall, led by the Northern Ireland Office, which then had not a single Catholic on its staff.

Prospects were clearly bleak. The following weekend was the Whit bank holiday. Wilson suddenly flew back from the Scillies to make his notorious broadcast attacking the 'scroungers' in Ulster. It was the only public speech of his in which Joe and I played no part. It was drafted in the Northern Ireland Office, with Wilson himself adding the sentence on 'scroungers'. Joe and I would have opposed the use of that language since it was bound to backfire, as it did. Three days later, on 28 May, the Northern Ireland premier Brian Faulkner and his fellow ministers resigned, followed by the announcement of the resumption of direct rule by the British Government. The Protestant strike had achieved its object in destroying the first brave attempt at a power-sharing executive in Ulster.

I was dragged from my lovely thatched cottage in the Suffolk sunshine back to a very gloomy Number 10. The Prime Minister was deeply depressed and angry at the clear demonstration that the British Government lacked the authority and the will to enforce its sovereign rights in Northern Ireland. On 30 May, he wrote a secret 'Prime Minister's Memorandum', copied only to the Cabinet Secretary, to Robert Armstrong and to myself. He stated that 'power-sharing' was now ruled out after the strike and that 'we are in the position of "responsibility without power"', with the army 'virtually powerless to maintain services.' He asked for his 'Doomsday Scenario' of 'withdrawal' to be considered, including a 'possible timetable'. He then proposed our 'Dominion status' option, which he had thought through in greater detail since we earlier discussed it. He said that financial support to the province should 'taper off' and be terminated within five years – by which time the military presence should be reduced to nothing. This demonstrated how our radical long-term thinking had been brought forward in the Prime Minister's mind to a short-term emergency exit.

But the immediate reality – reinforced by IRA bombs in Westminster Hall in June 1974 and at the Tower of London in July – was to return to sterile direct rule from London, backed by greater military force in Ulster. Our bitter experience taught me the lesson that Ulster was not then ready for quick constitutional 'fixes', and that when the time came for constitutional change there, it was essential to carry the Protestant majority (which might require radical reform of the Ulster Unionist party structure). This was a message I took forward when I was again to become marginally involved in the Ulster morass over twenty years later, as described below. By then, although much more actively Catholic, and still a lover of Ireland, I had also become more understanding of the root Protestant concerns. They have rights, too.

The success or failure of their economic policies have determined the fate of most modern British governments, though sometimes economic events are beyond the capacity of any ministers to control. I had, and still have, a deep interest in economics, though the more remote mathematical boundaries of modern theory have always been beyond me. To prepare for the economic storm which I was convinced lay ahead in 1974, I had recruited for the Unit some of the outstanding young economists in British academe. But for most of the time before the October general election we enjoyed little active engagement in that area. I was astonished that there was no serious Cabinet discussion of economic management and strategy until December 1974.

Yet horrors lurked and bubbled beneath the surface of our economic landscape. A perceptive paper prepared by Andrew Graham in mid May demonstrated that Britain was on course for hyper-inflation, reinforced by the fatal early decision to continue stage three of Heath's incomes policy, with its automatic triggers to enable wage increases to match price rises. Andrew's analysis pointed to a devaluation of sterling and the inevitable Treasury response demanding massive public expenditure cuts and statutory wage controls. I briefed Wilson verbally that we were heading in that direction, though the Treasury would not put forward any significant economic proposals until after the impending election and until the looming economic crisis had fully manifested itself. Then the Chancellor would introduce a major crisis package with statutory wage controls and a price freeze. Stunned ministers would unquestioningly accept whatever was proposed.

I suggested that the Prime Minister should immediately confront Denis Healey with these issues before they ran out of control and determine how best they might be handled while there was still time. However, the run-up to an election is not a time for grasping nettles. When Chancellor Healey came to Number 10 in late May to make a report to the Prime Minister on economic strategy, he did not stress any of his Treasury's real long-term concerns. He was characteristically buoyant, boasting that the Treasury was (incredibly, in my view) forecasting growth in GDP of 4 per cent per annum until 1979. (It barely surpassed 1 per cent per annum.) He also mentioned that they would like to see sterling depreciation of 3 per cent per annum to maintain Britain's competitiveness. (My observation was that currencies did not usually oblige by conveniently steady adjustments but in wide fluctuations.) This discussion between the two top men in the government was totally removed from the reality of the true medium-term prospects as so accurately forecast by Andrew Graham. This deliberate blindness to economic reality was understandable only in the context that both politicians knew they would face an election within two months.

I tried again before the August holiday to focus the Prime Minister on the economic storm ahead, sending a long brief, written with Andrew, arguing that he should begin to prepare ministerial and public opinion for the expenditure squeeze and switch to an incomes policy which lay inescapably ahead. He did not react. His mind was fully on the general election, now privately fixed for 10 October. Political prudence dictated to him that he should at least get the next election out of the way before proposing some version of the controls on pay which he himself had so recently opposed.

Not only did the government not grasp any economic nettles. Healey in his July budget actually manipulated the economy to produce a favourable climate for the October election with price controls, rising real incomes and increased pensions and subsidies. In September price rises were only 0.1 per cent and unemployment actually fell. Keynesian economic management made it possible to adjust the economy temporarily to suit election timing, as the Tories had done before in 1955 and 1959. But it did delay confronting the economic storm ahead and probably meant that the ultimate remedies would have to be even more severe.

In the absence of an explicit economic or counter-inflation strategy during the summer of 1974, Labour's proposals to reform British industry in the radical ministerial hands of Tony Benn constituted the new Government's most visible policies intended to improve the performance of the nation's ailing economy. The emphasis, which now seems to be from a remotely distant political world, was on greater planning and central direction. We had proposals to increase industrial investment through the new National Enterprise Board, for more central planning through Benn's planning agreements with individual firms, for greater direct public financial aid to industry (which in practice normally meant to bail out failing industry), and for establishing industrial cooperatives. Looking back, it is striking how most of us in that Labour Government, whether on the right following the French *dirigiste* model, or on Labour's left aping Stalinist centralism, still then believed that state intervention in the markets and the direction of capital would actually improve the performance of the economy over the longer term. Our subsequent experience in government provided a rude awakening and education.

My personal view was that, regardless of whether the industrial policy was sound – which I came to doubt – it was wrong for a minority government to try to impose a policy by statutory powers against the united opposition of Britain's industrial management. This view was not shared by Benn's left-wing supporters in the Labour Party, whose adherence to the principles and conventions of parliamentary democracy were often at best tenuous.

From this point in mid 1974, I made efforts to meet industrial managers and to visit my old friends at Grieveson Grant in the City to stay in touch with the financial markets which can break a government. I also began to follow the writings of free market economists, occasionally visiting Ralph Harris's Institute of Economic Affairs, where engagingly radical views were aired. I certainly did not share all their free market beliefs, but I did grow aware that Labour's statist, interventionist and nationalising approach to economic problems could make the problems worse rather than better.

So in the Unit our industrial approach was to support practicality and moderation, and to oppose the extremism of Benn. The latter seemed completely in orbit, quoting the views of his Bristol shop stewards as justification for all kinds of extreme industrial policies. Wilson was a ready listener on this topic and in June he told me that Benn was 'completely mad' and he would have to take control of industrial policy in his own hands. The result of the Prime Minister's intervention was a major crisis in Whitehall as Number 10 confronted the resourceful Secretary of State for Industry – with some of Benn's own civil servants supporting us against their own minister – and Benn effectively declaring independence from his regular officials and operating with his political advisers quite independently of his department.

The problem of 'Bennery' was discussed by Wilson, Callaghan and Healey at a 'prayers' meeting on 28 June. They decided that Benn had to be 'constrained' and the White Paper on industrial policy taken out of his hands. Callaghan said to me then that it would be politically risky to sack Benn outright, and more prudent take the policies out of his hands and hope he would feel humiliated and resign. That day Wilson abolished the existing cabinet committee handling the White Paper and established a new one, the Public Enterprise Committee, under his own chairmanship. At its first meeting to discuss the draft White Paper, which I attended, all the senior ministers tore into Benn's draft. Healey said it was 'irresponsible'. Shirley Williams asserted it 'would push Britain into a fatal economic crisis'. Crosland and Lever supported this view. Jim Callaghan was particularly savage and baldly stated that he would resign if the committee accepted Benn's draft. Wilson summed up, saying that the draft was rejected and another would have to be produced from elsewhere than Benn.

Afterwards Robert Armstrong told me that he had never seen a minister 'so mauled' in a cabinet committee. Yet Benn himself, with characteristic resilience, seemed quite unabashed by this mauling. I went into the lavatory for a chat with Healey afterwards and he perceptively commented that attacking Benn never had any effect – 'like cutting moonbeams', he said as he peed.

The Cabinet Office revised the White Paper, but while successfully removing the Benn rhetoric, they replaced it with vapid prose; just Whitehall guff. So the Prime Minister threw that draft out as well – and asked my Policy Unit to rewrite the White Paper. Andrew, Gavyn Davies, Richard Graham and I worked night and day on the redrafting to make it acceptable industrially and politically. I rewrote the whole Introduction, which set the tone in reassuring British industry of the Government's intentions. Planning agreements were made voluntary not compulsory; there was no more mention of nationalising the pharmaceutical and machine tool industries; and a firm commitment was made not to introduce any more nationalisation in the next Parliament. It was the Unit's most important contribution so far and the Prime Minister expressed to me several times his great satisfaction with our work. At a three-hour cabinet on Friday 2 August, our redraft was accepted by ministers with acclaim.

This tension over the industrial policy White Paper precipitated a long period of hostility and manoeuvring between Harold Wilson and Tony Benn. Convinced that his young minister was now a serious danger to political navigation, Wilson decided in the summer of 1974 to try to provoke Benn to resign, by demoting him from his beloved post at Industry to the lowly Department of Energy, thinking this humiliation would surely lead to his indignant departure. I never shared the Prime Minister's optimism on this point. Like most politicians, Benn enjoyed power and it seemed to me that there was no humiliation which he would not swallow in order to stay in the cabinet.

Having the Policy Unit rewrite his White Paper was one of the many affronts from the Prime Minister to which Tony Benn bravely turned the other cheek over the next five years. Wilson did indeed finally demote Benn to the Department of Energy a year later, but he swallowed that as well, and neither Wilson nor Callaghan ever carried out their occasionally mentioned threats to grasp the nettle and sack him. I assumed that, in the immortal words of President Lyndon Johnson, each Prime Minister on reflection preferred to have Tony Benn inside the tent urinating out, than outside urinating in.

It was a great relief for me to escape occasionally from the nightmare world of stopping 'Bennery' to areas of the social services where we were able positively to help underprivileged people. I gave maximum support to Maurice Finer's magnificent report on One Parent Families, having some personal experience myself of that subject. Surprisingly, Barbara Castle, the childless minister responsible for that area, seemed to show little interest in it. I also became very attached to her two junior ministers, Jack Ashley and Alf Morris, both totally dedicated to helping the disabled. I persuaded Harold Wilson to support Jack's plans to create a research Institute for the Deaf, and particularly to override mean opposition from our Chief Whip Bob Mellish to providing Jack, who was then stone deaf, with his own palantype machine, so that he could follow the proceedings in the Commons. I felt great admiration for Jack, as an old friend who overcame his terrible disability with skill and courage. I also felt a personal understanding, since my brother Clem was at that time descending into deafness. With Alf Morris, I persuaded the Prime Minister to support his successful campaign to provide motor vehicles for the disabled, which transformed their lives. All these good causes cost money, and the personal support of the Prime Minister is often decisive in obtaining the necessary financial allocation. It showed a human side of Harold Wilson that he was happy to give time and attention to such issues, which were politically small but very important to those living difficult lives who benefited.

At the beginning of August 1974 I was able to go away for a wonderful four weeks to my new house near Perpignan in France. It was an old Catalan farmhouse a thousand feet up above the pretty artistic town of Ceret, where Picasso lived before the First World War. It had no bathroom or lavatory and only one water tap – the outgoing farmer told me that he and his wife (the local pig-slaughterer) went out onto the five acres of vineyard for their bowel needs. The house and its six acres of vineyards cost very little but was beautifully positioned. From the terrace, we could see the glistening Mediterranean to the east above Collioure, and the Pyrenees ranging to the west, with Mount Canigou towering nearly 10,000 feet above us. The children adored it and I went there every summer, and at other seasons, for thirty years until sadly selling it in 2002 (finding the local habit of treating the truth as just one tactical option increasingly unacceptable). I often see the stunning view when I close my eyes to sleep on a cold English January night.

When I returned from France in early September, the Prime Minister and Number 10 were already gearing up for the general election decided for 10 October. A stream of White and Green papers poured out of Whitehall, giving an impression of Government achievement and promising more reforms once Wilson had the necessary majority. As it was, even without a majority and in the shortest Parliament since 1681, the Labour government had implemented most of Wilson's short-term promises from the February campaign – he kept a list of them on a crumpled piece of paper in his pocket and ticked them off as they were achieved. Some of our 'Little Things Mean a Lot' had already been enacted, including concessionary rail fares and my two personal contributions – protecting small breweries like my favourite Greene King from takeover (Wilson announced that such bids would not be approved), and preserving the pint measure for beer from Brussels 'litre-isation'.

The election campaign was fought against a background of looming economic crisis, and Joe and I wrote that phrase into many of Wilson's speeches. Heath was serious in his analysis, but since the three-day week few trusted his solutions. Wilson cleverly managed to suggest that with himself there was somehow an easy way out of the crisis. As he said in his Bolton speech eleven days before the poll, 'What the people want, what every family needs, is a bit of peace and quiet.' But it was not to be what they were to get over the coming years.

Parliament was finally dissolved on 20 September 1974 and our election machine swung into action. For Joe and myself in Wilson's team the situation was different from in February. We were now civil servants and had to remain mainly based in Number 10. Wilson, Marcia and Albert moved into Transport House. But in practice, much of the routine remained as previously, with morning meetings in Lord North Street where we decided the real tactics of the campaign, and gatherings at night to review the day's events over drinks, either in Lord North Street or Number 10.

However, this was only established after a pre-emptive strike by Marcia to eject Joe from the pole position as Wilson's speech writer. Without our knowledge she established her own team of Peter Davies and Denis Lyons, Wilson's long-standing public relations advisers, and temporarily persuaded Wilson to appoint them as his speech writers. Their opening contribution was to do the first draft of the Prime Minister's important speech to the TUC on 5 September which included a cliché reminder to the audience that 'no man is an island' and that 'the bell tolls for us all'. Most of it did not survive into the final speech.

Battle continued once the election was announced. A meeting of the campaign team was called that first evening in the Prime Minister's study. Joe, Albert and I sat around waiting for over an hour, but Wilson did not turn up. We then discovered that he was actually holding a separate meeting on the same agenda with Marcia, Peter Davies and Denis Lyons upstairs in the Prime Minister's flat. Marcia, who controlled the election expenses purse, also announced she would not authorise payment of Joe's London hotel expenses. Since he had to be present late at night, lived in Kent and did not drive, this put his participation in doubt. It was quite a pantomime and I soon got fed up, walked out and went to the cinema to enjoy watching *The Sting*, which was much closer to real life than the fantasy world of Number 10 that evening.

On the first Monday of the campaign Peter Davies and Denis Lyons arrived at Number 10 to replace Joe and sat upstairs in the cook's room trying to write the Prime Minister's key speech on the 'social contract' for the following evening. But by mid-afternoon they had completed only three of the necessary thirty or forty pages and they gave up. They sheepishly asked Joe to complete the speech and resume the speech treadmill, which with a wintry smile he rapidly did – that and every other day. From that time onward we at least did meet as a single team in the same place – though Wilson still conceded to Marcia's insistence that he did not have lunch with us.

Wilson himself sporadically intervened to dictate a few pages of his own rambling prose, frequently devoted to pointless attacks on our mean and biased press. Joe and I said nothing and waited. Later Wilson would silently read his typed text and simply throw it away and accept our version. Just before polling day, he touchingly said to me: 'You know, Bernard, I just have to get these things off my chest, then we can forget about them.' Basically, Wilson offered a quieter life than Heath, with fewer strikes and less confrontation. His speeches always referred back to the 'darkened streets' of Heath's three-day week, and forward to Labour's 'social contract', our cure-all for problems on the economic, industrial and social fronts. This social contract, which was to be so important in the next four years, had been endorsed by the TUC on 4 September and became an all-purpose political phrase, effectively conveying an image of social harmony and justice, and conciliation and cooperation in society at large. We also hoped that it would prove to be a specific anti-inflationary policy in which the unions would agree to postpone wage rises in return for favourable social legislation. It was a worthy aspiration and it worked for a while, helping to bring inflation down into single figures by 1978. But it contained no mechanism to enforce the limitation on wage rises, and it finally burst apart in 1978–9 when the unions showed that in fact they greedily wanted both the social benefits and the inflationary wage rises. Instead, as they deserved, they got Mrs Thatcher.

The actual campaign was dull and the electorate was clearly bored by a repeat show of the same songs and lead singers as eight months earlier.

In the opinion polls we were in the lead on every poll, usually by 5 to 10 per cent, but this shrank towards the end of the campaign. Wilson's personal lead over Heath was always around fifteen points – which shows how good was his reputation even a decade after he first entered Number 10. Bob Worcester's final poll correctly showed a general swing of 2½ per cent towards Labour, pointing to a small overall victory of under ten seats.

Election day offered the only cheerful weather of the campaign as we visited Wilson's Huyton constituency. From the moment the plane took off I sensed the increased tension in the atmosphere. Marcia was taking tablets and drinking brandy, and soon began to attack Joe and me. When we reached the Adelphi suite, she loudly accused me of 'leaking to the press as usual'. Just before we all set off to the count in Huyton, she summoned Harold into the bedroom and I heard her demanding that Albert – who most of all wanted to witness Wilson's final victory – should not be allowed into the count. She also insisted that Joe, Albert and I be excluded from the Huyton victory celebrations. Emerging from the bedroom with Wilson, she instructed Albert that he must give his ticket to Terry Boston, the team's bag-carrier. Wilson walked over to Albert looking rightly ashamed at what he had agreed, and gave Albert a large cigar as consolation. So we three loyal aides sat outside the count watching on television as the results evolved towards a Labour victory. After the count, Wilson came out and sheepishly told us that we were not allowed to go to the Huyton celebration party. Instead he took the likeable Terry Boston and scruffy Alf Richman, whose contribution I had never identified. I did not particularly care either way, preferring to watch the television coverage of the results. But Joe, who had written thirty-three speeches and two television scripts in nineteen days, was incandescent. Albert was deeply hurt and nearly in tears. We went together back to the hotel and watched television until the early hours, but the emerging narrow victory had by then turned a little sour.

The first results had in fact indicated a comfortable Labour victory, but then they slipped. The 145 seats declared on the Friday did not produce a single Labour gain. In the end we had a lead over the Tories of 3.3 per cent in votes, with a share of 39.2 per cent on a turnout down 7 per cent. We won 319 seats, giving a disappointing overall majority of three. But we had forty-three more seats than the Tories, whose vote of 35.8 per cent was their lowest in the modern electoral system (until their greater disasters in 1997 and 2001). This at least ensured us a longish term of office, since the fringe parties, with thirty-nine seats, were unlikely all to combine with the Tories against us.

Marcia renewed her attacks next morning when she tried to persuade Wilson to exclude Joe and me from the flight back to London. As we stood waiting to board the plane, Wilson asked for the list of passengers. He stared at it, blinking. He looked sheepishly at Joe and at me and we stared firmly back at him. He turned to look helplessly at Marcia – and then handed the list back to her without a word and we all silently boarded. On the plane, she bared her impressive teeth at me and returned to the attack. 'It is disgraceful,' she said loudly in front of the others. 'You are eating with these civil servants, joining with them instead of getting them sacked. And you appointed that cook to feed them. It has got to stop.' I said nothing and wondered what storms lay ahead in the new government.

Back in Number 10, Marcia turned on Harold and shouted at him: 'Now you are back ... you won't need me any more!' Wilson took the message and that evening told his Principal Private Secretary, Robert Armstrong, to sack the cook and to terminate the Number 10 team lunches henceforth. At least Joe had survived the most sustained attempt yet to squeeze him out. But he was to be punished further. In 1975, when Marcia produced the paperback of her book *Inside Number 10*, she eliminated the previous references to Joe in the hardback edition which had generously thanked him as a 'constant guide and friend to Harold Wilson'.

Wilson was naturally pleased with his victory. It meant he had won four out of his five general elections as leader. Since 1900, as he several times pointed out to me, only Baldwin and Attlee had fought so many elections, and neither had won nearly so many. He liked such statistics and surely had the right to his irritating habit of boasting about them. Certainly we were safely back in Number 10. But I quickly began to feel uncomfortable about our future there. The economic nemesis could not be delayed much longer. I also sensed signs of personal storms much closer to home. Marcia may have failed in her manoeuvre to oust Joe Haines. But she was a persistent lady. My shoulder blades felt vulnerable.

Ten

WILSON'S LAST GOVERNMENT

B ack from his fourth election victory, giving him a working if not a comfortable Commons majority, Harold Wilson acknowledged that he could not put off facing Britain's bleak economic realities for much longer. Five days after the election, he called in the TUC and CBI for talks about the situation. He then made a sombre broadcast in which he deliberately borrowed some of Heath's campaign lines in appealing for national unity to face the coming crisis, speaking to ' the whole of the national family' in which 'all of us should be partners'.

But inside Number 10 our political family was definitely not operating as partners. Having failed in her attempt to have Joe replaced during the election campaign, Marcia now turned her fire fully on me. She tried to get me and the Policy Unit evicted from Number 10 and banished to the remoter fastnesses of the Cabinet Office. My first detailed alert was on Tuesday 15 October 1974, when Bill Housden told both Joe and me that there had been terrible rows between Marcia and Harold at Chequers over the previous weekend. Marcia was demanding above all that I be sacked and that the Policy Unit be disbanded.

From then the atmosphere in Number 10 grew more tense as rumours flew. On the Wednesday Robert Armstrong told me that officials knew she was moving to expel me. Robert was supportive, frankly admitting that 'while you take the flak, the pressure on the rest of us is less.' He added worriedly that 'the appetite of this particular tiger will grow with feeding.' That evening Wilson hosted a victory celebration for his election team in the Number 10 drawing rooms. He profusely thanked 'my team', mentioning Marcia, Terry Boston and Alf Richman 'for their great contributions' but with no mention of Joe and me (not daring to with Marcia present). Next day, Bill reported to us that Wilson, after many rows in which he resisted the move, had finally capitulated to Marcia's demands and agreed to banish the Policy Unit to a remote part of the Cabinet Office. There I would be cut off from direct access to and influence over the Prime Minister. I would also lack access to the crucial information which flows through Number 10 relevant to all the policy issues concerning him. As such, I and the Unit would be effectively neutered and would be unable to do our job. We might as well go home. Bill reported that Marcia was jubilant at her triumph.

I discussed the problem with Joe and Robert. Joe agreed that it was a battle we had to fight together and win – because if I was 'shafted' by Marcia, his turn would follow. He said to me: 'This will test your steel.' I did not doubt his. Robert described Wilson's behaviour as 'utterly contemptible', strong words for a cautious mandarin in defence of an irregular civil servant. By now others knew. John Hunt, the Cabinet Secretary, told me that he was 'aware of Marcia's manoeuvres'.

The Foreign Secretary was also aware. Jim Callaghan approached me after a committee that day and said, 'Bernard, I hear things are bad again in Number 10 ... Harold seems haunted. But you know he will never get rid of her.' Harold Lever, to whom I spoke almost daily, reported that Wilson had told him that he was going to move me to the Cabinet Office. Joe saw little of the Prime Minister during this time. On a rare visit to the study, he found him drinking brandy and already the worse for drink. I saw him only once, at the Friday morning 'Prayers' meeting, when he did not speak to me, but launched off into an unprovoked and unrelated tirade against 'right-wing plots' (often a code for the 'Jenkinsites', including me). Callaghan and Healey looked puzzled and Jim told him it was all 'nonsense'.

The following week of 21–5 October, the crisis over the future of myself and the Policy Unit bubbled in Number 10 like in a cauldron and finally came to the boil.

Curiously, still nothing was ever actually said to me by the Prime Minister. Each day I sat in my office quietly working on papers, revealing nothing to my staff of the crisis. Wilson was in his study except when in committee or at the Commons. Marcia – almost for the first time since March – came to Number 10 every day and sat in her office. This symbolized her victory. There was no communication between them and me, though Joe, Albert and Bill shuttled regularly to my room with the latest news.

On Tuesday afternoon, the Prime Minister sent for the Cabinet Secretary to make the logistical arrangements for me to move to the Cabinet Office. John Hunt played it skilfully as always, having met Robert Armstrong beforehand to agree their united line. John loyally explained to the Prime Minister that unfortunately he did not at that time have room in the Cabinet Office for me and the Unit. That blocked the first line of attack. Robert then went to see Wilson and warned him, as I had told him, that I would resign rather than move and I would publicly expose all this nonsense if I were forced out.

Faced by those two big Whitehall guns – to whom I owe a great deal – and the possibility that Joe would walk out with me, Wilson began to back off.

On the Wednesday he finally spoke to Joe and revealed a change of direction and tactic. He told Joe that he was very pleased with my work and said that Marcia was going to withdraw from Number 10. He wanted me to have control of her Political Office and be in charge of virtually everything, including Albert. Joe and I immediately saw the trap: if I took the offer, that would prove my intention to oust and replace Marcia. I made it clear through intermediaries that I was not interested in Marcia's job and that I just wanted to continue my present job running the Policy Unit in Number 10 – and nor would I go to the Siberian wastelands of the Cabinet Office. I felt very cool about it and clear what the choices had to be. Having Joe and Robert standing with me made it much easier.

Throughout Thursday I sat in my office waiting for the summons to discuss all this with the Prime Minister. It did not come. But Wilson sent various messages through Albert, Bill and Joe to reassure me that Marcia had indeed capitulated and that when he and I did finally meet it would be, as Bill quoted him to me, a 'time for olive branches'. The Prime Minister told Robert to tell me that I was to have 'a peace lunch' with him and Marcia the following day, Friday, at his club, the Athenaeum. On the Friday morning, Robert confirmed to me that the club lunch had been booked. Bill Housden came to brief me, saying that the Prime Minister's intention was that 'everybody should be happy afterwards'. Bill again confirmed that a putsch had indeed been intended, but 'since you stood your ground, Marcia has been forced to retreat.' Bill had heard all the discussions and plans for my execution at Chequers and in the car.

On the Friday I went into Number 10 wearing my best suit, ready for my first lunch at the Athenaeum, and clearly likely to be one to remember. I went, as suggested by Bill and Albert, into Marcia's room, where she was drinking champagne with Albert. I greeted her politely. She was clearly tense and brittle. She explained that the Athenaeum lunch could not now take place – 'because I have come in the wrong clothes'. Then Wilson sent down a message summoning me up to the study. He ordered a bottle of champagne, already cool, and we drank it quite fast. He said that he wanted to assure me that there was no truth whatsoever in these curious and quite unfounded rumours which he gathered I had heard about my banishment from Number 10. However, he did want to suggest to me that I should 'replace Marcia as the Head of the Kitchen Cabinet' (he used those precise words). I quietly but firmly declined and without comment he moved us off into the small dining room with Marcia for an uncomfortable lunch.

There were long silences during which I could hear the seemingly loud scraping of our knives and forks on the plates. Wilson ate rapidly and left the room as quickly as possible. Then Marcia became irritable and again asserted – though for the first time to me – that I and the Policy Unit should be removed from Number 10. I quietly and politely resisted the Policy Unit move and she began to shout at me. As we left the dining room, she was still shouting abusively at me all the way down the stairs and along the corridor to the front door.

That was the end of the October diversions to banish – and effectively kill – the Number 10 Policy Unit. Before leaving for Chequers that Friday afternoon, the Prime Minister walked around the house and talked with me. He went out of his way to praise the Unit and me personally in front of the officials and staff. The following week he saw me often and was especially warm and friendly. Normal business had resumed. Over the next eighteen months until his resignation, I submitted to him 174 Unit papers on a wide range of policy areas.

The first government thistle which we had to grasp after this minor diversion was the renegotiation of the terms of Britain's membership of the European Economic Community. This was to dominate the Prime Minister's and our time over the next nine months, concluding with the referendum which had been promised in both recent election campaigns, and I and the Policy Unit were heavily involved throughout in detailed briefing to the Prime Minister. It proved to be a very delicate political operation in which Harold Wilson showed all his old skills in handling a totally divided Cabinet.

The political background was that in 1972 the Labour Party had been seriously split, with Roy Jenkins resigning the deputy leadership, over Edward Heath's successful application to join the EEC. A majority of the Labour Party in Parliament and in the country, and of the Prime Minister's senior colleagues, were against membership.

So in 1974 Wilson saw the issue not – as did Jenkins for the 'pros' and Benn for the 'antis' – as one of principle, but as a question of political party management. His twin objectives were to prevent Labour from inescapably committing itself to withdrawal from the EEC, and from breaking up the party over the issue. He successfully achieved these by offering at the two recent elections the immediate prospects of renegotiating better terms for Britain's membership, followed by a referendum of the whole British people.

Fulfilling this promise was not to prove easy, since Jenkins and many on the right were uncompromisingly committed to EEC membership while Benn, Shore, Foot and the left were opposed with equal dogmatism (or 'theology', as Harold described it). It was a pleasure for me to observe Wilson's skilful political management and timing in handling this delicate party situation.

He was also assisted by the use of two rare political devices. First he suspended normal collective responsibility and in the referendum campaign allowed dissenting colleagues to oppose whatever was to be the Government's formal decision on Europe without resigning. This so-called 'Agreement to Differ' gave Wilson useful political elastic to avoid splitting the Cabinet asunder. The referendum mechanism itself was also novel and convenient to Wilson. It was originally advocated by Tory and then by Labour anti-Common Marketeers seeking a way to block entry to the EEC – and was opposed by Jenkins because of that extremist support. In the event it sank Benn, who proposed it to Wilson, and confirmed the victory of Jenkins, who had passionately opposed it. Wilson at first rejected the whole concept of a referendum; but then on second thoughts he shrewdly saw its utility to him. He realised that a vote of the whole British people would dilute and swamp the opposition from Labour activists, who were strong in the party but small in the country as a whole.

Wilson typically approached the EEC renegotiations with the recent election manifesto permanently in his pocket to serve as his guideline. He often took out the crumpled document to show me the commitments which he had already ticked off as achieved. He knew that, providing he stuck to the manifesto and then secured a majority in Cabinet, he could not be attacked in the party.

The manifesto itself set out a shopping list of renegotiation objectives, some major, some minor. The first big issue was that the EEC Budget should be reformed so that it was less onerous on Britain. Next was amendment to the Common Agricultural Policy. The Prime Minister wanted radical changes to that burgeoning Alice-in-Wonderland lunacy, but knew that realistically he could only achieve minor amendments. So he concentrated on securing continued British access to cheap Commonwealth food, such as New Zealand butter and lamb and Caribbean sugar and bananas.

On the economic side, we opposed economic and monetary union, which Wilson saw would be dominated by the Germans, while our economy, linked to wider global trading, might never converge suitably with those on the Continent. His overall political strategy was to secure enough concessions to be able to claim at the end of the renegotiations that he had met his manifesto pledges (thus soothing his moderate left), while not causing a break-up with Europe (thus pleasing the Jenkins right). He was scorned in the press for these 'unprincipled' political priorities, but they were not dishonourable objectives and motives for a party leader – and they worked.

He showed impressive political skills which were often an education to me personally. On one occasion in the middle of intense negotiations to resolve the differences between us and the French over access to cheap Commonwealth food, my Unit came up with a very clever formula solution. I delightedly ran up to the Prime Minister's study and produced for him the answer. He looked at me with sad resignation and said, 'No, Bernard, no. Don't you understand? I don't want the solution, I want the grievance.' I then knew I was dealing with a professional in a different political league.

The renegotiations were thrashed out in broad principles at a succession of summit meetings of Heads of Government, while the critical details were settled at lower diplomatic levels under the shrewd leadership of Jim Callaghan, and these two experienced politicians worked together in close tandem. My Policy Unit was busy throughout drafting briefings for the Prime Minister. I attended all the Summits as his Senior Policy Adviser and also had regular discussions with Foreign Office and Trade officials to advance the Number 10 view.

Just before the Paris Summit in December 1974, Wilson held a critical private meeting with Germany's Chancellor Helmut Schmidt at Chequers. Schmidt promised to secure the necessary Budget reforms, providing Wilson agreed that he would then come out clearly in public in favour of Britain staying in the EEC. Wilson agreed the deal and decided to announce it in his next public speech, which was drafted mainly by Joe Haines, Robert Armstrong and myself, and we felt that we had expressed the Prime Minister's clear commitment. But when Marcia, passionately anti-EEC, saw the draft, she passionately denounced it. As so often, Wilson retreated under that particular barrage and told us that he now wished to drop the key sentences which committed him to personal support for our continuing membership of the EEC if the renegotiated terms proved reasonable. After heated arguments we finally persuaded him to restore the key sentences and not break his pledge to Schmidt. Once the speech had been made to the audience of unsuspecting mayors of London boroughs, the path was prepared for a successful summit conference in Paris.

There we made considerable progress, particularly on the Budget and the Regional Fund. Wilson was buoyant and in his bedroom in the early hours of the second day he sat in his voluminous underpants and listed to me the manifesto achievements already achieved. He also confidently described how he would complete the negotiations by March 1975 and hold the referendum by June. He told me that Roy Jenkins had agreed this timetable and so for the first time had implicitly accepted the referendum device. But Wilson still felt under pressure, especially from Marcia (who had telephoned him repeatedly during the session) to demonstrate back home that he was not, as he put it, 'in the pockets of the Euro-bureaucrats'. He summoned his team of Paris civil servants late that night and denounced them – unfairly in some cases. Afterwards he was clearly very pleased with himself and told me that he could now reassure Marcia that he was taking a firm line with officials.

My father and mother in the 1930s.

Aged four.

Brother Clem (left) and sisters Molly and Sheila.

Captain of the rugby XV at Northampton Grammar School, 1949.

Cricket First XI at Northampton Grammar School, 1952, with myself top left.

Harold Wilson's team of officials at 10 Downing Street, 1974-6, a photograph signed by the Prime Minister. Back row from left: Philip Wood, Nick Stuart, Tom Bridges, Nigel Wicks, myself; front row from left: Robin Butler, the Prime Minister, Mrs Wilson, Patrick Wright, Mick Forrester.

With Marcia Williams, 1974.

With Harold Wilson, tired on arrival on an overseas visit.

Wilson launching his incomes policy in 1975, with Joe Haines on his left and myself and
Albert Murray looking on from the back.

Passing inside information to Foreign Secretary David Owen at the 1977 Labour Party Conference.

On Prime Minister James Callaghan's visit to India, 1978,
with Roger Stott MP (left) and Tom McCaffrey.

James Callaghan's election campaign team in 1979.

Charity football at Stalybridge in 1979. Football luminaries included Dave Mackay (back row, third from left), Mike Summerbee (back row, second from right), Stuart Webb (front row, far left), and Nobby Stiles (front row, second from right), while the political players included MPs Roger Stott (back row, far left), John Prescott (front row, second from left) and Tom Pendry (front row, far right).

In New York at the eightieth birthday party of Aaron Copland (holding microphone), with Isaac Stern and Leonard Bernstein (right).

The second day in Paris we faced typical French hostility, but Schmidt privately reassured us that this was only a rhetorical gesture to President Giscard's nationalist constituency and that the Germans would settle the Budget problem through a 'correcting mechanism' (for which they would themselves of course pay, leaving the French as usual a net beneficiary).

The next summit was due in Dublin on 10–11 March 1975. Before then I accompanied the Prime Minister on a wonderful trip to snowy Ottawa and then on to Washington. The latter visit opened badly as our VC10 was wrongly brought into Andrews Airbase downwind and nearly stalled. But for our brilliant RAF pilot we would probably have crashed and lost the Prime Minister and Foreign Secretary, as well as many marginalia such as myself. As we landed I saw my shirt cuff covered in blood – the FCO secretary sitting next to me had in terror gripped my hand and dug her long finger nails into my palm. But all went splendidly after that, with a glamorous reception at the White House glittering with film stars. I walked around Washington in the sultry sunshine, enjoyed the great monuments and museums, and sauntered across pretty Georgetown. I went to a grand party and dance at Averell Harriman's stately house with all the political and media stars from Washington past and present. I also visited Congress with my old Oxford friend Paul Sarbanes, soon to be the impressive Senator for Maryland.

The final summit in wet and windy Dublin proved not too difficult, though it had its odd tricky moments. We met there in the small and elegant Patrick's Chamber within Dublin Castle – Harold Wilson (on his fifty-ninth birthday) was the first British Prime Minister to enter the Castle since 1914. Joe and I decided to walk to the Castle in the morning by way of the old junk shops on the Liffey quays. We were invited into the back of one by an eccentric owner who offered us morning whiskey by a blazing fire, gave us coffee, and told us mighty tales of desperate men he had known. He frequently began with the statement, 'I am a peaceable man ...' and then continued with some heroic description of how he had knocked some villain clean out of Murphy's Bar or the Hibernian Hotel.

But my happiest memory is of our Prime Minister holding a crucial briefing session with us officials in the large lavatory in Iveagh House, the Irish Prime Minister's residence where we had enjoyed a fine dinner. The lavatory was the only private location then available – and hopefully not bugged. When we all agreed to reject that latest version of the German budget reform formula, I ceremonially pulled the chain to flush it down the loo.

These summits were curious occasions, like oriental markets, with a buzz of different languages as premiers and foreign secretaries would come wandering out of the chamber to discuss briefs with their waiting groups of advisers. We had long slack periods which would be followed by a sudden rush of excitement as people emerged dashing out with news of some new development, progress or setback. On the final afternoon, all was deadlocked until Wilson came out smiling to tell us that the Germans had produced their helpful Budget mechanism and suddenly the tension lifted. Everyone was laughing and chatting – except Germany's Chancellor Schmidt, who would have to pay for our Budget achievements. I watched him drive away morosely in his Hamburg fisherman's cap. At the end, Joe and I sat on St Patrick's famous throne, last used officially by George V, happily drinking champagne, and then toured Dublin's bars until the early hours. Our EEC partners had delivered what the British wanted. Wilson and Callaghan now made it clear in private, though not yet in public, that they would recommend staying in the Community.

Wilson took his EEC package for approval or rejection to a tense two-day Cabinet on 17–18 March 1975. Roy Jenkins and Shirley Williams had made it clear in advance that they would resign if Cabinet decided not to approve staying in the EEC. Others in more junior ministerial office would certainly follow them. On the other side were Benn, Shore, Foot and Castle, weighty politicians who were equally passionately opposed to continuing our membership of the EEC. The atmosphere inside Number 10 was electric and unforgettable. The Cabinet seemed in danger of being torn apart. If that happened, the Government, with such a weak parliamentary position, would surely fall.

Wilson prepared for and handled his Cabinet with consummate skill. He chaired the proceedings with the express object of preventing any open confrontation and allowed everyone the chance to speak. He also provided – rare for a cabinet – a break for coffee. At the start of the concluding votes around the table, he and Callaghan gave a lead by announcing that they accepted the terms and would recommend Britain staying in the EEC. They personally swung several doubters, and the 'Yes' vote won by sixteen to seven – an encouragingly large margin, given that only a year earlier five of those 'Yes' votes – Rees, Peart, Morris, Prentice and Shepherd – had been opposed to our continuing membership. Jim Callaghan's personal influence almost certainly swung the first three. Without these five switches, the vote would have been lost 11–12.

Wilson's style of consensual agnosticism, legitimized by an election mandate, made it easier for him to hold the cabinet together – though a majority of Labour MPs, of the National Executive Committee and of party conference voted against the EEC.

In the study soon after that cabinet finished, Wilson told me that he was very angry with several of the 'Nos', whose political careers he had personally advanced – 'one or two possibly beyond their ability' – and who had now 'abandoned me'. These included three of his former PPSs – Barbara Castle, Peter Shore and Eric Varley. He said that Marcia had summoned Eric out of the cabinet during the coffee break to instruct him to vote 'No'. Wilson wrote off Castle's and Shore's opposition as 'theology', always incomprehensible to him.

The long referendum campaign was masterminded by a specially established Referendum Unit which met each day in the Foreign Office. Jim Callaghan, or, more often, his junior minister Roy Hattersley, took the chair, with other relevant ministers and FCO officials present, and the Prime Minister asked me to attend as his personal representative. Throughout the campaign our polls showed roughly two thirds of the electorate in favour of staying in the EEC, so we did not feel under great pressure.

Wilson himself showed little enthusiasm for the campaign, and for much of it made no speeches. Joe and I had initially set up a programme of speaking engagements for him, but Marcia intervened angrily to say that Wilson's diary was her job and she cancelled them all. So by mid May, Wilson had not made a single speech and still had nothing at all in his diary for the rest of the campaign. When this was queried by Jim Callaghan at the morning strategy meeting on 15 May 1975, I raised it with Wilson, who immediately blamed poor Albert. But he then at least arranged some engagements and spoke on each of the final days of the campaign, dictating his long and rambling speeches himself to demonstrate that he was not in the hands of the so-called 'Euro-fanatics' surrounding him.

In the referendum poll on 6 June 1975, 67.2 per cent voted 'Yes', and 32.8 per cent voted 'No', closely in line with our MORI findings. It was an overwhelming victory. Our 'Yes' majority was greater than the entire 'No' vote.

But Harold Wilson did not seem to enjoy the victory which he had secured. He spent the day of the result with Marcia at Chequers, from where he wired to us in Number 10 a flat and impersonal draft of his proposed victory statement, with no welcome for the result, as if he had never been involved. I telegraphed back to him some amendments, including suggesting that as the Prime Minister who recommended a 'Yes' vote, he should personally welcome the result. He accepted some amendments but still omitted any personal welcome for Britain taking a more positive position in the future of Europe.

He came up from Chequers in the evening and read out his little statement on the steps of Number 10. The Private Office arranged a celebration party in his study, but the Prime Minister did not turn up for it. He went instead to drink champagne with Marcia in her room – though it can hardly have been to celebrate a victory which she had throughout opposed. Wilson's own personal position was agnostic, mentally, but only at the cerebral level, accepting the arguments that it was on balance better to stay in. Over the past decade he had coolly taken many positions on the EEC. In 1967 he had first proposed Britain's entry to a sceptical De Gaulle, then had opposed the terms of Heath's entry in 1972, and at one time opposed a referendum while later supporting it. He never displayed strong feelings either way on the EEC itself. He supported the concept of a Community of Europe, never wishing again to see it wracked by nationalist conflicts. But he did not have a broad vision of the political future for the EEC, seeing it as just a trading organization, and was deeply sceptical that Britain would derive much net economic benefit from a more integrated Europe.

Wilson's main concern in my time with him on this issue was political: to trim, and to manage, the Labour Party mood so that he could hold the party together. During the negotiations he did his homework, constantly asking me for more Policy Unit briefings because he said that he did not trust the official advice – especially from the Foreign Office – which he saw as too 'Euro-bureaucratic'. But I felt that had we been arguing against these particular points and for the opposite, he could have accepted it and done it just as well, professionally and pragmatically, like the good civil servant he once was. Only on the issues of New Zealand food and the protection of poor Third World countries did he show any personal commitment.

He was never warm to things European – nor indeed to anywhere abroad other than through his sentimental attachment to the old Commonwealth, especially Australia and New Zealand. For holidays, the furthest he could usually be tempted was to the Isles of Scilly, which enabled him to go overseas yet remain in the United Kingdom. Indeed, he was probably mildly anti-European in the sense that he did not to like the continental style of life or their politics. The French and southern Europeans appeared particularly alien to him. He disliked their rich food, generally preferring meat and two veg with HP sauce. When he returned from a Paris dinner with the French President in September 1974 suffering from an upset stomach, he readily accepted Marcia's admonition that it was a proper punishment for going abroad. Politically, he believed that British democracy and the British Parliament were the most wonderful political systems and institutions ever invented. His observation of continental politics from the 1930s onwards did not convince him that very many Europeans were fundamentally democratic or had much to bring for Britain politically to learn.

Harold Wilson was, on my observation, basically a provincial, nonconformist puritan, with all the virtues, vices and inhibitions of that background, including touches of the 'little Englander' and a healthy suspicion of metropolitan glitz and cosmopolitan glamour. He would probably have preferred that the European Economic Community did not exist. Now that it did, he adjusted to that reality. He was also a sensible mainstream professional who was usually prepared to take the advice of Whitehall – and his official advice was to stay in the EEC. As a pragmatist, he knew that a 'Yes' vote was the most practical choice, because to stay in would be less disruptive – politically, economically, industrially – than to pull out.

As a national leader, he believed (as he often told me) that a victory for the 'Nos' would empower 'the wrong kind of people' in Britain: the Benn left and the Powell right, who were often extreme nationalists, protectionist, xenophobic and backward-looking. As a party leader, he saw the positive 'Yes' vote as the best way to hold Labour together – because Benn's antis would not finally leave the government over Europe, whereas the Jenkins Europhiles would and their resignation could effectively destroy it. Perhaps, as a statesman – which part, but only part, of his complex personality was – he sensed that Britain ought to be placed at the centre of Europe's future. Certainly, as a shrewd politician, he saw the 'Yes' position as the likely winner. So, for this mixed bag of reasons and motives rather than for any enthusiasm for the EEC, Wilson fought and won the battle to stay in. His whole conduct of the issue was, to me, deeply 'Wilsonian', consultative and consensus-seeking. His approach was flexible and not 'theological' (in Wilson's dictionary, always a bad word). Throughout, he fudged and ducked and weaved. But he succeeded. He kept Britain in the Community as he always wished; he achieved the terms which his manifesto demanded, and he held together by Wilsonian elastic bands his cabinet and party.

By his overwhelming victory in the referendum, he gave Britain's position in Europe a democratic mandate. Edward Heath had in 1972 taken the British political establishment into Europe. Harold Wilson and James Callaghan now brought in a majority of the British people. This positive outcome was a great relief to me personally. I had never been what Harold called a 'Euro-fanatic'. I opposed political union and was sceptical of monetary union. But I did believe Britain should be in the EEC, and when we came into government in March 1974 I was the only, very lonely, member of his personal team who was in favour of our membership of the EEC. Virtually all of the long list of his previous and present aides were against. Marcia constantly pressed Wilson to take a more negative position. She understood and tried to exploit his personal ambivalence, reflected in the flabbiness and lack of conviction in his few speeches when he did finally take an active part. But at least he remained – just – in what was, to me, the right position.

Harold Wilson often told me that in politics one should 'fight only one battle at a time', and with the referendum victory under his belt he was able to turn with visible delight to the long-festering problem of Tony Benn.

Wilson had decided to demote Benn during our clashes with him over the Industry White Paper in the summer of 1974, and had waited patiently for a suitable time. Now it arrived, with Benn severely wounded by his referendum defeat. Tony's stage army of the left had been blown out of the water by the democratic referendum of the British people (which Benn himself had suggested). The Prime Minister was now able to transfer Benn, who protested strongly but was impotent to resist and unwilling to resign, to the minor outpost of the Department of Energy. Wilson crowed to me in delight at his carefully executed victory over his colleague.

When I talked with Benn in November 1975 he was clearly still bruised and made a sharp verbal attack on the Policy Unit, accusing it and me of being 'unaccountable'. He complained that he frequently received 'unhelpful minutes from Harold, but I don't know how far you are behind them'. However, when I visited him in his office in early 1976 he seemed much recovered and back to his old lively self, and we had a good chat. I was always impressed by the range of his vision and by his sharp analysis of the problems facing this country. It was his solutions which to me seemed barmy. He was due soon to give a lecture on Herbert Morrison and wanted my help about points in my biography, especially about Herbert's approach to public ownership. He offered me tea in one of his famous tin mugs, but I declined. He seemed less tired and fanatical than in the hectic summer of 1974. I always admired his political resilience. He reminded me of a hard squash ball: you could stand a piano on him (which Harold Wilson had effectively done to his career), but when it was removed he soon bounced back into shape again, ready for the next game.

Often I observed and overheard on the telephone in the study him enduring verbal humiliation from two Labour Prime Ministers, and countless criticisms from his colleagues in Cabinet, but he always preserved his cool and courteous demeanour, indeed, an almost disturbing calm, with that peculiar and unwavering gleam in his eyes. He seemed not to mind the impending collapse of the Labour Government of which he was a member, perhaps operating under the bizarre assumption, propagated by the Trotskyite left then infiltrating the Labour Party, that he and his extreme left-wing friends, and not Mrs Thatcher and the right, would benefit from moderate Labour's demise.

Wilson had for the moment finally sidelined him and took pleasure from that. But Tony was biding his time and would give Callaghan much trouble in the years ahead.

Harold Wilson seriously mishandled the ministerial reshuffle centred on removing Benn. When he told Benn that he was to be demoted from Industry to Energy, the latter frostily said he must first discuss it with his wife. That evening the left-wing ministers gathered to lobby the Prime Minister, demanding that Benn be given twenty-four hours to think about it. That night Eric Varley wrote a curious letter to the Prime Minister saying that he would not take the job at Industry over Benn's dead body. At the same time there was trouble on the right wing, where Reg Prentice, supported by Jenkins, resisted being moved out of the Cabinet from Education to Overseas Aid (all part of Wilson's obsession with balancing pain and rewards on the two wings of his party). So the wheels were coming off the reshuffle, and late that evening Wilson began to mutter to us about his own resignation.

When Benn's twenty-four hours were up, he remained in hiding and sent Michael Foot fruitlessly to plead his case. Benn then arrived in person at 7 p.m. and launched an angry tirade at the Prime Minister, accusing him of damaging the Labour movement by demoting him – and then grumpily accepted his lowly new job at Energy.

But this did not solve Wilson's problems. Judith Hart then refused to accept Transport, feeling it was unworthy of her. In her place, Wilson offered Transport to his Chief Whip, Bob Mellish, who had let it be known that he wanted to have 'a proper ministerial job'. But he also turned down Transport, wanting to be Lord President, which was not on offer. Mellish, a vain man, also realised that he could not face the prospect of his wonderful deputy, Walter Harrison, finally getting his job as Chief Whip. So with tears in his rheumy eyes, Mellish decided to stay put. It was all becoming a shambles. Towards midnight on 10 June the cabal of left-wing ministers, led by Barbara Castle and Michael Foot, came like a deputation of shop stewards to the Prime Minister's room in the Commons to demand that Judith Hart should be restored to the cabinet now that Wilson had conceded to Jenkins's pressure and agreed to put Prentice in the cabinet at Overseas Aid. I sat outside the door with Joe and we could hear the shouting and ranting into the early hours, with a reference by Michael Foot to 'poor Judith's blood on the carpet.'

It was humiliating for the Prime Minister to allow himself to be treated in this way, and to me it illustrated the steady erosion of his authority and skills as leader. I felt that Wilson was like a fifteenth-century monarch being opposed by the feudal barons of the left and the right. Jenkins was like York and Castle like Lancaster. As Prime Minister, Wilson should not even have accepted such discussions with colleagues about the composition of his cabinet. But the shambles reflected how inadequately he had prepared for the reshuffle. The greatest British political manager of the twentieth century had initiated a small ministerial reshuffle, in his fourth administration, shortly after a smashing victory in the referendum, and he completely botched it.

Eventually the muddle was sorted out, and after the dust settled Wilson told me that he took some consolation from the fact that at least the press had not learned of the reshuffle in advance. Sadly, that was the kind of triumph which now seemed to matter most to him. I concluded that it was time for him to go – though that clearly could not happen immediately since he now faced the incomes policy crisis immediately ahead.

While the Prime Minister was absorbed with the Common Market and playing with Benn, the British economic situation continued to deteriorate. By January 1975, shop prices were rising at 25 per cent per annum and the latest Treasury forecast showed them soon to hit 30 per cent, with public borrowing rising possibly beyond the Government's capacity to finance it and the balance of payments heavily in deficit.

Robert Armstrong reported to me that the Governor of the Bank of England, Gordon Richardson, believed that the financial system was about to 'collapse' and that a wage freeze and massive cuts in public expenditure were unavoidable. In the Policy Unit, we shared that broad analysis without the Bank's underlying hysteria. We had already in November 1974 submitted to Wilson a powerful paper setting out the impending crisis and stating that the Chancellor and Treasury appeared to lack any coherent strategy for dealing with it. We concluded that the Prime Minister must himself now take a grip. He wrote back, 'Gloomy but difficult to fault.'

However, he did nothing. We returned to the charge in the New Year of 1975, when I submitted a paper by Andrew Graham and Gavyn Davies which again set out the harsh realities and choices facing the Government. We recommended a quick crisis package, with a mixture of expenditure cuts and wage controls. Again, no response.

The basic problem for Wilson was political. He knew that we had to curb wage inflation, but could not yet see a politically acceptable way of doing it. Neither of the two familiar mechanisms to curb wages seemed open to him. One was statutory wage controls of the kind introduced by Heath in 1973. Yet Wilson had vigorously denounced them in each election campaign. In the autumn he had returned one of our 'coming crisis' briefs by writing in longhand that 'I regard any attempts to regulate incomes by statutory means are out.' For Harold Wilson to revert to a statutory incomes policy would require quite a U-turn even by his own impressive and experienced standards in that activity. The second possible approach to cure inflation would be to impose a severe monetary squeeze. But when the Tory guru Sir Keith Joseph had floated this in September 1974, Wilson attacked him savagely because of the impact on unemployment. (He told me that he could not face in his final year the prospect of retiring and bequeathing record post-war unemployment.)

So the Prime Minister was in a tight corner. His political and electoral commitments ran directly counter to the tough measures against wage inflation which the deteriorating economic situation required. For a while his reaction was to turn his back on the problem and get wholly absorbed in Europe.

The Chancellor finally in March and May 1975 brought to cabinet his modest proposals for cuts in public expenditure. But they were resisted by ministers, Benn and Castle from the left opposing all cuts in public expenditure on principle, while some on the right accepted Healey's general argument for a cut in the deficit but rejected any particular proposals for cuts in their own departmental budgets. Tony Crosland, usually the best of them intellectually, appeared to view all public expenditure as good and all Treasury arguments as bad. Wilson sat on the fence and the Chancellor went away with no cuts and his tail between his legs.

But it could be only a matter of time to the inevitable day of reckoning. Especially as, simultaneously, ministers weakly approved a pay increase of 30 per cent for rail workers, justifying it fatuously by saying that 30 per cent was 'the going rate'. They did not seem to appreciate that each new and higher claim became 'the going rate' once they had conceded it. So the inflationary spiral rocketed onwards and upwards.

The day of reckoning came on 18 June 1975. With sterling under pressure, the Prime Minister summoned me to his study, said ominously that 'something must be done about wages', and asked me for my policy proposals. Next day I held in my room a brainstorming meeting of the whole Policy Unit, with Joe Haines attending to make sure that we did not lose sight of the political realities. Together we drew up and submitted to the Prime Minister the first of two substantial memoranda on the inescapable need for an incomes policy. We opened in a way which I knew would catch his attention – giving the stark warning that without a new economic policy initiative, sterling would fall from its present $2 to $1.65 over the coming year. Our suggested policy package to prevent this contained an incomes policy, but a voluntary one, not statutory, so as not to be in total conflict with Wilson's previous election pledges. We said the wage policy should be based on a simple 'norm' of a £5 or £6 increase for everybody.

Joe Haines proposed and David Piachaud strongly supported this on the basis that any incomes policy should be simple so that everybody could understand it for themselves. A flat rate increase also had the advantage for a Labour Government of being progressive, giving a bigger percentage increase to the lower than to the highly paid.

The Prime Minister responded quickly and positively to our paper. He told me that he was attracted to our proposals because the voluntary nature of the policy enabled him to promote an incomes policy without breaching all his past pledges not to have a statutory policy. We had therefore achieved our prime political objective in devising this crisis package.

The Treasury was informed of the Unit's initiative and immediately opposed it, officials there being hell bent on having a full statutory policy backed by the criminal law. So over the last two weeks of June there ensued a savage (though to me greatly enjoyable) Whitehall battle to capture the collective mind of the cabinet over whether the Government should take the statutory or the voluntary path.

The overall decision to have some kind of incomes policy was taken on 19 June at a cabinet held at Chequers to signify the importance of the issue. (This, incidentally, was the first full cabinet discussion of pay and inflation policy since Labour had taken office fifteen months earlier.) Healey opened by warning that Britain was 'heading for the precipice' and we had only a few weeks to get it right, or else there would quickly be two million unemployed. Ministers took the warning but also expressed a general reluctance to embrace a statutory policy, so the gate was at least open to our voluntary approach – though fighting off the Treasury would not be easy.

I sent Andrew Graham to this cabinet, though I often went myself and always enjoyed my visits to Chequers. Before meetings there, we usually gathered for coffee, served by WRENS, all of whom seemed to be stocky with very short hair. In winter there was always a blazing log fire in the main hall. Cabinet meetings took place upstairs in the long L-shaped room with dark wooden panels all round the walls and huge oriental carpets on the wooden floor. The oval table, longer even than that in the Downing Street cabinet room, could seat up to thirty. There were five large portraits in the main part of the room, including Walpole by Van Loo and two Van der Helsts, one of a lovely seventeenth-century lady and another of a courtier. I used to sit and gaze at them when the discussion grew intolerably boring.

The views from the four huge windows are over the rose gardens to the south and the parkland full of trees to the eastern horizon. Outside the brickwork is lovely, old, Elizabethan, and light, contrasting with the sombre and to me gloomy inside. I always found it slightly odd to meet in such beautiful circumstances and yet normally be discussing Britain's depressing problems. As the day wore on, the atmosphere grew heavy with cigar smoke. The sound of squeaking chairs as ministers shifted their stiff legs and cramped bottoms was like an accompaniment of modern tuneless chamber music.

Chequers looked particularly lovely on summer afternoons, with its old red bricks glowing. Then Wilson usually wore a light summer jacket and was often in sandals. But Chequers always seemed to me more an institution than a home.

Two committees, one ministerial, the other of officials, now embarked on exploring details of the possible forms of incomes policy. The Prime Minister also secretly set up a third ministerial Cabinet Committee (MISC 91) to discuss pay policy. On this he included some trusty senior ministers who were not members of the regular Economic Strategy Committee, and excluded from it some from the left who he did not trust. Thus pay policy came more directly under the control of the Prime Minister himself and his trusted inner cabinet.

Before the secret MISC 91 met on 26 June, I gave to Wilson a Policy Unit paper which set out in more details our proposals for a voluntary policy backed by sanctions. The Prime Minister told me on the 26th that he liked our paper very much and would take its line in the MISC committee – as did most ministers, broadly concluding that a credible voluntary policy was what the Government needed.

But the Treasury officials were absolutely committed to securing their full statutory policy and to making sure that our voluntary approach did not get a fair run with the Whitehall machine. I warned the Prime Minister of this. He grew angry and dispatched a 'Prime Minister's Minute' – the most commanding document in Whitehall's paper hierarchy. In it he formally instructed the Treasury not to proceed further with its statutory proposals and instead to cooperate in constructing a voluntary policy along the lines agreed by ministers in MISC 91. But the Treasury totally ignored the Prime Minister's instructions. Instead, at the end of June, the Chancellor submitted to cabinet a Treasury paper which dismissed out of hand the voluntary option and was wholly devoted to recommending only one approach – the full statutory policy backed by the criminal law to which the Prime Minister and his cabinet were formally opposed and which would certainly have split a cabinet whose bonds were already weakened by divisions in the recent referendum campaign.

The crisis, now both financial and political, finally erupted on Monday 30 June 1975. On that afternoon, MISC 91 was due to meet to discuss pay policy, with the above Treasury paper as its agenda. In the morning, the Prime Minister had gone to the Royal Agricultural Show at Stoneleigh, having beforehand warned me that in his experience it was 'at this point in the play when the Governor of the Bank of England enters from stage right.' Lo and behold, at 2.30 p.m., as Harold came back from the show through the front door of Number 10 to join the ministers gathering outside the cabinet room for the MISC 91 which he would chair, I saw the Governor and the Chancellor arrive together through the rear entrance from the Cabinet Office. The haughty and patrician Governor, Gordon Richardson, who had little understanding of the particular pressures under which a Labour Government then operated, came over to me looking tense. He said: 'This Government's whole credibility has gone ... We must end this nonsense of getting the cooperation and consent of others, the trade unions, the Labour Party. We must act now.' He then followed the Chancellor upstairs to see the Prime Minister in his study for a fifty-minute meeting, while the other ministers waited puzzled outside the cabinet room below.

There the Prime Minister was informed by his visitor that sterling was collapsing as they spoke. The Governor predictably concluded that only a statutory incomes policy could save sterling and the nation. The notorious 'Treasury bounce' which I had long expected had finally arrived – but bowled by the right-wing Governor. At the delayed meeting of MISC 91 Chancellor Healey said that sterling was 'crumbling', that we had lost most of our reserves, and 'we must halt the haemorrhage now.' His conclusion was clear – we must have a full statutory incomes policy immediately. He asked for approval for two White Papers: one to be published the very next day would propose a statutory policy with a 10 per cent norm; the second in the following week would set out massive cuts in public expenditure and rigid price controls. The committee of ministers listened in stunned silence. Only Jim Callaghan, still scarred and suspicious of the Treasury's conventional wisdom following his painful earlier experience there in 1964–7, offered any resistance. It was clear to me, sitting there watching the Prime Minister's face, that Wilson was in full retreat towards statutory compulsion. He had, as often before, been converted by the familiar mournful tolling of the sterling bell.

After attending MISC 91, Joe and I went up to the study and conducted a heated argument with the Prime Minister against allowing us to be bounced into a statutory policy. He admitted that that afternoon, coming back from Stoneleigh in the helicopter he had been determined to resist the expected 'bounce'; but he had now been completely convinced and converted by the Governor. We went together down to Private Office where the argument continued and Robin Butler – a Treasury man – bravely supported Joe and me against his own department.

The Prime Minister accused Joe and me of being 'too political' in pointing out the damage which a statutory policy would do in dividing the Labour Party – which I took as some tribute coming from someone who had never undervalued the political dimension. The argument continued that evening when the Prime Minister held a state dinner for Leo Tindemans, the Prime Minister of Belgium. Harold and Mary held a reception line for the guests, who included (at my suggestion) my friend David Sainsbury and the novelist John Fowles, whose books I was currently reading. Joe and I stood behind the Prime Minister and rudely interrupted his handshaking by arguing against the statutory policy which he was now defending. Understandably he grew irritable and between shakes he would turn round to snap a counter-argument and state that we were 'not being realistic'. At midnight, the next stage of the Treasury attack bounced into Number 10. It was a draft of the Chancellor's next day statement to Parliament, starkly setting out the statutory policy with its sanctions in the criminal law. Ken Stowe helpfully slipped us a copy and suggested that I might check it against the statement made on Heath's 1973 incomes policy, which Wilson in opposition had so roundly denounced. I went straight to my office and checked it and found it was almost word for word identical. Treasury officials had simply taken out of their pigeon-holes the earlier policy which had scuppered poor Ted Heath, dusted it down, and now placed it before Wilson for signed approval.

Wilson now seemed too far down the statutory path to recover. But I sat down with Joe Haines in his press office after midnight and we decided to make one last effort to convince the Prime Minister that a statutory policy would fail – because it would split his cabinet (Foot would certainly resign), divide his party, and by alienating the trade union movement would prove unenforceable on the mass scale necessary for success. As the last of the guests drifted noisily down the corridors and out into Downing Street, we drafted a joint memorandum to that effect and sent it upstairs to the Prime Minister. It read:

> We believe that the cabinet is being faced with an attempt by the Treasury to stampede it into a statutory pay policy, against every pledge which we have given …
> The proposed statement by the Chancellor is a straightforward announcement of such a policy. It has no reference whatsoever to acting against employers, it is solely concerned with legal constraints against pay. Paragraph 5, on dealing with prices, is so inadequate it will be laughed at in the House. Paragraph 4 sets the alternative to a statutory policy as the TUC policy. This is not the case. We have been formulating another alternative, part voluntary, part statutory, which stood a much better chance of success. The phrase 'using the law in the pay bargaining process' will lead to a split in the party. It is not, as we understand it, what the MISC decided today. It will lead to resignations from the Cabinet and the government. The commitment on public expenditure, which has serious implications, is being made in advance of any proper consultation or discussion with colleagues. We believe the Treasury are trying to bounce the Government along the same old path they have trodden before, with incalculable consequences for the Government and the party.
>
> [Signed J.H and B.D.]

Having read it, Wilson sent it back via a private secretary with his reply that we were 'wrong and becoming neurotic' in our opposition to a statutory policy; and that he had gone to bed in the flat. That seemed to be that. Joe and I were very depressed and we went our separate ways, he to Tonbridge, me to Kentish Town, to try to get a few hours' sleep.

However, all was not lost. My telephone rang in the middle of the night. Joe told me that the Prime Minister had just phoned him to say that he had reflected further and concluded. 'You are right and I now agree with every word of your brief.' He realised that he could not execute a statutory policy which he conceded would split his Government. So he said that he proposed to support the Policy Unit's approach to a voluntary policy backed by sanctions. He had already asked the Chancellor to come to see him early in the morning before the cabinet meeting which had been scheduled formally to approve Healey's White Paper and Statement to Parliament announcing the statutory incomes policy. I was delighted. After only four hours' broken sleep, I rose at seven and set off on my daily morning run around Hampstead Heath. It was particularly beautiful in the early sunshine that morning, rich with the smells of cut grass and shrubs. From the top of Parliament Hill, below stretched London waking in the haze. It had been quite a twenty-four hours.

Before the scheduled 9 a.m. crisis cabinet, Michael Foot went to see Wilson to inform him that he would immediately resign if Healey made his statement on the introduction of a statutory incomes policy. Wilson then saw what would have happened had he gone along with the Treasury bounce. Fortunately the Prime Minister was able to reassure Michael that there was now no such danger. After that Ken Stowe came up to me and said, 'You and Joe have earned your corn. There has been a monumental shift in the Prime Minister's attitude.' So Wilson held firm and told Healey he had changed his mind and was going for our voluntary approach. Healey was commendably accommodating, revealing a personal agnosticism about the policy choices, and readily abandoned his officials' proposals. Together the Prime Minister and his Chancellor went into cabinet to support the voluntary approach, even though the Treasury papers on the table before ministers were actually those announcing a statutory policy. After lunch Healey told MISC 91 of his plans to construct a voluntary policy. Sterling and the stock market rose.

The next critical stage was to get the trade unions on board, since without their support no voluntary policy could work. So Wilson summoned Jack Jones, boss of the then mighty Transport Workers' Union, to Number 10, where he suggested a £6 instead of a £5 norm as being more defensible to his members. Jones in turn converted Hugh Scanlon of the Engineers, and so the 'terrible twins' of the union left were on board. On 3 July the TUC formally approved the principle of a voluntary pay policy.

The only remaining problem was to convert the Treasury officials to the new policy which now the Prime Minister, the cabinet, the TUC and even their own Chancellor supported – and to identify £2 billion of accompanying expenditure cuts. For a time the Treasury arrogantly and stubbornly continued to pursue its own statutory policy, as if the will of the elected Government was of no relevance to it. On 2 July, I attended a meeting of the Official Committee on Prices and Incomes in the Great Conference Room of the Cabinet Office. It was chaired by Ken Couzens, a lively and bristly little man from the Treasury. He referred disparagingly to the MISC 91 meeting of ministers which had decided on a voluntary policy, and said that 'after that interruption, we can get back to serious business' – meaning back to a statutory policy. The other officials roared with laughter and showed an open contempt for the views and decisions of ministers and the Prime Minister. One Treasury paper before us opened with the statement that it was written 'on the assumption that a full statutory policy will be intro-duced.' Officials recognised that this was really a battle between the Treasury and Number 10. Afterwards I secured the support of Ken Stowe and of the Cabinet Secretary. Number 10 meant to win this battle. And we did.

On 4 July, we worked in the Unit for sixteen hours at a single stretch until midnight producing our own draft White Paper for a voluntary policy and as an alternative to the thin gruel coming from the Treasury. We sat in my huge room with the carpet covered in paper as we drafted, redrafted, and scissored pages, finally stapling dozens of sections together and feeding them for typing to my heroic secretary Brenda Phipps. Next morning, a hot and sunny Saturday, the Cabinet Secretary telephoned me at home to say that he would support our draft and then Joe rang to report that the Prime Minister had phoned him to say that he much preferred ours to the tame Treasury version and would instruct that it be used as a basis for the coming White Paper. I relaxed in my garden, facing over the Convent School towards the trees on the Heath, with Puccini flowing out through the door, the children playing on the grass, and the air rich with our honeysuckle and orange blossom. I was completely exhausted but felt satisfied and happy with life.

The following Monday morning I went with Robin Butler up that famous Treasury stone staircase and round those seemingly endless bleak corridors to join Ken Couzens, perky and baggy-trousered, with his then less fashionable estuary accent, and Andrew Graham and several bright young officials from departments across Whitehall, spending all that day drafting the basic new White Paper and the next three days hammering out the micro-details. I quickly came to like and respect Ken, forgetting our earlier clash. He was an indefatigable drafter and re-drafter and very funny when doing it. Once he had received the message that the Treasury statutory policy had been torpedoed, then like a true Whitehall professional he worked frantically to float the best possible version of our new policy.

The only remaining surprise for me was when I spotted a new footnote drafted by Treasury officials and Whitehall lawyers. It said that 'fees and increments' were to be exempted from the constraints of the new pay policy. I asked Robin Butler what this meant. He gave a typical Butler chuckle and said with a guilty grin: 'Well, fees are them [pointing to the lawyers], and increments are us [civil servants].' So those making and drafting the tough new policy were in principle excluding themselves from its rigours, though nobody in the media or Parliament noticed. In practice, of course, there was no prospect that civil servants would get an increase breaching the norm, while lawyers are always above the law.

On 11 July, the Prime Minister launched his new White Paper at a great conference in the Ministry of Defence. Because the policy was finally voluntary, he was able to announce that the trade unions fully supported the £6 norm increase – and that it was not a U-turn from his previous pledges. I went home that Friday to sleep through the weekend and restore my physical and mental batteries. It had been one of the most incredible fortnights of my working life: exhausting, at times frustrating, even infuriating, but in the end deeply satisfying to have been so centrally involved in the construction of a major government policy. I emerged from it feeling that perhaps I was no longer a just a new boy in Whitehall.

It later became fashionable to denigrate incomes policies in general, and our 1975 policy in particular, as if they inevitably fail. While myself now sharing the broad free-market reservations about such policies, I reject the dismissal of our policy. In fact Wilson's pay policy, as first continued by James Callaghan, was for a time (and nothing in politics is permanent) remarkably successful. Over the three following years it was a major factor in reducing inflation from nearly 30 per cent to single figures. To me it was a more humane way of controlling inflation than relying on the harsh deflationary impact of Mrs Thatcher's later four million unemployed. But the trade unions, who selfishly and foolishly destroyed our voluntary incomes policy in 1978–9, then left her as Prime Minister with no practical alternative to the tough monetarism from which the unions were to be the biggest losers.

After the pay battle was settled, Wilson said to me that without a Policy Unit, the Treasury's statutory policy would have been successfully bounced through frightened ministers (including the frightened Prime Minister). One consequence would have been that the then mighty unions would have fought against rather than for the new policy, which would almost certainly have destroyed the Government as well as the policy (as the Winter of Discontent demonstrated).

The existence for the first time of alternative economic advisers inside Number 10 gave the Prime Minister alternative options. It meant that he could meet his Chancellor fully briefed and with critical scrutiny of the Treasury's (then often dubious) figures and arguments and, most important in this case, to suggest alternative policy options. So the Policy Unit increased the Prime Minister's involvement in the conduct of economic policy – and thereby his power, which is presumably why succeeding Prime Ministers have retained the Unit.

Interestingly, after the cabinet which approved the final White Paper on 10 July, Denis Healey invited me into his small study in Number 11 and reflected on the development of this incomes policy with typical honesty and perception. He recognised that as Chancellor he had never been fully in control of the policy. He complained, with justice, that Harold Wilson as Prime Minister had never sufficiently supported him – something of which Jim Callaghan also complained to me. Finally Denis said to me: 'I am so pleased that we did not go ahead with our original full statutory policy last Monday. I am so pleased that cabinet stopped it. That would have been a big mistake.'

That was unwittingly a tribute to the Policy Unit. The development of the Policy Unit was good for government, as its inventor Harold Wilson intended, if not always good for the Chancellor's sleep. The Treasury was the most impressive single institution in government with (and occasionally against) which I have worked. However, it did have at that time limited vision, little political sensitivity or awareness of the needs of the real commercial markets which actually create the nation's wealth over which it stands as custodian. There was more than a touch of arrogance in the way it ignored any views other than its own. Other views and options certainly needed to be introduced into cabinet discussions of the economy. My Policy Unit secured that, via the Prime Minister. And from 1975 until 1979, the two Prime Ministers came to gain significant influence over broad economic strategy.

After its victory over pay policy, the Unit became more widely accepted in Whitehall. In the Treasury, a new generation of officials, typified by Robin Butler, Nigel Wickes, Peter Middleton and later Andrew Turnbull, emerged, less suspicious of outside experience and influence. I began to work regularly and closely with them. This made life in Whitehall much more congenial and satisfying for me.

Britain's economic problems did not go away over that summer, despite the counter-inflationary benefits of the new pay policy. By October, Healey was contemplating import controls and even asking for a loan from the International Monetary Fund. On 11 November 1975 he came to cabinet requesting £3.75 billion of public expenditure cuts, with Roy Mason threatening to resign if his wasteful Ministry of Defence was cut by a mere £450 million. Wilson told me before cabinet – in one of our regular discussions in the privacy of his lavatory – that his main objective was 'to avoid resignations'. (His own was only four months ahead.) Ministerial views on the Treasury package were balanced on a razor's edge and seemed marginally against, but Wilson exercised his chairman's right to count the views and announced that there was a majority of two in favour. Afterwards, he conceded to me that his sums were wrong, but he wisely decided that he could not always allow his Chancellor to be beaten in cabinet since this 'would demoralise him'. Shortly after, Healey applied for his first IMF loan.

The final decisive cabinet was on 15 January 1976. Healey achieved his £3½ billion cuts, with Defence resisting to the end, and the public expenditure White Paper was scheduled for debate on 8 and 9 March. Wilson mischievously left the unsuspecting Healey with the task of bullying his own rebellious backbenchers in the Commons – just before Wilson would announce his own resignation and the leadership election, which he did not want Healey to win.

Meanwhile the cabinet and the Policy Unit were also involved in a string of impending bankruptcies at the heart of British industry – Aston Martin, Ferranti, Alfred Herbert, Burmah Oil. In April the Government had to announce an injection of £1.4 billion into British Leyland in order to avoid imminent bankruptcy. Benn's subsidised pigeons began to come home to roost. Norton Villiers motorcycle company, which produced only fourteen machines per worker per year, compared with 150 by its Japanese competitors, collapsed, as did Benn's favourite Meridian cooperative. The National Westminster Bank was reported to us as being on the edge of insolvency and Burmah Oil's liabilities were reported to be a billion pounds, which gave Tony Benn the opportunity to demand the nationalisation of its North Sea oil operations.

Present-day British Prime Ministers have no knowledge or experience of what it is like to be faced with daily problems on the 1970s scale. Most dramatic for me was the threatened closure in November 1975 by its American parent of the Chrysler motor car company, which had been plagued with daily industrial disputes, especially in Scotland. At first the British political side, including the Prime Minister, myself, Varley and Kaufman from the Department of Industry, accepted the closure as inevitable – and Edmund Dell from the Treasury as desirable, in the hope that it would discipline British industry and its unions.

Wilson was as usual aware of the political dimension and wanted to leave the American management with the blame for closure. So at first he tried to give the impression that we were pressing the Americans to keep it open and that we were even willing to provide some small resources to persuade them to do that. But the Americans in turn played a clever game, pretending to want to keep it open providing we provided sufficient financing, so that when they did close it as they wished they could blame the British Government's meanness. Both sides were pretending to fight for keeping it open, neither meaning to win.

But in November the situation changed politically on our side when the two Scottish ministers, Willie Ross and Bruce Millan, told the Prime Minister that they would resign if Chrysler were closed. Wilson now switched tack and decided genuinely to try to keep the plant open – at least until after his planned retirement some four months ahead. So what started as a political game of pretending to try to keep it open became the reality of spending a fortune to do so.

The Americans also began to consider keeping it open providing they could get their hands on enough subsidy from the poor British taxpayer. The Prime Minister appointed Harold Lever to our negotiating team to try to invent a rescue wheeze, and asked me to be a member of our negotiating team with his specific remit to make sure that Ross and Millan did not resign. Our absorbing meetings continued through until Christmas, with Varley and Dell still assuming that our policy was still to close Chrysler as skilfully as possible, while Lever and I worked to keep it open and keep the Scots on board.

From the beginning I was fascinated by our Chrysler American counterparts. Boss Riccardo, known locally as 'the Chicago Flamethrower', sat opposite me with another Sicilian-looking henchman named Caffino. They both had menacing dark eyes, swept-back greased hair, sharp suits and flashy ties. They reminded me of stereotype night club owners from Hollywood thrillers of the 1940s. I expected them at any moment to put on dark shades, and assumed they had lethal violin cases under the table. They were quick and well informed. Compared with them, the negotiating officials from the British Department of Industry looked like a bunch of country vicars thinking they were coming to a village fete but finding themselves in a downtown casino.

At one tense moment in early December, Riccardo narrowed his eyes even further to slits, and threatened to bankrupt Chrysler immediately and to pay none of its debts or redundancy obligations. 'We came to play as gentlemen' – here he paused – 'but if you prefer, we won't.' At this point there was a quiver of silence on our side, and I expected Caffino to take the Tommy gun from his violin case and make us an offer we could not refuse.

Riccardo and Caffino now knew they had the Brits on the run, and by 8 December Lever had been squeezed up to £140 million – and still rising.

It was a bad deal for the British taxpayer and probably bad for British industry because it implied that the Government would always bail them out, however poor their performance. But it suited Harold Wilson, because it delayed the closure at least until after he retired and it kept Ross and Millan in the cabinet. Most important, it avoided making 30,000 car workers unemployed and vastly increased car imports burdening our already sick balance of trade. Anyway, the Prime Minister told both Lever and myself that we had done 'a good job'. Judgements of that kind, of course, depend on where you stand.

Housing was another major concern of myself and the Policy Unit, and on this subject I was often in disagreement with then current Labour thinking. To Labour, housing policy just meant building more traditional council houses. But the social environment was changing. The type of housing being built – still based on the earlier 'average' family – was not meeting the needs of the variety of new types of tenant: the young, the old retired, the single person and one-parent family, or the disabled. Local Labour housing policies were – like their national equivalents at Party Headquarters – increasingly out of touch with the changing wishes and needs of families in modern Britain. I was particularly concerned with housing.

In Roade, I had experienced truly bad housing at Waverley and had enjoyed our new council house. I knew the difference it could make to family life. Now I was a private owner-occupier in the Labour borough of Camden, and I observed with growing dismay the dogmatic lunacies of our local council. I witnessed how its hilariously titled 'Direct Works Department' was distinctly averse to doing any work, direct or otherwise. Its council house building and repairs were slow and expensive. Nor was this only a London problem. My brother Clem worked as a carpenter in the Manchester Works Department, and told me often how they spent most of their time drinking tea and playing cards. He became so frustrated that he resigned and emigrated to France.

I was keen for the Unit to take a radical approach to housing issues and pressed this on Wilson. The minister responsible was Anthony Crosland, who I had known since our days with CDS in the early 1960s. He was one of my political heroes and his *Future of Socialism* was the seminal work on social democracy for my generation.

Tall, dark and handsome like an intellectual Cary Grant, amusing, perceptive, indiscreet, arrogant, rude and phenomenally intelligent – it was impossible not to like Tony. But there was always something of the Oxford don about him, leaning back puffing his endless cigarillos and making detached, quizzical and amusing comments about current issues which excited everyone else. He seemed not really to enjoy getting involved at the pit-face of politics or government, and was a slow and reluctant decision-maker.

To some Whitehall insiders he seemed to have become lazy. Leo Pliatzky, Crosland's old Oxford friend, criticised him harshly to me in January 1976, saying he was 'a failed boy wonder, too lazy and with no political courage'. I suspect that worsening health may have been a major factor in these apparent faults. When I went to visit him in his office in November 1975 to discuss public expenditure cuts, he looked very tired and admitted to me that he had to sleep on his settee every afternoon. Next month he told me that he had had a medical check-up and was 'OK'. But in fourteen months he was dead.

Crosland had begun well at Environment in 1974, quickly setting up a Housing Finance Review to carry out an urgent survey of the chaos of public housing finance. But it soon ran into the sand, and no progress at all was made on the key issue of providing tenants with the right to buy their own homes.

Yet the evidence of public support for buying their council homes was overwhelming. Tenants throughout the country made it clear to canvassers on doorsteps in both 1974 general elections that they wished to obtain and exercise this right. Every opinion poll and social survey showed its growing political importance. Among council tenants, 64 per cent mentioned this right as being for them a very high priority, and one third wanted to own their own council homes. By 1978, opinion polls showed that 15 per cent of Labour voters preferred Conservative policies because of their commitment to council house sales and home ownership. In the 1979 general election, the Conservative firm promise to allow council tenants to acquire their own homes was a major factor in the defection to them of Labour voters, especially in the new towns and city estates. The sad irony is that if we in Number 10 had had our way, that would have been a Labour policy in time for the 1979 election.

My own early commitment to selling council houses was based mainly on my support for the principle of giving working-class tenants more choice and control over their own homes. With it went the freedom to decorate their homes as they wished and, very important, to move in pursuit of employment – many inner-city unemployed dare not move to seek jobs because it meant giving up their council homes and going to the back of the council queue elsewhere. Also, I could not see why the middle classes should have this freedom and not the working classes on the council estates. It infuriated me when I raised this issue with my local Kentish Town Labour Party and was dismissed out of hand by a bunch of mainly left-wing activists, many of whom were prosperously middle class and enjoyed the benefits of owning their own homes in nearby Hampstead and Camden Town (one of whom is in the Labour Government at the time of writing).

I was also concerned by examining the local authority housing costs and seeing the vast sums of public expenditure devoted to council house maintenance. If those houses were sold, many of their new owners would willingly do the maintenance themselves – and certainly do it better than the Camden Direct Works Department.

So I instigated a Policy Unit review of selling council houses, although a majority of its members were clearly worried about this breach of sacred Labour dogma. Key contributions came from the Press Secretary, Joe Haines. He had long believed in selling council houses and had worked out various 'life-leasehold' schemes for doing so without seriously reducing the amount of long-term council house stock. These schemes were to be offered permissively to local authorities, who would be free not to introduce the new measures if their local housing situation would be harmed by them – though they would naturally be influenced by demand expressed through the local ballot box.

I drafted the Policy Unit paper with a package of alternative schemes for tenants to acquire their own houses and submitted it to the Prime Minister in October 1975. He welcomed it enthusiastically, writing at the top: 'Yes, this is a fascinating study. The question now is how to proceed ... What we do not want is for it to get lost in the official machine for months.' When I talked to him about the scheme on 20 October, he said it 'could prove an historic document' and that it 'could change history'. He was very excited, showing it was still possible to kindle the fires of his political interest. We went through various stages of discussions and redrafting with officials and individual ministers and we seemed to make progress, but then it became clear that Crosland and his advisers were trying to block it. So I arranged a meeting with Tony and his special advisers, David Lipsey and Ann Carlton. They strongly objected to any sales of council houses, mainly on the grounds that it would alienate our local activists in next May's local elections. That was indisputable. My point was that while it would certainly alienate a few local activists, it would also attract many times that number of local voters – and that it was anyway right to do it in principle. But we could not bridge the gap.

Our scheme was submitted to a special cabinet committee (MISC 127) under the Prime Minister's chairmanship on 24 March 1976 – after he had announced his coming resignation. There most ministers liked it and – against the opposition of Crosland, Ross and Dell from the Treasury – concluded that the political and financial advantages were sufficient to justify asking officials to draft policies based on it. After the meeting, Wilson commented to me that Crosland and Ross had 'made up their minds on council housing in 1965 and their minds have been closed ever since.' He added that this was 'why old politicians should move on' – and 'I am setting an example.'

But these proposals which might have improved Labour's electoral fortunes became bogged down in the Whitehall machine, just as Wilson had originally feared. His retirement within days removed the scheme's most powerful and enthusiastic supporter. More opposition mounted within the Department of Environment and among the vested interests in local Labour parties, whose political bases were on the council estates. When Callaghan's new Environment Secretary, Peter Shore, who succeeded Crosland in April 1976, finally made an official statement on the Government's position in 1978, it was phrased very negatively, which delighted thousands of Labour activists and alienated millions of council tenant voters who wanted more freedom to own their own homes. It gave Mrs Thatcher a winning election card. The left-wing reactionaries in the party had won. In next year's general election we lost. Years later, Peter Shore told me with engaging honesty that 'I totally misjudged the policy of selling council houses. It had a dramatic effect.' That effect could have been in our favour.

It was my most important defeat in Downing Street and I was very angry. The heart of the problem, much wider than the issue of selling council houses, was that our Labour Government was trapped in the outdated prejudices and undemocratic structures of its own party organisation. Because of this, we failed to appreciate and respond to the changing priorities and aspirations of many of our own supporters. The fault did not really lie with Crosland and his advisers; they appraised correctly the hostile short-term response of party activists. The fault lay with the then outdated nature of the Labour movement itself, which, on this and other policy issues, made it difficult for its own Government to resolve the problems which faced it. It was thus again left to a Conservative Prime Minister to pursue the necessary change.

Harold Wilson had long decided to resign as Prime Minister at some point in 1975 or 1976, though he wavered over the precise final date, as the following chapter describes. But as we moved into late 1975, with his health deteriorating, he was personally a lame duck Prime Minister, with one eye on the exit, and this diminished his interest in policy matters.

However, several important issues did cross our desks during Wilson's fading final months and involved my time and attention. Devolution moved relentlessly and boringly along and I sat on its endless tedious committees. Ireland was also always on the agenda and Wilson remained interested in it, still playing with our 'Dominion Status' option while the Northern Ireland Office itself spoke of 'distancing'.

Two minor but important matters of great interest to me were settled in Wilson's final weeks.

I persuaded him to establish a Royal Commission on Legal Services. The Law had taken my interest at the LSE (I also then realised that I wished I had become a barrister, but it was too late to change trains). Law and justice – not always the same thing in Britain – are areas of the greatest importance to the conduct of a fair and democratic society, yet they seemed often to be being run mainly for the financial interest of that most powerful of all trade unions, the lawyers.

Wilson himself had radical views on the law, often using the collective phrase for its practitioners as 'a cheat of lawyers'. Together we overcame massive opposition from the Lord Chancellor, Elwyn Jones, and his notoriously reactionary departmental officials, and the new Royal Commission was approved in Wilson's last few days.

Another Commission report had recently been delivered by Lord Radcliffe on the subject of ministerial memoirs. This produced some impressive Whitehall manoeuvres. Radcliffe proposed that ministers should wait fifteen years before publishing their ministerial memoirs (an activity which many British politicians, being among the worst paid in the world, often saw as an essential pension supplement). He suggested that this self-denial should be voluntary and offered no sanctions to enforce it. The Cabinet Secretary, wishing to protect Whitehall's secrets, was very unhappy with taking politicians on trust and sent Wilson a 'Declaration on Ministerial Obligation in Relation to Memoirs', which required ministers to sign a declaration before leaving office that they would obey the fifteen-year rule, which could be used in the law courts as an instrument of enforcement.

In the MISC 89 cabinet committee which discussed Radcliffe, Roy Jenkins and Michael Foot opposed this authoritarian line on good liberal principles enthusiastically supported by Tony Benn and Barbara Castle (whose own diaries were being scribbled in the very cabinet committee discussing the issue). Callaghan and Roy Mason, both ex-military men, were in the small minority, along with the Law Officers (who usually favour all proposals which might generate legal fees), who took the tough disciplinary line.

Curiously, the Cabinet Office minute recording the MISC 89 meeting stated categorically that ministers had agreed to sign the Radcliffe Declaration. But I was present and witness to the fact that this was not so – and several ministers subsequently complained to me about the mistaken minutes. This error may of course have resulted from a temporary hearing aberration by the Cabinet Office minute-takers, though it also may have been another attempted 'Whitehall bounce'.

The Prime Minister himself, although under a strong whip from his Cabinet Secretary, was transparently and hilariously ambivalent – he and I knew that he

was at that very time negotiating his own memoirs deal with the ever-accommo-
dating publisher George Weidenfeld. At one point, John Hunt persuaded Wilson
to sign an answer to an arranged Commons written question confirming that
ministers would indeed have to sign the fatal fifteen-year declaration. But I intervened, referring obliquely to Wilson's own possible memoirs, and he agreed to
remove his signature. Wilson then wrote to the Cabinet Secretary saying that he
saw little point in asking ministers to sign declarations which were not legally
enforceable.

In the end, all was left unclear. The necessary Cabinet approval for the fifteen-
year rule was not in fact secured. Several ministers – Jenkins, Foot, Castle, Benn
and others – refused to sign any pledge. Yet I later saw references in official
documents to 'the fifteen-year rule' as if it was an established convention.
Anyway, it did not stop a string of ministers and Prime Ministers – including
Wilson, Callaghan, Thatcher and Major – from publishing their memoirs well
short of fifteen years after their resignation, with no reference to the Radcliffe
guidelines.

On this one, Sir Humphrey suffered a rare failure. I have myself waited
twenty-nine years since entering Downing Street before publishing these
memoirs (though my *Prime Minister* in 1987 was a discreet *hors d'oeuvre*).

Eleven

THE PRIME MINISTER RESIGNS

I t is very rare for a modern British Prime Minister voluntarily to resign, as Harold Wilson did in 1976, while in office and in reasonable health. Churchill, Eden and Macmillan resigned from office but partly under pressure and while in bad health. So Wilson's voluntary resignation was unusual. The London media predictably took a cynical view and universally assumed that he left because of impending personal scandal, but they were wrong on that as on much else about him.

Harold Wilson was electorally the most successful politician in twentieth-century Britain and was in 1976 unchallenged as leader of his Government and his party. The shocked disbelief which greeted his resignation was a reflection of his status in British politics. His closest aide, Marcia Falkender, in her 1983 book *Downing Street in Perspective*, reports how she had tried to persuade Wilson not to go. She describes him as then 'in the pink of health, able not only to endure, but to enjoy the physical and mental strain of the highest office in the land.' She states that he did not reveal to her his precise departure date until two days beforehand, at Chequers on 14 March 1976.

I do not accept that he was 'in the pink of health'. At the Paris summit in December 1974 he suffered from an attack of 'racing heart', and this recurred at times in the year ahead – at the Rome summit a year later he felt almost too ill to attend the meetings and was ordered by his doctor to reduce his workload. Nor was he always able 'to enjoy' the burden of his office, often complaining that he was bored. In the summer of 1975 he said to me: 'Bernard, I have been round this course so often that I am too bored to face jumping any more hurdles.' On another occasion, he said: 'The trouble with me now is that I only have the same old solutions for the same old problems.' But his resignation stunned the public and political colleagues. It is worth tracing how I saw it occur.

To me of course it was not a shock, since when I agreed to join him and set up the new Policy Unit in March 1974, Wilson had told me to get leave from the LSE until Easter 1976 because 'I will then retire.' Naturally I revealed that to no one except Joe. But many other signals emerged over the months ahead. In March 1975 he told Joe that he was beginning to find the job tiring and that he dreaded Prime Minister's Questions and hated the meetings of the party's left-wing National Executive Committee. (He often tried to arrange overseas visits to coincide with them.) The accession of a formidable new Leader of the Opposition, Margaret Thatcher, worried him and he now felt uncomfortable facing a woman. 'After ten years of studying my opponent like a hawk', he said, 'learning every part of his character, now, at my age, I've got to begin all over again.' He then poured himself a very stiff brandy. As an old dog, he didn't want to have to learn new tricks. It was surely better to go.

But he was still unsure of precisely when to retire. Two months later he discussed the 'succession' with me, with the clearly implied assumption that he would resign soon. He told me that Jenkins was now 'finished' and could not get the leadership; and also that Healey 'won't get it'. He felt that Crosland had improved his position – but this was before our clash with Tony over his resistance to council house sales, which damaged him in Wilson's eyes. In June 1975 he told Janet Hewlett-Davies, Joe's very able deputy, that he was fed up and thinking of going in October. He had mentioned this to Marcia, who became very agitated. She told Albert Murray (who as always told me) that everyone in the team should try to cheer Harold up and persuade him to continue on the treadmill. Albert said this was explicitly in the context of their own job-preservation.

After the referendum campaign was over in June, Wilson complained that he felt bored and again began to talk of resignation. Marcia put pressure on him and he again relented, but by the summer of 1975, although he was actively engaged for a time in the incomes policy, his real appetite for the game was dwindling fast. On 24 June he sat in his Commons room with us after Questions, drinking too much brandy and counting off on his fingers the number of Question Times until the summer recess. He seemed to assume there would be no more after that, with an October resignation. Bill Housden told me after a weekend at Chequers in late June that an upbeat Marcia had informed him that she had persuaded the Prime Minister to change his mind and he would now stay on beyond October. During July, always a stressful month in the Commons, Wilson grew more fed up with the job and he told Joe on 14 July that his resignation would be 'sooner rather than later. It is all déjà vu now.' The following week he tried to write his own speech for the annual Miners' Gala, but it was a terrible mish-mash of tired clichés. Joe told him straight that there was 'nothing new in it worth saying'. Harold touchingly replied, 'Well, I don't have anything new to say, do I?' So Joe rewrote it. Housden told me that he was totally convinced from all he heard that Wilson would still go in October.

But he didn't. Joe and I both learned from our usual sources at the end of July that during a Chequers weekend, Marcia had finally persuaded him not to resign in October. But Wilson was insisting that he definitely would not go on beyond Christmas – and had promised that to Mary. I felt very disappointed at this delay, believing that Wilson had very little left to give, and that now was an ideal time for him to retire, on the crest of a political wave after his recent successes over the referendum and the incomes policy.

But he dragged on. In September he was still talking sometimes of a precise Christmas departure, at others more vaguely of 'some time this year'. But on 27 October 1975 he instructed Joe Haines and Kenneth Stowe to prepare the detailed timetable for his retirement, to be announced on 14 February 1976 – the thirteenth anniversary of his election to the leadership of the Labour Party in 1963. The die was finally cast. He revealed to them that he had promised Mary that he would go at Christmas, but Marcia had been to visit him three times over the previous weekend to persuade him not to retire and he had conceded to her an extra three months. He thoughtfully found an outside job for Tommy Balogh and promoted Marcia's devoted fan Gerald Kaufman while he still had the power of patronage.

Wilson suffered a bout of ill health at the end of the year. On 3 December, after a difficult cabinet committee in which Healey had been brutally rude to him, he came out of the Cabinet Room for a pee and, as so often, called me into the privacy of the large washroom with him. He put his head in his hands and said: 'Bernard, oh I am so exhausted!' He then launched an attack on the Cabinet Secretary for burdening him with so many committees to chair. I felt so sad for him and saw that he really needed to retire soon. He went off next day to the Rome summit and there felt so ill that he nearly did not attend the sessions. He took his doctor Joe (later Lord) Stone with him and Joe told him then that he must cut down his work commitments or they would kill him. Instructions were given to Ken Stowe to clear his diary and to John Hunt to reduce his burden of committees. On his return to London, watching his unusually poor Commons performance on the summit, I wondered if the wild dogs of the Opposition would smell that the old lion was finally weakening; but apparently not.

He informed the Queen of his retirement intentions at his audience on 9 December 1975. By then he had pushed back the announcement date to 25 February 1976, chosen because it was immediately after a meeting of the National Executive Committee – 'I will enjoy keeping them in the dark', he said. Shortly after, already really 'demob-happy', Wilson was honoured with the Freedom of the City of London. This occasion exhibited and symbolized the curious financial network in which Wilson had become entangled. It also gave Joe, Albert and me some great entertainment. I can see now the colourful ancient ceremony in the Guildhall, with tiny Harold looking swamped and uncomfortable in his bulky robes. Marcia had herself drawn up 'The Prime Minister's Personal Guest List' of friends, which was published in the official programme I still retain. It included Joe Kagan (financier of the Political Office and later to be jailed for tax fraud), Eric Miller (financier of the Political Office and soon to commit suicide when accused of financial malpractice), Lord Brayley (financier of the Political Office and recently forced to resign from government for financial malpractice), Lord Plurenden (financier of the Political Office and described to me by a senior Foreign Office official as 'a double agent to the Russians'), Lord Fisher (described to me by Bill Housden as 'the original Godfather of the Political Office mafia'), Ariah Handler (manager of the offshore bank in which Wilson was alleged to have made an illegal deposit), and James Goldsmith (financier of the Tory Party whom Wilson had not then met and who anyway did not turn up).

Were these really Harold Wilson's close personal friends, chosen to attend his great honour? They were also an odd crowd to parade at the centre of British finance and its integrity. These personal friends were announced individually by name and marched in turn up the Guildhall aisle, with Marcia and her escort Gerald Kaufman bringing up the rear. Joe Haines commented loudly (not about Marcia and Gerald) that 'I assume Inspector Knacker of the Yard is keeping the ceremony under close observation', and added that 'if Albert shouts "police!" the hall will half-empty.' He was joking of course.

Over Christmas and the New Year of 1976 Wilson remained under pressure from Marcia to stay on longer, telling Janet Hewlett-Davies that 'Marcia would like me to stay on until I die in office.'

Even at this late stage he sometimes wavered before Marcia's persuasion. On 9 February she reassured Albert and Bill that they could relax, as their jobs were again safe. Next day Wilson was back on the brandy for the first time in weeks, hinting to Joe that he might delay his resignation because of the impending homosexual scandal concerning Jeremy Thorpe. On 1 March, Wilson told Joe that Marcia had been attacking him the previous weekend at Chequers, pleading for 'a few more months'. But he finally stuck to his commitment to go in mid March. He cancelled all planned trips abroad, thinned his diary, and handed over the chairmanship of some cabinet committees. He made few speeches. His red boxes were half empty, with some long papers unread for several weeks. He had almost ceased to function as an active Prime Minister except for chairing the cabinet and answering Questions in the Commons. He was a shadow of the man I had observed form his Government in March 1974. I discussed his retirement at this time with Albert Murray, who said that Wilson had told him that a new

Prime Minister would need a ministerial reshuffle and would 'have to get rid of Barbara [Castle]'. But he could not face doing it himself. Everything was being put off. Intellectually and psychologically he had retired. It did not feel to me in any way like some historic or cataclysmic ending. It was just like the slow tick of an old clock winding down.

In the week before his resignation announcement, Wilson had a lively social time. On Wednesday 10 March he attended Marcia's birthday party at George Weidenfeld's flat. He only just managed to scoot back to the Commons in time to vote when the Government suffered a big defeat. The next night he celebrated his own sixtieth birthday dinner, again at Weidenfeld's.

This was very entertaining, though the placement at table was curious. At the top table with the Prime Minister and Marcia was John (shortly to be Lord) Vaizey, who had often in his writings viciously attacked Harold Wilson, though he had recently become a friend of Marcia. Also in top places were the show business millionaires Lew Grade, who did a solo tap dance before a bemused Prime Minister at 1 a.m., and his brother Bernard Delfont (both of them about to get peerages). Mary Wilson sat at a lower table with Albert and me.

There was a strange atmosphere in Number 10 on the final evening as the small team in the know prepared for the next day's announcement. The media had no premonition of this closely guarded secret – which Wilson savoured as his final revenge on the 'reptiles'. Lord Goodman, who was in on the secret because he was already arranging the sale of 5 Lord North Street, had actually breached the Prime Minister's trust by alerting the chairman of the Express newspaper group. But when the latter informed his political editors, they dismissed it. The house was eerily quiet. Gavyn Davies drove me home late to Kentish Town after a dinner for the Royal Statistical Society. Like the rest of the Unit staff and most of Number 10, he was quite unaware of the bombshell about to burst.

Wilson feared there had been a leak of his plans from the Palace when he found that Lever seemed to know – though the latter's source was Goodman, who had also tipped off Roy Jenkins at a Christmas party. Roy sent for me on 29 January 1976 to try to get me to confirm it, but I declined. I hinted obliquely to him that all would be clearer by Easter but dare not say more. I knew that if I told Roy and, as was likely, he told his friend John Harris, it would surely then get back to Marcia – and I would be dead in the water as a 'leaker'. Wilson had actually alerted Jim Callaghan on the previous Thursday evening when in the car on the way from his birthday dinner to vote at the Commons. But Jim later told me that he thought Harold was just joking. So quite a few people knew, or at least were broadly aware that Wilson might be resigning soon. But, remarkably, the secret was held from the media and the public.

I did not get to bed until after midnight, slept badly, and was up at six on the morning of 16 March. I set off early for Downing Street, walking much of the way through Kentish Town and Camden Town because there were no buses. I was into Number 10 before 8 a.m. and found all the main staff already there. The policeman at the door knew something was afoot, queried me, and told me that they all assumed that 'Crosland is resigning'.

The Prime Minister did not come in from Lord North Street until 9.15 a.m., and left for the Palace to resign at 10.10 a.m. I went to the front door to watch a sad Bill Housden drive him off – not a single photographer or journalist was present to note him leave or return. (If I really did leak to Harry Evans, as Marcia and *Private Eye* believed, then the *Sunday Times* would certainly have had a man there at this time!) There was not a breath of rumour or speculation in that morning's newspapers. This was Harold Wilson's final triumph – he had cheated the press of the last great story of his political career. It was his best kept secret.

On his return from the Palace, Wilson sent for me to join him in the study. He was completely calm and relaxed. He said that the Policy Unit had been a great success, meeting all his initial hopes, and he intended to recommend his successor to keep it. He added with a grin: 'It depends who it is, of course – Denis Healey thinks he knows it all anyway.'

The cabinet had been specially summoned to learn the news at 11 a.m. I mixed with the ministers beforehand and it was clear to me that most of them had no idea of the bombshell which was about to explode. Lever was clearly in the know, sidling up to me on his walking stick and whispering: 'D-Day?' The Prime Minister sent for Jim Callaghan ten minutes before cabinet and confirmed what he had hinted to him after his birthday party the previous week. When Jim came down, he looked winded. Wilson then informed his loyal deputy, Ted Short, who afterwards appeared almost in tears. Marcia came out of her room looking very fraught and took Peter Shore to one side – I heard him loudly gasp: 'No!'

Then they all filed into the cabinet room, where the Prime Minister read his brief and dignified statement. I listened through the adjoining door from the Private Office. Ken Stowe told me afterwards that when Wilson finished, they all looked pole-axed. The man who had led them through their ministerial lives, about whom they all grumbled, who they expected to take the political flak and to lead them to election victories, was not going to be there any more.

Jim Callaghan, pre-warned, responded with an excellently pitched few words, concluding that Harold Wilson would be judged more kindly by history than by his own contemporaries. (I still wait for that and trust it will be proved true.)

While cabinet completed its sad proceedings I nipped up the small flight of stairs to inform my Policy Unit. They were totally shocked. Gavyn, never too healthy-looking, turned completely white and for a moment I thought that he would faint. Quite apart from their emotional sympathies for Wilson, whose remarkable career was now at an end, they were also understandably concerned that they would all be dismissed when Wilson ceased to be Prime Minister. Like me, their appointments terminated with him. I had arranged for three months' redundancy pay for them, which might cushion the pain. But my main hope was that Harold would keep to his word and persuade his successor to keep them on. They had done a superb job.

The rest of that day was an anti-climax after the long and tense build-up. The Prime Minister took Commons Questions from a subdued House. All the backbench rottweilers, who had snarled and snapped at him for years, seemed sad that their familiar target was to leave the stage. Edward Heath, instinctively sympathetic to another about-to-be ex-Prime Minister, rose above party prejudice and with his natural sense of an historic moment paid a superbly phrased tribute to Wilson. But Margaret Thatcher got the tone wrong, was graceless and point-scoring, and missed the mood of the House.

In the evening Carol and I went to the opera with our Hampstead friend Brian Knox to see Szymonowski's *King Roger*. But I found it difficult either to relax or to concentrate on the testing music. I kept thinking of my uncertain future with a family of four small children under eleven years old.

The prospect (unless Wilson's successor renewed my appointment) was of my either being out of a job, or having to return to the LSE, which I might find tame after the fascinating turbulence of Downing Street. But I did at least feel satisfied at having done a reasonable job over the past two years. Most important to me was that the Policy Unit was now clearly established in Whitehall with a good reputation – which had been my number one priority from the beginning. Ken Stowe and Nick Stuart had each come from Private Office to my room during the day to offer congratulations on the work of the Unit and to say that they hoped the new Prime Minister would keep it going. Ken, ever loyal, asked me to write a paper on the working of the Unit so that he could recommend whoever became Prime Minister to continue it.

I was also relieved that Harold Wilson had finally given up the huge burden of the highest office in the realm, whatever the implications for my personal career. In fact he was now a mere shell of that 'Rolls Royce' machine which Joe remembered joining in 1968. He had nothing more to give.

There followed three weeks of interregnum while the Parliamentary Labour Party conducted its elections to select Harold Wilson's successor as its leader – and hence as Prime Minister. It was for me a curiously flat time in Number 10. I recall returning there at 8.30 on the evening following the announcement, after a meeting with Roy Jenkins in the Commons. The house was dark and dead, like a morgue. Even the private secretaries had already gone home. Most lights were out. The flow of papers had ceased.

All serious policy issues were held over for decision by the new Prime Minister. Even during the following daytimes, the house was lifeless. The private secretaries sat there gossiping. My Policy Unit staff were edgy, uncertain about their futures. Joe showed the strains of worry about his own professional future. Number 10 was like a small liner whose engines had stopped, and she lay becalmed in the waters of Whitehall.

It was a strange period, in which Harold Wilson himself began to behave more strangely, with some of his odder traits becoming more pronounced and his suspicious side coming more to the surface.

Already in January he had begun to talk to me about dirty tricks by the South African security services against British politicians, especially against Jeremy Thorpe. When I was burgled at this time, he observed that 'somewhere in South Africa House there must be a room full of grandfather clocks and television sets, including yours.' I was not wholly convinced that he was joking. He was, as usual, not entirely off the mark, since some South Africans were indeed working to destabilise leading Liberal opponents of apartheid in Britain (and one had been courting Marcia's sister Peggy). But it was typical that he devoted so much time and attention to this diversion.

He and Marcia also at that time became obsessed with fears of a right-wing coup in Britain and talked of stopping the recruitment of mercenaries in Britain, since they feared these would execute the coup while the British army was overseas. On 10 February Marcia burst into his room in the Commons, where the team were having a foreign affairs discussion with Wilson, demanding that he intervene on the mercenary issue to prevent a coup.

He also became convinced that his study in Number 10 was bugged. On one hilarious morning in February when I was in the study chatting with him, he lifted a portrait (I think of Gladstone) up from the wall and pointed to a metal device planted in the wall behind. With his fingers to his lips requesting silence, he guided me inevitably to the lavatory in the corner of his study and there whispered to me that the device was a bug. Actually, given the Prime Minister's propensity for secret 'loo conversations', a shrewder spy would have bugged all the lavatories in Number 10. Anyway, he arranged for a private security agent to come into Number 10 and advise him if his study were indeed bugged. Regrettably, I did not enquire from him of the results of the investigation.

Harold of course loved all of this – the plots, leaks, conspiracies, agents and mercenaries – and this mild paranoia was both sad and amusing to observe.

But it should never be forgotten that Wilson did have real enemies outside who were trying to damage him. Right-wing extremists were discussing the need to overthrow the Labour government. Mercenaries were being actively recruited in Britain to fight in Africa. I never entirely dismissed the suggestion by an old friend of Wilson that my own room was indeed bugged. One day I passed the Head of MI5 in the corridor. I had never met him before, yet he said to me, 'Enjoy your football on Sunday?' I suddenly had a feeling of being watched and have never entirely dismissed Harold as being completely barmy on this subject. Not completely.

During his final days the Prime Minister still held the occasional serious meeting, especially on setting up a new statutory body to help the film industry, one of Marcia's pet projects and described by Healey in committee as 'Harold's retirement benefit'. (Marcia sat on the Interim Committee of the Film Industry from 1977 until 1982.) But our main remaining activities were social, especially the formal farewell dinners with first his cabinet on 22 March, and then with the Queen on the following evening. For the former, twenty-three Cabinet ministers gathered beforehand in the handsome White Reception Room, together with John Hunt and Burke Trend as the Prime Minister's two Cabinet Secretaries over the past twelve years, Ken Stowe as his Principal Private Secretary, Douglas Allen as Head of the Civil Service, and Joe, Marcia and myself from Wilson's personal team. We all filed into the gloomy State Dining Room, where I had a marvellous seat at the head of the table. I could observe it all like a fly on the wall.

The ministers were in high spirits, having fun, and with no apparent tensions between the candidates for the succession – Callaghan, Foot, Jenkins, Healey, Benn and Crosland. Wilson's after-dinner speech was disappointing – ragged, off-the-cuff, without the weight of a prepared speech or the virtues of sparkling spontaneity. Then Tony Benn, who was cheekily taking photographs of the great occasion, leaped to his feet and made a brash but quite amusing speech. Roy Jenkins followed with a few measured words, which I could not hear because Barbara Castle, perhaps not unwittingly, was talking loudly throughout. Roy came over to me after dinner and said some kind words about the high reputation of the Policy Unit. He seemed a little resigned and sad that he would clearly not win the election to be the next Prime Minister running the Unit. I was sorry not to work under him. Overall, it was a remarkable occasion.

The dinner with the Queen was inevitably more formal, though not excessively grand. It was the first time she had dined with a retiring Prime Minister since Churchill in 1955. Wilson was the fifth Prime Minister to whom she had bid farewell (with three more to follow so far). She was quietly dressed with less glitter than at her usual state banquets, wearing a lovely dark shawl. The dinner was good and the wine superb, with a 1945 claret and a 1931 port (two important years in Labour history, the first a great electoral victory, the second a terrible defeat). The reception afterwards continued quite late, no one able to leave until the Queen herself departed after midnight. Guests were ferried to her for conversation, and I chatted to her about racing and to Prince Philip about Ireland, continuing a deep conversation we had started at Buckingham Palace a year earlier.

Marcia hovered nearby with her escort George Weidenfeld, but I did not see her included with the monarch. In fact Wilson had earlier been concerned about Marcia's presence and had asked Ken Stowe beforehand to clear with the Palace that Marcia would be acceptable as a guest. I was told that Marcia believed she herself had royal blood, being descended from the illegitimate brood of Edward VII – hence the peerage name Falkender, referring to the courtier who took responsibility for the child. Wilson had indicated to Ken Stowe that if Marcia were excluded, whether as a competitor for the throne or for other reasons, he would not invite any other outside guests.

Apparently the sovereign was undaunted by the prospect of the presence of such a powerful relative, and it all passed off peacefully. It was a splendid occasion which I enjoyed immensely, especially the great 1945 claret with its deep and rich taste.

But perhaps my best social engagement then was to play in one of the most memorable football games of my life, a charity game arranged by my old Labour MP friend Tom (now Lord) Pendry in front of over 5,000 spectators at the Stalybridge ground in his constituency. Tom brought in a group of veteran international stars, mainly from the great Manchester clubs, and I – a veteran of forty-two but definitely not a star – played at old-fashioned right half, alongside the 1966 World Cup hero Nobby Stiles and the mighty Dave Mackay of Scotland and Tottenham Hotspur, with England international Mike Summerbee in front of me on the right wing. Opposite were a number of Manchester United heavyweights, including the notoriously tough Scottish international Tommy Docherty. When Docherty tackled me painfully long after I had released the ball, Mackay came up to me and said in a thick Scots accent, 'Don't worry, Bernard, he'll no do that again.' A few minutes later Mackay tackled Docherty with such ferocity that I could hear the crunch from forty yards away. As Dave predicted, Docherty did not come near any of us again. I had the bruise for weeks but was proud to have taken part with so many great players.

The Number 10 farewells followed the big dinners, and the Unit had a farewell party on 30 March, with all the top Whitehall mandarins present. The Prime Minister was detained for some hours in Marcia's Political Office party, where she handed out most of the jewelled bracelets which Eric Miller (soon to be knighted) had provided for her. Harold did not arrive at the Unit until 7.30, nicely sloshed, his face vacuous and his eyes glazed. But he stayed for an hour chatting happily with everyone. When he left, he had to ask Janet Hewlett-Davies to point him the way towards the Private Office. He had no sense of direction even when sober.

Labour's leadership election was very significant for me, since if the Unit were retained, it would determine who would be my next political boss. One potential candidate, Tony Crosland, came with Susan to supper at home in Brookfield Park on the Saturday before the first ballot. He was as always amusing and endearingly indiscreet – including attacking the likely winner Jim Callaghan as 'too bloody conservative'. He admitted to me that his main ambition was 'to beat Roy on the first ballot', but was still not certain whether to stand in the coming round. I advised him to do so, to demonstrate his political seriousness, but to be prepared to be annihilated – which he was. At the last moment he approached Jim Callaghan and offered to withdraw from the ballot and declare his support for Jim (whom he had supported in the 1963 leadership election) in return for a promise to be made Chancellor of the Exchequer in the new Government should Jim win. But the latter refused, making no pledges or alliances.

I visited Roy Jenkins on 17 March, and his frantic team knew that his chances of the leadership were not good. Like Crosland he had not done enough in the recent Government to impress and win over the 1974 intake of MPs. When Roy spoke in Cabinet it was with great authority, but he did not get involved often enough, seeming at times like a sleeping partner in the Government, as if trying to avoid contamination from the debris of his own fracturing party and awaiting the unfolding of some scenario of nemesis for Labour. Wilson thought that he was preparing for his role as a leader of a future national coalition. I always liked and respected Roy and felt that he understandably found much of the left-wing nonsense in the party too distasteful. But the result was a diminution of his personal support in the parliamentary party, leaving him little chance of winning the leadership.

Denis Healey was another major ministerial figure with little chance of success. A man of immense physical and mental energy, he was also an intellectual by inclination with a vast range of interests and talents, and a genuine internationalist who was engagingly frank and funny. He understood the economic issues, but wasted time in theoretical arguments with his economist advisers, which took his eye off the political practicalities of the immediate problems. His instinct, as when at Defence between 1964 and 1970, was to bury himself in his department, where he was always admired. He did too little political networking, making little effort to win over his cabinet and parliamentary colleagues – as during the battle over incomes policy in 1975. He seemed to believe that a mixture of a powerful intellectual argument and bullying would suffice to win the battle.

Denis, often described as 'Labour's lost leader', was in fact too much of a 'loner' – and in some respects too apolitical – to achieve the very top in politics, which is essentially a 'tribal' game. He did not suffer fools gladly. But there were a number of fools among his colleagues who all had votes and he did not get them. On 17 March, before the nominations closed and when Denis was still undeclared as a runner, I was outside the cabinet room talking to Roy Jenkins, when Denis came bouncing up. Roy asked him with a smile if he was 'keeping us guessing about your leadership bid, or keeping yourself guessing?' Denis replied disarmingly, 'A bit of both, actually'.

Jim Callaghan had the best organised campaign, and the early canvasses by the Whips' Office suggested that he would win comfortably. On 17 March he had a serious talk with Wilson, who told me afterwards that 'Jim was very confident, almost measuring the curtains to Number 10.' Reassuringly to me, he reported that Jim had accepted his advice to retain the Policy Unit. He added with a smile that 'you realise, Bernard, that I have retired in order to give the opportunity to an older man.' (Whereas Harold had just turned sixty, Jim was sixty-two.)

After the first ballot on 25 March, Jenkins was in third place behind Callaghan and Foot with a vote in the fifties, and withdrew honourably. Benn also announced his withdrawal to throw his support behind Foot. Crosland went out with only a couple of dozen votes. At the second ballot, on 30 March, Callaghan led Foot and Healey dropped out with only 38 votes – fewer than Jenkins had got on the first round. In the final ballot on 5 April, Foot picked up a few of Healey's soft-centre supporters, but Callaghan rode home with a vote of 176 and a majority of 39 – the number precisely predicted to me by Wilson.

Number 10 was very subdued on that day of the final ballot. It was the last day of Harold Wilson's nearly eight-year rule. No government business was being transacted. The Private Secretaries were reading newspapers. The Policy Unit was still. I met Wilson standing near the Press Association ticker tape and he said it was 'a relief not to have to think about my colleagues'. His face seemed already to have gone flabbier as the tension and pressures of office lifted. He took me on a last tour of the cabinet room, which he had known for over thirty years since first serving in the Cabinet Office secretariat. He searched through the bookshelves – full of books donated by outgoing Prime Ministers and cabinet ministers – looking for anything from Stanley Baldwin, the last Prime Minister to resign, like him, truly voluntarily.

He paused to touch on my personal future. He had alerted Ken Stowe and Janet separately beforehand, as they told me, that he intended to offer me 'something big', which could only mean a peerage. I had discussed this with Joe and had decided to decline graciously, as Joe had done on Friday when offered to go to the Lords. Neither of us wanted to be part of the unsavoury 'lavender list' of Retirement Honours currently under discussion. There were long pauses and silences after he mentioned 'your future'. He clearly preferred me to ask. I said nothing. Then, to my relief, a Private Secretary came in and the moment passed.

The Prime Minister hosted a final lunch for his personal team in the small dining room: for Joe and Janet from the Press Office, Ken Stowe and Patrick Wright from Private Office, for Mary, Albert, Marcia, her sister Peggy and myself. We assembled beforehand in the White Reception Room, this small group standing and waiting for the last rites, quietly and with little more to say to one another before going our separate ways, staring at our shoes. None of us wanted to drink. The sun streamed in from over St James's Park and Horse Guards Parade, with in the background the hum of traffic from Whitehall and The Mall. We all stood with the Prime Minister dutifully waiting for Marcia, who was having drinks in her room, to join us. We waited and waited, often in complete silence, the Prime Minister, his wife, his devoted staff on his last day in Number 10. We waited until two o'clock when Marcia finally arrived, with poor Albert shamefacedly in tow.

So Harold Wilson finished in office as he came in, too often humiliated by this relationship from which for some reason he could not escape. The lunch was brief and sombre, none of us having much appetite or much more to say. Peggy Field sat next to me, friendly and twittering like a bird. At one point, she leaned towards me and whispered: 'My God, you have some steel in you, the way you have stood up to my sister.' I was not sure if it was praise or a complaint. We all drifted away as quickly as politeness allowed.

Joe gave his Press Office farewell party at 4 p.m. Wilson arrived with Marcia at 5.30 and we all sang 'For He's a Jolly Good Fellow'. Then he walked back down the corridor to the front lobby. I followed and watched him go out through the big black front door, nearly twelve years after he had first come into the house as Prime Minister and nearly thirty after he had first entered as a cabinet minister under Clement Attlee. He did not turn to acknowledge those Number 10 staff who were waving him out for the last time. After calling in at the Palace to hand in his resignation to the Queen, he was driven straight to Chequers for his final stay there.

I still have a clear picture of him leaving through the door – slightly stooped, with his hand brushing back his always distinguished grey hair in the breeze, a plump little man in a slightly crumpled suit, apparently casting aside, without a backward look, the famous house, the supreme office which is the ultimate objective of any British politician's dreams.

The sharp contrast with Margaret Thatcher's tearful departure fourteen years later is striking. As with much else, Wilson seemed not really to care. His driver Bill Housden, a perceptive observer of the scene and a man who knew him longer and better than most, once said to me: 'Nothing sticks with him.' Except for Mary and Marcia, personal relations did not usually survive beyond their current utility. Today's and tomorrow's headlines too often mattered more to him. That evening of 4 April 1976, he seemed to have no regrets and no proud memories. Ultimately, I suppose, he saw himself as he once described to me an apparently close colleague whom I loved, Harold Lever: just 'a ship that passes in the night'.

I felt personal concern for Harold Wilson as I saw him leave Number 10. I could not imagine what he would do with his time, deprived of the flow of crises and meetings and papers and colleagues to manage, on all of which he thrived. He had too few genuine personal interests to keep him busy and satisfied. Chairing his coming Royal Commission on the City of London and writing his colourless story of his administration would not be enough. Like many politicians, he had made countless acquaintances around the moving picture of the political world. But he had few real and permanent friends. When he had received the Freedom of the City of London his published special list of 'personal friends', apart from his family and staff, was filled with those who financed Marcia's Political Office. There was not another person who constituted what many more ordinary people would recognise and cherish as a personal friend. And his social hangers-on were bound to desert his ship once he no longer had the glamour of power or the rewards of patronage to offer. He seemed to me to be disappearing through that black door into a black hole, with Marcia guarding the entrance.

I knew that his departure meant that Joe and I would no longer have access to him. Joe saw him again only twice, for cool lunches in their first month away. I saw him occasionally, never by arrangement. He came into Number 10 for a party at the end of July 1976 and we had a friendly chat, him telling me all about his new book. He returned three months later to report complaints from Marcia that our new regime was no longer treating the Israelis well enough. It was an echo of the diversions from which we suffered in days that now seemed so long ago. I chatted with him while he waited to see the new Prime Minister, who only gave five minutes to his predecessor's strange final mission to Number 10.

When I met Harold more often a decade later in the House of Lords he was a shrunken figure, soon afflicted with dementia which rendered him unclear who I was. He did not deserve such a sad decline.

Meanwhile, James Callaghan had travelled from Transport House to kiss hands with the Queen at Buckingham Palace, before arriving to take over the reins at Number 10. There was a pandemonium of journalists, photographers, tourists and general political commerce outside in Downing Street. Earlier, on 19 March, Jim had sent his political adviser Tom McNally, an old personal friend with a marvellous sense of humour, to inform me that he wanted me to stay and run the Policy Unit for him. Tom said, 'You must be at your desk when Jim comes in', before adding with a wide grin, 'But he is not making a similar offer to Marcia.'

So I could relax about my job security for a while longer. Tom occupied Marcia's room, enquiring, 'Should I have it exorcised?' Tom McCaffrey, Jim's wary and wily Press Officer, took over Joe's office with the bow window looking over Downing Street. He cleaned away the empty bottles and told me that he proposed to sack all of Joe's assistants and 'make a clean start'. I wasn't sure about that. I also chatted with Jack Cunningham, Jim's smart and straight Parliamentary Private Secretary whom I came to like more and more over the years.

I went up to the study and carefully knocked before entering – Jim was reputed to be much more formal than Harold – and he warmly welcomed me into the team, which was basically the two Toms and Jack Cunningham. Audrey Callaghan was very friendly and supportive. After his first television broadcast was done, he announced that they were now going home to their modest little flat in unfashionable Kennington 'to have an early night'. So I went home early too. We had changed trains in Number 10 without too many hitches. But life there was clearly going to be different.

Twelve

HAROLD AND MARCIA

S adly, Harold Wilson did not retire in the warm glow of approval for the remarkable political career which he had chosen voluntarily to bring to an end at the age of sixty, departing from Downing Street amid a crescendo of media and public disapprobation of his final honours list which undoubtedly left a stain on the rest of his life. How on earth could he have allowed this to happen? As a close witness deeply saddened by this final great error (and as someone who, along with Joe Haines, made it clear that I did not wish to be part of this particular list), I shall try to record the background to how it developed in the context of his relationship with Marcia Williams.

Firstly, it should be understood that this was a Resignation honours list, traditionally reserved for personal service to the Prime Minister. Usually it contains devoted *personal* staff – political aides, personal secretaries, chauffeurs and such like. It is partly a recognition of past personal services to the Prime Minister, partly a compensation for the career disruption (sometimes terminal) which the Prime Minister's resignation usually imposes on his staff. The Resignation List is quite distinct from the regular annual honours lists which are supposed to recognise contributions made by members of the public to political and public life.

Some of the shock which greeted Wilson's Resignation List (which began to leak to the media before it was officially published) derived from the fact that many of its constituents did not fit into this category of service to the Prime Minister. Those of his staff who were honoured – the driver Bill Housden, the cook Mrs Pollard, three secretaries from Marcia's Political Office and a few of the Number 10 regular civil servants – were on a separate 'personal list'. Apart from Albert Murray, most of those on the main Resignation List were outside figures. Indeed, some were barely known to Wilson and were identified as enemies of the Labour Party.

But they were mostly close to Marcia. Among the controversial peers was Joseph Kagan, a textile manufacturer who had met Wilson and Marcia two decades earlier and, along with such other Wilson peers as Lords Plurenden, Kissin and Schon, shared an interest in trade with the Soviet communist bloc. Kagan helped with major donations to finance Marcia's Political Office (and his secretary married Marcia's brother Tony). He had also provided Marcia's first house in Wyndham Mews. He was an unpleasant thug who threatened with physical violence anyone – including women – who stood in his way. Peter Jenkins, the distinguished journalist, told me that Kagan tried to use him to procure young women for him. His former secretary said to me that he was 'a nasty and unprincipled man'. Certainly Kagan was not an ideal member of a retiring Prime Minister's honours list – as was confirmed when he was jailed in December 1978 for serious currency offences.

Less controversial, but still surprising, were the two show business brothers Lew Grade and Bernard Delfont, whom Marcia had included in Wilson's sixtieth birthday party. Several stars from her film world were also honoured. Most surprising in the list of peers was the economist John Vaizey, a friend of Marcia who in print had been a savage critic of Harold Wilson. When Harold Lever had recently visited Vaizey's Brunel University to receive an honorary degree, Vaizey ostentatiously boycotted the formal lunch and wrote to Lever afterwards saying it was because of his total opposition to Harold Wilson and all he stood for.

Least surprising among the new peers was George Weidenfeld, a generous publisher and social host to both Wilson and Marcia. Weidenfeld, publisher of my Morrison book, gave glittering parties at his home on the Chelsea Embankment, to which I was at first invited. But I always felt nervous there, like a moth approaching the flame. The atmosphere was heady, with publishing deals being done in corners and beautiful middle-aged ladies being tempted to display hitherto unsuspected literary talents writing books for George. Young women with upwardly mobile aspirations trawled the room. I was aware of Marcia's hawk eyes watching me disapprovingly, waiting to pounce if I made a false social or political move. Later, when my relations with her were totally hostile, I was usually excluded from George's treasured invitation list. He was Marcia's man.

The knighthoods in the list created even more media astonishment. James Hanson and James Goldsmith were outstanding in commerce, and Hanson certainly deserved recognition in a less personal list. But neither knew Wilson personally and both were vociferous in denunciation of his policies. Each had given large sums of money to finance the Tory party fighting against Wilson in the two recent general elections. Over dinner with me in 1974 the buccaneering Goldsmith denounced Wilson, his politics and all he stood for. Goldsmith's knighthood was intriguingly described as 'for services to exports', which was curious in view of the fact that his company, Cavenham Foods had only 0.4 per cent of its sales overseas. His contact point was Marcia, who had sought in recent months to arrange meetings for him with the Prime Minister.

On 9 January 1976 Marcia arranged dinner between the Prime Minister and Goldsmith and later that month the latter went to Chequers. There he pressed the PM to intervene with the Singapore financial authorities to persuade them not to prosecute his friend James Slater over alleged malpractice at his company Haw Par – which Wilson did.

Next month she pressed the Prime Minister to appoint Goldsmith to the new National Enterprise Board. Shortly before Wilson retired, Marcia arranged for Goldsmith to have lunch in Number 10 with the Prime Minister. Afterwards, Harold told Joe that 'Jimmy' had promised to make Marcia a non-executive director of a private subsidiary of his Cavenham Foods. 'Paris is worth a mass', he said, showing commendable knowledge of French history.

Many years later, one of Goldsmith's relatives told me that Jimmy had paid towards the cost of the private education of Marcia's sons. She added that Jimmy had expected a peerage and was very angry to get only a knighthood in 1976. He owed that to Marcia.

A final story about Goldsmith, who was a remarkable character, was told me by Arnold Goodman at lunch in the Athenaeum in July 1977. He related how in 1976 Wilson had asked Goodman as his lawyer to set up a charitable trust for himself, Wilson, as beneficiary. The Prime Minister explained that Jimmy Goldsmith would pay in a large amount of money, but had insisted on it being to a charity so that he could claim the tax relief on his contribution.

Goodman refused, saying gently, 'My dear Harold, you have many qualities, but you simply are not a charity.' Wilson had indicated that the money was not for him personally but would be 'passed on'. Goldsmith was an odd relationship into which the Labour Prime Minister had been introduced.

Another knighthood went to Eric Miller, the attractive Jewish boss of Peachey Property Company and a close friend of Marcia, who helped finance the Political Office. According to Lord Goodman, whose law firm was the vehicle for the transaction, Miller purchased Marcia's second house in Wyndham Mews – which Wilson told Albert Murray was intended to be 'a love nest for Marcia and Eric'. The two were very close during 1975, wining and dancing together. He arranged to take her to Israel with him in the company aeroplane but that somehow fell through. Many in the know in Number 10 expected them to marry.

Marcia wrote a touching letter to Albert stating it was quite impossible for her to see Eric Miller for football, dinner etc. unless surrounded by friends because, to put it quite frankly and bluntly, 'he turns me on!' She wrote she was too old a lady to be thrown in this way, adding that she would leave it to Albert to think up a story for him and she would speak to him about money matters as soon as they could do it in crowded surroundings. Meanwhile, she requested Albert to ask Miller for a paper on local rating because she wanted to prove to Wilson that Eric really could produce the goods, as well as the 'goodies'.

When attractive Mrs Miller understandably intervened in late May 1975, complaining about the friendship with her husband, Marcia collapsed and took to her bed – from where she telephoned the Prime Minister in the middle of a conference in Brussels to ask him to persuade Eric not to give her up. Bill Housden told me he overheard a terrible row between Marcia and Harold, sitting in the car outside Lord North Street, when Harold claimed he had a nine-page letter from her asking him to intervene and persuade Eric to divorce his wife and marry her and to reward him with a peerage – a story which Harold repeated to his Deputy Press Secretary next day. Apparently the Prime Minister declined to get too involved in these domestic diversions.

The friendship continued for much of the rest of that year. When the police later investigated the affairs of Peachey Property they discovered payments to 'clients of Goodman, Derrick solicitors' made in November 1975, which were traced through Number 10, though the money was repaid soon afterwards. The administrators also later enquired about the large amount of time Miller had spent away from his company and with Marcia and Number 10. But a rift emerged and Marcia excluded Eric and his wife from the annual Number 10 party for disabled children (they usually provided and personally wrapped the presents). When the Board of Trade began investigating Peachey's affairs in early 1976, Marcia approached the then President, Stanley Clinton-Davis, effectively telling him to stop the enquiry into Miller's company. Stanley, a courteous and able lawyer, told me in 2001 that the letter was signed 'PP Harold Wilson, Prime Minister'. He telephoned Marcia to explain why he could not stop such an enquiry. She angrily demanded that he must listen to the arguments of her friend and expert on corporate affairs, James Goldsmith. Stanley saw Goldsmith and told him it would be improper for him to intervene in this way, which the latter accepted.

Miller remained on the Honours List, although, like Goldsmith, with a knighthood not a peerage. He shot himself in 1977 before the censorious DTI Report on his role in treating Peachey as his personal fiefdom appeared. I liked Eric, and especially the way he always arrived in Downing Street in a London taxicab, which he sensitively felt more appropriate for a Labour Prime Minister than arriving in his Rolls Royce – though in fact his company had purchased both the cab and its driver for his personal use. But he was another odd one on Wilson's personal list.

Wilson's team in Number 10 had been aware for some time that Marcia was formulating proposals for an honours list which might create difficulties for the Prime Minister. Early in December, Wilson and Marcia had a row over honours, with her insisting on certain names and him resisting them. Afterwards he told Janet Hewlett-Davies, his Deputy Press Secretary, that Marcia had insisted that he had obligations to her from long ago. He claimed to have replied that 'because of that doesn't mean that I have to spend twenty years penal servitude afterwards'.

On 17 March 1976 Albert Murray told me that he had seen in her office Marcia's long list of candidates for peerages. That same day Ken Stowe came to see me, very worried about the proposed list, which he said was much too long and quite different from a normal Resignation List, 'which is supposed to be small and for those personally linked to the outgoing Prime Minister.' Joe Haines came to my office on 30 March after the PM's final session of parliamentary questions. He was deeply disturbed. He had seen the Resignation List. He said it was a very long list of peerages and knighthoods, in Marcia's handwriting on a sheet of her coloured notepaper – which he then described as 'lavender' (she later said it was 'pink'). He commented that 'some of them are people that Scotland Yard might in due course wish to interview'.

The names on the list, written out by Marcia, had been ticked by Harold in his familiar green ink. The only name which he had apparently crossed out was that of the PR friend of Marcia, Will Camp, allegedly a gossip and too close to *Private Eye* for Wilson's taste. Heading the peerages were David Frost and John Vaizey, followed by George Weidenfeld, Joseph Kagan, Illtyd Harrington (a London politician friend of Marcia's) and the tap-dancing Grade brothers. Others on the long list were James Goldsmith, James Hanson, Jarvis Astaire the boxing promoter, John Terry from the Film Board, Donald Gosling (a tycoon from National Car Parks) and various stars of stage and screen.

That evening, after the Policy Unit farewell party, Joe and Janet begged Harold to take a more responsible attitude to his list. But he seemed uninterested, as if he had washed his hands of it, and responded by talking of awarding himself a Companion of Honour – rather as if that was the only honour in which he was personally involved. On the day in April when he left Number 10, with honours 'leaks' already in the press, I talked to him beside the ticker tape and he said that he could not understand why he was being 'personally attacked' over the honours list. 'Bernard', he said, 'I barely know half of them.' He seemed to take it for granted that it was not really 'his' list and was surprised that the media did not know that.

Actually the capacity of staff in Number 10 to influence honours lists was apparently only a recent development. I then knew little of the history of honours in Britain but I received a background briefing when on a quiet Friday evening, 19 March 1976, after Wilson had announced his resignation, I dropped in to see the famous Freddie Warren, who had run the Chief Whips' Office for many years under many administrations, starting when Ted Heath was Chief Whip.

I always enjoyed talking to Freddie because he, together with his beloved assistant Dot, knew where all the political bodies were buried. I walked along the corridor which links Number 10 through the Chancellor's house to Number 12 (then the Chief Whip's office), and in the half light of dusk I saw Freddie sitting at a desk covered in papers, glasses and bottles, including an empty champagne magnum. He was fast asleep, upright in his desk chair, looking like an old bird with his glasses slipped down to the end of his beaked nose.

I spoke. His eyes blinked open and he immediately said, 'Have a drink, old man', then poured us both huge whiskies. He was already full of drink, but his eyes and mind were bright and clear. He began by praising Joe and me for doing 'a great job and keeping that Harold Wilson on the rails'. He said that we should both have 'something big' in the coming honours (he himself had a well-deserved knighthood in the 'personal' list). I replied that Joe and I would both decline since we did not wish to be part of Marcia's patronage list. He then explained how, when he first joined the office, the Chief Whip was the Patronage Secretary and handled most political honours. But he claimed that in 1966 Wilson took patronage away from the Chief Whip and brought it into Number 10: 'That gal Marcia insisted on it.' He said that no Chief Whip other than the young John Silkin would have agreed to it, and that Whitehall had been against. Freddie asserted that Silkin was 'over-promoted' in return for handing over the patronage. I have no idea if this was true, but it is intriguing and Freddie was in a strong position to know.

The list continued to create waves inside Whitehall and Westminster as well as in the media. The Political Honours Scrutiny Committee challenged eight of the names, especially Goldsmith and Kagan. Its chairman Lord Crathorne, who was the source of some of the advance information in the newspapers, was quoted in the *Sunday Times* as saying that it was 'an abuse of the system' and that 'these fellows have never done anything'. Several Whitehall departments were consulted and reacted with hostility. Ken Stowe showed me their official responses in Private Office: there were strong objections from several official quarters to some of the recommendations. One immediate consequence was to slow down the publication of the list – which Wilson had hoped to do the next (Maundy) Thursday because there would be no newspapers on the following day,

Good Friday, and no meeting of Parliament the following week. There were also late efforts to improve the quality of the list with the inclusion at the last minute of highly respectable names. Max Rayne (who certainly deserved recognition for his great charitable donations) only received his offer letter from Wilson on a Tuesday and was asked to accept by return of post for an announcement forty-eight hours later.

When the Resignation List finally appeared at the end of May, certain names had been demoted or dropped. Goldsmith, Hanson and Miller were demoted from peerages to knights. Others were removed altogether – David Frost following objections by Lord Goodman because he currently had a television contract with the Prime Minster. The Labour Party was predictably enraged at the list. Over 100 Labour MPs signed a Commons motion attacking it for containing 'the less acceptable faces of capitalism'. Jeff Rooker, the splendid Birmingham MP of impeccable integrity, spoke for the PLP when he said: 'I have fifty people in my local party who have each done more individually than this lot put together.' The regrettable fact to a Labour person is that of the total of 103 Labour peers appointed by Wilson as Prime Minister, only one third proved to be regular Labour supporters in the Lords lobbies, and one in ten never voted with Labour at all. (Marcia herself does sometimes attend and vote, but in twenty-nine years so far has never contributed in the Chamber.)

The Times in its main leader on 27 May described the list as 'a bizarre one for a socialist ex-Prime Minister', saying that a majority of the honours went to 'capitalists of a tough risk-taking type ... These are the very people whose lives are the contradiction of everything for which the Labour Party stands ... Are they really his friends for whom he feels the warmth of personal gratitude?' The answer to the latter of course is 'No'. As Harold said to me on the day he left office, he barely knew half of them. It was a sad way for Harold Wilson to go. One of his cabinet colleagues was quoted in the *Sunday Times* of 30 May 1976 as saying with clear regret: 'A pity about Harold. Such a graceful exit – and then he had to do this on the doorstep.'

So how on earth could Wilson have allowed it to happen? The notorious honours list clearly reflected, and can only be explained by, the great influence of Lady Falkender over Harold Wilson. Wilson often took her political advice, which in my time with him was sometimes – and earlier was usually – shrewd and perceptive.

But it went far beyond that. Her behaviour towards him and others who worked for him was often unusual, even intolerable, yet he always tolerated it. He was at times clearly afraid of her, as I illustrate below, and I quickly realised that for some reason he dare not correct or rebuke her. He certainly did not dare to get rid of her. When she refused to go through the process of security clearance required for employment in government, he took the risk of signing her 'PV' – Positive Vetting – clearance even though she would not allow the security forces to interview her. Whenever under attack by her, he would increase his intake of brandy. Then by evening he became strange and aggressive, his brow lowered, with a scowl on his face and a curious hunted look in his hooded eyes.

I experienced the extent and curious nature of her influence very early in the 1974 Government. In the last weekend of March she phoned me from her country house in Buckinghamshire. She complained that Harold was already becoming 'happy and complacent' and she was 'punishing' him, refusing to take his telephone calls, and when he visited her in Wyndham Mews 'I gave it to him with both barrels.' She said (and I noted it): 'I'm getting him worried. He knows that I am up to all his tricks. I will keep playing with him and he will come out here soon. He knows that I've got his number.'

I took on board her clear and true message that none of the rest of the team in Number 10 had influence over Harold Wilson to compare with hers.

Her sphere of activity was restricted after 1974 by the existence of my Policy Unit and also by the exceptionally close alliance between the other two senior members of the Prime Minister's triumvirate of personal advisers, Joe Haines as Press Secretary and myself as Senior Policy Adviser. But she remained the person closest to Harold Wilson, and when she chose to intervene he usually gave her wishes priority over all others. At Chequers at weekends she enjoyed and exploited unrestricted access to him.

He often indulged her wildest whims almost like a daughter (for example treating honours like chocolates given to her to keep her quiet and happy) and, equally, seemed to fear her like a fierce mother (as when he physically hid from her intimidating telephone calls). She had the magical power both to switch on and switch off his lights. She was also very adept at mobilising his demons and evoking his alleged enemies. Somehow, over the previous twenty or so years, she had frightened Harold Wilson and reduced him to a dependence which was sometimes pathetic to observe. He occasionally showed resentment at that dependence and tried briefly to shake it off. But in the end he for some reason needed it and always reverted into subjugation.

Harold and Marcia's relationship was one of great intensity and complexity, which no one coming late to the scene, as I did, can presume fully to analyse and understand. But its existence mattered to everyone who worked in Number 10 trying to serve the Prime Minister. It inevitably pervaded our lives, sometimes intruding merely as rumbles of distant thunder, sometimes striking centre stage like lightning. It was an influence which clearly met some deep need in Harold and may well have assisted him greatly in his rise to the top of British politics, providing the necessary aggression and jagged edge which was lacking in his own rather soft personality.

But it also had a debilitating effect on our everyday life working for Wilson. The reality was that anything we did or proposed for the Prime Minister – giving policy or media advice, suggesting meetings, fixing appointments, writing speeches, travelling with him to overseas negotiations, or indeed attending any engagements in relation to our jobs, was always likely to be subject to the intervention of the Political Secretary. Because she had such influence over the Prime Minister – though only fitfully exercised in my time with him – these activities or proposals were likely to be changed or rejected, often without apparent rational cause. Working for Wilson was like walking through an endless minefield, constantly wary, looking and listening for any signs of where the next hidden explosive might lie.

Exercising influence on the Prime Minister in Downing Street requires above all access to his ear and, to a lesser extent, the capacity to determine who else has access to him. The endless throng of claimants wishing to talk to the Prime Minister is enormous. It has to be sifted and in many cases resisted. Those who have access have influence on the levers of power. Marcia controlled access to and from the whole political and personal side of Wilson's life, including all aspects of the Labour Party, much of his finances and his patronage. Any one of the team who inadvertently trespassed on her broad territory, did so at considerable personal and professional peril.

In my time she tightly controlled the political and personal area of communication to and from Wilson, on paper or in person. She received his mail, often at Wyndham Mews where she drafted replies and often signed on his behalf. With the exception of civil servants, his governmental colleagues, the press and a few special acquaintances, anybody wishing to see or talk to the Prime Minster was advised to make contact with and through her. Her disapproval meant exclusion. This strategic position ensured her considerable powers, since others had to please her in order to reach the Prime Minister. From her critically located offices, one opening on to the Cabinet Room lobby in Number 10, the other adjacent to the Prime Minister's office in the Commons, she acted as an impressive and effective dragon at his gate. A number of people he respected (such as Lords Goodman, Kissin and Lever) attempted to wean Wilson away from this dependency. He told them that he neither wanted nor dared to face the consequences (whatever that might mean) of the liberation which they advised. I never made any such suggestion to him.

I never underestimated Marcia's abilities – her determination, her manipulative skills, her sharp political insight – nor the permanence of her influence over him. Of course these abilities were certainly more in evidence in earlier times than mine. I had not seen her whole life's journey as Wilson's main confidante during much of his climb to the top of the slippery pole of British politics. But I did see the dramatic power of her personality, exercised both creatively and destructively, and not only exercised on the Prime Minister himself. Once launched against any human perceived personal enemy (such as myself at times), her tirades were very impressive. Her victims were at times reduced to shivering and even blubbering wrecks. Wilson himself fled to the solace of the brandy bottle. The sad experiences of the Prime Minister's lovable personal assistant, Albert Murray, a former Member of Parliament and government Minister of State, a kind and decent man, and of Wilson's official driver Bill Housden, whom she often borrowed for her own personal use, were but two examples of grown men who I saw reduced to trembling fear.

The basis of her aggressive power lay of course in the realisation by her victims that she could normally mobilise the support of the Prime Minister. Without that guaranteed backing her style would have been less effective – indeed would have been unacceptable in any normal working or social context. Those who refused to be controlled by her, such as Arnold Goodman (whom she described to me as 'evil', he in return calling her influence 'poisonous'), Joe Haines, myself, Robin Butler and Robert Armstrong could find themselves subject to remorseless hostility and attack. As her sister had commented to me at that final lunch, it required some degree of steel to keep Marcia at bay. Harold Wilson lacked it.

As private individuals, Harold's relationship with Marcia, however odd it might seem to some, would have been their own affair and nobody else's business. But he was not just a private individual. He was the Prime Minister of the United Kingdom and Leader of one of its two main political parties.

So it had a public importance. It was also very important to me and to others on his staff because Marcia's problems absorbed so much of his time and energy. Above all, they diverted him from important matters of government. So it may help future historians and biographers if I describe their relationship as I saw it and the many diversions of the Prime Minister's and our time which resulted from it.

The notorious 'land deals scandal' in April 1974 was the first major such diversion which I observed in his Government. For two weeks, the Prime Minister, Joe, Albert and I were almost totally absorbed in what seemed a jungle of hysteria. None of us could focus on the major problems facing the new Labour Government – on Northern Ireland, Rhodesian sanction-busting, or the current industrial relations conflicts. I was able to give too little time to the urgent need to establish the staffing and working routine of my new Policy Unit. For the Prime Minister it was much more serious. Marcia insisted on constantly involving him in the land deals affair, insisting he talk to her, talk to her lawyers, and attack the press.

Her style of language when referring to him often seemed to me shockingly aggressive, especially relating to someone who was the Prime Minister of our country. She several times threatened in my hearing to give the press information which she claimed would 'destroy him', once ominously tapping her handbag and implying that it contained the fatal ammunition to destroy him. Wilson was visibly intimidated and frightened by these threats. They clearly agitated some fears deep within him, real or imagined.

For most of these early weeks in government I was genuinely sympathetic to Marcia, especially because of the intolerable harassment of her by the press, although deeply resenting the diversion of the Prime Minister's precious time away from the critical problems facing the Government and the nation.

Several critics have claimed to me that she (like Wilson) was 'paranoid' about the press. On my observation, she was indeed obsessed with the press, but she was justified since parts of it were clearly trying to destroy her (and, through her, Wilson). The journalists and photographers simply behaved like hooligans. Also, part of the *Daily Mail's* central 'evidence' for the 'scandal' was based on a Wilson letter and signature forged by Ronald Millhench, soon to go to jail for the offence. Their later adding to the attack the cruel story of her two illegitimate children was a further sewage tactic in which sadly part of our press specialises. But feeling sympathy for her treatment by the press should not disguise the basic question of whether a Prime Minister should be diverted, or allow himself to be diverted in this way.

The 'land deals affair' broke on 3 April 1974 with full-page spreads in the *Mail* and the *Express*. The 'allegation' was that Marcia had joined with others to form a company to speculate in land development of some coal slag-heaps near Wigan in Lancashire. Also involved in the company were her brother Tony Field, Lord Arwyn (elevated by Wilson in his previous Government) and a partner who was a tax exile in the Isle of Man. The scheme's profitability allegedly depended on the company's getting planning permission to develop the land and for a new road through the site linking it to other local main roads, and there were hints of links between someone in the local planning department and Wilson's Huyton constituency. The main accusation by the press against Wilson, though later withdrawn, was that he had used his position as Leader of the Opposition to help the company to try to obtain planning permission. This was particularly damaging to Wilson in view of his frequent attacks on property speculators and on anyone becoming rich through financial speculation rather than through the Victorian values of hard work which he personally advocated, and indeed personified.

For most of that first day of the crisis the Prime Minister was totally involved in the affair, sending his lawyer Arnold Goodman to issue libel writs against the *Mail* and the *Express*. In the evening he took Joe, Albert and me into the Cabinet Room to discuss it. He was violent against the press, saying: 'If they want it dirty, they can have it dirty.' He made wild references to Jeremy Thorpe's alleged homosexuality, to the sexual activities of two newspaper proprietors, and how in the Lord Lambton sex scandal the Heath Government allegedly improperly kept a prostitute witness abroad so that she could not make embarrassing statements in this country. He demonstrated how unfair criticism from the press always drew the worst out of him.

Joe and I argued strongly that he must not stoop down into the sewer with the press, not least because it was much more familiar ground to them and they were better at it. Joe warned that if he did, journalists would hit back at Marcia, high-lighting her various houses and illegitimate sons. But Wilson found it hard to listen to us. He was clearly hurt, at times pathetic. He said to me: 'She has been with me for twenty years. You have been here for only a few weeks. She gets all this.' He begged me to go to see Marcia, 'if only for a few minutes'. He asked me also to write a kind letter to her. He showed no awareness that her own behaviour might at times expose him to criticism and divert him from performing his job as Prime Minister.

The following day's press was dominated by the 'land deals scandal' and Wilson faced heavy questioning over it in the Commons. Before Cabinet, he drafted a personal Commons Statement which I thought was terrible, full of attacks on the press and unconvincing justifications. I sent a memo to him in Cabinet stating that it was 'inviting disaster'. He came out of Cabinet to see us in the study and reluctantly agreed to pressure from Joe and myself to change it. I also phoned Marcia, who was weeping over the phone. She then phoned Wilson and demanded his help in removing the gang of journalists who were blockading her house. So he asked Albert and me to go to remove them, 'physically if necessary'. We took a taxi to smart Wyndham Mews in Marylebone and found hordes of journalists and photographers completely blocking the road and the entrance to her house. This was my first experience of what is known as 'doorstepping', a euphemism for press hooliganism. The journalists were constantly ringing the doorbell, beating on the door, shouting and pushing written demands for interviews through the letterbox, climbing on the window sills and trying to take photographs through Marcia's curtained windows, including her bathroom.

I had attended many rough football matches but had never seen worse hooligan behaviour. Had they been any group other than journalists parading under the spurious protection of 'freedom of the press' they might have been arrested for breaches of the law. Until recently I had been an enthusiastic supporter of the freedoms of our vibrant press. Experiences such as this, and others later, rapidly converted me to the need for an effective law of privacy. I concluded that no society which allows people such licence to abuse fellow citizens could be considered fully civilised.

I forgot my earlier clashes with Marcia. When Albert and I had fought our way to and through her door, we found her in tears, totally distraught. I quickly pushed out again through a volley of abusive questions – one hack shouting with the customary malicious ignorance of the trade: 'Are you fucking Marcia, Donoughue?' – and went to buy her a bottle of champagne and some ice cream.

But I was surprised to find that her main reaction was to blame and violently attack Harold Wilson, who seemed to me to be spending his whole life trying to support and console her. She claimed that was all his fault, that he had abandoned her and left her alone to look after herself.

When Albert and I returned to Number 10, we found the Prime Minister still totally involved in Marcia's concerns. He was incandescent against the press and proposed to Joe as his Press Secretary a new strategy to 'freeze them out', including ignoring or even abolishing the parliamentary press lobby. He said he would now bring in a Privacy Bill (though regrettably he did not carry this out). He had also naively claimed that Marcia was innocently involved only in 'land reclamation' and not 'land speculation'. He as always began to think in terms of plots, and saw Marcia's old sparring partner George Wigg as behind the whole story, still plotting to have revenge.

What concerned me most was that the Prime Minister's mind was totally taken up with these Marcia diversions, and he was not focussing at all on his official duties. In the middle of a discussion on 'land reclamation', the Irish Prime Minister Liam Cosgrave arrived for official talks on Northern Ireland. Power-sharing was disintegrating, but I could see that the Prime Minister's mind was wholly elsewhere, on the 'Wigan Alps' in fact.

Just before going into the Cosgrave lunch, he asked Joe, Albert and myself to return to the siege of Wyndham Mews. From there we took Marcia to her lawyers in Grays Inn, where we wasted several hours waiting for four libel writs to be issued. Returning together to Wyndham Mews in the late afternoon, we learned that the *Daily Express* would publish tomorrow the story of Marcia's two illegitimate children – whose father was Walter Terry, a journalist on the *Express* itself. It was growing very murky.

Marcia then collapsed in tears. We arranged for police cars to intercept the Prime Minister en route to Oxford (no mobile phones then) to address the University Labour Club. The atmosphere in Wyndham Mews verged on hysteria, with Marcia ranting against the Prime Minister for having 'deserted' her and for having 'fled to Oxford to hide'. Her ever-loyal elder sister Peggy made endless cups of tea. Maids loitered, clearing away dirty cups and glasses. Joe, Albert and I tried to offer support. The gang of journalists was still rampant outside. With all the curtains pulled, to me it seemed like being in a military bunker under direct attack. I sensed what it was like in the cellars in the last days of Berlin as the Russians moved in.

Fed up with it all, I fought my way through the mob to go home to Brookfield Park, very late for a dinner party with friends already at table. Just as I began to eat, the telephone rang. It was the Prime Minister, calling from a public call box at the Oxford University Labour Club meeting.

Noisy students milled around him and I could hear him repeatedly shouting 'close the bloody door'. Apparently Marcia had just contacted him and said she was 'desperate'. He told me that she was threatening 'to reveal all' – whatever that might be – if he did not help her. So he asked me to return to her house and 'pull the telephone wires out of the wall to stop her speaking to the press.'

I was not sure if this was appropriate behaviour for the Prime Minister's Senior Policy Adviser, but I swallowed hard, again apologised to my guests, and left for the battlefront at Wyndham Mews. There I found Albert nicely 'sloshed' and Terry Lancaster from the *Daily Mirror* persuading Marcia to sign an article Joe had drafted for her. Marcia herself and Peggy were in a state of near nervous collapse. I decided not to attack her telephone lines since she seemed unlikely to communicate coherently with anyone that night, and returned home again to my bewildered dinner guests as rapidly as politeness would allow.

It had been an incredible day, much closer to fantasy or nightmare than to normal political reality. I was rapidly learning that working for Harold Wilson contained more diversions than I had originally anticipated.

The following Monday, 8 April 1974, the Prime Minister made his statement to the Commons about the land deals affair. Joe, Robert Armstrong and I worked on it most of the morning. Wilson was concurrently holding talks with the Prime Minister of Jamaica, but he kept leaving that meeting to rush into us with fresh paragraphs angrily denouncing the press (which we fought to exclude). He was completely distracted and in no condition to deal properly with Jamaica or any government business. On the Wednesday, when at Harold's request I telephoned Marcia to try to cheer her up, she was far from appreciative, becoming verbally abusive, threatening and at times incoherent. She said that she would insist on going to the Scillies for Easter with the Prime Minister. 'That will embarrass him.' She described Harold as 'the King Rat. That is what he is. A King Rat.'

I was appalled and kept a detailed note. Albert was then sent round to Wyndham Mews again to try to help her, but she abused him and threw him out of the house. Poor Albert, a gentle and affectionate soul, returned with tears in his eyes. By this time, I had virtually exhausted a whole range of emotions in relation to Marcia: from sympathy and support, to irritation and impatience, and now being quite fed up. I decided from then to have as little as possible to do with her and to get on with my Policy Unit work, which had been completely neglected for the past week.

At times in this land deals crisis Wilson completely lost his control, yet at others he seemed to view it with quiet detachment, as if it had nothing to do with him. In the middle of the saga, with the media and the Conservatives in uproar, demanding his resignation and Marcia's dismissal, and with his own party deeply offended, Wilson summoned me to discuss the situation. He was not annoyed with those who had brought this terrible racket down on his head. In a curious way he seemed to be positively enjoying it. He said to me that it was 'just like Agatha Christie. We are still at the last but one chapter. It could be any one of five who did the forgery.' (Unaccountably in his mind the quintet included Marcia and her brother.) He asked me how I thought the final chapter would finish. He had absorbed almost every detail of this saga and had spent the whole of the earlier cabinet mentally trying to fit the final jigsaw pieces into place. To him it was a fascinating game, and he behaved as if he were not really part of it and had no control over the action nor the characters in it. I am not really an Agatha Christie fan, much preferring Elmore Leonard, and was anyway more concerned with the total distraction of our precious time from the serious business of government than with who actually did the forgery. But Wilson's approach was to me fascinating and certainly, for a Prime Minister, different.

Marcia's and the Prime Minister's 'gagging writs' effectively took the land deals affair off the front pages. But the affair occasionally bubbled to the surface in Number 10 and diverted Wilson's attention over the following two years. In the New Year of 1975, when her libel action against the *Evening Standard* was approaching settlement, Marcia suddenly exploded at Joe and said she would 'bring you all down'. She threatened to 'destroy' Wilson and claimed that he was 'up to his neck' in the land deals. She said that if she was forced to resign she would spend her life writing books exposing Harold, Joe, Albert and me. Joe responded that he would 'earn my living reviewing them.' That frisson passed. In June the transcript of the Ronald Millhench forgery trial showed that he claimed to have paid the Field company £340,000 and that they had put up £130,000 of their own money.

Fresh eruptions occurred in September over the tax consequences of the 'land reclamation'. Marcia had apparently been assessed for around £20,000 for her share of the large profits, and her brother Tony for more. Albert and Joe witnessed and reported Marcia's efforts to get the tax deferred or paid by others. The Prime Minister and Lord Goodman were involved, with her pressing the PM to get the Inland Revenue to loosen its grip, and to give Tony a job on the new British National Oil Corporation to help him financially. In November she drafted a letter for the Prime Minister to send to Prince Fahd of Saudi Arabia recommending Tony, who was about to visit that country seeking contracts. The foreign affairs Private Secretary in Number 10, Patrick Wright, objected to it as being an improper use of the Prime Minister's influence.

In March 1976 Wilson sent for Harold Lever to help with these tax liabilities, asking (as Harold explained to me) that Lever's own private bank open an anonymous account to receive donations towards paying off Tony's tax bill. He then changed the proposal and asked Lever to give Tony a loan of £60,000 and in return receive the Wigan slag heaps or Tony's house in Blisworth as collateral. Lever was assured the interest would be paid by a group of long-standing associates, including Frank Schon and Kagan (both elevated to the peerage by Wilson shortly afterwards) and Lord Plurenden (elevated by Wilson in 1975), who all visited Wilson during his final week in Number 10.

But Lever's bank assessed the value of the slag heaps (without the planning permission) as inadequate, and Lever, who told me that he did not wish to get personally involved, withdrew from the affair. Wilson then grew angry and said that 'this sum is only a book-keeping transaction for you.' I have no idea what happened after that, since a few days later Harold and Marcia left Number 10 and the land deals affair went with them.

I apologise for having devoted some space and detail to the 'land deals affair', which might seem trivial. But such trivia had considerable significance. The affair dogged Harold Wilson from the beginning to the end of the time that I worked for him, and it illustrated the complex relationship between my Prime Minister and his closest assistant. It showed that her concerns could dominate his professional life and divert him from the serious task of government. It also demonstrated that Harold and Marcia each shared an extreme sensitivity over and hostility towards our press.

Wilson was fascinated by newspapers. Yet by 1974 he also loathed them for their treatment of himself and Marcia, and the journalists returned this feeling with contempt. Most newspapers and most journalists were by then hostile to him, writing him off as unprincipled, sleazy and weak. Even his unrivalled skills at party management were dismissed as simply further evidence that he was not interested in policies or principles. But above all, journalists were bored with him. He had been on stage for ten years and they wanted a different singer with different songs. Nothing he could do would ever again impress them. One morning in the study after reading a typically malicious piece in the *Mail*, he turned and said to me almost pathetically, 'You know, Bernard, if this afternoon I walked on water like Jesus Christ across the surface of the Thames from the Commons to St Thomas's Hospital, the headlines in the *Mail* and the *Standard* would be "Wilson cannot swim".'

His paranoia had a rational base since they were genuinely out to destroy him. But it was partly his own fault. I told him that he should not read the malicious rubbish in those newspapers and then he would not be hurt. But he was addicted to newspapers and to journalists, even while hating them. He grabbed the first editions late at night, went back for more punishment at breakfast, and spent too much of each day complaining about the rubbish he had read. During my time with him between 1974 and 1976 I felt that somehow he always hoped that the journalists would change tack and again be fair and kind to him as they were in his glory days of 1963–4. He did not realise that journalists are not in the business of being fair and that he could never again be a fresh subject of novel headlines. He was by then just boring copy. Too often, his first instinct when anything went wrong for his Government was to blame the newspaper messengers which reported (and often distorted) the disaster. He could not grasp that among the newspaper malice and lies there actually sometimes was also a real story. With the land deals, it was a genuine story that staff close to the Prime Minister had been speculating in getting planning permission to develop land at a time when Wilson himself was denouncing that very activity, and journalists were justified in writing about it.

After that affair had blown over, his obsession with the press continued. He told me he wanted 'revenge for the press attacks on Marcia'. He launched a Royal Commission on the Press and told me of his intention to abolish the press lobby (finally executed by Joe in June 1975), and he did not hold a single Prime Minister's press conference in Britain for over a year. For the Commons debate on the press in mid-May I urged him not to devote his whole speech just to attacking the media. I said, 'You must rise above that.' He replied significantly, 'I cannot rise above Marcia if I don't attack them.'

There were fresh eruptions in our camp on the first weekend of the October 1974 election campaign when the *News of the World* carried a story announcing that Wilson proposed to make Marcia a minister for the Civil Service in his next Government. Marcia went ballistic, demanding that Wilson order Lord Goodman to issue more writs and himself devote much of that evening's opening

big speeches at Portsmouth and Southampton to attacks on the press. He rushed
back from Chequers to Number 10 to do this, bringing with him some terribly
long and rambling text, which he dictated.

As he left the study to deal with a resigning minister, he said to us, 'Take out
all that stuff attacking the press. It is not a good idea to do it.' But while he was
out of the study, and I was working there alone revising the speech, the telephone
rang and the operator said to me: 'Lady Falkender is phoning from home and is
demanding that the Prime Minister speak to her immediately.' I went straight
downstairs to tell him and reported back to the operator that he would call her in
a couple of minutes. Marcia cut into my call and insisted that the Prime Minister
come to the phone 'straight away or there will be trouble'. A couple of minutes
later she was back on the line demanding that the Prime Minister must give up
everything to talk to her. I saw Wilson scurrying to the privacy of her room to talk
to her.

He returned to the study five minutes later looking very harassed. He said to
me, 'She is in a terrible state.' She had insisted that he restore to his speech all
the attack on the press, with its reference to cohorts of journalists scouring the
nation's dustbins for gossip, which Joe and I had persuaded him to omit from the
first draft. So the secretaries had to prepare another press release restoring all the
original attacks on the press. Wilson meanwhile began to knock back several stiff
brandies. Then he was phoned by Dr Stone and I heard Wilson say, 'Yes, she is
in a terrible state. You must give her plenty of them.'

Wilson was now in not too good a state himself, looking hunted and glazed. He
left Number 10 late for his opening campaign engagement at Portsmouth and in
such a flap that he forgot to take with him either Albert or the speech. So his big
black Rover 3.5 skidded noisily to a halt at the end of Downing Street and driver
Bill Housden came running back into Number 10 to collect both of the forgotten
items – and then nearly missed the train to Portsmouth from Waterloo. As my dad
would say, 'It was quite a circus.'

As a newspaper addict, Wilson inevitably took a close interest in my own clash
with *Private Eye*, which in 1975 alleged that I had leaked government secrets to the
Sunday Times and also that I was giving to the City advice on how to evade taxation
(not until then thought to be a speciality of mine). In reality, my main sins in their
eyes were that I worked for the hated Harold Wilson and, worse, was a close friend
of *Sunday Times* editor Harry Evans, of whom the *Eye* hacks were corrosively
jealous, partly because he was so successful, partly because as an editor he was
firmly committed to accuracy (a form of journalism some of them despised), and
partly because he was courting Tina Brown, a beautiful young writer who was
actively desired by the married Catholic *Eye* journalist Auberon Waugh.

My initial reaction was to ignore these bizarre allegations. But the Prime Minister pressed me to sue, saying that if I did not do so, 'some people' would believe that the allegations must be true (clearly having Marcia in mind there). He also pointed out that the particular allegation of leaking official secrets, if unchallenged, could lead Whitehall to suggest that I should not be allowed to see secret documents.

So I went ahead. However, I did not take action on another *Eye* suggestion that Harry and I were homosexual lovers. Both of us enjoyed that one. The legal procedures which followed taught me the expensive horrors of our libel lottery system and why it is so often no protection for the majority of victims defamed. I heard that *Eye* hacks were phoning up my friends and acquaintances 'digging for dirt' on me – meaning to use it to try to intimidate me to withdraw my case against them. I also received a phone call in Number 10 from an *Eye* scribbler (later employed on the *Daily Telegraph*) threatening that if I did not withdraw my writ they would 'stake out your house, your wife and your children' and would 'destroy you'. Nice people! I offered to meet him personally to thrash him, and was sorry that he did not accept my offer since I suspect a few old Northamptonshire techniques of 'duffing up' would have quickly settled the case. In the New Year of 1976, the *Eye* admitted to my lawyer that they had no evidence whatsoever for any of its allegations, and to Harold Wilson's delight, just before his retirement, settled on me substantial damages and costs. They also settled with Harry Evans on a dozen similar fantasy-based-on-envy defamations.

Marcia's elevation to the peerage in May 1974 as Lady Falkender led to further minor diversions. Wilson told Joe and me that she had been pressing for it and he 'could see no reason to say no'. Joe urged Harold to wait until after the imminent election, when it would be accepted as a fair reward. But Harold said, 'Well, I have promised it and that is that.' In fact the media treated it surprisingly lightly, with 'Lady Marcia' headlines and suggestions that the honour had come to her as 'a complete surprise'. She certainly appeared much happier afterwards, so Harold may well have been right to give it.

Through May and June 1974 after the land deals crisis, Marcia rarely ever came into Number 10. Her mail was ferried from there to Wyndham Mews by the dutiful Bill Housden in the Prime Minister's car. On the return journey, Bill carried messages and papers to Wilson, usually according to Bill including a number demanding my dismissal.

The diversions continued to be launched from afar. One evening in the middle of the Ulster crisis, Wilson went off to have a private dinner with George Wigg, leaving behind in Number 10 a gathering of ministers and top military brass who were discussing the total collapse of civil order and authority in Northern

Ireland. The reason for his expedition was that Marcia and he blamed Wigg for the spate of press stories attacking her. Wilson took with him as ammunition some information on Wigg's mistress and second family, collected by private detectives. He threatened to expose Wigg if he did not lay off Marcia. The visit was a curious priority for a Prime Minister in the middle of the Ulster crisis. He spent much of Sunday 9 June preparing a press statement denying an unpleasant *News of the World* story suggesting that Marcia was a security risk and that the stress of working with her had caused the death of Wilson's earlier Principal Private Secretary, Michael Halls. When Marcia finally came into Number 10 on 10 July it was to discuss with the Prime Minister her writs against various newspapers over the land deals affair. A week later he spent the hours before flying to Paris to see President Giscard talking to Arnold Goodman about trying to stop *The Times* publishing a profile of Marcia.

After a quiet late autumn in Number 10, the New Year of 1975 saw the Prime Minister again engulfed in Marcia's concerns. He went away to the Scillies over the Christmas break, and did not, as she expected, telephone her on New Year's Eve and could not visit her on New Year's Day as he was travelling back to the mainland. She blamed the wretched Housden for not having reminded Harold to do so and threatened to stop him going with the Prime Minister on the overseas trips which Bill so enjoyed. Poor Bill was visibly shaking when he related this to me.

On 16 January she summoned the Prime Minister out of his briefing for Commons Questions and when he returned to us he looked black and slammed the door angrily. At times Wilson escaped to Joe's room knowing that she dare not intrude there. Wilson described January 1975 to me as 'her worst black period'. He said, 'She is going through the roof about everything.' Bill reported that she was 'threatening to bring Harold down.' On 28 January Harold asked me to go to see her at her house 'to try to calm her down' (optimistic, since I usually had a quite contrary effect on her). He said, 'Tell her about any Civil Service plots which you have discovered. That will please her.' In mid-May, Harold told Albert that he was 'completely fed up' with her attacks on him and he was thinking of throwing it all in. Next day he was beginning a meeting on Northern Ireland when she phoned him. At first he refused to take the call, and took a stiff brandy instead. Then he went to his private room and locked the door to keep out intruders who might overhear. When Patrick Wright finally saw him, he reported that the Prime Minister was 'not with it at all'.

For his last few months, Harold was under constant pressure from Marcia to extend his time in office, as described earlier. She also then repeatedly attacked him for being friendly towards Joe's deputy, Janet Hewlett-Davies. On 21 September he was suffering such strong attacks over Janet that he retreated to hide in the flat. When he left Number 10 that day he used the special flat lift and not the main stairs so that she would not see him pass her office door. On 2 November, Harold suffered what he described to Joe, me and to Bill Housden as 'my Black Sunday'. According to Bill, when he drove Wilson over to Marcia's country home, she attacked the PM about Janet and demanded that he instruct Joe never to send his deputy to meetings with the Prime Minister. Wilson rightly and courageously refused to interfere in Press Office arrangements. On the Tuesday, Harold told Joe that when discussing Janet, Marcia's face 'went red with that mad look'.

Certain kinds of occasions were particularly prone to provoke outbursts from Marcia and diversions of the Prime Minister's time.

Visits abroad were an unfailing source of tension and diversion for him, and his first overseas visit of the 1974 administration was to see Chancellor Schmidt in Hamburg on 18 June to discuss our EEC renegotiation. As he was about to board the plane, Marcia phoned to demand that he talk to her. The flight was held up while he called her from an open telephone in the reception hall and I heard him apologise profusely for not having spoken to her earlier, explaining that he had tried several times. There were long silences on his part, with his face growing more cowed as he took the barrels of shot. On his return next evening he went off dutifully to see her in Wyndham Mews.

On the second morning of the Paris Summit in December, when the Prime Minister was renegotiating our EEC terms, Marcia phoned a message to him in the conference hall. She said that her brother Tony was unwell and therefore she required that both Wilson and Dr Stone leave the summit and return from Paris to London immediately. Joe Stone then said to me that it was his professional opinion that she was not always 'properly balanced'. As he had before in Germany, Stone floated a very shocking solution to relieve the Prime Minister of this pressure on him, referring puzzlingly (possibly, though not clearly, humorously) to 'putting her down'. Wilson quickly showed signs of stress and in the afternoon he had to be treated by Dr Stone for an attack of 'racing heartbeat'. During what he called his 'Black New Year' of 1975, the Prime Minister made an official visit to Canada and Washington – my first big trip beyond Europe with him. As Joe Haines and I passed Marcia's room at lunchtime before flying off, we heard her berating Harold because he was going abroad in the hands of the Foreign Office – and especially because he was taking me with him. Albert was in the room and told us later that Harold did not escape until after 2 p.m. When we reached the Washington Embassy, Wilson quickly launched an unprovoked attack on Ambassador Ramsbotham and his officials. We had often seen this kind of response to pressure from the Political

Office, with him demonstrating from afar that he was not actually under the control of the hated diplomats.

In May 1975, Wilson went to a meeting of Commonwealth Heads of Government in Kingston, Jamaica (Marcia vetoed my attending, as I describe below), and then onto Washington, where I joined him. On our return to Heathrow, Harold told us that he would not be going back with us immediately into central London because Marcia had asked to meet him at the airport. The tired party of senior officials and the Foreign Secretary began to disperse for home. I saw Jim Callaghan saunter up to the waiting Prime Minister and say, 'Hard luck, Harold, hard luck. But if you will arrange for these women to meet you ...' The rest of us began to depart from Heathrow one by one in the line of waiting official cars. I was almost the last to leave, sharing a car with Dr Stone, who remained fierce in his anger at the pressure which Marcia put on the Prime Minister (and again referred mysteriously to the need to 'dispose' of her). I looked through the rear window and saw Harold Wilson, the Prime Minister of Great Britain, standing alone, pathetically waiting beside his car.

Next day Bill Housden and the Principal Private Secretary told the rest of the story. Harold finally climbed into his car and asked Bill to drive him around and around the perimeter of Heathrow, so no random photographer would see him waiting. On the completion of each circuit they called in to see if Marcia had yet arrived. She finally turned up an hour later. Joe concluded that this whole farrago was to punish Harold for taking me with him.

Wilson's last official visit abroad was to the Rome summit in November 1975. (I was again vetoed by Marcia at the last moment.) He was far from well, suffering more 'racing heart', and had an exhausting final day of unsuccessful negotiations over oil. Marcia phoned to demand that, late at night, exhausted and unwell, he call her from the airport. The Private Secretaries, who reported all this in great detail next day, stood beside him on an open telephone and overheard them have 'a blazing row'.

State and social occasions often created the same tensions and diversions for the Prime Minister and his staff as did his visits abroad. The Trooping of the Colour and the Beating of the Retreat in June 1975, held just behind Number 10 on Horse Guards Parade, were prime examples. The Saturday of the Trooping ceremony was a beautiful sunny day, and I took Carol and my four small children. Just before the Trooping began, Albert came up sadly to me and revealed that Marcia had persuaded the Prime Minister to issue a humiliating instruction that Albert, I, and our wives and children should not be served any drinks after the ceremony. I shrugged it off as par for the course, but Albert was ashamed to have to tell his lovely wife Anne that she and the boys were forbidden to have a drink on that very hot day.

We were only a marginal part of the diversions at the Trooping. The property developer Eric Miller, then a close friend of Marcia, decided at the last moment not to attend. Marcia was visibly distraught and left the stand in the middle of the Trooping to phone Miller to try to persuade him to come. She tried to get the Prime Minister to do the same. After the ceremony, she went to her room with Harold and, according to Albert Murray, who was present throughout, she shouted at the Prime Minister through much of the afternoon, demanding that Wilson should not retire from office, as he was then planning for the autumn, and making threats about some alleged long-ago financial deal involving Joe Kagan and Frank Schon. Albert tried to leave, but Harold ordered him to remain in the room and 'stay as a witness'. Albert's wife then had to return home by train without him. Marcia finally announced that Harold had now sacked her and she left, though over the next hour repeatedly phoned in to him. Wilson refused to take the calls, lurking across the room away from the telephone and leaving Albert to try to fend her off by claiming that he could not find Harold. It was a curious day all round.

Before the Retreat, six days later, Marcia submitted her version of the Prime Minister's guest list, with over fifty names, including Eric Miller, Rudy Sternberg (Lord Plurenden), others from the Political Office trust and several Israelis. Joe and I were excluded. The only guest personally chosen by the Prime Minister was General Gowan of Nigeria: as he had just broken off all diplomatic relations with Israel, the party was likely to have political interest. On the evening of the Retreat, a long line of Rolls Royces cavalcaded into Downing Street to deliver Marcia's guests. It was an odd prelude to the Prime Minister's imminent introduction of his pay policy of a £6 limit on wage rises for the nation.

State dinners also created diversions. On 15 May 1975, the Prime Minister gave an official dinner for the visiting Prime Minister of Fiji. Marcia arrived twenty minutes after the dinner was scheduled to start and the distinguished guests were kept waiting in the reception rooms. When we finally sat down in the State Dining Room, the food did not appear immediately, having been delayed. Marcia strode across to Patrick Wright, the Private Secretary for foreign affairs, and shouted, 'Don't you dare ever again allow people to sit down if their food is not ready to be served immediately ... Go and do something about it.' Patrick, a civilised man who was later Head of the Foreign Office, just sat still and silently ignored this outburst. He afterwards explained to me that 'I have not come across that kind of boorish behaviour before, so I simply did not know how to respond.' At the end of the meal, as the Fiji Prime Minister began to respond to our Prime Minister's welcome, Marcia rose and marched out of the room – later to return to the post-dinner reception, accompanied by her friend Eric Miller and the singer Frank Sinatra, together with some Italo–American bodyguards. Albert explained to us that she desperately wanted some tickets for Sinatra's coming concert.

Our lunches at Number 10 were a frequent cause of major diversions, involving the periodic sacking of whoever happened to be cook at the time. On our first evening Marcia had appointed me as supremo of the kitchen, with the initial task of ensuring that there were regular lunches available for the Prime Minister and his personal staff. Many previous occupants had complained of the lack of nourishment in there while engaged in very long working hours. The basis of the derided 'beer and sandwiches' with the trade unions in Number 10 during Wilson's previous Government was that there was nothing to eat there and sandwiches could be bought in.

Marcia was soon unhappy with the lunch situation. On our first team lunch we were eating with the Prime Minister in the small dining room, when Marcia suddenly complained because we were eating whitebait. She said seriously that she could not tolerate them looking at her from our plates. Harold solemnly consoled her that the fish were actually 'from the National Home for Blind Whitebait' and so she need not worry because they could not see her. I chuckled at this and added that anyway they were all volunteers, proud to be on offer for the Prime Minister's lunch. She was not amused, attacking the Prime Minister in strong language and then walking out. Harold immediately abandoned his lunch and meekly followed her. The rest of us finished our meal in silence. It was to me an early warning of the storms which lay ahead. Afterwards I went to her room, where she put on her coat and said 'I am leaving for ever.' It was a curious opening performance.

Marcia soon announced that she would refuse to attend any more lunches. Instead, she – their original author – tried to stop them taking place. Wilson capitulated and from late March he virtually ceased to have lunch with his team, a serious loss of contact with our Prime Minister at which we could, during his busy day, usefully discuss serious policy issues.

However, on 1 April, Harold suddenly suggested to us that we all have lunch together. Marcia was not in at Number 10, but she heard of it and telephoned me in the afternoon in my office. In strong language she accused me of conspiring 'to organise a lunch with Harold and without me'. I tried to explain that it was a spontaneous occasion at the Prime Minister's suggestion, but she continued in this vein for half an hour until I finally put the telephone down, needing to get on with my Policy Unit papers. Next day she launched another telephone attack, accusing me of being idle and doing nothing in Number 10. I received the clear impression that she expected me to be intimidated or frightened by her attacks.

From this time onwards, the Prime Minister rarely dared to have lunch with his team in Number 10 and usually, if in the house, he ate alone off a tray in the flat above – often eating the same food which we were eating in his dining room just below. Sometimes Wilson bravely sneaked in to join us for coffee (thus able to assure Marcia that he had not had *lunch* with us). He would quickly slip away saying, 'Don't mention that I was here.' He did break ranks once, on 10 May 1974, when he was in great form all morning as we discussed arrangements for the coming general election campaign. He beamed and said to Joe and me, 'Let's have lunch upstairs.' We did so, planning important details for the coming campaign. As he was finishing his cheese, the phone rang. It was Marcia, demanding that he talk to her immediately. For ten minutes he stood listening silently until he finally slammed down the phone, looked suddenly hunched and his face black, all his buoyancy gone, and he retreated, saying only that he was going to take his coffee in his study. Joe followed and Harold asked him if he thought 'she is going round the bend.' After lunch he slipped out of Number 10 to Chequers without saying a word to any of us. It seemed a pity that when Harold Wilson was feeling in such good form, she had intervened to depress him. After that episode, the Prime Minister never again that summer lunched with his team.

Having successfully banished the Prime Minister from the dining room, Marcia now focussed her anti-lunch campaign on our excellent cook, Paddy. In September she demanded that Paddy be sacked as a security risk. Wilson capitulated and instructed Robert Armstrong (who many years later married Paddy) to dismiss her. Before Paddy went, on 12 September, Harold tip-toed into the dining room where his team were lunching and informed us of something that he wanted included in a speech which we were writing for him. He opened by saying loudly, 'I am not lunching here', as if fearing that the room was bugged and the message might get back to Marcia. Shortly afterwards he informed Joe that he would not – as previously promised – be lunching with his team during the election campaign, but would be eating with Marcia in the flat, and that we could join him for coffee afterwards.

Lunches, which should have been a convenient vehicle for discussing policies and tactics, had become a weapon in some curious war of influence over access to the Prime Minister's ear. And the issue simmered on. At the end of 1974, Wilson announced that the Number 10 lunches were to be terminated. But we all missed their collegiate utility, and in February 1975 Robert Armstrong relaunched the lunches, only on Tuesdays and Thursdays (then Commons Questions days), with his then wife Serena, about whom there could be no security risk questions, to cook us some wonderful roast chickens. In April, Marcia announced that Serena's use of the huge kitchens was interfering with the occasional work of Mrs Pollard, Wilson's domestic cook. So Serena went and the lunches again ceased.

But Private Office was reluctant to be defeated by Marcia, who most of the time was sitting out in Wyndham Mews issuing her war instructions. A month later we resumed with another excellent cook, found this time by Robin Butler. (Future Cabinet Secretaries clearly have a good eye for cooks.) But as a concession to Marcia we were forbidden to eat in the official small dining room, and were banished to the shabby pantry. Even this modest compromise arrangement did not last very long. In the New Year of 1976, a new regime was imposed, with lunch attendees strictly limited in numbers, and poor Albert, who had offended in some minor way, permanently excluded. The whole lunch affair was trivial in the extreme, but it was yet another persistent diversion which consumed Wilson's time and nervous energy.

The Political Office itself, which Marcia ran, often from afar, was the nerve centre of such tensions and diversions, with poor Albert and Bill often still shaking when they reported the latest episodes to me. There was actually nothing new in these experiences in the Political Office in 1974–6, as is made devastatingly clear in the unpublished diaries (of which I have a copy) of George Caunt, one of Marcia's office managers in the previous decade.

The furore surrounding the death of Michael Halls, Wilson's Principal Private Secretary in the late 1960s – leading to a court case with allegations that his demise was accelerated by stress – also involved earlier evidence of the tense atmosphere surrounding Wilson's private staff. Worst in my time was when Marcia withheld from Albert his monthly pay cheque as a punishment for some alleged misdemeanour. He had two small children and was permanently short of money on his low office wage. Joe and I saw him virtually in tears because he dare not go home to Anne and tell her that he had no wages. Once Wilson offered to give Albert a personal cheque as replacement for his withheld pay. Albert's widow, who later led a distinguished career in local government, told me that she believed that the stress of working in the Political Office was a major factor in his ill health and fatal early stroke in 1981. His doctor told Anne that his haemorrhage derived from a weakness in an artery related to stress dating back some five to seven years.

Bill Housden, Harold's driver for many years – though he spent as much time working for Marcia as for the Prime Minister – overheard the conversations between Harold and Marcia in the car, often witnessed what occurred at Wyndham Mews or in Buckinghamshire at weekends, and himself regularly experienced Marcia's wrath – and reported regularly to Joe and myself. One example was in early July 1974 when Marcia attacked him for being friendly with

Joe and myself – apparently itself an offence. She then forbade him to enter her house and ordered him to leave her letters on the doorstep and collect the replies from there. Bill often to me threatened to 'go to the newspapers' or to 'record everything on tapes' (which he may have done) – 'that will be my pension', he said. He often drove Marcia shopping, to social engagements, or to her country house on Fridays or at weekends, and this eventually soured his relations with the other pool drivers in Number 10, since they sometimes had to take the Prime Minister on long and late journeys to his Liverpool constituency or to other distant engagements at weekends, getting back late for their families. They formally complained to their employers in the Civil Service Department in November 1975. I found as a government minister in 1997–9 that Whitehall drivers are often the best source of information about their ministerial employers. Bill Housden was certainly in that tradition.

The periodic mayhem inside Number 10 was of more than passing interest to me because the diversions emanating from the Political Office affected the Prime Minister – and so they affected me in my work as his Senior Policy Adviser. When he was distracted, it was difficult for me to get him to focus on policy issues and on the Unit's advice on those issues.

I was also particularly concerned because so many of the offensives launched by Marcia were directed at me personally. My own relations with her had been good during the 1974 election campaign, when I found her contributions perceptive and helpful. I readily accepted her as being in a special position in relation to Harold Wilson, having been closer to him for much longer than any of the rest of the team, and saw myself as the peripheral new boy ready to learn from her long experience of working with Wilson.

But our relations deteriorated the moment I moved into Number 10. At the end of the first week of our Government, in March 1974, I arrived home very tired and found a message waiting that I must telephone Marcia immediately. I did so, but barely managed to speak a word. She shouted at me for seventy-five minutes, attacking Joe, Albert, the Private Secretaries, and especially me. She claimed that we wanted to appoint and run the Government without involving her and that Wilson was no longer consulting her; that Joe, Albert and I were 'ganging up' against her; and above all that 'you are out to replace me.' I found it quite disturbing, not least because I had no intention of replacing Marcia. The Policy Unit's job was quite different from hers in the Political Office.

I certainly did not want to be the cause of trouble for the new Labour Prime Minister. So that night I wrote out my resignation and next morning gave it to

Wilson outside the Cabinet Room, with a brief verbal explanation. He put it in his pocket with a smile and said, 'The fact that you have done that means that it does not have to happen. We can now forget about it.' He added, 'I am very happy with you', and then explained that Marcia had in the past demanded the resignation of all his aides, including Joe Haines and Gerald Kaufman, but he never took any notice. He said he knew that if he did sack them, she would 'threaten to tell the press that I am disloyal to my staff'. He pressed me to try to maintain good relations with her and to phone her at home.

But I continued under pressure from her, with abusive phone calls and reports from Bill and Albert of her criticisms of me to the Prime Minister. I was not confident that he had the backbone to resist them.

In early May 1974 she told Wilson that she was going to issue a public statement saying that she was resigning as his 'Political' Secretary and would remain only as his 'Personal' Secretary – because he was now taking my advice and not hers. Afterwards, Harold told me about it and relaxedly reassured me: 'Don't worry about it, she is very disturbed at the moment.' Next day she left a message for me to phone her and, when I did, launched an attack on me for trying to 'steal' her job. In June, Bill Housden told me that she regularly sent letters by his hand to the Prime Minister demanding that I be sacked. At the end of June, Harold Lever told me that he had been summoned to Chequers to answer some Marcia accusations. She alleged that Lever, Harry Kissin and Arnold Goodman were conspiring to separate Wilson from her, using me as both the instrument and her replacement. She claimed that George Weidenfeld had overheard this plot and had passed it on to her. Lever said that he had denied it all, while confessing to me that he now wished it would come about. But he knew there was no chance of that happening. Kissin confirmed this to me.

Fresh evidence of my alleged plot to replace Marcia emerged in early July 1974, when the *Spectator* published an article by Dr George Jones, the distinguished LSE academic and my co-author on the Morrison biography. It was a work of pure political science, describing the functions of the Policy Unit and its place in the Whitehall machine, but Marcia reacted angrily, complaining to Wilson that the article implied that I had influence over policy in Number 10 and did not fully acknowledge her role. Wilson sent for Joe and said that Marcia was 'raving' about the article. She had summoned him to Wyndham Mews the previous night and given him a real 'hammering'. Joe said that Harold was 'still shaking in his boots'. I went immediately to Wilson to explain the background to the article and that it had been fully cleared through the Press Office prior to publication. I also pointed out that in his original text, at my suggestion, George had included a quote from me describing Marcia's separate and important role, but that the *Spectator* had cut this out at the last moment.

Harold was very friendly towards me but looked hunted and haunted. He rambled on about how Marcia was jealous of all of us on the staff, but she had suffered a hard life and this was why 'she often behaved in this strange way', then told me all about the Lever–Kissin–Goodman plot to oust her and replace her with me. He did not blame them but explained that they were wrongly 'trying to save me [Wilson] from myself.' (At his earlier discussion with Joe he had said that 'they must not try to separate me from Marcia – that would be fatal.')

Harold begged me to try to find Jones's original text for the *Spectator* article with its favourable reference to her important role. He asked me to get it to him before he came under her whip again later that night. So at nine o'clock in the evening, I travelled from Number 10 to George Jones's house in Hornsey to collect the text, which fortunately he had kept, and then sped back to the House of Commons. I found the Prime Minister in the dining room eating with Tony Crosland and Peter Shore. I did not want to expose the ludicrous situation in front of his ministers, so sent him a note saying that I had the text for him. He leaped to his feet before his bewildered colleagues, beaming and waving an excited thumbs-up sign to me, like a schoolboy who had just found his lost wallet. I had survived the guillotine again. But I wasn't convinced that the head of the Number 10 Policy Unit should be spending his time on too many such diversions.

Having survived the attack in October 1974 to banish me and the Unit to the Cabinet Office, described above, I enjoyed a fairly quiet autumn on the Marcia front. But hostilities flared up again during what Harold called the 'Black New Year' period. Bill Housden told me on 8 January 1975 that she was attacking me heavily to the Prime Minister. 'It is all jealousy', said Bill.

A few weeks later, Wilson told Joe that Marcia was 'behaving wildly' and blaming me personally for everything. I had also committed a grave tactical error, due to my ignorance of Marcia's royal lineage. On 11 February I went to dinner at Buckingham Palace and conversed with Her Majesty the Queen. On learning this, Marcia exploded and dispatched the Prime Minister to the Press Office to demand from Joe Haines to know why I had been invited. (Actually it was through my good friend Lord Porchester, the Queen's Racing Manager.) That afternoon in the Commons, poor Harold looked very hunched and drank five brandies.

As with the Prime Minister, my own official visits overseas were for me a recurrent provocation of Marcia's hostility. In June 1974 Harold took me with him to Germany and she attacked him for doing so. At the end of that month I was due to go with Harold to Brussels and he asked me to draft his speech for the

NATO meeting there. Marcia erupted and persuaded him to strike me off the list, although I still had to labour on the speech. I was also excluded from his next trip in July to talk to Giscard in Paris.

More vetoes were imposed on trips abroad in the following year. Harold put me on his official list to go to Moscow in February 1975, then took me off at the last moment to placate Marcia, who was going through her 'Black Period'. I was also due to go with him on his final overseas visit to Rome at the end of 1975, but he had lunch with Marcia just beforehand and returned to Number 10 to instruct Private Office that I be excluded. By now, Number 10 officials understood the background to these exclusions and no longer interpreted them as a reflection of my declining influence with the Prime Minister – a barometer which civil servants watched closely.

To me these exclusions were mere irritations and just part of the small price of working for Harold Wilson. The worst 'exclusion crisis' occurred over Wilson's visit to the Commonwealth Leaders' Conference in Jamaica in April 1975. Ever since our return from the successful EEC summit in Dublin in March, Albert and Bill had reported to me that she was demanding of Harold that I do not go to Jamaica, and that she and Albert should go instead as the Prime Minister's advisers.

The case for my attending was particularly strong since the two main items on the agenda were Commodities, where I and the Unit had produced the Prime Minister's main briefing, which he had praised extensively, and on the role of Special Advisers in Government, where I was then the senior special adviser in the British Government and was, together with Tom McNally at the Foreign Office, writing his formal paper to present to the Conference.

On 9 April, I had my smallpox jab from Wilson's personal doctor, Joe Stone, and was all packed and ready to go to the Caribbean. But that evening an embarrassed Robert Armstrong took me aside and said that Marcia had 'triumphed'. Although the Foreign Secretary Jim Callaghan had expressed a particular wish that I go, Wilson had capitulated and had instructed Robert to take me off the list, but did not dare tell me himself. Actually, I did not mind about missing the trip, which would give me some free time to rest and spend with my family, whom I too rarely saw. But I did resent the possible damage to my credibility in wider Whitehall. So I decided to confront Marcia when we were alone in the Prime Minister's room at the Commons on the evening of 9 April.

I was deliberately cool and polite, simply asking her directly about her role in my exclusion from Jamaica. She shouted and denied that she had ever discussed it with the Prime Minister – contrary to reports from Albert and Bill, who had witnessed her pressures against my going. She ran from the room and shouted abuse at me in the corridor as John Silkin and Harold Lever passed by. It was not a comfortable experience, but I was satisfied to have finally – and for the only time in those two years – confronted her with a direct question about her behaviour towards me.

When Harold finally spoke to me about my not going to Jamaica – he never attempted to explain why, presumably assuming that I understood only too well why – he said that he wanted me 'to keep an eye on' all that went on in government here while he was away. He referred with approval to 'your espionage network in Whitehall' (he always assumed that there were spies and plots everywhere and was obviously pleased to have a spy on his own side), and said with feeling that 'there is nobody here on the political side that I can trust.' He said that he wanted me to go to the United States as his personal representative to negotiate on various financial, trade, energy, and Middle Eastern issues, and he would arrange for me to talk to Nelson Rockefeller and Henry Kissinger. He grew ever more expansive. 'Go to Washington. Go to New York. Stay on after I leave.'

I was very pleased to go to Washington, where I had a wonderful visit in the spring sunshine. I also felt that here in this tiny episode were illustrated all the complexities of Harold's character and his ambivalences towards Marcia: his weakness in giving way to her demands; his attempts to compensate for this weakness by other kindnesses; his minor deceptions and self-deceptions; his perception of the realities of her control over him, yet his unwillingness or incapacity to deal with it. In that conversation, I felt touched by him and warm towards him for his human fallibilities, while being unable fully to respect him.

Perhaps the most bizarre of the episodes involving me and illustrating the Harold–Marcia relationship concerned her efforts to get me excluded from the development of Labour's incomes policy in the summer of 1975. I have described above in Chapter 10 how in the Policy Unit we developed a voluntary incomes policy and through it helped to defeat the Treasury's plans for statutory action. Yet afterwards I learned that I might not have been involved in this issue at all. Joe Haines and Ken Stowe later told me the background, with extra information from Albert and Bill. Apparently right at the beginning Marcia had persuaded Wilson to stop me from seeing any papers on incomes policy and also to exclude me from the key cabinet committee which formulated the government's pay strategy. The Prime Minister instructed Ken accordingly about the papers and the committee, but Ken courageously omitted to pass the instruction on to me. He ensured that I received all the papers and I went blithely ahead attending all the meetings chaired by the Prime Minister who had ordered my exclusion. In the end we shaped the White Paper and its policy. Moreover, when it was completed, the Prime Minister repeatedly praised our work to me.

He never mentioned that he had given instructions that I should not be allowed to take part and he proceeded as if it had never happened. From the beginning he saw me in the committees from which he had excluded me and chatted with me about the latest policy developments of which I was supposed to be unaware. Every few hours he discussed with me the committee papers which on his instructions I was supposed not to receive. He responded to and regularly praised the Policy Unit briefs which I was supposed not to be in a position to provide. Finally he instructed the Cabinet Secretary that the Unit's draft White Paper was the one which he preferred and which should be the basis for the Government's policy.

On the Monday after it was all settled, he came up to me at the ticker-tape machine in the lobby across from Marcia's door and said loudly, 'I hear that you had something to do with the good drafting work that has been going on.' He pretended that he really did not know of my constant and central involvement and had not authorised or approved any part of it. He worded it as some kind of rumour, after the event, of which he had no previous knowledge and over which he had no control (or he would have been required to put a stop to it as Marcia demanded). In that one bizarre episode is again encompassed the whole complexity of Harold Wilson's character, like the many layers of an onion, and also the strange nature of his relationship with Marcia: initially obeying her demands, agreeing at her behest to distrust those closest and most loyal to him, yet not minding if he was disobeyed, ultimately suppressing totally that he ever gave such nonsensical instructions and finally praising the banned person for doing the forbidden work.

It was a kind of Walter Mitty fantasy world in which I was working. Fortunately, Joe and Ken shrewdly decided it was best if I was kept in the dark until the policy business was successfully completed. Anyway, nothing could take away the satisfaction of our policy success.

In September 1975 Wilson told Janet that Marcia was 'obsessed' with me, and he repeated this view to Joe in December. Wilson's explanation to Janet, as she and Joe conveyed to me, was that Marcia had originally supported my appointment on the assumption that she would be able to 'control' me. But 'she found that she could not control Bernard.' Wilson added that 'she is a monopolist and disapproves of everything she does not control.' More frivolously, the explanation may also just possibly have been in the stars. Marcia is a volatile Pisces and I am the stellar opposite, a pedestrian Virgo. Virgos are said by those who believe in this kind of thing either to match very well with their opposite Pisces (as I do now with my partner Sarah Berry) or, most often, they don't. With Marcia, I didn't.

For the Prime Minister, Marcia's interventions frequently diverted him away from what seemed to be more important business of government. For me personally, the kind of diversions described above added to the existing stresses and strains of working in Number 10. Unlike any other department of government, Number 10 was then very small. There was no hierarchical structure to cushion tensions between staff. Less than a dozen of us worked directly, personally, and often hourly to the Prime Minister. The Prime Minister's mood and reactions at any particular time determined what we could or could not help him to achieve. Anything, however extraneous, however seemingly trivial, which affected the Prime Minister's mood or concentration, which diverted his attention or pre-empted his thinking, also affected our and especially my capacity to serve and advise him on the major policy issues of the day. Any pressure which affected him affected all of us in his team. It is my view that his Political Secretary was at times a major source of distraction for the Prime Minister away from what I saw as his main government responsibilities and priorities. From her position, she undoubtedly saw it differently.

These distractions and tensions added to the ceaseless treadmill of work which burdened the Downing Street team. I was often deeply exhausted. The long working days; the need to scan and quickly absorb a huge flow of paper; the endless conveyor belt of high-level committees; the pressure of having to take positions, make judgements, and give hurried written or verbal advice on matters of considerable complexity and importance and for which one could be held accountable if it went wrong – all these accumulated over time to deplete my own innermost physical and nervous resources.

The strains were undoubtedly made worse by the conflicts and tensions of our internal office politics. Fortunately this burden was often eased and erased for a while by the countervailing sense of exhilaration derived from operating at the centre of political power and by the satisfaction of working together with a small band of very high-calibre people. Occasional success, whether personally in my job or by the government as a whole, also often eased the pain of exhaustion and helped the adrenaline to keep flowing. But always in the background there was a nagging sense of deep exhaustion, which fully surfaced only when stepping off the treadmill and taking a holiday, the first part of which was always in my case spent sleeping. It must have been worse for Joe Haines – and even worse still for the modern Press Secretary in Number 10 – bombarded with telephone calls day and night.

Having experienced, suffered, and above all enjoyed the pressures of Downing Street under Harold Wilson (and then more calmly under James Callaghan), I was finally impressed that there are not many more errors made in British government. The overload at the centre is great.

My observation of politicians also led me to conclude that to reach and survive at the top of politics requires more stamina (and luck) than genius. During my years in Number 10 I was blessed with relative youth and considerable physical and mental energy. My admiration for those, such as Harold Wilson and James Callaghan, who survived those pressures when much older and less obviously physically fit, was and is boundless.

I am often asked how and why Marcia came to have such a powerful influence over Harold Wilson. My simply answer is that I do not really know, though the fact that she had worked so long (nearly twenty years before I joined him in 1974) and so effectively, guiding him during his long climb up the political greasy pole to become Prime Minister, must have been a major factor. Her Field family became deeply entwined with the Wilsons, with Marcia, Peggy and Tony at times employed by Harold or Mary. This appearance of a 'dual' family was symbolised at Wilson's memorial service in 1995 in Westminster Abbey, where at the end Marcia stood apart from Mary at the west door and shook hands with the line departing down the south aisle.

Some apparently plausible but unproven explanations of her control over Harold have been offered, sometimes possibly inspired by political animosity or envy. Sex and money are two common routes by which women influence men. The sexual innuendo – that Harold and Marcia had enjoyed, or were still enjoying, a sexual relationship, and even that he was the father of her two sons – was often raised by Tory canvassers and hintedat by many journalists in the 1960s and 1970s. Some people closer to Harold Wilson also believed in some kind of sexual relationship at some time. Albert Murray and Bill Housden, from the centre of Marcia's entourage, both believed that there had been an affair and muttered darkly about St George's Day 1956, close to when Harold and Marcia had dinner with the Russian leaders Kruschev and Bulganin.

Joe Haines, a man of unfailing veracity and memory, has published that Wilson told him how he took his wife to lunch to celebrate her birthday in 1972 and Marcia was so angry that she summoned Mary to Wyndham Mews and claimed a brief affair with Wilson in 1956. By this account Wilson commented to Joe that now Marcia had used 'her nuclear bomb', she could not threaten him any more. However, I observed that she did continue to threaten him.

Most sexual relationships, in my view (not shared by our press), should be private matters of concern only to the people involved. In any event, unless there are witnesses, confessions or progeny, there is no proof. But interest in Wilson's sexual life can be justified if it influenced his conduct of the public office of Prime Minister, such as by fear of exposure. Certainly in my hearing Marcia threatened to 'destroy' Wilson, tapping her handbag ominously (though I never saw its contents). And certainly, in my presence and hearing, Wilson showed acute fear of these threats. Why? Why did he ask me to go to Marcia's house to tear out her telephone wires to stop her talking to the press?

He had, of course, a provincial nonconformist mentality, moulded in pre-war mores, which would suffer guilt and fear shame from exposure of offences against conventional morality. He would especially worry about being shamed before Mary, the daughter of a provincial clergyman whose disapproval he feared. Certainly he had experienced enough to know how our seedy press would have hounded him over it. But it is hard to believe that the revelation of some minor sexual peccadillo two decades earlier would in fact 'destroy' Wilson. The resulting embarrassment would hardly justify the extremes of fear which I observed in him. Could it, however, have been linked to his successful suing for heavy libel damages in the early 1960s of an American newspaper which suggested he had had an affair with Marcia? If he had sworn there had been no affair and taken money, whereas actually there had been – and Marcia would be a decisive witness – then he would have a well-based fear of charges of perjury, which would destroy him politically (as Jeffrey Archer and Jonathan Aitken have recently discovered). But I have no evidence on these sexual explanations. Certainly on my observations in 1974–6, I was convinced, in so far as an outside observer can be, that there was no sexual affair then.

All of that is to me mere speculation. The other common speculative explanation of her control over Wilson concerns money. For example, Arnold Goodman, who knew more than most about Wilson's financial affairs, told me over a long club lunch in 1977 that he was convinced that Marcia's control over Harold (which, from a bitterly hostile position, he described as 'blackmail') was related to money and earlier episodes when Wilson was involved in trade with the Communist bloc. There have often been suggestions of financial 'sleaze' surrounding Wilson's affairs. If true, this would have been ironic, since of all successful men I have known, Wilson had the least personal interest in money for himself. He often seemed naive about personal finance (as opposed to macro-economics), happy to leave such matters in Marcia's shrewd hands. Yet of course as party leader he needed money to finance his political life, and especially his Political Office which Marcia ran in every aspect. In those days there was no state aid for such activities. (It was Wilson's Government which introduced the 'Short Money' which alleviated the financial pressures on opposition parties.)

Contributions from the Labour movement were inadequate and often came with strings attached. So money was needed for his political activities – and that explains some of the curious people around Wilson and especially around Marcia.

Marcia controlled all of Wilson's office income and expenditure. Albert Murray, her formal deputy, said that in his time neither he nor Harold ever saw the office accounts. I witnessed Wilson sign a whole book of blank cheques and hand it over to Marcia. Much of the finance for her office derived from the so-called 'Office Trust', containing at least five people (Kagan, Fisher, Plurenden, Kissin and Schon) who were made peers in the two years 1974–6 – and two, Miller and Gosling, knighted at that time.

Marcia's own personal finances also excited interest within the team and in the media. Bill Housden often reported her impressive spending on shopping expeditions to Harrods (usually driven there by Bill, who carried the shopping bags, in the PM's official car). Over a relatively short period she acquired two houses in Marylebone and had a country retreat, which seemed ambitious on her office salary of £4,000–£5,000 a year. However, she additionally received into trust, with Goodman as trustee, a significant share of Wilson's book royalties. Goodman, who handled the legal side of her housing, told me that Joseph Kagan had financed one of the houses and Eric Miller another. Miller gave her jewellery, as did John Cordle, the Tory MP forced to resign from the Commons over the Poulson corruption scandal. Other friends were later financially generous to her – when she had a prolonged spell in a top private hospital in the 1990s, the distinguished film producer David Puttnam paid her fees. A 'respectable' peer on the lavender list told me that in the early 1980s he had received a curious letter from Marcia, referring to his peerage and asking for a contribution towards the cost of one of the houses, but he declined to chip in.

So there was around Harold and Marcia a network of odd financiers and financial transactions which may have gone back to their relations with East–West trade in the 1950s (when Wilson met Kagan, Plurenden, Schon and Kissin among others). This may have given him some reasons to fear exposure by Marcia or others, which is what Goodman believed. But I personally saw no direct evidence of it as the source of Marcia's controlling influence over Harold. It needs much more evidence and understanding to explain that conundrum. Wilson's longstanding trust of her earlier good political judgement was surely a major factor.

Future historians and biographers will have to explore deep into the pair's long and complex relationship (and none of his biographers have so far entered that tricky legal minefield). Future narrators might also consult professionals from the fields of personal behaviour to explain why she so energetically instructed and punished him; and why he so readily accepted that degree of control and suffering. That is territory beyond my expertise. I was merely a puzzled observer (and recorder) during that very intense period of my life.

Some of the above descriptions of events in Harold Wilson's last two administrations may not always seem to reflect well on him. In particular, he was too often and too willingly led into company inappropriate for a Prime Minister and occasionally into petty actions unsupportive of his most loyal staff. Much of the detail is trivial and only included in this book because of its importance in illustrating how as Prime Minister he was often diverted from important issues of state to deal with what I and others saw as indeed trivia.

But I do not wish to leave a portrait of him which closes on a negative note. He was a most complex man who led a remarkable life and career, and I was fascinated and privileged to watch him in action. I grew in many ways to like him, but not always to admire everything he did. His character showed many light sides as well as the dark shades on which London newspapers concentrated in the last twenty years of his political life.

Harold Wilson's approach to politics and government is best understood through his upbringing. His Northern, nonconformist, lower- middle-class and middle-brow background and his meritocratic education at grammar school continued to shape him throughout his long career and was clearly reflected in his personal style of life, which always remained authentically and commendably provincial in the best sense of the word. He retained his Yorkshire accent and was never personally interested in 'abroad'. Unlike some of his political colleagues, he was never seduced by the glitter of the metropolitan establishment into which he moved but of which he never became a paid-up member. He was not religious in the spiritual sense, but the chapel tradition of Christian good works inspired his early politics. He was an active Boy Scout, remaining in contact with that movement even when party leader, and the Scouts gave him solid standards and a belief in self-improvement and clean living. Observing him much later, I felt that in a way the Labour Party manifesto was his adult version of the Boy Scouts' Code, to be learned by heart and obeyed.

When I joined him, although he seemed tired and old for his fifty-eight years, his character struck me as basically unchanged, with the virtues and limitations of that background, still committed to the nonconformist work ethic, to self-improvement through education, to respectability, thrift and discipline. In that guilt-ridden puritan background, there was little sexual liberation, arty-crafty culture or social climbing. It was very much Gilbert and Sullivan and not Bach or Benjamin Britten. To his credit he stuck to those values.

Politically, he always in private derided as 'theology' the dogmas of both the left and right wings of the party. He was probably never a 'socialist' in any meaningful Marxist sense. Rather his 'socialism' was a mixture of nonconformist suspicion of wealth, genuine concern for the underdog, and *dirigisme* based on his wartime experience of Whitehall planning, all dressed up with a veneer of technological modernisation. His most lasting achievement in government was supporting in 1964–70 the remarkable raft of social reforms – on capital punishment, homosexuality, racial discrimination, censorship, divorce and abortion (despite his Roman Catholic constituency) – which adjusted British laws to the more libertarian values of the younger generation. The initial impetus for these reforms lay elsewhere, mainly with Roy Jenkins as Home Secretary. But it is to Wilson's credit that, against all his nonconformist conditioning, he supported and promoted them.

Wilson had been deeply scarred by his unexpected election defeat in 1970 and the party split over Europe in 1972. His final premiership in 1974–6 was conducted with much more modesty and low profile than the triumphal days of 1964–6. There was now a touch of autumnal mellowness and Stanley Baldwin's 'quiet life' about him. But he still displayed all his old skills in holding his fissiparous party together over incomes policy and the Common Market referendum. He was always an impressive chairman of the cabinet, seeking to find the common ground which maintained unity. His achievement in winning four general elections out of five was remarkable, especially when set against the disasters afflicting the Labour party in the years after his retirement.

On the negative side were the constant allegations, not always easy to refute, that he lacked deep political principles or consistent policy objectives; that he was almost wholly the brilliant political manager and operator, with too little sense of strategy; that it was because he apparently believed in so little that he had few real policy commitments and objectives; and that he appeared solely concerned with managing the party to achieve and remain in power. Certainly there was in him something of the Whitehall mandarin, administering rather than believing in policies. I saw evidence supporting those criticisms, but do not accept their totality. For instance, in my brief time he showed great interest in policies toward Northern Ireland, council house sales, legal reform and the Open University. He was also a genuine moderniser within a limited framework.

When he was engaged, and before ill health hit him, he still had a quicksilver mind and an astonishing appetite for work. But he was not an intellectual in any sense, with little interest in abstract theories or the high arts. Most attractive to me was that he had absolutely no side to him, nor any of the pretensions to grandeur which sometimes grow in office. He showed no trace of snobbery, racism or chauvinism – he instinctively treated women and blacks as his equals and he automatically advanced women in his governments as did no other leader of the western world. He showed none of the patronising politically correct claptrap (PCC) which blighted later Labour generations. When the media referred snootily to his liking for steak and kidney pie and tomato sauce, they were actually touching on one of his most engaging qualities, which no amount of high office corrupted.

Unlike many other nonconformists, he was not puritanically sanctimonious nor censorious. He was astonishingly tolerant of the sins, foibles and human weaknesses of others, including (except among journalists) his political enemies, towards whom he displayed virtually no vindictiveness.

Much of government and politics he saw as mild entertainment. During the first week of his 1974 administration, with the nation's industry still in turmoil as we strove to settle the miners' strike and head off hyper-inflation, Harold invited my wife and me to have drinks with him in the study of Number 10. (She had come in for the election victory party which Marcia had cancelled at the last moment without informing us.) Harold was laughing and joking and described the whole situation as 'a riot'. He said that 'nobody outside would believe it. It is a total pantomime.' It was impossible not to like him in that mood, with no trace of the dark demons which sometimes took him over. The words 'pantomime' and 'circus' often cropped up in his vocabulary. He saw himself in politics as the pantomime producer or the circus ringmaster, running the show and himself having to ride three horses at the same time. It usually emerged as an attractive and boyish mischievousness which I always found engaging. Yet at other times he took the business of politics very seriously indeed. He had many layers.

Among his sayings to me on politics, the ones I liked best were: 'I never go into a room without first working out where is the alternative exit'; 'It is no good just having an answer – in politics you have usually lost once the question is asked'; and 'Don't give me a solution – I want the grievance.'

Wilson's private personality was as mixed as his public persona. He could be kind, though not truly warm; humorous, though suddenly moving into dark moods. He was soft, almost feline, and sought to avoid personal confrontations. He loved gossip and the small change of politics and the marginalia of government – appointments of bishops and such like – on which we whiled away many hours in Number 10. That was very human, although it could make him frustrating to work for.

In a way his 'kitchen cabinet' was a substitute for his personal family, with whom, like many politicians, he spent too little time. He could also be boringly boastful. In this boasting, as in his delightful mischievousness, he was like a schoolboy, sometimes engagingly innocent, sometimes like the boring 'swot' from the lower fifth.

Much darker was his obsession with the press and his constant suspicions of plots against him by political colleagues or imaginary enemies, and his constant suspicion of 'leaks' of information to the media by his own staff. The latter added to the immense work pressures in Number 10. He was not always loyal to those who served him, perhaps viewing them (as he once said to me of wonderful Harold Lever) as 'ships that pass in the night'.

Such an approach is common in the jungle of politics, where too close a personal attachment can become an obstacle to a politician's career mobility or advancement. Party politics is certainly tribal and it is necessary at any particular time to hunt in packs with the comfort and support of numbers: Wilson, Callaghan and Jenkins all nurtured their political tribes successfully. But on my observation, most politicians have limited lasting personal loyalties. It may explain why so many politicians appear lonely and dissatisfied in later life. Often on the way up they make few real and lasting friendships and have also neglected their close family in the tumult of Westminster politics.

Harold Wilson certainly appeared to lack close personal friends in retirement and became a sad and lonely figure. But he was an engaging, if deeply complex man who experienced – I am not sure if he enjoyed – a remarkably successful political career, for which he deserves more honour than he is currently given.

Thirteen

CALLAGHAN MAKES HIS MARK

ollowing Jim Callaghan's arrival in 10 Downing Street, at first I had difficulty in adjusting to a new regime and to a quite different personality as Prime Minister. Ken Stowe told me that Private Office found the transition stressful. We were all watching the new man very carefully, trying to assess his personality and what was his particular style of working. Whenever he displayed a preference or individual way of working, we would discuss it together and amend our styles of servicing him accordingly.

Jim Callaghan also took a while to find his feet in the special atmosphere and under the unique pressures of Number 10, since there is no training or preparation course for being a Prime Minister. On his second day in office he called me to his study for a chat and said he felt 'isolated' and 'bewildered' and finally 'a prisoner'. He was to learn that isolation was in the nature of the Prime Minister's job. Wilson accommodated it by encouraging a constant flow of staff to visit and talk with him. Jim did not want that and so was always more alone. Early on, he told me: 'I am not sure how to make my mark as a Prime Minister.'

Anticipating his uncertainty, I had already prepared my first 'green paper' to him headed 'Themes and Initiatives', setting out the various ways in which a Prime Minister can make an impact. It opened:

> Any new Prime Minister faces a paradox. He is the pre-eminent minister and yet – because he has few statutory functions and less policy-servicing than any of his Departmental Ministers – he may find difficulty in making a commensurate impact on his Government's policies ... He can choose to take personal policy initiatives, which leave his own stamp on the Government, and possibly on history. But if he is to intervene personally, he should be selective, well-informed, and visibly effective ... It may be a question of the themes in your speeches, and of emphasising certain priorities within an already committed range of policy options, which gives your Government its final edge.

I set out a shopping list of policy themes from which he might choose – including stressing social 'responsibilities' as well as 'rights'; reducing welfare dependency, increasing the incentives to work, and restoring values and standards to our education system. All reflected my own personal preferences and are strikingly close to Tony Blair's New Labour platform twenty years later. I suggested to Jim Callaghan that he choose one of these policy areas to which he was personally attached and make a radical speech on it. To my delight, from the list he first chose education. So the path was set towards his famous 1976 Ruskin speech launching the Great Debate on Education.

Watching James Callaghan over the months and years, I observed a very commendable man, quite different in style and character from Harold Wilson, not just in that he was nearly a foot taller (and walked with a curious gait, tilted towards one side as if compensating for the lurch of one of the ships on which he served during the war). Most different from the previous regime was his strong sense of values – really like those of a nonconformist Victorian, with deep feelings of responsibility towards the underprivileged and a strong sense of right and wrong (where Harold was always ambivalent).

When in the Unit we produced a paper for his first Easter holiday reading about the restoration of responsible values in our society, another of my personal concerns, he telephoned me from his farm to say how much he liked it and asked me to join in the writing of his future speeches to incorporate this dimension. Sometimes these 'values' emerged as a touchingly old-fashioned prudery. He once cautioned Tom McNally and me not to tell bawdy stories in front of Audrey (not that we had any such intention), and he told me that he had been totally unaware of homosexuality until well into adult life, adding: 'It all puzzles me. There have always been so many pretty girls.' But he was more comfortable in male than female company and was not as good as Harold in promoting women.

Although apparently an agnostic, his Baptist upbringing showed through when, especially during a crisis, he would suddenly burst out singing hymns. Before he left his Commons room for the big debate on our pay sanctions policy, he sang to us one of his favourites – 'We'll Meet Again with the Lord'. I often heard him humming a hymn to himself as he set off for a critical meeting.

He was much more of a family man than Harold. Audrey played a key role in his life, and we always knew that a parliamentary situation was serious when he asked her to travel with him in the car over to the Commons from Number 10. We were aware that his children and grandchildren mattered greatly to him. On Trooping of the Colour day in 1976 – different from our experience the previous year when our children were deprived of drinks! – Jim toured the reception room and talked with each messenger, waitress and child in turn. My children still remember it with affection. He also had more of the common touch than Harold, helped by his tougher upbringing and his time in the Navy as well as a trade unionist. He shared many of the pleasures of ordinary people, often going to the popular theatre and watching television, on which he was very knowledgeable about the various series and the actors who starred in them.

My observation over the coming three years was that James Callaghan had three layers of personality. On the surface was the familiar bluff and avuncular Jim. Below that was a shrewd, secretive and even wily politician. And beneath those layers was an authentic and very decent person who really did believe in the straight honest values in life. By comparison, Harold Wilson had only two main layers. On top was Tricky Harold, the clever and devious political manipulator. Below that was a kindly, weak and insecure man. But I am not sure that there was anything at all beneath that perhaps just a void where Jim had his root values. To me, as his personal adviser, what mattered most about the Callaghan regime was that it was sane, sensible and balanced, with none of the hysteria (though of course less of the colour and fun) which afflicted the fringes of Wilson's reign.

Callaghan's needed a lot of time and space for his working process. He did not like a crowd of advisers around him, preferring them to approach him singly, by prior arrangement and having sent in a paper in advance so that he could prepare mentally. He often took a while to return papers – some of mine were found under his bed – and told me that he did not like too much sudden pressure, nor 'all the problems to come together. I like to take issues one at a time.'

That may be why he sometimes appeared to be overwhelmed by the avalanche of problems in the pay crisis in 1979. In such crises he tended to withdraw into himself and cut off communication with his team, instead of involving them even more to share the burden. That, perhaps, reflected his insecurities and that he did not have a freely outgoing personality. He did not pretend to be 'cosy' and did not often chat openly as Harold did, disapproving of what he saw as 'gossip'. He usually played his cards close to his chest.

I admired the way that he took serious issues seriously and had an acute sense of the likely public and political reaction to any proposal. He could be extremely severe and I would not have wanted to be on the wrong end of one of his critical rebukes. Having been Chancellor, Foreign Secretary and Home Secretary, he knew how to make Whitehall deliver. He once told me that he viewed Number 10 as an old-fashioned railway signal box: he had to pull the right levers to make the policy trains reach the right Whitehall destinations on time.

He was also skilled at using the appropriate civil servants for the appropriate tasks. On one occasion, I thought that I had a wonderful idea in the social policy area which would have great political benefits. I explained it to Jim on paper and he ticked it and arranged a meeting in the study to discuss it.

When we gathered, I saw that a senior civil servant, Ken Stowe, was present. I politely questioned this since, although Ken was a good friend, I felt that my proposal was very political and civil servants should not be present. Jim disagreed, explaining: 'You see, Bernard, I have been around in government for a long time and I have been tempted by a lot of very clever political wheezes like yours. Sadly, they don't all work as well as it looks at first sight. So I have found it is better to have someone present who says: "Wait a minute." Ken is my "wait-a-minute" man.' Ken did indeed say 'Wait a minute' to my clever wheeze, spotting a fundamental flaw, and I was pleased that it was allowed to die without further embarrassment. That was the Civil Service at its best – not being simply obstructive but detecting genuine downside in a proposal.

Callaghan's personal political style was magisterial (helped by his height), even authoritarian at times, and his occasional grumpiness and severity meant that some colleagues and staff could be nervous in dealing with him. But he was good at handling his ministerial colleagues and he was not afraid to confront them and their political problems head on. He was said to be anti-intellectual (some of his early political allies were not impressive), possible arising from having left school in his early teens, being then the only British Prime Minister born in the twentieth century not to have been to university. I like to think that he was simply impatient with the pretentious arrogance with which some self-professed intellectuals surrounded themselves. His mind was powerful, based on practicality and honed by very great experience. He had a devastating capacity for asking simple but central questions which did not allow for anything but simple and straight answers – which I often did not quite have.

He was always nervous before a big speech, telling me that he felt 'terrible, for two days it is like a big black cloud. I get irritable and say to Audrey: "I cannot do it. I've nothing to say." But she keeps me at it. Then ten minutes beforehand I feel OK.' In delivering his speeches, he was a true professional, always dominating and yet involving his audience. He had a strong and commanding style in the House of Commons and it is now often forgotten how he usually dominated Mrs Thatcher there. Even in the depths of the Winter of Discontent he was personally well ahead of her in the polls, when his party trailed the Tories by up to 20 per cent. He told me that from his experience of the Commons it was essential 'always to be accurate, always understate, never exaggerate. Remember there is always somebody who knows better than you do'. This was typical of his natural modesty, shrewdness, prudence and caution. He never wanted to show off or to 'showboat'.

Like Harold Wilson, Jim grew to dislike Commons Questions. He said to me: 'This is my worst fifteen minutes of the week. I hate this silly game we have to play.' At first he abolished our pre-Questions briefing on Tuesdays and Thursdays, preferring to take his post-prandial nap instead. He said: 'It is better to be well rested than well briefed.' But he found that he could not do without his briefings for Questions and soon resumed them.

Jim was also good on television in a solid, reassuring and old-fashioned way. Before broadcasting about the Winter of Discontent in 1979, he asked me, 'What demeanour should I adopt?' I replied, 'Be natural. Be yourself.' He said, 'Yes, that is the only way. There is no point in trying to adopt a false style.' That was authentically Jim. He was quite unsuited to modern 'spinning' or presentation with a 'celebrity' style. I always liked the fact that he was just himself.

The change in prime ministerial working style also meant a major change in work routine for myself and my Policy Unit. Life was more regular, less Byzantine than under Wilson. I saw Callaghan in person less frequently, spending much less time gossiping in the study. My time with him was simpler and more direct, mainly concerned with the central business of policy advice. The rhythm of my daily office diary was more predictable. I had a little more space for my family – though this was still minimal, since I usually left home shortly after eight in the morning and was rarely back before nine at night, and I often stayed in town much later for social activities.

I was not at first clear how Jim would use the Policy Unit. Some political colleagues had suggested that he would make little use of it at all, since he was allegedly wholly a politician, not interested in policy ideas. This was unfair. In fact, he was often more *seriously* interested in getting the right policy approach than Wilson had been. But he was initially uncertain how to make best use of the Unit. On his first day, I went to the study to discuss with him the continuance of the Unit. He was unaware that we had all been sacked and, in fact, he did not have a Policy Unit at all until he reappointed it. He looked quite shocked by this information and said, 'I want the Unit to continue: bring them back in double fast.' He went on: 'I am not very clever, as you will know from the newspapers. I don't have Harold's brains for bright ideas. In fact I need the Policy Unit more than Harold did. So I want a lot of intellectual input.' That gave me confidence for the future. A few days later, he came personally to the Unit and talked to each member in turn – something Wilson had never done even though he invented the Unit. My staff were delighted and felt renewed commitment to their work.

Callaghan's first priority was to appoint his new cabinet. His main changes were to drop Barbara Castle (Health), Ted Short (Lord President) and William Ross (Scotland), all significant figures in the party, though probably having served their time. I met Barbara Castle descending the stairs, glowering from her dismissal. She and Jim simply did not get on well, even before their clash over trade union reform in the late 1960s (when she was basically right). Even her old chum Harold Wilson had told me in 1975 that she ought to go, but he lacked the courage to sack her himself.

The most important promotion was of Michael Foot to be Lord President. (He hoped for the Northern Ireland Office but was refused.) His vital role for Callaghan was to hold the Labour Government and the TUC together under the increasingly elastic bands of the social contract, and his loyalty to the Prime Minister was also a beacon signalling to many on the moderate left that the Government should be supported by them. (The lunatic and disloyal left could be influenced by nobody.) I often chatted with Michael in the early mornings as I was on my run and he was taking his dog for a walk over Hampstead Heath. It was not his fault that his trade union allies finally collapsed under militant pressure and betrayed the Labour Government.

Tony Benn asked for a 'more political' job than Energy and again demanded twenty-four hours 'to consult my wife'. Callaghan told him to take Energy now or leave it – and Benn of course took it, looking very sour when I observed him leave Number 10. John Silkin tried the same tactic and the Prime Minister told him: 'You have got two minutes or you are out.' Silkin, probably lucky to be in the cabinet anyway, immediately accepted. By the end, Callaghan had made it clear who was boss and there would be no more tantrums of the kind which Wilson had encouraged by his softness and pliability.

Callaghan's most difficult handling was again of Roy Jenkins. Fortunately, I was not involved as I had been in the embarrassing episodes under Wilson in March 1974, since Jim believed in doing his own tough work. Even so, it did not go well. Roy's position was quite complex because President Giscard of France had already indicated to Wilson and to Roy that the French wanted him as the next President of the EEC. Roy had been to see Wilson on 22 January 1976 and, according to Wilson, said that he was fed up with being Home Secretary. To Callaghan he seems to have enquired about the Foreign Office, now vacant with Jim moving to Number 10. The new Prime Minister refused this and floated the possibility of the Treasury. But he apparently withdrew that offer – if it ever was a firm offer – the next day.

When I met Roy in the Commons corridor soon after, he told me that he did not really want the Treasury anyway, and his preference was for Europe if he could not have the Foreign Office, and perhaps over it. I sensed that, although they shared some of the same political enemies, Jim and Roy were simply not made for one another, with totally different lifestyles. I imagine that the ruthless side of Callaghan also saw it as a way to squeeze out his main rival on the right by denying him the top cabinet positions and leaving him with Europe as his only senior option. Politics can be rough.

Their separation in the mid-1970s was a pity in many ways, certainly for the Labour Party. Jim later admitted to me that he had not handled Roy as well as he should have done. Working together, they might have been more successful in resisting the party's lunatic left. But that was in neither's stars.

Part of Callaghan's problem was that he was personally unclear how to fill the vacancy at the Foreign Office created by his own promotion; and this was linked to doubts about when to relieve Denis Healey of the exhausting burden of the Treasury. During the leadership campaign he told Wilson that he really wanted Healey for the Foreign Office, but the latter had to remain at the Treasury until the inflation crisis was under control. Till then, he would have a stopgap Foreign Secretary (and possibly saw Crosland as that). Probably he had in mind later switching Healey and Crosland, since each would have been more at home in the other's job. But before long Crosland died, and Healey remained at the Treasury throughout the Government since the inflation crisis never seemed sufficiently under control to risk a change and there was nobody else – now Jenkins had gone – big enough to shoulder that burden.

Overall, Callaghan's new cabinet was solid and experienced, but it struck me as lacking in political charisma. I do not think that he quite got his appointments right first time round. The departing Castle and Ross and the soon-to-depart Jenkins and Crosland were all major political personalities and as such were a political loss to the Government. The newcomers to the cabinet – Albert Booth, Bruce Millan, David Ennals and Edmund Dell – were greyer men who did not replace the lost personality. Ennals was certainly a mistake, not up to the big political job at Health. Of the continuing incumbents, Fred Mulley, Eric Varley and John Morris were not significant political figures. I believe that it would have been better to try to keep Jenkins (who left for Brussels in September) to add weight to the central departments and to promote more of the better young ministers.

On his second day in Number 10, Jim discussed with me the qualities of his younger colleagues, confessing that he did not know all of them well. I pressed strongly the case for John Smith, Roy Hattersley, Bill Rodgers and David Owen to go straight into the cabinet to refresh it with more vigour and imagination. I also suggested promotion to higher posts for Philip Whitehead, Betty Boothroyd, Neil Kinnock, Jack Ashley and Alf Morris. From the left I supported Stan Orme as having working-class roots.

Jim responded positively, especially towards John Smith, but he did not really show his hand. Over time, he did put most of the first group into the cabinet, but only slowly and too often into very junior cabinet posts – Hattersley and Rodgers in particular were wasted at Prices and Transport, and John Smith waited on the fringes far too long. In my view, it would have been better to put straight into the cabinet John Smith at Scotland instead of Millan, Hattersley or Owen to Health instead of Ennals, Rodgers to Employment instead of Booth, and any one of them instead of Silkin and dear Fred Mulley.

Such moves would have altered the cabinet balance against the left, something Wilson would certainly never have done. But I believe it would have paid off when the great crisis arose in 1979. Then it was proved that there were far too many tired mediocrities in the cabinet and Callaghan and Healey were left to shoulder too much of the burden alone. But in the current unstable situation in the Labour Party, Jim Callaghan felt that he had to balance representatives of all sides in that unstable coalition. The price was paid in lower quality.

Our reappointed and remotivated Policy Unit quickly moved into action for its new Prime Minister. Over the next three years I sent him over 500 memoranda covering a wide range of policies, though with economics as ever dominating our concerns. As always I kept a very low public profile and during over five years running the Policy Unit (except during the furore over Joe Haines's book, described in chapter 14 below) I was mentioned in the press only half a dozen times – quite a different approach from my recent counterparts.

I made a few changes in staffing. Andrew Graham, whose skill and experience had helped us to launch successfully, returned to teaching economics (and later to be Master) at Balliol College, Oxford, though I continued to consult him. Given the economic storms ahead, I quickly reinforced the economics side. Gavyn Davies took over from Andrew as our chief economic adviser. To work with him I recruited Richard Smethurst (future Provost of Worcester College, Oxford) and David Gowland, Professor in Economics at York University. Jim Corr came in from the World Bank to work on industrial and energy policy, Elisabeth Arnott from the Labour Party research department to cover social policy and, a little later, when Tony Crosland died, his adviser David Lipsey came to bring a valuable range of economic, social and drafting skills. It was a high-powered group.

Our first major policy focus was on education. In my initial memo to the Prime Minister, I had suggested education as a target area for one of his personal policy initiatives and I was delighted when he bit on it, since it was a subject of passionate interest to me. I then had four children under the age of twelve at inner London state schools and a wife who taught in state schools and was later to be a Schools Inspector. In my memo I had said that what was worrying most parents was not the ideological structure of our system – grammar schools versus comprehensives, etc. Their main concern was more basic: 'Will their children be taught to read and write and to add up; be protected from bullying and intimi-dation; will basic educational skills and discipline be maintained and some social values inculcated?' I went on to set out what in time was to become his – and in some way's Mrs Thatcher's and Tony Blair's – approach to restoring standards in our schools: 'This is surely an appropriate time to restate the best of the tradi-tional and permanent values – to do with excellence, quality and actually acquiring mental and manual skills; and not only acquiring these qualities but also learning to respect them.'

Jim responded enthusiastically, asking us to draft a major speech for him focussing on quality and standards in education. It was to be delivered in the early autumn of 1976 at Ruskin College, Oxford, an adult education college with a great tradition of producing successful Labour MPs who had dropped out early from formal education.

I worked long and hard on this speech, together with Liz Arnott from the Unit. I included all my parental feelings and frustrations about the need for more rigorous standards in our schools, for more concentration on the basic skills of literacy and numeracy, and to give greater priority to technical, vocational and adult education. (In the previous eight years, the number of engineering students in Britain had increased by only 5 per cent, while those in sociology increased by 38 per cent, in theology by 51 per cent, and in general arts by 169 per cent.) We had embarked on a radical course of great difficulty, and it would not be easy to change the entrenched direction of Whitehall education policy or to persuade the 'liberal' educational establishment to change its habits.

This Labour government had rarely showed much interest in education, and the issue had rarely broken the surface under Wilson since 1974. The two ministers hitherto responsible, Reg Prentice and Fred Mulley, were minor figures in the cabinet with no agenda for educational reform (though Mulley was a lovely man and brighter than his media reputation). The Department itself revealed little initiative in any part of its territory – Harold Wilson described it to me as 'little more than a post-box between the teachers' unions and their local authority employers'. Most politicians who expressed any interest in education seemed concerned only with its 'structure', with being for or against the ideology of comprehensiveness. Too few were concerned with the daily experience of actual children in actual schools. Too many on the left had no children of their own.

Worst of all were the main teaching unions, which were then often dominated by left-wing militants primarily concerned with reducing teachers' responsibili-ties and workloads and removing all standards and disciplines from education, which they seemed to wish to turn into a kind of voluntary hobby with the prime purpose of making children socially well adjusted, with nobody ever failing at anything, even if seriously undereducated. For some of the leaders of the National Union of Teachers, the ideal teaching life appeared to be spent passing endless motions denouncing the Government in a permanent union conference at some seaside hotel.

Jim Callaghan's speech was delivered at the Ruskin 'Rookery', an appropriate venue because its students were from those who had 'missed the opportunity to develop their full educational potential at an earlier age' – with Jim himself a perfect example. Ironically, his great education speech was disrupted by an outside group of boorish militant university students demanding more money for themselves at Oxford. Here were the privileged demanding even more privilege. Jim's speech was concerned with the educationally underprivileged. It received enormous coverage in the media and clearly touched a chord among the nation's parents. He concluded with a clarion call for a Great Debate on education and this did indeed follow among the public.

But the educational establishment reacted, predictably, with less sympathy than the general public. The National Union of Teachers denounced the speech with furious hostility, clearly feeling threatened by any requirement for higher teaching standards.

The Department of Education was deeply shocked that a Prime Minister should have the impertinence to trespass into its own 'secret garden'. The senior Inspector of Schools (an unmarried lady I had met twenty years earlier when she was a don at Oxford), peremptorily summoned me to the Department to conduct a severe investigation into my motives, making it clear that she held me personally responsible for this whole disastrous development. She wished me to take back to Number 10 the clear message that education was not the business of the Prime Minister – and especially not my business.

When the Prime Minister minuted the Education Department instructing them to produce a Green Paper following up the themes which he had identified in his Ruskin speech, officials there made it clear that they were not inclined to take any notice. The draft Green Paper took nine months to emerge and then it was sparse in content and was deeply complacent about the existing state of British education. Only three of its 200 paragraphs were devoted to the growing public criticisms of the current system, with only three bland paragraphs on 'standards' and 'discipline'. Such vital questions as the content of the curriculum and the role of schools in the community were ducked completely. Parents were mentioned only in terms of their being on the receiving end of information handed down from the Department and the local education authorities, rather than as participants with a direct personal interest in the educational process because they had children being educated in our schools.

The draft Green Paper represented Whitehall at its complacent, self-satisfied, condescending and unimaginative worst, and I was furious. However, I kept in touch with Shirley Williams, the new Secretary of State for Education, and she indicated that she was prepared to take on the entrenched educational establishment providing that she could rely on continuing political support from the Prime Minister when the left-wing education unions inevitably kicked up rough. I secured that promise from Jim.

I had come to like Shirley during the 1975 debates over incomes policy. We often had lunch together in Covent Garden, away from the Westminster jungle, and that was, for me, usually the highlight of a tough week. She sometimes appeared disorganised, which led unfriendly colleagues, not all of whom in those days approved of women as ministers, to describe her as 'muddled'. In fact she was not muddled on what mattered, on the key areas of politics and policies. Apart from being politically sound and sensible, she also had a quick and imaginative mind and a lovely open smile. She giggled engagingly, as if still an Oxford undergraduette, blue stockings and all. I grew enormously fond of her and came to value her views.

Over time, the Department of Education did slowly adjust its stance a little more in the direction of the principles and proposals set out in Jim Callaghan's speech. But little change was visible in the schools and it awaited Mrs Thatcher's – and Tony Blair's – new and radical broom to make any serious practical progress. Had the Labour Government demonstrated the will necessary to implement the Ruskin proposals, I believe they would have made teaching and schooling (in my view the most important of human endeavours) a more satisfying experience for teachers and children alike, without the battles and demoralisation which resulted from the later Tory tactics of confrontation in the field of education. But at least James Callaghan had, as he sought when coming into Number 10, 'made his mark' on a chosen policy area. It was very satisfying for me personally to have played an active part in that process and in the field of Education which has mattered to me so much throughout my life.

In 1976 the British economy was slipping towards another of its then familiar crises. This time the basic problem was not inflation, which was improving under the constraints of the previous year's incomes policy, with pay settlements reducing in line with the £6 norm. The difficulty lay with the other financial numbers. The domestic debt was huge at £12 billion and growing, with the whole of the 1976–7 contingency reserve spent in the Prime Minister's first month in office. The external balance of trade deficit was also alarming and consequently confidence in sterling was being rapidly eroded.

The medicine which had to be prescribed to reassure the money markets was a significant reduction in public expenditure. So at the end of April 1976 I submitted to Callaghan our Unit's first major economic policy paper. It warned him that a sterling crisis was imminent and that he should be prepared to go to the International Monetary Fund and accept their tough conditions for a loan.

Soon afterwards, the Prime Minister summoned his main economic advisers, including myself from the Unit, to Chequers to discuss the looming crisis. He concluded: 'We have to have more expenditure cuts and we had better get it over with soon.' Healey came back in July asking for £2 billion, which was discussed and agreed at a fascinating series of seven cabinets throughout July. At these Jim Callaghan established his style and his authority over his colleagues, taking the discussion round and round the cabinet table, encouraging all ministers to have their say, including the left wing, and in the process educating them on the difficult economic dilemmas which faced the Government. From this time he effectively took over the conduct of economic policy.

Immediately after this first round of cuts was finally agreed at the end of July, I was in the study with the Prime Minister when Tony Benn phoned. He informed Jim that he would have to consult his Bristol constituents and shop stewards before deciding whether actually to resign or just to continue campaigning in public against the cuts which had been agreed in cabinet. Jim snapped down the line that if Benn spoke in public against a cabinet decision 'you will be sacked immediately'. Benn chose to remain in cabinet.

I enjoyed a wonderful August in Ceret with the family. Before setting off from London, six in a small Ford Cortina, I gave each of the children £5 to buy paperback books, and they soon established a lasting reading habit. In France we had a daily routine of going shopping to the village in the mornings, sleeping and reading in our rooms after lunch, and walking around the hills and vineyards or narrow streets of the village in the cool of the evenings. We also began to make wonderful local friendships, especially with Jean-Francois and Eliane Leger and with Josef and Dikkie Caritg, the former being French and Josef a proud Catalan.

On my return from France in September, with sterling plunging, it was clear that the crisis was about to break. The Chancellor was formally authorised to apply to the IMF for a large loan. For the next three months the Prime Minister and his cabinet – and we in the Unit – were totally absorbed in the battles which followed. They might have brought down the Labour government, but fortunately that did not happen, mainly because of the political ability and strength of Jim Callaghan, who emerged very dominant over his cabinet, as over the House of Commons, and remained so until the final sad debacle of the Winter of Discontent.

The main question facing the Chancellor and the Prime Minister and the rest of us in Number 10 concerned the size of the inevitable cuts in public expenditure necessary to secure the IMF loan and rescue sterling. That question was at first not easy to answer since the IMF team which slipped quietly into a London hotel that autumn remained invisible, and for two months refused to make clear to us precisely how much they required in cuts as blood money for their blessing and loan. The Treasury mandarin Leo Pliatzky told me the following year that the IMF had commenced by privately demanding to the Treasury cuts totalling between £9 billion and £12 billion over the next three years. Leo claimed he had opposed accepting this enormous figure because 'it would have destroyed the Government' (little doubt of that), but added that several in the Treasury and the Bank supported it – possibly for that very reason. Certainly such cuts would have meant mutilating the public sector on a scale never achieved or sought even by Mrs Thatcher in her butchering heyday. Had Jim Callaghan accepted that target, the results would have been a major economic slump, massive unemployment, the reversal of most of the social policies for which the Labour Party stood, and the almost certain collapse of the Government.

During October and November, we entered a curious period of phoney war. The IMF officials had secret meetings with the Treasury and the Prime Minister privately discussed the situation with his Chancellor. But it was all fencing in the dark while in Number 10 we did not know what the IMF was precisely demanding. They were exploring to find out what was the maximum figure of cuts that the cabinet would accept without rebelling – and we were waiting to discover what was the minimum figure they would accept in return for the loan. It made for a febrile, suspicious, almost paranoid atmosphere as rumours flew around Whitehall and ministers waited week after week to learn what number to discuss.

My own relations with the Treasury deteriorated temporarily during this phoney war, mainly because of their attempts to prevent myself and the Unit from having access to any information about the progress of the negotiations with the IMF. Remembering our role over incomes policy, they feared that we would influence the Prime Minister – as we indeed did, and as it was our job to do. The main differences between us were both of analyses of the current situation, and of the prescription of remedies. We believed that the Treasury forecasts were too pessimistic (as they proved to be), that there were no economic grounds for major expenditure cuts since Britain was in recession, and that we should aim for the minimum cuts necessary to restore market confidence in the short term. We particularly disagreed with those (who were not all) in the Treasury and in the

Bank of England who sought to exploit the opportunity to impose a massive deflationary squeeze on the British economy regardless of the unemployment and political consequences.

Instead of dealing openly with our arguments, the Treasury tried to exclude us from the debate, by cutting us off from information on what was actually happening in the IMF negotiations, and falsely accusing me of leaking confidential information. I refused to accept this freeze-out, seeing it as my job to discover the full information for the Unit in order to brief the Prime Minister. I checked through every possible source in my information networks around Whitehall, and Gavyn Davies energetically did the same, and so I ended up with a fairly full picture and was able to brief the Prime Minister and discuss with him the latest developments in the secret saga. The whole business again demonstrated that access to information is a primary weapon in Whitehall, and no adviser without it can ever hope to win a serious battle there.

The political side of the IMF crisis came to a head at the end of November 1976, with the first serious cabinet discussion of the issue, and concluded in the first half of December. At that opening cabinet, ministers were finally shown the £5 billion of flesh which had to be extracted from Britain's public spending in return for the IMF loan and seal of approval for our policies. Ministers wisely said 'No, thank you' and from that time the Prime Minister took over the responsibility of finding a compromise acceptable to both the financial and the political sides. On 25 November my unit submitted a paper setting out our proposed compromise package which would reduce the Public Sector Borrowing Requirement by £3 billion with the minimum consequential deflation.

The Prime Minister liked the paper and next morning he summoned myself and Gavyn Davies (who had done most of the detail) and grilled us severely on our proposals. He then passed the paper to Denis Healey and said he wanted the Treasury to give it positive consideration (a tough request).

Gavyn and I then went to discuss it with Treasury officials. They immediately said that it did not contain enough 'blood' in terms of expenditure cuts to satisfy the IMF. When we responded with extra proposals to cut public service manpower and freeze Civil Service recruitment, the shocked officials (who by 'blood' did not, of course, mean Whitehall blood), brought in a senior mandarin from the Civil Service Department. He resisted our proposals as 'totally unacceptable' because they involved more work and less jobs for the Civil Service, threatening that protesting civil servants would 'bring the country to a halt faster than the miners'.

I blew up with anger at the way these cosseted bureaucrats, comfortable with their job security and inflation-proofed pensions, could advocate in such a cavalier manner that half a million workers in harsh private sector jobs be made unemployed, but refused to share any of the sacrifice themselves. So we ended in a bad mood all round, which did not advance the prospects of our paper getting a positive reception in the Treasury. But I did note that our next priority might be to abolish the Civil Service Department (another Unit idea which awaited Mrs Thatcher for its execution).

Four major cabinets decided the IMF issue at the beginning of December. At the first, the ideological left showed its hand with a paper by Benn and Shore on their proposed 'Alternative Strategy' of a 'fortress Britain'. Beforehand, I had put to the Prime Minister a list of precise questions to ask Benn about this paper, which he did very effectively. There was a big majority against the left's socialist Alternative Strategy, with only Foot, Booth, Silkin and Orme supporting Benn and Shore.

But Callaghan was shrewd to give the left its full opportunity to make its arguments and to realise that they were a small minority in cabinet. The Prime Minister then ordered Crosland and Lever, never men of steel, to give up their opposition and agree to support a smaller package of cuts. That effectively killed off any rebellion from the right. At two more cabinets on 6 December ministers agreed a final package of £800 million cuts and £200 million extra taxation for the coming year and another £1 billion of cuts after that. So Jim Callaghan had finally delivered ministerial support to Healey – and the IMF accepted this compromise.

The final ribbon on the IMF financial package was the Letter of Intent which recipients of IMF loans always have to write to the Fund promising future good behaviour. This produced another sharp clash between the Treasury and us in Number 10. Treasury officials had refused all week to show us the Letter, claiming unconvincingly that they had secretarial problems. I stayed in Number 10 until late on the Friday evening hoping to see the draft, but it did not appear. In fact, they were deliberately waiting till the weekend before showing it to the Prime Minister. No doubt they hoped that it would then bounce through without questions, since the Unit members would be at their homes and the Prime Minister was ill in bed with bronchitis. If so, the tactic did not work.

On the Saturday morning, 11 December, the Prime Minister telephoned me at Brookfield Park from his sick bed and asked me to come straight away into Number 10 with Gavyn Davies to advise him on the Letter of Intent. We quickly spotted that the Letter actually omitted all the key figures on money supply, domestic credit expansion and the Public Sector Borrowing Requirement. The Treasury brazenly proposed to insert these after the Prime Minister had signed the Letter – and these figures, if made very tight, would give them the means of actually achieving the massive and destructive deflation which they had sought in their opening huge cuts package and which the Prime Minister and we had resisted from the beginning.

I went upstairs to Jim's bedroom in the flat, gave him our brief and verbally explained to him what would be the consequences if he simply agreed and signed off on this Treasury 'bounce'. I then went off to play football at Crystal Palace for our Parliament team against the Belgian Parliament. (I was not, of course, then a member of either of the Houses of Parliament, but by now, aged forty-two, played football as a kind of hired gunslinger for whoever would select me.)

While I was away damaging Anglo–Belgian relations, a very hoarse and grumpy Prime Minister telephoned Healey and blew him out of the water for attempting this latest 'bounce'. Jim threatened to call a special cabinet unless the Letter was changed.

On Sunday morning I returned to Number 10, where the Prime Minister summoned me up for tea in his flat. He was lying in bed surrounded by his boxes, and Audrey produced pots of tea and plates of cakes. He told me that using 'our paper' he had forced Healey and the Treasury to promise not to tighten the monetary targets in the Letter of Intent. He was very pleased with our work, and especially Gavyn's, and it was a satisfying conclusion to an exhausting weekend.

Callaghan's personal achievement over the IMF crisis was considerable. He had kept his ministerial team together while allowing sincere differences of views to be expressed. Ultimately he delivered united cabinet support for a package of cuts which was sufficient to restore market confidence in sterling, without being so deflationary as to destroy his Government. He both led the Chancellor on the policies and at the same time fully supported him in cabinet (the kind of prime ministerial support which, he complained to me, Wilson had not always given him as Chancellor in 1964–7). The Treasury, which tried some silly tricks on him, had clearly at the beginning underestimated him, remembering the broken Chancellor of the 1967 devaluation, not realising that since then he had recovered, grown in confidence and toughened up. When the Treasury later complained that Jim was 'trying to be his own Chancellor', he commented to me that 'I was only trying to be Denis's political adviser'. Probably, Healey would have benefited from having a Policy Unit of his own in the Treasury to protect him from internal official 'bounces'.

One final interesting aspect of the 1976 IMF crisis was the way in which the agreement, by forcing us to publish specific monetary targets, helped to entrench monetarism in the mindset of British government. This was not, of course, a sudden conversion under duress from the Fund, and the intellectual background to it in Britain had been the steady erosion of faith in traditional Keynesianism

With Jim Callaghan in 1995.

Twin sons Stephen (left) and Paul . . .

… and my daughters Rachel (left) and Kate.

Sailing down the Nile to the tomb of Tutankhamun with the Earl and Countess of Carnarvon.
The Earl's grandfather had led the excavation of Tutankhamun's tomb in 1922.

Meeting Nelson Mandela, with Alan Simpson MP,
on a parliamentary cricket tour of South Africa, 1995.

Above: Receiving the 'Top Tipster' award from John Prescott at the Labour Party-sponsored race meeting at Brighton, 1997.

Left: With Anji Hunter, Tony Blair's influential secretary.

Below: With Tony Blair and comedian Stephen Fry (and, partly obscured, the writer John Mortimer), 1998.

The minister from MAFF in 1998 – with my beloved terrier Honey at a County Show;
promoting British food specialities;
and on one of my more enjoyable overseas trips, to Indonesia.

With former Cabinet Secretary
Robin Butler in the Pyrenees,
1997.

Opening the sports hall at Roade
School with headmaster Will
Adams, 2001.

Introducing Jeff Rooker to the House of Lords with Joyce Gould, 2001.

With Sarah at Ceret, 2001.

With Sarah and our friend
the actress Anna Massey.

Two racing superstars: Jim
Culloty and Robber Baron
winning comfortably at
Taunton, 2002.

The minister at his desk at MAFF, 1997.

which I had observed over recent years. At the same time the monetarist theories gained rapid ground in the intellectual debate conducted at our universities and in the press, where Samuel Brittan in the *Financial Times* and the Prime Minister's son-in-law, Peter Jay, in *The Times* led the charge. On the Tory benches in the Commons, Keith Joseph, Geoffrey Howe, Nicholas Ridley and John Biffen ensured that the role of monetary factors in creating or controlling inflation was in the forefront of the economic debate. Most Labour politicians were then unaware of this seemingly academic warfare. Jim Callaghan and his colleagues had grown up since the 1930s with a prime commitment to full employment and a belief that Keynesian demand-management provided the essential techniques for providing and maintaining that full employment. But during the harsh experiences of 1974–6, some of the more interested ministers – especially Callaghan, Healey and Jenkins – were made increasingly aware that the Keynesian approach was simply not working in the new economic world of 'stagflation', where the economy remained in recession and additional public expenditure produced more inflation but no more economic growth.

I was particularly aware of this dilemma and continued to follow the academic debate. I never swallowed the whole monetarist mumbo-jumbo of the Chicago school, nor believed that there was a precise mathematical link between growth in money stock and the future inflation levels. But I was aware that monetarist colleagues at the LSE, such as Harry Johnson and Alan Walters (later Mrs Thatcher's guru), had made a broad case that was convincing to me: that at the very simplest level a lax monetary stance in government resulted ultimately in higher inflation; that high public expenditure beyond our capacity to finance it caused high interest rates and high taxation; and that high inflation, high taxation and high interest rates caused high unemployment. That had been our diet in 1974–6.

So the crude Keynesianism practised by both parties in government since 1945 was no longer working beneficially and in some ways was creating unemployment. Public expenditure had grown inexorably by 20 per cent in 1974–6 and by 1976 it had reached a peak of 60 per cent of Gross Domestic Product. While over those two years national output rose only 2 per cent and unemployment surged. We were suffering higher taxes, interest rates, inflation and unemployment without enjoying much higher growth. Additionally, due to the particular inefficiencies of our then public service sector and the negativism of its trade unions, we were increasing public service expenditure without even getting better public services. That was a seriously bad deal. We were paying for Keynesianism without getting the benefits. This created a growing disenchantment with that approach, reflected in James Callaghan's remarkable speech to the 1976 Labour

Conference at Blackpool, when he told a stunned and resentful audience: 'We used to think that you could spend your way out of a recession to increase employment by cutting taxes and boosting public spending. I tell you in all candour that that option no longer exists.'

I agreed with every word he said. After only two months in office, in May 1974, I sent Wilson a paper drafted by Andrew Graham alerting him to the need to come to grips with the monetarist issue and suggesting that he should set up a cabinet committee specifically to consider monetary policies. But Wilson had already by then lost interest in contemporary developments in economic thinking and he did not respond positively.

So we returned to the attack in December 1975. Andrew and Gavyn wrote for me a compelling paper on the need for the Prime Minister to initiate a stricter monetarist approach to government finances, rather than to allow it to seep into policy by a series of *ad hoc* decisions by the Treasury and the Bank of England. Wilson said he agreed but did nothing. However, the IMF agreement and James Callaghan's personal dedication to defeat inflation ensured that from 1976 the Government's approach embraced the broader principles of monetarism – though not until Mrs Thatcher's succession did it become for a while the strict theology of Downing Street.

Fourteen

QUIETER TIMES

With the IMF agreement successfully under our belts, I enjoyed a satisfying eighteen months in Number 10, with few of the crises and little of the turbulence which had characterised the whole period since I entered government in March 1974. It was cheering to see the economy stabilised, with inflation moving down into single figures for the first time since early 1974 – the Unit was deeply involved in the tricky phase 3 of the incomes policy – and unemployment was at least steady. Our precarious position in the Commons was eased when Callaghan formed a pact with the Liberals in March 1977, and the Government's ratings improved in the opinion polls. James Callaghan became nationally respected as Prime Minister and I was proud to work with him.

One arcane problem dealt with by the Unit was the periodic drying up of the market in government gilt-edged stocks, making it difficult for the Government to finance its large debt without regular hikes in interest rates. It was clear to me that the inefficient market mechanisms for selling gilt-edged stocks needed reforming, though this would not be easy to introduce since the Bank was very attached to a system which gave it great power in the City. In June 1978 I sent to the Prime Minister a paper with a list of suggested technical reforms to the marketing of public debt. We suggested issuing index-linked gilts, variable-rate stocks, and particular ways to encourage unit trusts to buy gilts. We also proposed the introduction of a tender system to replace the traditional poker game between the Government broker and the investment institutions.

The Prime Minister agreed with our suggested reforms but the Bank of England was extremely hostile and blocked them. In due course innovations such as index-linked gilts, variable-rate bonds, and tender-selling were introduced under successor governments. I suppose that can be counted as a partial success for the Unit, though our members were long dispersed by the time the reforms came about.

Apart from the remorseless treadmill of economics, the Unit was involved in several social policy areas. We strongly supported the introduction of a new child benefit paid to the mother (against Jim's reluctance). For the NHS, Callaghan rescued an extra £50 million from the IMF cuts – but he ran up against a familiar obstacle from the public sector unions. I had intervened with Private Office to make sure that the letter to the Department of Health offering the money included a condition that the extra resources should be used only 'for improving patient care', but the health unions, backed by the mediocre minister David Ennals, insisted that all the money go directly to their members. The Prime Minister summoned a meeting of health unions in Number 10 to explain to them why his priority was to give money to treat the sick, an objective with which they were not particularly sympathetic.

This episode illustrated our problem with the public service unions – that they saw health expenditure as only for the benefit of the NHS workers and not the patients, and education expenditure as being for teachers and not children, and local government activities as for the benefit of municipal employees and not the citizens. (Tony Blair must be careful they do not take the same approach today to the financial bonanza being given to the NHS.) It then seemed to me inevitable that those unions would some day get their comeuppance from a Government representing the interests of the whole general public. When Mrs Thatcher delivered that blow, from a much less sympathetic position than ours, there were understandably few disinterested people ready to speak up in the unions' defence.

In the area of industrial policy, the inefficient and under-invested British motor car industry continued to dog us with its troubles and to absorb vast public subsidies which might have gone to a better cause. British Leyland was a particular disgrace, producing in 1978 fewer cars from more workers than it had done in 1972.

Even Rover let the Prime Minister down. By 1979 his noble old Rover 3.5 had done over 200,000 miles and was not fully equipped with the latest anti-terrorist devices. So officials persuaded a reluctant Jim to get a new car. It had to be British for political reasons and could not be an ostentatious Rolls – only privileged ambassadors, obviously more important than elected Prime Ministers, could enjoy them abroad. So two new Rovers were ordered, with £250,000 worth of security 'extras': bombproof, bulletproof, special communications equipment – the lot. When the new cars came, they were found to have thirty-four serious mechanical faults and had to be returned immediately to Rover for repairs. Returned repaired, the Prime Minister took one for his Friday journey back to the farm. Reaching sunny Sussex, he decided to open the windows for some fresh air and pressed the then-modern electric button. The window slowly toppled inwards and fell onto his lap. His driver told me that 'the Prime Minister's face turned dark, but he did not say a word until we reached the farm'. Then he simply handed the driver the window and said, 'Don't bring this car again.' So it was back to the old Rover until a new and hopefully less unreliable Jaguar became available later. Ken Stowe now had the task of disposing of two new yet dodgy Rovers with few miles on the clock and a quarter of a million pounds' worth of security extras.

Northern Ireland remained an apparently insoluble problem. Callaghan appointed as Secretary of State Roy Mason, a right-wing toughie who was very acceptable to the Ulster Unionist majority, with the broad instruction to keep the lid on the Irish cauldron – which he basically did achieve. This stance was reinforced when Callaghan forged an understanding with the Ulster Unionist Party which gave us a slim majority in the Commons even after the termination of the Lib–Lab pact.

Perhaps to balance matters, he appointed me as his personal representative to the Roman Catholic Church hierarchy in Britain. I dealt with a sensible Bishop Konstant, who was acting directly on behalf of the saintly Archbishop Hume (one of my later heroes but seen by the Church hierarchy as 'too unworldly' for such discussions).

My most practical and enjoyable involvement in Anglo–Irish affairs at this time was to organise, with my close friend Professor Trevor West of Trinity College, Dublin, the first ever official football match between the British and Irish Parliaments. The Irish side included a future Prime Minister, Bertie Ahern, whom I personally marked (though hopefully not for life), and Michael O'Kennedy, later to be Foreign Secretary. The British won comfortably as the Irish team, which had enjoyed a very good and liquid lunch before the game, faded in the second half.

As a fascinating piece of history, I saw the denouement of the policy of economic sanctions against white South Africa introduced by Harold Wilson in the 1960s. Secret papers made it clear that the Cabinet Defence Committee (OPD) and Foreign Office officials were aware in 1968 that British oil companies were evading sanctions by supplying oil to South Africa. In 1978, the Bingham Report revealed much but not all of this scandal. Wilson, who had chaired the OPD Committee, announced on the front page of *The Times* on 4 September that he had known absolutely nothing about sanctions-busting in 1968. One of my golden rules about Harold was that 'he only bothered to deny that which was true', but perhaps his dementia was sadly already affecting him.

One additional aspect of the affair concerned the submission of relevant Foreign Office papers to Bingham's enquiry. I overheard an agitated discussion between FCO and Number 10 officials revealing that it had been official policy to withhold from Bingham the key documents that revealed that ministers and officials had indeed known of sanctions-busting in 1968. But these papers were 'inadvertently' included with the submission to Bingham, and not excluded as intended. An internal Cabinet Office paper stated that 'unfortunately' Bingham did receive 'a full picture'. In desperation, officials approached the Bingham team to ensure that there were no specific references to these key papers in his report. This was apparently agreed.

My personal and social life under Jim Callaghan was as busy as under Wilson, though with more predictable routines, reflecting the Prime Minister's own more routine life. I rose most mornings by seven and went for runs of three to four miles across Hampstead Heath, usually with my friend John Carrier who lived nearby. In winter it was dark, with us often running under a moon and on paths and grass covered in frost. But in summer the Heath was luxuriant and rich with the smells of leaves and flowers and I loved the vast views over London and down the distant Thames as we rose towards Kenwood or up the steep and punishing climb to the top of Parliament Hill.

I lunched regularly at the Gay Hussar in Soho, then run by Mr Victor, its proprietor, like a private club for Labour politicians and journalists. I often ate there with Joe Haines, who updated me on the latest Fleet Street rumours. There were always a mass of political friends at other tables, especially Michael Foot (who like me had his regular table in the window), Roy Hattersley, Tessa Jowell, publisher friends such as Graham Greene, and a spattering of journalists. Before sitting down we usually toured the tables to say hellos and exchange gossip.

Apart from enjoying together Downing Street social engagements, I saw too little of Carol in the week. As with many professional people where both partners work, our time together too often comprised hurried discussions of domestic arrangements, such as who would stay in to receive the builder or who would take the children somewhere (usually Carol). It at times turned the marriage into a kind of domestic business partnership and occasionally produced the kinds of strains familiar to modern working parents, though she uncomplainingly bore the bulk of the domestic burden.

Not that we had much choice about both working to earn money. My salary at Number 10, around £9,000 a year, was still paltry given my responsibilities. I was summoned by my bank manager in 1978 to justify my huge overdraft and consequently had to sell an Epstein watercolour and many of my books from the LSE, going sheepishly down the Charing Cross Road to find the best price. I saw even less of the children than of Carol during the week. I regret that omission and have tried to make up for it since – but life is not a film where one can later roll it back and refashion it a different way. I lost some of their precious childhood forever.

Fortunately, holidays were always spent together as a family: Christmas, Easter and many other weekends were spent at our pretty Suffolk thatched cottage with its big garden and wonderful views across fields to Wickhambrook church and to the rustic local pub with its fine Greene King beer. Our summers in Ceret were also entirely family affairs, with books and walks and swimming in the river, but no telephone or television for a whole month.

My lovely girls, Rachel and Kate, each joined Camden School for Girls while I was with Callaghan. The twin boys were also progressing well. Paul was sweet and kind. Stephen was particularly forward and funny. He wrote to Harold Wilson suggesting better designs for naval uniforms and especially that I might be better employed spending more time at home. Aged just six, he wrote (without consulting me) to the Secretary of State for Defence with various of his inventions to improve the nation's military arsenal. The Private Secretary, John Mayne, wrote back a delightful letter commenting that these inventions 'will, of course, be of profound importance to our future research, development and production programmes' – providing that the Government did not carry out the Labour National Executive's current disarmament proposals.

Shortly after, when I went with Callaghan to visit President Ford in Washington, Stephen wrote separately a simple note to the President requesting, 'Please look after daddy in America.' On the 22 December 1978 he wrote at greater length to the Head of MI6:

I am only nine (just) but I am very interested in the INTELLIGENCE services. I am trying to set up a spy ring but nobody seems interested. I have got my sisters' Wendy House for a HQ, but I need information about what I should do. I have bought Osbourne Spybooks, the Know How book of Spycraft, Spys Guidebook, and the Know How book of detection, but they just show codes, disguises, nothing about setting up a spy ring and training and equipment which are the most important things to show in a spy book thats why I wrote this letter so I could get some help from the Top Intelligence people. If you please be so kind and send me a training manual for spys, information about spying and setting up a Spy Ring and some files to fill in about myself and friends. And if it wouldn't be too much a test to test myself on the art of spying. Yours sincerely

Stephen Donoughue Age 9.

Stephen received a suitably cautious reply:

I was most encouraged to learn of your interest and hope that we can keep in touch. As between professionals, you may like to see how the Chinese were organising themselves in the 4th century BC. Much of their tactics remain of use today. I hope the attachment [by Sun Tzu] will help you identify the sort of people you should be looking for.

                                    With my best wishes. M. [Sir Maurice Oldfield]

By far the most exciting of several official visits we made abroad was undoubtedly that to India and Pakistan, touching Burma, in January 1978. It was very exhausting, but the beauty, variety and the vibrant colours of the subcontinent, together with the friendly courtesy of the local people, kept me 'lifted' throughout. Every day seemed to be a highlight, but best I recall the lovely trip on the river at Dacca, another river trip at Chittagong (a name resonant of BBC news broadcasts in the war), the Taj Mahal floating in the smoky air, a fabulous picnic at Fatipur Sikri served by turbaned soldiers and feeling like a scene from the height of the Raj, a boat trip among the waterlands and birds of Gujarat with Prime Minister Desai, a test match in Lahore, a two-hour after-dinner speech without alcohol by the Pakistan President (soon to be assassinated), a visit to the Khyber Pass with frontier guards silhouetted on the hilltops, and simply the relaxed pleasure of residing in the old Governor's House in Bombay, with breakfast on a sunny veranda overlooking the Arabian Sea. It seemed a long way from Roade.

On our flight back, we landed at Aswan and had a late supper with President Sadat of Egypt (an impressive statesman soon, sadly, to be murdered) at his holiday residence, with views towards the great Nile dam. Having landed back in London at 2 a.m. on the Saturday, I went off that afternoon to play football at Crystal Palace for the British Parliament against the German. I was still high with the intoxication of our Indian visit, scored a goal which was subsequently shown weekly in the introduction to BBC TV *Grandstand*, and was given a yellow card for an instinctive tackle on an innocent German striker named Adolf.

Ghosts from my Wilsonian past occasionally flitted by to remind me how much saner my life was under Jim than it had been under Harold. When Joe Haines published his book *The Politics of Power* in early 1977, with descriptions of our battles with Marcia, it received tremendous coverage throughout the media, which made me uncomfortable since I loathe publicity. I sent Jim a copy of the book, and when I went nervously into the study was greatly relieved to see him with the book on his lap chuckling with pleasure and saying, 'My God, that Marcia, she was quite something' and then, 'I wish I had somebody here who could write like Joe.'

Just before Christmas 1978, Bill Housden joined me for supper in the cafeteria of the House of Commons and reported that Wilson's memory was deteriorating very badly and that he often could not remember where he was supposed to be going that day. He said that Harold spent most of his days sitting and staring vacantly in his room in the Norman Shaw Building. 'Nobody visits him. It is very sad.'

During a happy family August in Ceret in 1978, I felt modestly confident about the Government's political future. The economy had stabilised, although there was bound to be a tricky time ahead with the next round of pay policy. The Tory lead in the polls was steadily diminishing, while Jim Callaghan's personal lead over Mrs Thatcher was huge. The next general election had to be held by October 1979, and like most political colleagues and commentators I assumed and hoped that it would be during the coming autumn of 1978. Just before Christmas 1977, I had sent Jim a long paper analysing potential election dates, which concluded that October and especially November of 1978 promised best, because there would then be a brief opportunity when the economy would be good, and many people would also then receive significant increases in welfare benefits. After that the forecasts grew murky, with growing pressures likely against our pay policy. These economic forecasts proved correct, with growth at 2½ per cent, price inflation in single figures, take-home pay rising at 6 per cent and unemployment steady at below one and a half million. Victory now would give Callaghan the authority of an election mandate to back his anti-inflation policies. So I returned from France at the beginning of September 1978 expecting soon to fight an election, and with reasonable hopes of success.

Events were not to unveil in the way I expected, and the following turbulent eight months saw the nemesis of this Labour Government.

It was like a drama in the usual three acts. The first act saw the Prime Minister take a finely balanced decision on election timing which proved to have closed the last opportunity for a Labour victory. Act Two displayed unprecedented trade union militancy and lunacy which destroyed the credibility of Callaghan's Labour Government. The final act saw us defeated in Parliament and at the polls. This later event was to push my life into another dramatic change – this time certainly not for the better.

Fifteen

NEMESIS: THE WINTER OF DISCONTENT AND DEFEAT

While I was holidaying in France in August 1978, Jim Callaghan was at his Sussex farm cogitating over whether to call a general election. If he wished to hold one in October, he needed to announce it in early September to allow the party organisation time to prepare. If he chose delay, he had to make that clear soon in order to end the speculation and get the Government moving again.

He took with him to the farm some MORI polls showing that Labour was not doing well in its key marginal seats. He also took the *Times* election books with the results of the 1970 and 1974 elections, and analysed them constituency by constituency to try to establish what the results might be now.

Jim returned to London for a special cabinet on 1 September to take the views of his colleagues. No officials were allowed to be present, though from the written record it appeared that a majority of ministers were in favour of an early election, especially the younger ones (with the exception of David Owen). Older members such as Michael Foot, Merlyn Rees and Harold Lever, to whom Callaghan listened more readily, were against dissolving this year, and Healey was ambivalent.

Callaghan did not show his own hand, though he later claimed to have made up his own mind against an early election on 17 August because of his electoral analysis at the farm. He did not consult his personal staff, Tom McNally, Tom Macaffery and myself, and none of us knew his decision until the last moment.

Over the previous months, he had carefully kept his options open. By ending the Lib–Lab pact in the summer of 1978, he had cleared the decks to fight an election unencumbered with formal alliances. He recruited Roger Carroll from the *Sun* newspaper as a speechwriter, knowing McNally would be fighting his own constituency and unavailable to write for him. He asked his Cardiff party to print his leaflets ready for an autumn election. As late as Sunday 3 September he asked Geoffrey Goodman of the *Mirror* to join his election team as liaison to the TUC.

That Sunday, before the announcement of his decision, he had lunch with six trade union leaders who formed the clear impression that he intended, reluctantly, to fight – and expected to lose. Yet he had also kept open the option to soldier on in government. So he could jump either way and may indeed, as his daughter believed, have left the final decision until very late in the day.

He played his election announcement with an uncharacteristic sense of drama. He took none of his personal team with him to Brighton for his big speech to the TUC on Tuesday 5 September, and none of us really knew what, if anything, he was going to say about the election. My only involvement was on the day before the speech when he telephoned me from the farm and said that he wanted discreet help in discovering which star of the Victorian music hall had sung the famous song, 'There Was I, Waiting at the Church'. I checked the answer with the Policy Unit's music hall adviser, Joseph T. Haines (by now working as the chief leader writer on the *Mirror*). He immediately said 'Vesta Victoria'. I conveyed this information to the Prime Minister, who thanked me but offered no further comment. Next day, he sang the song to the assembled trade unions, though to my surprise ascribing it to the more famous Marie Lloyd. He was immediately criticised in the press for this error and later apologised to me, explaining that he made the mistake on strong advice from officials in Private Office.

I watched Jim sing his song very impressively on my office television, but its message was too subtle for his audience, including me. Few if any among the trade unionists grasped that he meant that Mrs Thatcher would be left for some time longer waiting for her election opportunity to cross the threshold into Number 10. Virtually everybody assumed that he was just playing cat-and-mouse with the press and with the Tories, and that the television broadcast which he had arranged for Thursday 7 September would announce the election.

The *Daily Mirror*, firmly steered on insufficient evidence by McNally and Macaffery, announced that the date was fixed for 5 October. (I had more cautiously told Joe Haines that I simply did not know.) The Prime Minister returned from Brighton, summoned a special cabinet for the Thursday morning, and there informed his colleagues of his decision not to hold an election. No officials were allowed in. I sat waiting in the outside lobby, and when the cabinet door swung open ministers streamed out, looking puzzled and distracted as they headed silently down the corridor and out into Downing Street. William Rodgers glared at me and snapped. 'That was the most disastrous cabinet in this Government.' Several of the key Number 10 staff did not learn the news until watching the television broadcast early that evening.

I felt shocked and deeply disappointed (as was Tom McNally, who had firmly arranged for various cabinet ministers and trade union leaders to speak in his

Stockport constituency in the expected coming campaign). I normally knew all that was happening at the centre of government, and it was a strange and frustrating experience to be kept so completely in the dark.

I was already psychologically adjusted to the prospect of an election and had firmly decided while on holiday in France that I would leave Number 10 even if we won. It was not easy to recreate new commitment and momentum to our work over the winter months ahead. I was also disappointed because I sensed that the Prime Minister had taken the wrong decision. I had set out the reasons for an autumn 1978 election date in our Unit paper to him at Christmas 1977. The predicted window of economic benevolence had indeed now arrived, with good growth in the economy and in real incomes and with inflation down into single figures, whereas the prospects further ahead through the winter looked more tricky. The opinion polls were also moving encouragingly. Having been 4 per cent behind (only 2 per cent in England) in August when Jim took his initial decision, Labour moved to 5 per cent ahead of the Tories in October. We also then won the Berwick and East Lothian by-election with the first by-election swing to Labour since 1966.

Callaghan himself was miles ahead of Thatcher in the polls as 'best Prime Minister'. The country still seemed not quite ready yet to risk her radicalism. In my view then, the chances of winning an election that autumn, though far from certain, were probably better than the risk of soldiering on through the winter with our fate in the hands of an increasingly irresponsible trade union movement.

Lacking the average journalist's gift of twenty-twenty hindsight, I cannot be absolutely sure what would have happened had we fought the election in the autumn of 1978. Nor was it then clear what political horrors lay ahead. Certainly it would have required an exceptionally pessimistic view of human nature in general, and almost clinical doubts about the mental balance of large numbers of left-wing Labour and trade union activists in particular, to have foreseen that the Labour movement would behave with such suicidal lunacy in the eight months ahead; or that they would make such efforts to secure the defeat of their ally James Callaghan and the election of a Mrs Thatcher committed to the emasculation of the trade union movement. The Prime Minister did not have that degree of pessimism and cynicism. He had grown up with the trade union movement and had great faith in its collective common sense. He could not realise that that common sense would shortly evaporate in a period of collective madness.

Jim Callaghan probably had a whole mix of reasons for making a different decision from what I and most Labour colleagues would have done. Certainly his election analysis had been a prime factor discouraging him. He later told me that he had concluded that at best we could win 325 seats against the present 310, and might even fall to 303, with the Tories on 304. And the polls, though moving our way, still showed Labour behind the Tories, especially in the marginals, at the time of his decision. So since he believed we were unlikely to improve our parliamentary position very much, he saw no point in holding an election. He believed, perfectly sensibly, that a Prime Minister should dissolve for an early election only if he was confident of winning, otherwise he should soldier on and hope for a better opportunity.

Possibly he was also influenced by other more personal factors. My impression was that his innermost preference throughout the previous year had been to continue government into 1979. In September 1977 he had told me that he did 'not want an election next year [1978] if I can help it'. Tom McNally, who knew his boss better than most, thought that Jim wanted to complete three years as Prime Minister simply because 'that sounds more substantial historically that two years'. Having observed Harold Wilson ticking off dates and achievements, I do not dismiss this understandable motive. Certainly an older man, knowing it is his last lap at the top, views these decisions differently from a younger man with decades of opportunity ahead.

It is interesting to note that the colleagues he consulted personally on the decision were Foot, Lever and Rees, who were also among his older ministers. Above all, as a deeply cautious man, he saw the safer course as soldiering on, in the sense that to go early and lose was the worst of all election decisions for a party leader. He also wanted to make more significant progress in conquering inflation before he retired and he knew that his 5 per cent policy for the next pay round, if successful, would achieve that.

Finally, he believed that he had stitched together a political survival kit for the coming parliamentary session. He had arranged the support of the Ulster Unionists, still had the sympathy of David Steel's Liberals, and could hope that the Scottish and Welsh Nationalists would return some gratitude for what the Government proposed on devolution. Together, on balance, they made to him a case for doing what I suspect he all along wanted to do anyway.

The day after his television broadcast, I saw the Prime Minister in his study. He asked if I was surprised by his decision and I replied: 'Yes, because I had come to believe what I read in the newspapers.' He claimed there were 'plenty of clues' pointing to his decision to delay. True, but there was also plenty of evidence of his preparations to fight the election. Anyway, he said that he wanted my Unit 'revitalised' and he wanted me to feed in more ideas 'like the great education debate'. He knew that it was fatal for a Government to be seen to be just 'hanging on'.

I then arranged a series of brainstorming sessions in the Unit to identify our new policy themes. It was not easy for me since I had already psychologically retired from Number 10 and it took a while to sharpen up my appetite again. But the Unit discussions revved up my engines. I included in them several outsiders. Tessa Blackstone spoke very well on the NHS and Tessa Jowell on housing, and both were to be successful ministers in the Blair Government twenty years later.

I sent the Prime Minister a paper entitled 'Themes and Initiatives' and he responded most to our suggestions on 'Responsibilities as well as Rights', on reviving the NHS, and on guaranteeing jobs to the long-term unemployed.

So we were successfully relaunched into Unit activity and I tried to forget my disappointment at the lost election opportunity. I also felt it would help if the Prime Minister now carried out a major reshuffle which would revitalise the personnel of the cabinet. I sent him a memo suggesting a range of ministerial changes, mainly devised to drop the tired old warhorses and promote able and energetic young ones. I suggested Roy Hattersley to Education, David Owen to shake up the Health Service, Michael Foot as a libertarian at the Home Office, John Smith to Scottish Secretary, Bill Rodgers to Defence, Denis Howell for Transport or as Chief Whip (his great political talents were never fully used), and Joel Barnett to be Chancellor if the PM could risk moving Healey to the Foreign Office in the middle of the pay policy crisis. Out would go Ennals, Silkin, Mulley, Millan, Morris, Booth, Peart, etc. It seemed to me particularly damaging that senior ministries which were key policy areas to Labour, such as Health, Housing, Industry and Employment (Ennals, Shore, Varley and Booth) were not in the hands of first-class political ministers. At that time Mrs Thatcher looked young and fresh and we looked old and tired, and the Prime Minister knew that his cabinet needed improvement. At the 1977 Brighton conference he admitted to me that there was 'too little political sex appeal' in it and that 'even the young ones are too grey.' He praised Healey as 'the biggest member of the cabinet' and said that Owen, Hattersley and Rodgers were doing well, though he felt Rodgers was 'not subtle enough in his right wing views'. He felt that Foot had 'slipped', Shore was 'too rhetorical' and Booth 'very wooden'.

He did not dissent when I said that it was politically dangerous to carry so many second-division players in the cabinet. But Jim politely declined my impertinent interference in the Prime Minister's prerogative over the disposition of his political troops. He pointed out that 'the trouble with reshuffles is that the people who are promoted believe that they deserved it anyway and they no longer have to behave well in anticipation; while those who are dropped or ignored are made enemies for life'. I saw his point and understood that he didn't want to risk rocking the ministerial boat. But it did mean that his cabinet was not refreshed and that three of its outstanding younger members – John Smith, Roy Hattersley and Bill Rodgers – were left in junior posts below their political capacity.

We were quickly absorbed in a decision with momentous consequences for the future of Britain in Europe, and one which reverberated through the following decades. In July 1978 the German and French leaders, characteristically without consulting Britain or any other EEC members, launched the 'Zone of Monetary Stability in Europe', soon to be called the European Monetary System and later to evolve into the Euro. It was a major political step towards further European integration. Ministers discussed this radical European initiative at a special cabinet committee on 10 October, with the Governor of the Bank of England (and myself) present, and again in full cabinet on 2 November 1978.

In the Unit we briefed the Prime Minister not to join, with Gavyn Davies strongly against and I (probably the most 'pro-European' of the Unit) more reluctantly so. But the Prime Minister did not need any steering since he saw no financial or economic attractions in the scheme for Britain, and certainly no political ones in dividing his cabinet. He said to me that the only reasons for entering the new monetary mechanism were international – 'to help build Europe, and to stabilise the world monetary system' – and that in writing his speeches we must now 'prepare the way for our staying out of the EMS ... The more it goes on, the less attractive it seems to me ... Do not make the mistake of trying to make a success of a system just because we have embarked on it. That is always the danger in Government.' He was supported in his opposition by a large majority of his ministers, with only Harold Lever and Shirley Williams in favour of plunging in. The Treasury and Bank of England officials were also deeply sceptical, so there was little prospect of Britain joining the new monetary system. At the December Council in Bremen, Callaghan tried to soften our antagonism by supporting the construction of the EMS 'snake', while opting out of the grid mechanism and any day-to-day management of it.

But by the time the European monetary issue was settled in December our concerns were again dominated by our domestic pay policy to defeat inflation. The trade unions had accepted the five per cent pay policy during the summer only on the assumption that they would not have to deliver it – because an election would intervene and would change the game. Callaghan privately preferred zero per cent but accepted five per cent as the maximum increase permissible if we were to stop inflation from rising above the current level of eight per cent in the following election year. For me that is the basic defence of Callaghan's five per cent policy. It was the only way of avoiding high inflation – and avoiding the monetary squeeze and high unemployment which would inevitably follow such inflation. So, however difficult, it was worth pursuing. But once the trade unions destroyed that five per cent target, they ensured that we would lose the next election and that Mrs Thatcher, after her victory, would have no policy alternative other than to introduce the monetary squeeze which made over 3 million people unemployed – most of them trade unionists.

In the autumn of 1978 we were quickly faced with a string of high wage claims, with Ford and British Oxygen opening at fifteen per cent and many public sector unions seeking to outbid them. The Labour Party Conference voted massively to reject the Government's five per cent policy. But the Prime Minister remained resilient. In mid-October he told me that he did 'not propose to yield'. He was comforted by a Gallup Poll which showed massive public support for our incomes policy, with a majority of individual trade unionists for it. But the problem was that the trade union organisations had come under the control of a minority of extremists and the union leaders, not a distinguished bunch at that time, were responding to these militants, not to the majority of their members. On 14 November the TUC rejected an agreement we had already made on pay with their own Economic Committee. A month later our legislation to provide sanctions to back the pay policy was defeated in the House of Commons when five hard-left Labour MPs refused to support the Government and so made another of their contributions towards electing Mrs Thatcher. The Prime Minister's political credibility had undoubtedly been damaged, and I sensed that it was a major step towards the Government's demise.

Despite the growing political gloom, I enjoyed a wonderful family Christmas in Suffolk. Eight of us, including my brother Clem and his impressive new French wife Agnes, crowded into our tiny wattle-and-plaster cottage and sat around its blazing log fires. I always loved tiptoeing upstairs late on Christmas Eve and putting the children's presents in their pillow-cases. Clem said it was just the kind of Christmas which he and I had missed in Waverley long ago. There was no telephone nor television to interrupt us at the cottage. (If Number 10 wanted to communicate with me in Suffolk, the local policeman was dispatched to my door to bring the message and then I went up the hill to the public phone box and dialled to Downing Street, pushing my coins in the slot.)

Suffolk was a last haven of peace before the political horrors which faced us in the New Year. Ominously, there was a terrible blizzard on New Year's Eve, which froze everything – water pipes, the car, the lot. I drove up to London with the car windows icing on the inside. Only one lane of the motorway was clear of snow and there had been no attempt by the local authorities to grit the roads, so we often skidded frighteningly. The local government employees and their employers had totally lost sight of their responsibility to serve the public and I sensed that there were large numbers of the British electorate slithering around the roads that day and beginning to agree with Mrs Thatcher's robust views on the subject. The public service trade unions were about to bring down a deserved nemesis upon themselves.

Back in Number 10 on 3 January 1979, the Prime Minister sent for me before he set off on his trip to Guadaloupe. He liked the paper which I had submitted over Christmas on the prospects for our pay policy linked to price sanctions, but he said that I was 'too optimistic' (actually I was deeply pessimistic, but wanted to lift this morale). He told me that he felt that 'it is all falling apart.' He was very suspicious of the 'calm' in Whitehall: 'I don't like the smell of it. We shall wake up in a few weeks time and find that it is too late, everybody is settling for 20 per cent ... This does not look good.' He said that he did not trust the Whitehall machine to tell him the truth and feared that 'ministers and departments are selling out.' So he wanted me to monitor the pay policy for him in his absence and asked me if I thought there was anything more that the Government could do about the crisis. I returned to our paper on price sanctions, suggesting that if employers granted excessive wage increases then they should be required to recoup the costs not out of inflationary price increases but out of profits or cutting other costs. I said that a mixture of price sanctions in the private sector and true tough pay-comparability in the public sector would at least give him a coherent pay strategy to replace the demolished 5 per cent.

He grew more enthusiastic and telephoned Healey in Sussex, telling him to get moving quickly on the price sanctions side, convinced that it was a policy on which he could rebuild his alliance with the TUC and make a platform on which he could fight an election. Then he set off for the Caribbean sunshine, though his departure from Heathrow was delayed an hour while they dug his VC10 aircraft out of the snow and defrosted it.

I quickly met Healey and Hattersley and worked to construct the new pay policy linked to price sanctions. Hattersley was particularly constructive and struck me as shaping to be a future Chancellor. But the situation on the wages front was deteriorating by the day, with food and oil supplies interrupted by the transport strike and some ports closing. A railway strike loomed to join the road transport workers. The electricity and gas workers and the local authority manuals were queuing up with huge wage demands and the public service nurses, teachers and social workers were preparing to ride on their backs. There seemed to be madness in the air as unions announced their intention to strike almost before they had laid their pay claims on the negotiating table. Their leaders displayed a teenage machismo, competitively boasting of intentions to bust the pay policy by the biggest amount (and by implication about who could create the most inflation). Each day I wired the Prime Minister on the disturbing situation at home. He phoned Healey from the Caribbean on 8 January to say that something 'tough' would have to be done about 'union power', but it was not clear precisely what that might be.

It felt to us in Number 10 as if an avalanche was sweeping away our central counter-inflation policy. It also did not look good in a freezing London paralysed by strikes, when the newspapers frequently published huge photographs of the Prime Minister, McNally and Macaffery basking in the Caribbean sunshine.

Jim Callaghan then made an uncharacteristic mistake on landing in London on 10 January, breaking Harold Wilson's golden rule that a minister should never speak about the British domestic situation when arriving from abroad, since he is likely to be out of touch and to miss the nuances. Jim Callaghan never said 'Crisis, What Crisis?', the notorious *Sun* headline which the Tories used damagingly against him. Nothing has ever deterred some newspapers from making things up, but sadly Jim gave them the opening and the opportunity for this invention. He tried to convey an 'unflappable' image, but it came over as complacency in the sunshine and he never recovered from that.

The Prime Minister was quickly put in touch with the seriousness of the domestic situation. Next day, in cabinet committee and then full cabinet, he saw ministers such as Ennals and Booth already waving the white flag even before the union panzers had arrived on their lawns. Following the Prime Minister's lead, cabinet decided to try to stick to the 5 per cent policy; but we knew there was no serious hope of success in that endeavour.

The trade unions were loudly abandoning the policy and their Labour Prime Minister. Jim said to me with deep personal regret: 'Bernard, here is this great trade union movement in this great crisis, and it has nothing to say. It is completely leaderless.' Certainly the unions were depressingly weak. Apart from the pathetic Moss Evans of the giant Transport and General Workers' Union, who was at best a third-rater, there was the appalling Alan Fisher of the Public Employees, who Jim rightly described as 'just a left-wing windbag'. Daly, the mineworkers' leader, and Basnett, the weak and vain boss of my own General and Municipal Workers' Union, were little better. A few of the union men had good qualities. Terry Duffy of the Engineers was brave on policy but often fatally unfocussed. Roy Grantham on the white-collar side was excellent. So was loyal Sid Weighell of the Railwaymen, still primly and socially respectable in his black homburg hat.

Sid came to my room one morning for coffee after a meeting with the Prime Minister and affirmed he was 'in the business of saving the Labour government'. He brought with him colourful Frank Chapple, the former Communist and now anti-Communist leader of the electricians. Frank was, to me, one of the few cheering union lights in the encircling gloom. He spoke with justifiable contempt of Alan Fisher, adding that 'most of his members have never done a single fucking day's hard work in their lives'. Frank explained that his biggest problem was with his own union. 'My Executive are enemies of mine and they are a fucking 'orrible lot. In fact my members are a fucking 'orrible lot too.' But he promised to do what he could to help Callaghan. 'I don't actually support any fucking incomes policy, but I will support one now if it will help this fucking Government.' I liked both Sid and Frank in their different ways, and felt that if more of our trade union leaders had their authentic and honest qualities the Government might not have been in quite this mess.

For a time I enjoyed being deeply involved in the battle. I wrote a dozen pages of the Prime Minister's big Commons speech on the crisis and worked with Gavyn on his paper on pay policy. But in the following week, starting 15 January, our policies and morale were collapsing together. The road haulage strike was bringing many industries to a halt. The water strike had deprived many parts of the North of fresh water for ten days. The railways were closed and the London Underground at a halt. The weather continued to be dreadful and I walked the three miles into Downing Street through the freezing slush.

In cabinet, Healey, Hattersley, Owen, Rodgers and Shirley Williams were still showing some backbone, but other ministers were clearly 'bottling out', as Albert Murray would say. Weak decisions were taken to capitulate to the lorry drivers, encouraging others to copy their intransigence, to finance any level of local authority pay settlement through higher rates, and not to pursue price sanctions. At one point the Prime Minister directly asked Benn: 'What should we do now, Tony?' But Benn had a different agenda and did not reply.

Ken Stowe reported that the flow of official papers had entirely ceased. The machine was paralysed and departments were afraid to confront their own sectoral clients who were striking against the government. Ken told me: 'It is just like it was in February 1974. Whitehall is waiting to see which way the cat will jump politically.' So the great crisis was not as I might have expected, with ministers and officials dashing from meeting to meeting desperately trying to rescue the situation and papers flowing in with policy suggestions from every direction. Number 10 was silent, the atmosphere one of quiet despair, like a ship fatally holed and slowly sinking. Neither the Civil Service nor ministers had any ideas on how the Government should go forward. In the Unit, we tried to reconstruct a credible policy, though I realised that the day of the centralised incomes policy was probably at an end. Without the consent and cooperation of the unions it could not work in a democracy. This left tough monetary policy and unemployment as the only levers which would work. I wrote to the Prime Minister that he 'must demonstrate some authority soon' and that 'the nation does not want to hear what the trade unions might promise to do next; it wants to know what the Government will do now.' When I spoke to him about it, he just grunted. He didn't need telling. The problem was how to do it.

In the Commons debate about the crisis on 16 January, the Prime Minister spoke with statesman-like gravitas for nearly an hour. But Mrs Thatcher put on her best performance yet, with slashing attacks on the excesses and abuses of trade union power. Sitting in the Prime Minister's box beside the Speaker's Chair, I perceived that she really could be the next Prime Minister. But it was our trade unions who had provided the ideal platform for her to perform. Moss Evans, Alan Fisher and their allies had made her. The Tory backbenchers were for the first time ecstatic in greeting her speech. It was clear that the silent Labour members could smell defeat.

After a depressing cabinet on 18 January, the Prime Minister grimly asked me: 'How do you announce that the Government's pay policy has collapsed?' His confidence and morale were now clearly undermined. The trade union onslaught against a Labour Government had clearly stunned him. He could not bring himself to fight his old trade union allies – yet without fighting and beating them, his personal battle against inflation was lost. On 19 January he summoned his staff for a rare meeting together and he told us: 'we have been gravely damaged politically this week', adding that we must prepare for an election 'in March or April'.

The following week saw the nightmare continue. It began with a strike of over nine million public service employees, headlined as a 'Day of Action' (an active experience previously unfamiliar to some employed by Camden). On Tuesday the trains were on strike, while the roads and Heathrow airport were blocked by more blizzards. Once again I walked the three miles to work slithering through the snow and ice. Many people in the capital did not get to work at all. Ministers met and looked bewildered, with even the robust Healey silent. Only the younger ones – Hattersley, Owen and Rodgers – showed the fight to toughen it out. I could smell 'Pétainism' in the air at cabinet. The left wing and soft-centre ministers seemed to have simply given up. They all supported a policy of 'give 'em the money', as if the inflation problem would then go away.

The reality was that there were far too many marshmallows and too few vertebrae in Jim's cabinet. Ennals and Shore were particularly weak in dealing with the trade unions organising workers under their own Health and Local Government departments, each effectively conceding up to 15 per cent in prior discussion before even coming to cabinet for approval. After Ennals waved his ready white flag, Jim told Tom McNally: 'Ennals is finished, busted.' Actually, Ennals should never have been promoted so high by Jim.

At the beginning of March the Prime Minister met with the Cabinet Secretary and agreed with the latter's suggestion that Ennals and Shore could not be trusted to negotiate toughly with the unions, and they decided to put in

Hattersley (their junior in cabinet rank) to oversee the negotiations and ensure they did not always capitulate in the opening round. As for Tony Benn, who frequently made clear his disapproval of the Government's policy, the Prime Minister told him in mid February that but for the coming election he would sack him now. Jim told me afterwards that he would anyway drop Benn if he won.

To a considerable extent Callaghan's Government was beaten from within the Labour movement – by the irresponsible behaviour of the left-led trade unions; by the left-wing Labour MPs who voted in December to defeat our sanctions policy; and from within the cabinet by the group of ministers who capitulated at the first sound of union gunfire. It was also undermined from within Whitehall by officials in departments who would not oppose their client workforces in the public sector. It was not a question of conspiracy or betrayal – and it certainly can be seriously argued that the Government had now done its time and was fated to fall anyway. But an internal demoralisation developed along with internal failures of will. It reminded me of my studies of the fall of France in 1940.

February 1979 opened as bleakly as January had passed. The weather continued to be awful, with widespread sleet and snow. When the road hauliers settled for 20 per cent, the cabinet finally agreed to abandon the 5 per cent policy and to try desperately to establish 10 per cent as a norm. But the public service sector was committed to defeating that endeavour, insisting on 15 per cent to the health workers, while members of Fisher's National Union of Public Employees were refusing to carry the sick to hospitals or to bury the dead. This had nothing to do with trade unionism as Jim Callaghan or I had known it. It was just greedy capitalism with a union card. The Government was looking increasingly ragged and the Prime Minister was far from his best, still making tough general statements but then agreeing to weak decisions on excessive particular settlements. The political damage was reflected in the opinion polls, where by 15 February we were 20 per cent behind – this compared with a 3 per cent lead in the New Year. Significantly, a majority of the public supported the tough Thatcher approach and 94 per cent supported her on having a compulsory ballot before a strike. They included the silent majority of trade unionists who both we and the trade union leaders were failing to mobilise.

Now the civil servants joined the shameful public sector gravy train. They went on strike on 23 February even before their 26 per cent claim was properly on the table. They offered to accept 2 per cent in staff cuts to pay for a tiny part of the cost of their claim – but we spotted that 2 per cent was their annual staff wastage anyway, so it was not a very painful concession. Some of the Whitehall officials involved in preparing the Government's own 5–10 per cent policy were among those pressing for their own pay claim at four times the national policy.

The Civil Service claim, now averaging 24 per cent with some getting 45 per cent, finally came to cabinet on 21 March, and the Whitehall machine went into top gear to ensure that the claim went through in full. At first our Private Office, certainly under pressure from the rest of Whitehall, refused to let me or the Unit see any of the papers for the cabinet. Gavyn and I exploded at them. We had been sent virtually every secret paper for five years, but they drew the line at their own pay. They wanted no independent briefing of ministers, just civil servants briefing on their own pay (which was also my pay, though I tried to view it independently). The Chancellor's adviser, Derek Scott, came in to tell us that the Treasury was refusing to let him see the papers either. When I finally secured the cabinet papers, I noticed that they did not even mention the actual figure of the 24 per cent average increase – presumably lest it prejudice ministers against the settlement. Ministerial friends told me that each had received an identical departmental brief pressing the minister to support the deal. We were deep into pure *Yes Minister* territory. So Gavyn and I wrote a brief to the Prime Minister setting out the true figures and the costs of the proposed settlement. This did not make us popular around the house and anyway did no good. Ministers again surrendered. When I spoke to the Prime Minister about it after cabinet, he resignedly asked: 'How do you take these civil servants on, Bernard? It is always very difficult to beat them.' He was right, of course, but I could hear in Jim's voice that some of the fight had gone out of him. I began to conclude that there was not too much point in our continuing.

Really, as a Government, we were now simply just hanging on, presumably on the assumption that we might do less badly in an autumn 1979 election than in the spring. The weather continued to be dreadful in the first half of March. Number 10 remained silent and becalmed. There was a sense that the Government had already ended its active life and was merely going through the final pre-burial preparations. Whitehall now certainly assumed that there would soon be a change of Government. The Prime Minister remained upstairs in his study or in the flat for much of the time when he was in Number 10. McNally and Macaffery complained to me that he did not discuss any serious issues with them. He did talk regularly to me, especially about pay policy and about our problems with Scottish devolution, but his conversations were mainly with individual ministers and with civil servants from Private Office.

His personal team no longer functioned as a real collective unit at this time. Tom McNally was often away nursing his Stockport constituency. Macaffery's 'bottle' seemed to have gone, with him reminding me too often, though realistically, that 'the game is over'. In fact the Prime Minister had only two meetings with his personal team in the whole first three months of the year. All his major decisions – on the big pay capitulations, on devolution and on handling the fatal vote of confidence – were basically taken alone or after private consultations with some civil servants. I felt that as the crisis deepened he retreated into himself.

He was clearly very tired and often edgy. He held a special cabinet of ministers only, with no officials present, on 14 March and told his ministers that he was fed up with living from week to week with our authority draining away. So he now wanted to aim for a spring and not an autumn election.

My own personal feelings during these final weeks were of depression and political impotence. Sitting quietly in Number 10, I felt that somehow its walls were closing in on me. However hard we tried in the Unit, I could not see a way through – and was not convinced that anyone would now be listening if we pulled a policy solution out of the hat. In March 1979 I privately wrote: 'So we survive, stumbling on possibly till the autumn, often humiliated but never quite brought down, achieving little in policy terms, just surviving, until, with our credibility and self-respect eroded, with our ministers tired, with no platform and few friends, we are finally beaten in October. Hanging on until we are hanged.' That summed it up, except we were to be hanged not in October but in May.

I was deeply aware of the particular role which our then trade union movement was playing in Britain's economic decline in those dreary late 1970s. The unions seemed to operate under the curious assumption that everybody could get big increases in real wages while the nation as a whole produced little or no extra real resources. The public service unions added to this the belief that more and more people could be employed in the 'non-productive' service sector and be paid as much as the productive sector without any damage to the economy.

Although I was always a strong supporter of the principles of a welfare state, I began to see the dangers of 'welfarism' when it became an individual or national way of life. Our welfare system itself had matured to the point where it needed radical reform. Its internal practices were now dominated by what the Conservatives accurately described as 'producer-socialism', whereby those who worked in it were given priority over the millions of ordinary citizens who paid for it and were its users. This imbalance was wrong in principle and politically damaging to our Labour Government. I occasionally tried to write this theme into some of the Prime Minister's speeches over those years, arguing that schools were for the benefit of children as well as of the National Union of Teachers, that the NHS was for the sick as well as for the Health Service workers, and that public housing was for the homeless as well as for the local authority housing departments. The Prime Minister nibbled at it, but needed the unions too much for his pay policy to want to open up too many other fronts of controversy with them. So I made little progress with this approach – though Mrs Thatcher soon did.

In the event it was not pay policy but our proposed constitutional devolution of powers to Scotland which finally precipitated the general election and the fall of our Government. In the referendum in Scotland on 1 March 1979, we did not secure the necessary 40 per cent support for the 'Yes' resolution. As Tom McNally said next day, 'I wish the bloody Scots had told us in the past five years that they did not really want devolution.'

On 13 March the Scottish Nationalists told the Prime Minister that unless he moved the order to introduce devolution within two weeks, they would put down a motion of No Confidence in the Government. He refused to do any kind of deal with them, so they were committed to vote against him. The Liberals and Ulster Unionists also now moved firmly into opposition. So the dice were steadily falling against us on the coming Confidence motion. Personally, I felt detached and recalled William Empson's lines about 'Waiting for the end boys, waiting for the end.'

The Prime Minister became surprisingly sensitive about accusations of 'wheeler-dealing' and he instructed his whips and ministers not to make any deals to win votes. On the morning of the great Commons Confidence debate on 28 March, he stayed in his room alone finishing the drafting of his speech. He slept after lunch. As he left with Audrey for the Commons, his staff gathered in the lobby of Number 10 and cheered him on his way into a Downing Street crowded with cameras. It was a kind of early farewell. In the Chamber, Mrs Thatcher spoke flatly and sat down to a moderate reception from her own side.

By contrast, Jim was superb and received a standing ovation which went on so long that the Speaker had to intervene. But afterwards he received a note from our whips. I saw his face drop and he swiftly left the Chamber. I followed to his room. The news was that Dr Broughton, a sick Labour member, could not be brought to the Commons to be nodded through in the vote. Jim told his Parliamentary Private Secretary, Roger Stott, to go immediately to tell Audrey that we would now lose. I tried to cheer him up by telling him how good was his speech. He replied: 'I am sorry, Bernard, but speeches don't make any difference now. We won't get the votes, and that is what matters.'

At the conclusion of the Confidence debate, Private Office reported to us that officials still expected the Government to win by one vote, or at worst to tie – which would mean we would survive. Nobody seemed to realise that neither of our Irish MPs, Gerry Fitt and the wayward McGuire, who had each been personally alienated by Roy Mason's ultra-Unionist regime in Belfast, would support the Government. We did not get the Unionist votes either, so in the end we suffered for our Irish policies without getting any compensating advantage for them.

We lost by one vote – 311 to 310. The Tories leaped to their feet cheering. Our side looked stunned. The Prime Minister rose and briefly informed the House that he would announce his decision about the date of the Dissolution tomorrow, and then left the Chamber to summon his closest ministers – Rees, Foot, Healey and Michael Cox, the Chief Whip – and his election team from Transport House. They fixed on 3 May for the election.

After he left to go back to Number 10 at around 11.30 p.m. I wandered around the House of Commons talking to shocked Labour colleagues. I went to John Smith's room and chatted with Ann Taylor and Roy Hattersley, whose future careers were now to be clouded by long years in opposition. Then I went to the Whips' Office, where the atmosphere was very tense. They felt guilty they had failed to deliver the majority. Some blamed the Prime Minister for not allowing them to buy votes with peerages, etc., until too late. (One Tory MP's vote was on offer in return for a peerage.)Walter Harrison, a wonderful man, explained to me why – mainly on sentimental and humanitarian grounds – he had decided not to bring in the sick Dr Broughton, who had been willing to attend, even if it was the last thing he did in life (he died two weeks later). The junior whips, Ann Taylor and Jim Marshall, later said this was a big mistake. That was the crucial one vote by which we lost. It was a vote which we controlled, whereas we could never be sure of controlling our Irish.

I stayed at the Whips' wake until the bitter end, drinking more and more whisky and becoming more and more sober. I was deeply angry that we had lost, as it seemed to me to be a self-inflicted wound. Firstly, Fitt and McGuire had been alienated, though that may have been an inevitable price of winning Ulster Unionist support over the previous two years. Secondly, our Whips were too squeamish about bringing in Dr Broughton. Thirdly, the Prime Minister had been too sensitive about 'wheeler-dealing' to win votes. When I had said to him the previous day that it was 'worth two Dukedoms to win some Liberal votes' and that there were 'no prizes in losing', he had bridled but admitted that it was 'personal priggishness' on his part to deter our Whips from buying or fixing votes. It was also sheer bad luck that two of our MPs, Tom Swain and Sydney Irving, had recently died and their two Labour seats were vacant pending by-elections. There were so many 'if-onlies' – but history is full of 'if-onlies'.

Anyway, defeat almost certainly lay at the end of this path even if we had scraped through on 28 March. I went home and into bed at 3.30 in the morning, setting my alarm for 6.45 a.m. I awoke feeling shattered, exhausted and still furious that we had lost a vote which with more luck and professionalism we might have won.

Although I felt that the coming election was lost from the beginning, I and the Unit decided to give it our best shots and at least to go down fighting. We quickly prepared a small Handbook of Policies, one page for each policy area so that the Prime Minister could keep it in his pocket and refer to it when travelling. I also submitted to him a memorandum on election campaign themes and suggested that he go onto the attack from the beginning and try to expose the unpopular aspects of Thatcher's monetarist approach by each day asking her to answer three basic questions : what would be the consequences of her policies in terms of jobs, of prices and of public services?

At the opening of the campaign, on 8 April, the latest poll showed the Tories 21 per cent in the lead. That day I had a private chat with Jim and he said that he felt confident and was enjoying the battle enormously now that it was engaged – though adding that his one worry was 'whether I have the stamina'. He admitted that Thatcher was 'the dominant personality of the campaign. If we win it will be because the people cannot take her.' In fact, we lost because they could not stand us being run by the unions – and were prepared to take a risk on Thatcher.

I soon slipped into my third general election routine. I rose at 6 a.m. (having returned home around midnight the previous evening) to drive in for an initial 7.15 meeting in the Political Office to discuss the latest press coverage and plan the day ahead. Then we went upstairs for breakfast in the small dining room with the Prime Minister, Audrey, their son Michael and the new election team – which seemed to me to lack experience. Beside the table were trays of sizzling bacon, eggs, sausage and coffee, floating lovely smells around the corridors in Number 10. I usually chose to sit next to Audrey, a marvellous person who quietly looked after Jim and was clearly very important to him.

At 8.30 a.m. Jim went off to Transport House for the Campaign Committee and the daily press conference. At first I did not go to the conference, feeling I would be an exposed civil servant, but Jim quickly noticed and asked me to go along with him. That was quite nostalgic for me, again walking up Lord North Street each morning, past Wilson's former house where I had my opening apprenticeship at the start of the February 1974 campaign, and on to Transport House, with the mob of journalists milling around like bloodhounds looking forward to the kill of our Labour Government.

After each press conference I returned to Number 10 and worked with the Unit on hasty speech drafts or finding facts and figures for Jim. In the second half of the campaign he changed that routine and decided to hold a mid-morning strategy meeting in Transport House, which I always attended. He often returned to Number 10 for lunch and usually took a nap afterwards, once saying 'to quote my old skipper, I am going to examine the rivets in the ceiling.'

One central problem, which derived from Jim's secretive style, was the recurring lack of communication within the team, who seemed to operate in little isolated cells and did not communicate enough with one another. For myself, I never felt a central part of the team as I had in 1974, but I had the advantage of direct and regular access to the boss himself. Party headquarters in Transport House provided its usual obstacles to Labour's campaign, often refusing to cooperate with the Prime Minister's team. The vain General Secretary, Ron Hayward, went to see Foreign Secretary David Owen to ask for a Colonial Governorship for his retirement – David and I agreed that certainly the cocked hat and feathers would suit him. The Party Press Officer, Percy Clarke, was again, as in 1974, in tears and again threatened to resign in mid campaign. Party headquarters often gave the impression that it did not wish to allow minor diversions such as a general election to interfere with its habitual way of life. The reforms in Labour's party organisation later begun by Neil Kinnock and mainly introduced under Tony Blair and Peter Mandelson were long overdue and should never be mocked by those who apparently hanker after the more personal and infinitely more inefficient style of the past.

The 1979 campaign was unusually long, covering nearly six weeks, including Easter when I had to work in Number 10 while Carol and the children went to Suffolk to enjoy some of the first sunshine of the year. Jim was often edgy in the opening two weeks, clearly unhappy with the erratic service from his team. He was particularly critical to me of Roger Carroll's *Sun*-style speeches, saying he wanted 'less flip sentences and more policy substance'. After one meeting, Jim asked me to write 'a philosophical speech' dissecting Thatcher's right-wing views on society. 'Put a towel round your head, Bernard,' he said, asking for the completed speech 'by the end of the day'. I sat down and wrote it straight off in four hours. I needed the towel because I had one of my regular terrible colds, with my eyes streaming and my temperature heading higher.

On 18 April the Prime Minister announced a radical reorganization of the speech-writing process. He said that he wanted the Policy Unit to write the basic drafts, with Roger to spice them up with punchy *Sun* aphorisms, and David Lipsey, a skilled writer, to oversee the final drafting and make sure that the policy substance was not lost in the spicing process. After that, life became much more satisfying for the Unit. Gavyn, David and I wrote large sections of Jim's final speeches and he seemed happier with them.

I accompanied Jim on the final Monday evening to hear him speak at Gravesend – so far in three election campaigns with Wilson and Callaghan I had never until then heard either of them deliver an election speech. It went well in Gravesend, though as usual the microphones failed to work. I concluded that the Labour Party in those days used a special type of microphone devised to silence its leaders. Tuesday 1 May was for us in London the last day of the campaign and I worked on Jim's eve-of-poll speech for the next evening in Cardiff. Team morale rose in the last few days, helped by a weekend poll which showed us closing the gap with the Tories. At the last press conference, Jim again used my three basic questions to Thatcher about the impact of her monetarist policies on prices, jobs and public services and he pointed out that she had never attempted to answer them in the campaign. (She would answer in practice in her first Government, with prices rocketing, unemployment doubling and the public services slashed – but taxes were indeed cut, the unions were confronted, and the electorate liked it.) That evening I watched him go out through the big black door, still with that curious lop-sided gait and his arms swinging loosely, for the last time before his defeat.

On the eve of the poll the weather was as awful as it had been for most of our final four months in Government, with widespread snow, hail and rain to remind the electorate of the horrors of the Winter of Discontent. I concluded that God was, if only for the time being, a Tory. With the Prime Minister in Cardiff, Number 10 was totally quiet. Private Office had already prepared the thick briefing files for the incoming Tory Government.

I felt completely drained as I overheard Ken Stowe on the telephone discussing with lovely Caroline Stevens, Mrs Thatcher's Diary Secretary, how to arrange her positive vetting to get security clearance to work in Number 10. Later in the day I spotted Ken showing round the house Mrs Thatcher's future Chief Whip Richard Ryder, a very decent man who was in due course to marry Caroline. The last rites for us and the first rites for them were being executed.

It was my view, shared my many journalists covering it, that we clearly won the election campaign. The opinion polls confirmed that. There was a swing of 3–4 per cent of voters from Tory to Labour over the campaign. Jim Callaghan had done particularly well. Tactically, he did not put a foot wrong throughout. He was 7 per cent ahead of Thatcher as 'best Prime Minister' at the start of the campaign and surged to 19 per cent ahead by the end. Even 43 per cent of the Tory voters said he would do a better job as Prime Minister than Thatcher.

But the polls also showed that the Tories were ahead on most policy issues and were most ahead on the two issues which mattered most to the electorate –

taxation and trade union reform. Some 78 per cent of all voters, including 40 per cent of the Labour ones, believed it was 'time for a change' and that was the crucial message from the campaign. Jim himself described the result as 'a vote against the events of last winter'. People were now ready to gamble on Thatcher's new face to replace Labour's boring old familiarity.

Jim had put his finger on it on 12 April as we drove back together in the car from Transport House to Number 10. I reported the optimistic improvements in the recent opinion polls, which suggested that we could still just conceivably scrape home. He said that he was still worried 'there has been one of those deep sea-changes in public opinion. If people have really decided they want a change of Government, then there is nothing you can do.' Such a sea-change in public opinion had in fact already taken place before we even got to the starting stalls of the election campaign.

On election morning, with the newspapers showing the Tories around 7 per cent ahead in the polls, I left home for Number 10, calling in on the way to vote at our local polling station. It was very quiet inside, with just a trickle of old ladies voting. I could tell from the look in their eyes that they had not come to vote FOR any political party. They had come to vote AGAINST. Against Alan Fisher and every NUPE thug who had prevented their sick from getting to hospital or their dead from getting buried. Against every Labour local authority, such as ours in Camden, which for weeks past had left piles of rubbish rotting on the pavements as these ladies tried to shop. And against every trade union leader who had stared at them out of their television screens and said to hell with them and the rest of the public, he just wanted to grab as much as he could for his members by whatever means were to hand. I realized that whereas I had been writing in the Prime Minister's speeches attacking Mrs Thatcher for preaching the harsh doctrine of 'weakest to the wall', in fact, as far as these old ladies were concerned, Labour's union allies were daily practising that doctrine – and these ladies were voting against going to the wall.

I sat around in a silent Number 10 for most of that polling day. At three in the afternoon the Prime Minister telephoned from Cardiff to Private Office to say 'we have lost', and that he wanted us to be prepared to leave Number 10 by 3.30 tomorrow.

At least it would not be a humiliatingly hurried eviction. I had earlier in the week discussed with Ken Stowe the need to have what I called 'a civilised transfer of power'. Ken had already put that into effect. There would be no middle-of-the-night dash by the beaten Prime Minister from Cardiff to resign at the Palace in the morning, with Mrs Thatcher arriving through the front door of Number 10 as Jim's belongings departed through the back, as happened when Ted Heath pushed out Harold Wilson in 1970. It was arranged that we would all have time on Friday to gather in Number 10, collect our remaining belongings, have lunch together, say our goodbyes, and leave in a dignified way.

During the evening of polling day, I watched the predictable early Labour losses on the television set in my office with Gavyn Davies and Jim Corr. After midnight, I went to watch at the ITV studios. As the last overnight results were coming in, I moved to sit near to Michael Heseltine. He was naturally enjoying the prospect of approaching power, as I observed it slipping away. I ticked off our losses on my list of key Labour marginals. Many good friends lost their seats. In the final tally, the Tories had 339 seats, up 62 compared with 1974. Labour lost 50 seats and fell to 269, with 36.9 per cent of the vote, our lowest share since 1931. The Tories had a comfortable overall majority of 43.

At the end of broadcasting, I was the only person still remaining in the dark room. Leaving the ITN building, I walked along Wells Street and past the Middlesex Hospital to where my car was parked. It was already getting light. We were beaten, and from tomorrow I would be unemployed. I did not feel at all tired. I was beyond sleep. Nor was I genuinely disappointed, since I had never seriously believed that we could win. But physically, I did feel deeply numbed and I was completely flat mentally and spiritually. It was as if the electric motor running my life for so long had failed. Or as if I were bereaved, somebody close to me having died, leaving a void.

At home, when I walked upstairs to my bed and exchanged a few words with Carol, it was already past five in the morning, with light streaming in through the window and the birds singing in our garden. I slept lightly for a couple of hours. The children buzzed in and out of our bedroom to kiss me on their way to school. I heard Rachel, the eldest at fourteen, say: 'Daddy has got the sack.' Stephen, aged nine, was clearly delighted by the news, observing that now I would 'be at home more', and especially that I could cook his lunch (optimistic) and he would 'not have to stay at school for school dinner,' which was one of the main burdens of his young life.

I drove back to Number 10 and walked in through the big black door for the last time. I called on Private Office, where the Private Secretaries looked nervous, working on the briefs for the new Prime Minister, who was reputed to be 'difficult'. I went to my office and found Linda, our devoted secretary, sitting on the floor shredding our official files and putting the proceeds into big black plastic sacks. All five years of the Unit's efforts and concerns – about pay policy, inflation, sterling, sales of council houses, child allowances, industrial strategy, renegotiating the EEC terms of entry, the European Monetary System, Ireland, Scottish devolution, North Sea oil, down to saving regional pubs and the pint of beer measurement – all this disappeared in shreds into plastic bags. Fortunately I had kept many personal notes.

The Prime Minister had returned from Cardiff at 7 a.m. pursued by the usual pack of press hounds smelling blood. He went off for a walk in the Number 10 garden with Ken Stowe, who had been a wonderful Principal Private Secretary to him – and a good friend to me and our team. Later Ken told me that Jim was 'a bit emotional and wounded – feeling that he had been rejected'. Ken wisely advised him to resign the party leadership as soon as possible and 'play a presidential role in politics'. In 1981 Jim told me that he regretted not taking Ken's advice. He said that 'I was misled by a foolish sense of duty' and so stayed on to suffer all the horrors of the subsequent civil war in the Labour Party. 'I hope I just about got out with my reputation intact,' he reflected. He did, but Ken was right and he should have gone quickly. Later in the morning, he toured the house and said his goodbyes to all the staff. He shook my hand and said. 'Thank you, Bernard, for everything.' He asked me to come to see him at the Commons about my future. But for some reason which I do not recall I never did go. I suppose I preferred not to think about my future, which was not looking too bright.

We all went upstairs to the small dining room for a farewell lunch of cottage pie – my last meal ever in Number 10. I was a little sad but not gloomy. We had adjusted to the trauma of defeat well in advance. At least Jim had fought an honourable battle. His daughter, Margaret Jay, a long-standing friend of mine, had flown in from Washington to join us. It seemed a long way from the early days when Marcia always wanted to sack whichever pretty girl was cook at the time. Jim said he did not think there was anything more that we could have done to win: 'the people wanted a change', and 'the unions did it. People could not forget and would not forgive what they had to suffer from the unions last winter.' Then we all drifted downstairs. When the Prime Minister left for the Palace to resign the staff cheered him off through the door, some weeping.

I went back for a last look at my handsome room and collected the photographs of my children scattered around it. A remarkable chapter of my life had been spent there. It was almost as if I had been married to Number 10. Five years and two months, usually ten to twelve hours a day, sometimes more. A relentless treadmill of excitements and miseries, victories and defeats. Being at the centre of affairs is always invigorating and it kept my adrenalin flowing, however exhausted I was. But it had not all been wonderful. At times, as when the environment around Wilson seemed trivial and tacky, I had hated it and longed to be out of Number 10. I swung continuously from 'wishing-in' to 'wishing-out', a cycle familiar to politicians who experience the political stage. I experienced the 'wishing-out' more often than most because I am really a private personality, disliking the public spotlight or appearing in the media, valuing privacy as the greatest asset with which we are born.

I realised in Number 10 (and again twenty years later as a minister) that ultimately I prefer my private life, my private pleasures and interests, my private friends and being with those personally closest to me. That is why I never went into the House of Commons, despite some attractive offers. Public life is more suited to people with predominantly 'public' personalities, as have most successful politicians. They usually love the public stage, relishing the spotlight of publicity, enjoying the crowds and the battles, liking people to be interested in what they do, courting journalists – and sometimes avoiding personal intimacies. I am not like that. The strong sense of privacy which I think I have, is a positive disqualification from public life. In that sense I have always been disqualified, and when in office have often longed to get out. It was typified by the way I loved my long holidays in France and weekends with the children in Suffolk, always sad to get back to London. In 1975, I noted that these private territories seemed to me 'a small flourishing oasis of affection and generosity, shelter from the appalling desert of human meanness and envy' which I often saw in the world of politics and the media, whereas Harold Wilson – an example of the classic 'public personality' – hated his holidays and often found quite phoney excuses to return to the Downing Street treadmill.

I did not feel that we had done a bad job in the Labour Governments of 1974–79, given the huge and often insuperable problems which confronted us, with the world economy in recession and the fact that for most of the time we lacked a secure parliamentary majority. We left inflation just below the level which we inherited, with the balance of payments in rare surplus and our currency reserves replenished. But these were just cold statistics. On the deficit side, we left a country where society appeared divided, national morale was low and group behaviour depressingly bad.

It is easy today to forget how dismal certain aspects of life could be for many people in the late 1970s, especially in the large conurbations. Few public services, especially at local government level, worked adequately or as well as they had done twenty years earlier. Travelling on public transport (still today no paradise) could be a nightmare. Strikes were frequent in the public and private sectors. Manufacturing products were often shabby and unreliable, with our domestic cars particularly prone to failure. Basically, customers were badly treated and so daily life for ordinary citizens could be very frustrating. In this dreary national context it was very frustrating to be in Number 10 feeling that we could do very little to improve matters. I felt completely hemmed in by constraints preventing any reforming action. Labour's policies were either sectarian or conservative. No attempt was made in the party or the government to appeal and adjust to the new society emerging in Britain, the growing new middle classes and the new young with their aspirations. We were umbilically tied to the old-fashioned unions and the shrinking old working classes. There was not a touch of vision in the Government's approach. It spent too much of its time looking back to try to preserve the achievements of the post-war Labour Government and looking over its shoulder to appease the left, which was itself a strong force of conservatism.

In the Policy Unit, too much of our time was spent on damage limitation and too little on exploring new policy horizons (which had no chance anyway of pursuit by the Government). It felt like being locked in a political cage. That was all part of the background conditioning our electoral defeat.

So I privately understood that the general public wanted political change. I realized that Mrs Thatcher, with no such historical baggage, might be better placed than Labour to resolve some of these problems: to restore some efficiency to our economy, some discipline to the public sector, some priority to the consumer as opposed to the producer, and some sense of responsibility in society as a whole. So from the national interest point of view I was not totally depressed by the prospect of a Conservative Government, even though it would leave me unemployed and penniless.

Although I was to remain a member of the Labour Party through all its troubles in the coming years, I also watched with sympathetic interest as Mrs Thatcher did try to redress those particular faults. I had learned in Number 10 how, in Britain, Prime Ministers have less power to change society than their electorates believe, hope or fear. So I was to be surprised at how much the new premier was to achieve against the built-in inertia of our system. Ironically, it was the Conservatives who provided the radicalism necessary to break out of the policy cage.

I slipped out of Number 10 at 3 p.m. on 4 May 1979. As I crossed Horse Guards Parade to pick up my car from its privileged parking place, I was held up by a cavalcade of black cars speeding over the gravel towards Horse Guards Gate to turn right down Whitehall. Mrs Thatcher waved royally to me as she flashed by in the first car. The rear vehicle was driven by Mr Callaghan's former driver. He peeled off right to the back gate of Number 10 and I saw Ken Stowe jump out and sprint through the garden, as he had in April 1976, to be inside the house to welcome the new Prime Minister, with her staff lined up to greet her in the hallway. The familiar ceremony of changing office continued. I climbed into my battered Ford and drove slowly northwards home to dear old Brookfield Park. I faced new and not very comforting chapters in my life.

Sixteen

CAREER TURBULENCE: MURDOCH AND THE CITY

I had unfortunately made no firm arrangements for future employment when I left Number 10 in May 1979. This was partly because I had been too preoccupied during those final devastating months in Government, but it was mainly because I knew that the media would parade any job enquiry I made as evidence that I believed that Callaghan would lose the election and so I was deserting the sinking ship. (I had equally made no job preparations ahead of Wilson's departure in 1976 because that might have alerted the press to his resignation intentions.) This failure to protect my future left me in a dire financial position in the summer of 1979. I was forty-four, with four children and a large overdraft.

My redundancy pay covered me until July, but after that I was seriously broke. So I signed on 'the dole' at the Kentish Town social security office. This was for me an emotional experience and something which my father (who had died in 1971) would have hated. He had believed that one of the rewards of my education, for which he had made so many sacrifices, was that I would never, like him, suffer the dreadful threat of unemployment. It also brought home to me the price which I was forced to pay when in 1976 the LSE had given me the ultimatum (unthinkable in any American or European university) that either I left Number 10 immediately to return to teach at the School or resign. Resenting the ultimatum, I had resigned my life tenure and surrendered a valuable asset in a world of growing employment uncertainty. Jim Callaghan was appalled by the LSE ultimatum, which appeared to confirm some of his views about the pettiness of the academic world.

Anyway, it meant that now I had no job to fall back on. So I began to look around, beginning a decade of career mobility and turbulence in which I had five employers in ten years. With one exception, in the City, I was not to enjoy them. In personal terms, the 1980s was not a good decade for me.

After the election I was physically exhausted from over five years on the relentless treadmill and my spirits were very low. Usually vigorous and curious, I now

felt languid and mentally flat and found it very difficult to generate any enthusiasm for any new pursuit. The shock of leaving Downing Street, with its daily
excitement and its stimulants to my adrenaline, and moving into the flat desert of
unemployment was very painful. I suspect that my subsequent sallies into unsuit-
able jobs, such as working for Murdoch and for Maxwell, were in part an attempt
to get back into worlds of greater excitement.

I sat at home unconstructively for several weeks until I found my first job,
kindly arranged by my old friend Claus Moser, as Development Director of the
Economist Intelligence Unit, the research agency owned by *The Economist*
magazine and based in beautiful Spencer House, overlooking St James's Park. It
proved a valuable source of income but the EIU, gentle and cosy, and I were not
suited to one another. So I was ready to move when a more challenging and
dangerous opportunity arose. Harry Evans, the distinguished editor of the
Sunday Times for the past fourteen years and an old Highgate friend, asked me to
join him at *The Times*, where the new proprietor Rupert Murdoch had offered
him the editorship.

There was a complex background to Harry's offer. Lord Thomson, the benign
Canadian owner of *The Times* and *Sunday Times*, had finally tired of the endless
battles with the greedy print unions, and in the autumn of 1980 put the celebrated newspapers up for sale. Harry and I decided to put together a consortium
which could buy the *Sunday Times* and to offer the journalists and print workers
an equity stake of around a quarter of the enterprise, hoping that this would help
to resolve the appalling industrial relations problems which had for so long
dogged the industry, and we brought in Don Cruikshank, the thirty-four-year-
old Finance Director of Times Newspapers and later influential in the City of
London. A business plan was quickly put together and we set about getting wider
financial backing. The *Guardian* agreed initially to take a 24 per cent stake and to
share in our printing (though it later pulled out).

By December 1980 our consortium was loosely knitted together and we
submitted our offer through Morgan Grenfell to Warburgs, who were acting for
the sellers. But Thomson and the board of the old Times Newspapers decided
they would sell only to Murdoch, because he was the only bidder who was interested in acquiring both *The Times* and the *Sunday Times*. To try to match
Murdoch's advantage as a single bidder for the whole package of journals, we
joined together with the group of employees already bidding for *The Times* and
in January 1981 together made a single bid for the titles in what we described as
'a business train which would decouple later'.

But Warburgs refused to discuss our offer. The seller had decided that there
should only be one candidate, Murdoch. Yet the game ought not to have been

over. The acquisition should have been referred to the Monopolies Commission under the 1973 Fair Trading Act, since it gave Murdoch control of over the threshold 30 per cent in both the daily and the Sunday markets, an excessive concentration of media power by any definition.

But here politics intervened. Mrs Thatcher was apparently worried about the *Sunday Times* slipping into hands which were not reliably Conservative, so she intervened to stop the reference to the Commission, reportedly saying: 'Rupert supported me in the last election and I must support him now.' Her Secretary of State for Trade, John Biffen, did his Prime Minister's bidding and wafted the merger through in a matter of days. He used the highly questionable excuse, provided for in the Act, that the newspapers were loss-making and faced imminent closure without Murdoch's rescue. This was balderdash, of course. Others were willing to pay more than the Australian to rescue them. And Biffen's claim that the *Sunday Times* was loss-making could not survive any rigorous and fair scrutiny of the figures. It was forecast by the seller's bankers, Warburgs, to make a profit of nearly £5 million in 1981 and £12 million in 1982. Among its many assets, its headquarters in Grays Inn Road was worth more than the whole Murdoch bid of £12 million – less than half of the bank valuation of the company's tangible assets. Labour MPs protested against this 'scandal' in the Commons chamber, but the whipped Tory majority ensured that the deal was rushed through. (This manipulation of the Monopolies Commission procedures is frankly acknowledged in the published diaries for June 1981 of Woodrow Wyatt, a close acolyte of both Murdoch and the Prime Minister.)

Murdoch brought to these papers his own particular brand of media genius, tough management and serious depreciation of non-monetary values. Under his control, substantial investment in technology and marketing together with the effective annihilation of their trade unions have made them commercially very successful, with a valuation today of probably some one hundred times what Murdoch paid.

Having won the two newspapers, Murdoch characteristically set about desta-bilising their existing editorial and management teams. He sacked all the executive directors and editorially he happily let go the editor of *The Times* William Rees-Mogg, asking Harry Evans to replace him.

My political instincts told me that this offer to Harry was such a poisoned chalice that I advised him against taking it, because it would move him from a supportive environment on a financially successful paper to one forecast to lose £10 million in the coming year and inhabited by a different breed of more tradi-tional journalists whom he did not know, who owed him no loyalty, and many of whom considered themselves socially and intellectually superior to this son of a

Manchester train driver. But Harry could not resist the challenge of the most prized editorship in British journalism. He was excited by the prospect of creating a modern quality newspaper on *The Times* venerable foundations.

Harry also naively believed Murdoch's initial promises of support for him and his guarantees to Parliament that he would not interfere with the editorial content of the paper or the editor's long-established prerogative over staff appointments. He also believed that providing he did a good job of creating a better newspaper, then the old-guard *Times'* staff would give him credit and back him (a few did). So he decided to drink from the poisoned chalice – and immediately asked me to join him. Having myself advised Harry why it would be suicidal for him to go, it would have been logical for me to have declined his offer. Instead, I ignored my own advice and actually joined with him on the doomed enterprise. I did it with my eyes wide open, absolutely clear in the back of my mind that it would all end in tears.

Before leaving beautiful Spencer House for the dismal *Times* building in Gray's Inn Road, I consulted the Editor of *The Economist*, Andrew Knight, a very smooth and measured man who understood the world of newspapers far better than I did. He wisely advised me against the move, explaining that 'Rupert is ruthless, with no sense of personal loyalty.'

I thought it prudent to meet the notorious new proprietor before going to work for him, and was not encouraged by our first encounter. Murdoch produced for my benefit a string of snappy right-wing slogan-solutions to Britain's ills (which he clearly blamed on Labour practitioners such as myself). He asserted that the British were all lazy; that Britain's establishment was effete and too snobbish about commerce and making money; and that Mrs Thatcher alone had the right policies and approach to put all these faults right. I could see why he was so at home with his *Sun* newspaper and felt that he had given me my instructions for the next year's *Times* editorials. Harry reported afterwards that Murdoch had said; 'Get him on board, can you?' – and now I sensed that the ship already had the gangplank in place.

My reasons for taking the fatal leap into Murdoch's clutches in June 1981 would not have convinced anyone more sensibly concerned with the security of their own future career. I was bored at the EIU and I also missed involvement in the excitements of political life. Journalism promised to offer that involvement, even if only as a voyeur – it gives some of the pleasure of playing with the political scene without ever being held accountable. Hence Stanley Baldwin famously described it as having 'Power without responsibilty – the prerogative of the harlot through the ages.' It is indeed a form of prostitution, but to me *The Times* at least seemed to promise to be an above-average brothel.

As so often, I was tempted by doing something new, however dangerous. Above all, I was attracted by working more closely with Harold Evans. Small, quick and springy, looking like a jump jockey, with enormous energy, boundless curiosity and an impish grin, Harry was an inspirational editor who over fourteen years had made the *Sunday Times* a model for lively but accurate and responsible journalism. He was also a delightful personal friend. Companionship in a job has always mattered greatly to me, and I find it difficult to work anywhere happily without friendships at the workplace.

My position at *The Times* was Assistant Editor, at a salary of £25,000 a year. In practice I had three specific functions on the newspaper. First was as leader writer – 'thundering' as we called it. I wrote thirty-one editorials – mainly first leaders – during my eleven months on the paper. I came to share the role of first leader writer with the long-serving Owen Hickey, a donnish associate editor who I respected intellectually for his analytical skills but whose chilling personality was beyond my reach. But I soon began to hear through the grape vine that Murdoch and his eccentric henchman Gerald Long were upset by my occasional suggestions in leaders that Mrs Thatcher's Government was not totally perfect and that the new Social Democratic Party was of political interest.

My second function on the paper was to prepare feature articles covering topics of current interest in much greater depth than is normal on a daily newspaper. Working with me in the features team were two outstanding young writers, Peter Hennessy, an expert on Whitehall and later a distinguished Professor at the University of London, and David Walker, who became a leading media commentator on social and governmental affairs. We produced serious analyses on Britain's defence, its inner cities, on the family, the Trotskyite infiltration of the Labour Party, and a string of features on Whitehall departments.

My third and less specific function was to work for the Editor on whatever issues arose to interest the paper. I worked directly to Harry and not to anyone else in the *Times* hierarchy, and hence I handed my editorials directly to him, which apparently upset Hickey. These entrenched sectional heads ran quite separate and seemingly unaccountable baronies on the old *Times*, usually viewing passing editors with patronising tolerance.

One of my most fascinating roles was to assist Harry in his efforts to modernise the newspaper. He cautiously changed the antique layout, taking the personal advertisements off the front page. He brought in brilliant writers such as Anthony Holden, Peter Stothard and Frank Johnson, promoted reliable Brian Macarthur to executive editor and made Fred Emery, the Whirling Dervish of news, to be Home Editor. Harry's ultimately most fatal move was to promote the Foreign Editor, Charles Douglas-Home, to be his Deputy Editor. Douglas-Home promised Harry to be a 'bridge between the old *Times* and the new'; we did not then realise that his bridge could easily convert into the gangplank which I knew must exist somewhere in Gray's Inn Road.

But I quickly realised that Harry's individual style and the deep-rooted culture of the old *Times* were on collision course. Some of the old-guard editorial staff were openly resentful of his attempts to change their ways of working. One day, one of the senior journalists in the City section snapped at me, 'What is this silly little man doing running around trying to tell us how to do our jobs?' In his voice was all the snobbish contempt of the southern public school old-*Times* for the son of a northern railway driver.

The chief resisters to Harry's reforms saw their role as that of the famous Black Friars (an allusion to the old *Times* location at Blackfriars), protecting the lasting values and traditions of liberal conservatism, on *The Times* itself as well as in British society as a whole. They viewed both Harry and Murdoch, in their different ways, as threats to those traditions and values. They also believed that Harry did not appreciate that editing a daily newspaper six times a week was quite different from editing a Sunday such as the *Sunday Times*, requiring mechanistic systems of news management quite different from the individual energy, inspiration and input of any particular editor, as had been Harry's style at the *Sunday Times*. They did see off Harry, but Murdoch beat them in the end, changing the paper in some of the ways which Harry envisaged and showing scant regard for their Black Friars' values.

The personal attitude of Rupert Murdoch to all this turbulence was crucial but never clear to me until towards the end. I met him early on at dinner, where he and Harry discussed the future of *The Times* with much mutual agreement. Murdoch expressed deep contempt for the traditional *Times* establishment, typified to him by Rees-Mogg, as he did for the rest of the traditional British establishment, including the monarchy. He seemed fully supportive of Harry's plans to modernise the paper. But I found him hard to read. His face looked curiously like a walnut, brown in complexion, heavily wrinkled and clearly very hard. On the back of his hands were mats of black, hair like some marsupial from the outback. I detected no trace of human warmth, feelings or humour. He was impressively clear in his thinking and punchily brief in expression, showing impatience with anything which did not have practical, commercial or financial justification.

As a businessman he was clearly superior to any other newspaper proprietor or manager I had so far met, with a strategic vision of the global future of the media. But I sensed that he had no deep values or principles and I recalled Andrew Knight's comment that Murdoch was ruthless and had no personal loyalties. Perhaps the best description of him was that by the *Sunday Times* Features Editor

John Barry, who referred to his combination of 'lethal charm with the habits of a shark. One minute, he's swimming along with a smile, then snap! There is blood in the water. Your head's gone.' Beneath Murdoch's surface energy heat there rested, as Harry remarked, 'a cold centre'. The charm was cosmetic, the sincerity deceptive, the lively style manipulative, and the centre ice old. I concluded, and warned Harry, that Murdoch would use him to shake up the *Times* old guard; but would also abandon him without a second thought when it suited him. I was, of course, aware that I was bound to be an incidental casualty in that looming scenario. From the beginning, as Harry documents in his riveting book *Good Times, Bad Times*, Murdoch found it difficult to restrain his instincts to interfere in the editorial side of the newspapers, in direct contravention of the pledges he had given to Parliament. His main concern was that we ought to be uncritical cheerleaders for Mrs Thatcher. He criticised headlines which were not supportive of the right wing and exploded when we allowed a left-wing trade union leader to express his point of view. He particularly disliked my editorial on Thatcher's 1981 reshuffle, commenting that all the Tory ministers who stood up to her were just 'hypocrites' and 'pissing liberals'.

Managerially he announced he would close *The Times* unless he achieved 600 redundancies. He also tried to transfer some of the company's most precious assets, its titles, to the News Corporation, which could have enabled him to retain valuable assets from any imminent liquidation, which John Smith in the House of Commons described as 'a breathtaking subterfuge'. John Biffen had earlier promised Parliament that Murdoch would face criminal sanctions if he breached the terms of his acquisition, but the so-called guardians at the Department of Trade remained silent. Interviewed by Fred Emery in March 1982, Murdoch, with commendable candour, described his parliamentary undertakings to Biffen as 'not worth the paper they are written on'.

In early 1982 Murdoch's campaign against his Editor intensified. While Harry was away with influenza for some of the key weeks in February and was depressed by the fatal illness of his father, Charles Douglas-Home took over the editorship of the paper and events moved to a crisis. Anthony Holden, who was to prove loyal to Harry and brave in confronting Murdoch, told me that he had learned on sound evidence that Douglas-Home was scheming to evict and replace Harry. Brian Horton, the Foreign Editor who had direct lines into Murdoch, confirmed this manoeuvre to me and warned me to prepare to abandon ship.

I was surprised by this news about Douglas-Home. During the previous eleven months I had gone out of my way to work closely with him, consulting him on my editorials. I believed that I had created a relationship of trust, almost of friendship with him. In my naivety, I invited him to my room and informed him of the rumours, asking him directly: 'Charlie, are you after Harry's job?' I would not have minded too much had he said 'Yes', since that was an understandable ambition and anyway I had concluded that Harry's term at *The Times* was nearing its end. But Douglas-Home rebutted the suggestion with great indignation. He said (and I took a note immediately afterwards) that 'I swear to you, Bernard, that not only am I not after Harry's job, but I would never wish to edit *The Times* under this destructive monster Murdoch'. I reported this reassuring conversation to Harry, who told me next day that Douglas-Home had again reaffirmed to him that he would not under any circumstances take the editorship. When I saw Douglas-Home in his room that evening he said, 'I am pleased to have killed that canard.' He reaffirmed to me his determination never to serve as an editor under Murdoch, again described Murdoch as a 'monster', and explained to me that Murdoch was like a cancer agent – when he entered an institution he infected and killed all its living cells. (He himself was suffering from the disease which was to kill him three years later.) He added that it was Murdoch's nature to divide and destroy any vital organism in his empire, such as a happy editorial or management team. This was a perceptive view, and I was completely convinced by Douglas-Home's repeated claims that he had no ambitions to be Editor. When Holden and Horton returned separately again to assert to me that Douglas-Home was playing a devious game, I strongly refuted this and defended him. Clearly my naivety was (and still is) boundless. I have always believed what people tell me unless and until I have strong reasons to do otherwise. I do not know how to conduct my life in any other way.

On the afternoon of Tuesday 9 March 1982, the day after he returned from his father's funeral in North Wales, Harry came to see me in my office and reported that Murdoch had just demanded his resignation. Douglas-Home had already agreed to take the editorship of *The Times*, even before it was vacant. Harry looked shattered and I felt deeply sorry for him. I advised him not to resign precipitately and to take good legal advice before doing anything.

My own emotions were disturbed and my brain racing, since I knew that I was bound to share Harry's fate. That evening, as I completed the first leader on Geoffrey Howe's impressive budget, Douglas-Home walked into my room and asked for the copy of it. He read it, said it was good, and that it should go up straight away for setting. I thanked him for his approval and suggested that as usual my editorial should also go to the Editor for final approval. Douglas-Home ignored that suggestion and sent it up for printing. This was presumably his statement to me that he was already in charge, even though Harry had not yet resigned. He made no reference to his recent declarations to me that he would never take the editorship.

Charles Douglas-Home – or 'Charlie' as he was usually called, a touch patronisingly, by *Times* staff – was educated at Eton, served in the army, and was the
nephew of the 14th Earl of Home, who was briefly an unsuccessful Tory Prime
Minister in 1963–4. Charlie had a worthy career on *The Times* and in 1981was a
serious candidate for the succession to Rees-Mogg (whom he frequently criticised to me). One of his more intriguing earlier activities had been to prepare a
secret dossier on each *Times* journalist with details of their private lives –
referring to one as having 'a chaotic love life' and to another as 'not a gentleman'
(which he would certainly have written about Harry and me). When this earlier
spy work became known on the paper, Charlie was censured by the NUJ chapel
and forced to apologise, and he promised to destroy his archive of scandalous
dossiers. He had clearly been unforgivably guilty of applying to fellow journalists
the low practices which they regularly apply to members of the public. But apparently he could not kick the habit.

When the Editor asked me to conduct a weekly meeting of the specialist
writers to try to energise them, Douglas-Home helpfully and discreetly handed
me a large brown envelope saying, 'Don't let anybody know about this.' It
contained the relevant sections of his notorious dossier (the very one he had
promised to destroy) relating to the specialist writers. From the few I examined,
the writers emerged as much more interesting people than I had imagined from
their stolid feature articles. I concluded that 'Charlie' would clearly have been
happier in MI5.

Douglas-Home was short and sandy-haired and walked stiffly as if on wooden
legs. His appearance had a curious mixture of the appearance of a boyish army
officer with the weary look of an old man, and he had an engaging air of studied
nonchalance. I had enjoyed his book on Rommel and immediately liked him and his
intelligent wife. From the beginning he presented himself to us as a trusty figure
representing the 'bridge' to old-fashioned decent establishment values. He told
Harry on his appointment as Deputy Editor that 'you can depend on me'. Rees-
Mogg confirmed this assessment, telling Harry that 'Charlie won't let you down.'
I believed that assurance. But in fact I had no experience of handling this kind of
Etonian from a long breed of Scottish border politicians and (more distantly)
cattle-rustlers. They can be smooth and charming on the surface but are ruthless
in pursuit of their ambitions and bite like a snake in a corner. (My experience with
'Charlie' might make me reassess the history of how his apparently disinterested
uncle secured the premiership in 1963!) Those sharp and deceptive qualities have
enabled various generations of Douglas-Homes and their social equivalents again
and again to make their way to the top of the greasy pole of British political life,
preaching clubbable team spirit while practising ruthless opportunism to advance

their careers. I respect, and nobody should underestimate, their calculating political skills. But personally I lack the character to emulate or even cope with them. One evening in Nuffield College, a distinguished Oxford economist who had known Douglas-Home well since Eton days took me on one side and with concern asked me: 'How well do you know Charlie?' I said that I thought we were becoming friends. He responded sharply: 'Bernard, you have little experience of these kind of people. Watch out. Don't listen to what they say, watch their eyes.' It was a shrewd warning, but I was not equipped to act on it.

Once the opportunity of the editorship emerged, Douglas-Home ceased to be a loyal adjutant. He began openly to criticise Harry, once saying directly to him that 'You are finished' (not untrue, but unnecessarily heartless). He suborned one of Harry's assistants to report on his activities and visitors (more ammunition for the dossiers?), and began to strut around the editorial floor, his thin lips curved in a new-moon smile: the cat knew he had the cream. He forbade staff to persist with the planned petition in support of Harry. He admitted to Harry with languid candour that 'I would do anything to edit *The Times* ... I've worked fourteen years for this newspaper. It is time I was rewarded.' When Tony Holden grilled him in a dark corner about his 'treachery', Douglas-Home replied with a smile that it was simply because he wanted the editorship, and that any bridge player would appreciate the finesse which he had played to achieve it. When Holden resigned in protest, he handed Douglas-Home a written quotation from Shakespeare's *Macbeth*, where Banquo says to Macbeth, who had murdered Duncan to gain the crown: 'Thou hast it now ... and I fear thou play'dst most foully for't.' They were bloody times.

Over the next few turbulent days, while Harry held out, refusing to resign, I spent much of my time discussing the situation with him. He was under constant pressure, sometimes amounting to hooligan harassment, from Murdoch's managerial and legal associates trying to intimidate him into resignation immediately. Harry's moods swung and at times he seemed on the edge of a breakdown. He wanted to fight on the issue of editorial independence and the pledges which Murdoch had given to Parliament, and to reinforce this principle he said he would resign only to the National Directors, who were supposed to symbolise editorial freedom on the paper. As far as I could see being a National Director on *The Times* seemed to involve only interesting lunches and welcome fees, with no power or responsibility. One of them, Lord Robens, railed against Murdoch in most unflattering terms. But the others kept their heads down and somehow failed to meet to discuss or to receive Harry's resignation.

On the afternoon of Friday 12 March I was with Harry when Murdoch's Australian henchman Richard Searby burst into the room, thrust some documents at Harry and shouted: 'Now get on with it!' When Harry's own genteel solicitor took a call from the Murdoch legal side, I heard him complain politely about 'this shouting and ranting' from the other end, warning that if they continued to 'behave like ruffians' he would call off the proceedings and go home. Harry sat white and exhausted with his pen in his hand as if about to sign the resignation documents, but I said that he need not give way to the Murdoch bully tactics. So he did not sign, and with his wife Tina Brown, who was impressively strong and supportive, we went out to a restaurant for supper.

On Monday morning, 15 March 1982, Harry looked much better and told me: 'I am fighting on. I am editing the paper today.' He was strengthened by the recent flow of scores of letters to *The Times* supporting his stand. But then he discovered that Owen Hickey, another guardian of traditional integrity at the paper, had selected to print the only letter received in defence of Murdoch – predictably from the former Labour minister Hartley Shawcross, as ever anxious to reassure the political right that he had buried his distant radical past. Harry and I both attended the mid-morning editorial conference, which had an eerie atmosphere, since everyone present knew that Harry was under irresistible pressure to go and that Douglas-Home was already carrying out some of the functions of Editor. Then we lunched together at the Garrick Club, where Harry again insisted that he intended to fight on to establish the principle of editorial independence. But I knew the battle was lost.

Back at the newspaper in the afternoon, as Harry buzzed around the news desk the news reporters were preparing to write a big story on the plight of their own Editor. To them he still insisted on resigning to the hidden National Directors and publicly stating his views on editorial independence. Murdoch was at this time vetoing Harry's own draft resignation statement because of its reference to the issue of editorial freedom. At a little after eight in the evening I went to Harry's room, where he was still actively editing copy in the paper – including the story of his own imminent departure. The atmosphere in there was unreal. Murdoch's henchmen were beating on the door demanding action. Harry's lawyers were anxious to catch their trains home. Harry was white and nervous, often appearing about to resign and then backing off, as he had the previous Friday. We all knew that the *Times* board had gathered upstairs to accept his formal resignation – but until that point he would still technically be Editor.

It is difficult even now, nearly twenty years afterwards, for me to convey the intensity of my feelings that evening. I maintained an outward calm but was inwardly overwhelmed with emotion, and exhausted after days of pressure and nights of poor sleep. I felt sorry for Harry, whose great editorial career had come to this concussive end, and my own career had also come to another juddering halt. I would again be unemployed, at forty-seven, with no financial resources and four children between the ages of eleven and sixteen.

Shortly after nine on that Monday evening the legal proceedings were complete and Harry's resignation went to the waiting *Times* board. The television cameras were summoned to his room where he nervously read his resignation statement, his voice almost breaking. We left the building together. He took me first to the ITN studios, where I gave a restrained interview with no personal recriminations to Alastair Burnett on *News at Ten*; and then I continued on to the BBC, where I did the same for John Tusa on *Newsnight*.

Next morning I returned to *The Times* and was immediately summoned by John Grant, the mediocre Managing Editor whom Harry regretted not sacking at the beginning. He carried an ominous file on his lap (was it borrowed from Douglas-Home?) and told me menacingly that he was considering firing me, allegedly for my 'not having informed the news desk the previous evening that the Editor was proposing to resign'. At a further meeting with him and Douglas-Home, the latter explained coldly that as the new Editor of *The Times* he proposed to take disciplinary action against me.

The formal disciplinary proceedings took place that afternoon with lawyers present from both sides – mine from Heald Nickinson, the firm of my old friend Jack Black. These proceedings were to me farcical. I felt that they could only be adequately described by my literary hero and satirist of totalitarian methods, George Orwell. The pigs had certainly taken control of the farm. This was the British right-wing behaving like the Russian Communists at the time of their purges. The accusation which Douglas-Home read out, impressively without laughing, seemed to me and to my lawyer to be clearly a fabrication. It alleged that on the previous Monday evening I had allowed a false report that Harry would not resign as Editor to go forward for publication in the first edition of the newspaper. It was by Don Macintyre, whom I liked and respected, and at one point indicated that Harry might stay on. I had spoken to Don around six in the evening and had actually said that I thought the Editor would resign that evening, but after his U-turn the previous Friday I could not be sure. That was quoted accurately in Don's article. But subsequently Harry had told him that he expected to stay on and that shaped the opening of the story. I never saw the full and final version. Douglas-Home conceded to my questioning that the only quotations from me in the text were accurate, but he alleged that I should have gone to the news desk and informed them once Harry had resigned around nine.

This accusation – which Douglas-Home refused to put on paper despite repeated requests by myself and my lawyer – was bizarre and would have been hilariously funny had the circumstances not been so serious. I had not misled the

journalist nor told him that Harry was staying on – apparently Harry had
suggested that to him. Don confirmed this to me later. I had never been shown
the final story and had no way of knowing that it contained the suggestion that
Harry was staying on. My editorial responsibilities as set out in writing when I
joined were to work directly to the Editor and I had never worked to the news
desk. The implication that somehow I possessed and withheld from the news
desk some secret information about Harry's resignation was incredible. Harry's
impending resignation was known to everyone in the country who was interested,
having dominated the news headlines throughout the weekend. The hallway of
The Times was full of journalists and cameramen waiting to report his resignation. The management and board of *The Times* were in the building throughout
the evening waiting for Harry's resignation and received it at the same time that
I knew. If the *Times* news desk, and Douglas-Home himself, somehow remained
unaware of this surrounding cacophony, then it demonstrates how much they
were in need of modernisation.

The 'kangaroo court' met again on the Wednesday morning in a small and
dingy room in the *Times* building. Douglas-Home assumed the gravitas of a
judge as he sat flanked by the wretched Grant (still clutching his Stasi-style file).
Douglas-Home pronounced his verdict in a curiously slow and pompous tone.
He said that 'we' – I don't know if that was the royal use of 'we' or a reference to
him and Murdoch – 'have slept on the matter overnight.' His verdict was that 'we
dismiss him here and now', and without payment of any contractual redundancy
compensation. I had to leave the building immediately. The National Union of
Journalists representative was Paul Routledge, then a fan of Arthur Scargill, the
far-left mineworkers' leader in the process of leading his great union to destruction. He gave me the impression that he may have quietly enjoyed the sight of a
Labour right-winger in distress, but he finally raised the important point that the
charge bore no relationship to anything in the *Times* code of rules. But Douglas-
Home dismissed that out of hand and also ruled that I would not be allowed any
appeal. It was a kangaroo court with an Etonian gloss, concocted to punish me for
standing by Harry as Editor.

Of course, I fully realised that after our clash with Murdoch my position on
the newspaper was unsustainable and I would have to leave. I would certainly
have been happy to negotiate my own speedy departure in a civilised way and on
my legally contractual terms. But it was totally unnecessary to conduct my
inevitable departure in such a vindictive manner. I understand now that I had
naively underestimated Douglas-Home's deep Conservative hostility to all that
Harry and I stood for in terms of class, politics and attitudes to modernisation,
etc. He may also have been trying to demonstrate his willingness to do Murdoch's

dirty work. I was personally very hurt by his behaviour, but I appreciate that he was already suffering under the dark clouds of cancer and that he may have seen this as his final career opportunity to get to the top. I saw him only once after that depressing morning. A year or so later, I was lunching at my usual window table in my favourite Gay Hussar when Charlie, still Editor, walked in looking gaunt. Mr Victor, the proprietor, immediately pointed him upstairs, which was viewed as second-class accommodation by us regulars. Victor then came over to me and said: 'I won't have him downstairs after the way he treated you.' (From his clientele of journalists and politicians Victor knew everything that went on in those worlds.) That was serious revenge.

After the trial verdict, I went to my solicitor's office in Bedford Square. He specialised in employment dismissals and told me, with a show of personal feeling unusual among professional lawyers, that he could not remember a case so outrageous. Next day he wrote to Murdoch's solicitors setting out the basis for our claim for wrongful dismissal. He also firmly stated that if *The Times* ever published the outrageous allegation that I had committed any serious misconduct then we would sue the paper for defamation. They responded defensively, promising that they would make no public comment on my dismissal, their lawyers obviously not confident about a legal scrutiny of the management's rash action. But they remained otherwise as aggressive as ever, dismissing my lawyer's telephone call with near-abuse and asserting that they would fight me through the courts 'with all of Murdoch's financial backing against Donoughue's'. That was a serious threat, since I had no money at all. I also heard from a *Times* colleague that they had trawled through all my expense claims hoping to find evidence of fraud, but found nothing. Despite my tuition from Godfrey Smith at the *Sunday Times* twenty years earlier, I had still not acquired the journalists' skills at cooking expenses.

I also appealed for help to the trade unions. My National Union of Journalists leadership pressed the *Times* management hard to withdraw its action because it breached the existing disputes procedures. But we made very little progress until June when, still looking for a job, I decided to broaden my trade union attack on *The Times* and went to the TUC to see Bill Keys, General Secretary of the print union SOGAT and Chairman of the TUC Printing Trades Committee, whom I had known and liked since my days in Number 10. It was teatime when I arrived at Congress House, but Bill had clearly drunk well at lunch and was continuing to enjoy whisky for tea. He appeared to have some difficulties in focussing on the details of my problem and I finally rose, somewhat impatiently, to go home. As I left the room disappointed, Bill said: 'Bernard, don't worry, my members at *The Times* will wish to discuss the principles involved in your case. They will probably do that each day next week between six and ten in the evening' – the crucial printing time for newspapers. I realised that Bill was more focussed than I had supposed. I do not know what happened between him and *The Times*, but the following afternoon my solicitor phoned me to report that he had received a call from the newspaper's management. Their bottle and bluster had gone, and they suddenly wished to settle my case on amicable terms, meeting all our demands. The summary dismissal was withdrawn, to be replaced by a mutually agreed termination of contract with full payment of my contractual compensation. The often denigrated – and now emasculated – print and journalist unions clearly did have a purpose.

One rare happy moment in this drama was in the aftermath when Harry came to visit me in Brookfield Park and presented me with a beautiful silver goblet from Aspreys. On it was inscribed: 'To my loyal friend Bernard, who warned me of the Ides of March, and stood with me.' Despite the pain, I was proud to have worked with him and I miss his friendship now that he lives across the Atlantic.

While I concluded my settlement with *The Times* in the spring of 1982, I once more scanned the employment horizon for a new job. At that time the choice for a forty-seven-year-old with the wrong politics was limited, and some of my past experience was as likely to be held against me as in my favour, while my clash with Murdoch ensured that I was unlikely to get another newspaper post in London. Employment in public or political life was also closed, since Margaret Thatcher was in Downing Street and for her first eight years in office she refused to appoint any Labour supporters to any vacancy which arose. (In my time there Wilson and Callaghan had appointed several of their able Tory opponents to public posts.) Academe, suffering a punitive financial squeeze, also offered little prospect to me. So three of my trades were blocked. I therefore turned to the City, to Grieveson Grant, one of our top stockbrokers, where I had previously acted as a consultant and where the partners and staff were among the nicest people I knew. Of course, Labour stockbrokers were thin on the ground, but the next four years with Grieveson were to offer me among my happiest working experiences in my four careers so far.

At Grieveson, I worked first as an investment manager on large, mainly local authority pension funds, and then as Head of the Research Department, where I was in charge of up to fifty analysts. (Two of my staff, the businessman Luke Johnson and journalist Bronwen Maddox, later achieved some fame.) My own particular role was equity strategy, both domestic and global, and I wrote monthly articles analysing the British economy and the implications for shares. I became especially interested in the new discipline of Quantitative Analysis – the use of modern mathematical techniques to establish and monitor market values –

and we were among the first City firms to use it on any scale. I also studied hard for the London Stock Exchange examinations – covering arcane areas of the back-office administration of certificate transfers and forms and procedures I had never witnessed. Aged nearly fifty, I just managed to pass. It seemed much harder to me than getting a first at Oxford. I have been told that I am the only Labour politician and minister ever to have passed those examinations and become a full member of the Stock Exchange, which I suppose is some kind of distinction.

Membership of the Exchange enabled me to become a capital partner at Grieveson – sharing the profits and the financial windfall when we were taken over by Kleinwort Benson in 1986, but also risking unlimited liability for losses. My partners were very straight and fun to work with and many were highly intelligent. Colleagues such as Michael Bedford, John Brew, Brian Knox, Peter Ellis, Peter Clark, Jim Hamilton and Michael Beaumont (all educated at Oxbridge) were, contrary to the views in academe, brighter, more hard-working and more interesting than many university lecturers I had known.

While in the City I kept in regular touch with many of my former academic, media, arts and political worlds. I rejoined the Standing Committee of the LSE. My relations with my Oxford college, Lincoln, grew ever warmer, and they elected me to an Honorary Fellowship in 1986. My only remaining media activity was in advising the authors of the wonderful television series *Yes Minister* and *Yes Prime Minister*. I lunched regularly with Jonathan Lynn and Anthony Jay and we discussed possible plots based on my experiences at Number 10, though the real genius lay in the way in which they would pick up a side remark or recollection of mine and convert it into a hilarious television story. They also – mainly through the mouth of Sir Humphrey Appleby, the fictional Cabinet Secretary – deftly created a language which was both recognisably 'Whitehallese' and yet distinctly theirs. Sir Humphrey is a creation of pure genius, a kind of Downing Street Jeeves to Prime Minister Wooster-Hacker, silkily subservient but brighter and really always in control of him.

I also appeared on *Desert Island Discs*, something which Herbert Morrison had always coveted, carrying in his wallet his list of records ready for when the occasion arose, though sadly for him it never did. I was interviewed by Michael Parkinson, a real 'pro' who did the programme in one relaxed and unrehearsed take. Each of my eight records to take to the desert island meant something special to me. 'Love is Here to Stay' by Gene Kelly was a reminder of my teenage years in love with Hollywood dance musicals. 'Something' came from the best of the Beatles in the 1960s. 'Gentle on my Mind' by Glen Campbell usually opened our day in sunny Ceret. *La Bohème* with Mirella Freni was from my days in the royal box at Covent Garden with Lionel Robbins and Claus Moser. The clarinet concertos of Mozart and Brahms were played by Jack Brymer, star of the London Symphony Orchestra. Richard Strauss's song 'Morgen' sung by the statuesque Jessye Norman always moved me, and Schubert's string quintet brought back sad memories from Jack Kennedy's funeral onwards. Today I might be marginally more adventurous musically, with some Shostakovich, Berg and Tom Waits. For my luxury to take to the desert island I chose linen sheets, delivered fresh by parachute every week, and my book was the collected poems of W. B. Yeats.

One of my then most satisfying musical pleasures was my long association with the London Symphony Orchestra. I was elected Chairman of the Executive Board in 1979 and remained with the Orchestra for over a decade. Our initial task was to plan their move to be resident orchestra at the new Barbican Arts Centre under their new principal conductor, Claudio Abbado. We also had to strive to create a whole new audience in the bleak Barbican. The LSO, soon brilliantly managed by ex-cellist Clive Gillinson, never, as some orchestras did when under commercial pressure, abandoned its pursuit of the highest musical excellence. I travelled the world with the LSO, hearing them play and seeing them celebrated in Tokyo, New York, Boston, Washington, Berlin, Paris, Dublin and Salzburg. It was a privileged musical education for me.

My most vivid LSO memory is of visiting Oman at the invitation of the Sultan to play some specially commissioned (and to me quite incomprehensible) Omani classical music. On the night the hall was packed with Bedouin men in flowing white robes and carrying long knives. While awaiting the Sultan's arrival I stayed outside, as instructed, with the many wives of the LSO instrumentalists who had come on the trip. When he had taken his seat, I entered the hall with the forty-two wives filing behind in a fashion which clearly seemed familiar to the Arab audience. There arose gasps of admiration from the Bedouin, ripples of whooping and then outbursts of clapping. The Omani man escorting us to our seats leaned over to me and said: 'Sir, they are impressed by the size of your harem.'

My most serious diversion while in the City was to publish in 1987 a book on the previous Labour Governments in which I had served: *Prime Minister: The Conduct of Policy Under Harold Wilson and James Callaghan*. It was deliberately academic in style, omitting all personal gossip and background noise of scandal which had clouded the Wilson years, and it made only three passing and bland references to Lady Falkender. The book was generously reviewed, and for one week in June 1987 rose to third position in the *Sunday Times* list of bestsellers, but it soon disappeared from the publisher's list.

I remained spasmodically involved in Labour politics, attending my Kentish Town management committee. But the party was an unattractive sight. The 1979 election defeat led to a bloody battle for the control and soul of the party, with left-wing minority activists led by Tony Benn exploiting the undemocratic structures and procedures of the party to make a bid for power, which came within a hair's breadth of success. They pressed Labour into ever more leftish postures, despite the overwhelming evidence from every election and opinion poll that the electorate wanted the very opposite.

Meetings of my local party became very unpleasant, with militant activists trying to abuse and intimidate anyone who spoke against them. I shall never forget a sweet and elderly working-class lady who had been in our party all her adult life attempting to speak up against the zealots and in favour of concentrating on the practical issues of housing, schools and the NHS. She was loudly abused, with one left-wing woman ranting, 'Sit down and shut up, you old bag!' The lady sat down in tears and I never saw her at meetings again. When I spoke in favour of selling council houses to tenants, I was repeatedly interrupted and overwhelmingly outvoted – by left-wingers (including one who went on to serve in a Tony Blair cabinet), many of whom owned their own smart homes in privileged Hampstead but did not wish to share that pleasure with working people on the council estates.

Labour was massacred by Mrs Thatcher in the 1983 general election, the electorate rejecting our Bennite manifesto, which was rightly described by Gerald Kaufman as 'the longest suicide note in history'. We lost a quarter of our losing 1979 vote, and our 27.6 per cent share of the poll was the lowest since 1918. Holding only three seats in the south of England outside London was the culmination of years of left-wing lunacy and ignoring the electorate's wishes. Labour came close to polling fewer votes than the new Social Democratic Party, and at the party conference in 1981 Benn came within a fraction of beating Healey for the deputy leadership: had those two polls gone the other way, that might have finished the Labour Party as a serious political force.

I was furious at Labour's idiocies. When our branch held a review of what lessons should be learned from the 1983 election defeat, I made a brief statement suggesting that we should listen to the electorate and devise policies to meet their wishes, mentioning the sale of council houses, and reforming the NHS and the nationalised industries. I was loudly interrupted and abused by the militant claque. Two stout young women with short hair and thick sweaters shouted, 'Who is that bastard? Kick the fucker out!' The meeting's formal conclusion was that we should pursue even more left-wing policies, so far were they removed from political reality in a democracy (a political system to which they had only tenuous attachment).

I quite understood why so many longstanding Labour 'moderates' left the party to join the new Social Democratic Party, led by Roy Jenkins, David Owen,

Bill Rodgers and Shirley Williams, all old political associates of mine. It must have seemed to them like escaping from lunacy to sanity. Most of my Hampstead friends and my wife moved across, but I did not go. I shared their hostile view of much that was happening in the current Labour Party but, unlike some of them, my deepest roots were in the old Labour movement and I did not intend to abandon it. I also sensed – as my old friend Denis Howell often said – that the SDP might prove ephemeral.

I became more involved in the party scene when I was elevated to the peerage in early 1985 and took the Labour whip in the Lords. The possibility of a peerage had been first floated obliquely to me by Wilson when he resigned in 1976, and James Callaghan had made a direct enquiry to me about it in 1978. Jim returned to the subject in 1982, getting the support of Cledwyn Hughes, then our Lords leader. It took some time to filter through Mrs Thatcher's hostility to any Labour appointments, but our Welsh mafia finally delivered for me – and by the time I took my seat another Welshman Neil Kinnock was party leader. Cledwyn and Harold Lever introduced me to the Upper House in the operatic old ceremony of doffing hats, and Jim Callaghan wrote to me afterwards that he had looked for me sitting for the first time in the elegant Lords chamber (a daunting experience), but he could not see me because I was 'hidden behind Denis Healey's eyebrows'.

At the time of my elevation to the Lords, my private life entered a period of great instability. In the summer of 1986, during the time when Grieveson Grant was being taken over by Kleinwort Benson, I separated from Carol. Soon after, at her request, we divorced. Such deep emotional disturbances are not easy to explain and are really only the business of the partners involved. I had been with Carol for thirty years – and before that was with Jill for five years and have later lived contentedly with Sarah Berry for over a decade, so I don't have particularly itchy feet. Our intensive professional careers led Carol and me to drift apart. When Rachel and Kate left home for university and the boys were heading there, 7 Brookfield Park, once so vibrant and noisy, now seemed silent and empty. Often I was away on business. At other times, with Carol similarly absent, I returned home from work to spend the evening alone with Pushkin the cat and the clarinet I was trying to learn.

I moved to a flat with the impressive address of 1 Sloane Square to try to rebuild some satisfaction and stability into my personal life. The move had the additional advantage that I would never again have to make use of the dreadful Northern Line. I never have. Our divorce was conducted in a civilised way, very much to Carol's credit, and I have continued close to my children. But it was a traumatic experience which I do not propose to repeat. One of the main prices of divorce, as with bereavement, is the loss of a shared history and memory together. I cannot understand how some friends undertake it more than once. But it was emotionally the correct step for me.

After Kleinwort Benson took over Grieveson Grant in 1986, I never felt secure or comfortable with their very impersonal and deeply Tory style. I also began to feel frustrated, wanting to pursue my interest in the new technique of index-tracking investment. This meant using computer techniques to construct an investment portfolio to replicate the content and the performance of a whole market index, such as the *Financial Times* All Share or the FT 100. This approach has the dual advantages of low management costs and also the likelihood of above-average performance, since some 80 per cent of City fund managers usually underperform the relevant markets.

But the senior Kleinwort managers turned down my request to initiate such an approach. They apparently did not believe that 'tracking' had much future (it soon became the fastest growing investment technique) and anyway saw it as conflicting with their traditional (underperforming) management approach, for which they charged much higher fees.

So I began to enquire elsewhere in the City. The first opportunity came from an unexpected quarter when I met Kevin Maxwell, son of the publishing tycoon, at a *Daily Mirror* reception at the 1987 Labour Party conference. I barely knew him, but he revealed that he proposed to establish a new company devoted to index-tracking, and suggested I join him. I was intrigued, seeing a way out of Kleinworts and a way to practise my new interest. Association with the Maxwells, even though Robert appeared at that time to be rehabilitated from his earlier sins, was clearly not without dangers. But, as usual, I found the combination of novelty and danger irresistible.

Seventeen

MORE TURBULENCE: WORKING
WITH ROBERT MAXWELL

I left Kleinwort and joined London and Bishopsgate, a new part of the then Maxwell empire, in the summer of 1988. It was to prove my most mistaken but not my least interesting career move so far, and it projected me into another bout of life turbulence. Before departing from Kleinwort, I had consulted our previous Senior Partner at Grieveson Grant about Maxwell. He was properly circumspect but reported that during all the years in which Grieveson had acted for Maxwell as one of his stockbrokers 'he always delivered what he promised and never reneged on his word to us.' My old friends at the *Daily Mirror*, especially Joe Haines, were very keen that I should join the Maxwell team. They of course knew of Maxwell's past sins and present faults, but the general view among those working for him was that his previous painful experience with the 1971 DTI Enquiry and his recent commercial success in building a media empire, together with the army of City lawyers, bankers and accountants which permanently surrounded him, would ensure that he did not deviate into serious trouble again.

However, two of my closest friends, Graham Greene, Managing Director of the publishers Jonathan Cape, and Michael Bedford from Kleinwort, argued strongly against my going to join Maxwell, believing that this leopard had not changed his spots and presciently foreseeing the dangers involved. In the end, I took the wrong decision.

I was attracted by the challenge of the new index-tracking business and by the fact that Maxwell was already a big player in the media and political worlds, enjoying ready access to top politicians and statesmen at home and abroad. The very danger of the move gave it a spice which appealed to something in me, even if that something may not have been very mature. Looking back over my speckled life, I can see that the challenges of novelty, political excitement and career danger have always proved difficult for me to resist. Anyway, I reasoned, I would not be taking the Maxwell risk for very long. My plan was to be working full time in the House of Lords by the time of the next election, expected by 1992. So I instructed my lawyers to draft my Maxwell contract on the assumption, as it actually turned out, of a short three years' involvement.

My position was to be Vice-Chairman of two new small companies: London and Bishopsgate International, which was concerned with index-tracking investment (my main involvement), and London and Bishopsgate Holdings, which did financial derivatives trading and took financial stakes in other businesses. Robert Maxwell was Chairman of both companies, holding 75 per cent of their shares, though for most of the first two years he remained fairly distant from the businesses. The remaining 25 per cent of the shares were divided between the Chief Executive Andrew Smith, the Finance Director Larry Trachtenberg, and myself with the smallest holding. I had never before met my two young American colleagues, who were longstanding friends of Kevin Maxwell – the active representative of the controlling Maxwell family on our boards. Smith was sharp (too sharp, it proved) and had taught at Oxford, while the amiable and plausible Trachtenberg was an LSE graduate, so at least their educational pedigrees seemed initially to be OK to me.

They were centrally involved in the financial trading and management of the companies. My responsibilities were defined and published as being 'Investment Strategy, Marketing, Public Relations and Public Contacts' and I had no hands-on responsibility on the financial trading side. Over time I grew less confident that I could believe the Americans' word, and increasingly conscious that Smith, Trachtenberg and Kevin Maxwell were operating closely together and excluding me – of a very different generation, style and background – from some of their thinking and operations.

We worked hard to establish the fledgling business. Our offices were never based in Maxwell House, nor part of the main Maxwell operations at the quoted Maxwell Communications Corporation, so I visited the headquarters only when having specific business, usually with Kevin. In early 1989 we took over the quoted New Tokyo Investment Trust and converted it to track the Japanese Topix market index, renaming it the First Tokyo Index Investment Trust (FTIT) – the first investment trust 'tracker' ever quoted on the London market. LBI's young team of quantitative analysts was excellent and its techniques very advanced at the time, tracking its relevant market indexes within a small technical margin of error plus or minus. In addition to the First Tokyo Investment Trust, we also secured management contracts for one section of the Sun Alliance investment funds, where in 1990–1 we performed better than any of their internal portfolio managers, and also managed some 10 per cent of the pooled Maxwell pension funds, including the *Mirror* Group, which were under the separate corporate control of Bishopsgate Investment Management (BIM).

During early 1990 I had a series of disagreements with Smith over his risky derivative trading operations. I was also concerned at my exclusion from details of financial transactions conducted by him and Trachtenberg together with the Maxwells. Therefore before Easter 1990 I had decided that the clear incompatibilities between myself and my colleagues' 'Wall Street' style were such that I should quietly leave LBI. Nothing had occurred which to my knowledge was in itself wrong, but I was not confident that I knew everything that was happening in the company.

I discussed my potential departure with Kevin, who did not discourage me from leaving, acknowledging that we were 'like oil and water'. So I instructed my solicitors, Heald Nickinson, to prepare my exit. Unfortunately, as it turned out, I did not execute my resignation. Firstly, Smith, the main source of my concerns, launched a New York version of LBI and transferred himself to it. His replacement, Mark Tapley from Shearson Lehman, was a man much more of my own taste – straight and technically competent – and I felt that I could happily work with him, for a little longer at least. We also recruited a compliance officer from LAUTRO, the City regulatory authority, so I felt more relaxed about the supervision of the financial trading side. Most significantly, I then contracted debilitating hepatitis on a visit to Africa in March 1990 and was away from the office a good deal until much later in the year.

On returning to full-time work at the end of October 1990, the basic divisions within LBI came to a disruptive head. There was what Tapley and I described in several memoranda as a 'dualism' between him and me on one side, and Smith (who continued to interfere in LBI's financial trading from New York), Trachtenberg and Kevin Maxwell on the other. Over several acrimonious weeks we negotiated a complete split in the company – though it never became fully operative since it soon became clear that the Maxwells actually wanted Smith and Trachtenberg to continue to be involved in our operations. I became completely fed up with these games and at a memorable lunch with Robert and Kevin Maxwell on Tuesday 18 December 1990 I arranged my own imminent resignation, which they were clearly happy to accept. Robert Maxwell for his part revealed that he proposed anyway to close down LBI in London. My solicitors negotiated with the Maxwells the terms of my personal resignation and these were engrossed in a formal document dated 23 March 1991 and confirmed to me in a personal letter from Kevin Maxwell. But my long anticipated withdrawal from the Maxwell operation was to my annoyance once again suddenly delayed. A serious crisis arose with the First Tokyo Investment Trust, putting it into conflict with LBI, and so both Maxwell, as Chairman of LBI, and Alan McInroy, as Chairman of the Trust, asked me to stay on to help to sort it out. Very reluctantly I agreed, feeling I had a responsibility to do so, being a director of both companies. But I was deeply disappointed since I was by now very keen to move on into the Lords, where I was already arranging to take front bench responsibilities. Consequently my resignation contract, which had been agreed only a week before the crisis broke, had to go on hold.

This FTIT crisis had such important reverberations later that it is necessary to describe it here in some detail, and I hope that the reader will bear with that.

The problem first emerged in January and February 1991, when concerns were expressed to us in LBI that First Tokyo was at risk of losing its privileged tax status as an investment trust because the revenues it had received from lending its equity stock to the market – some £650,000, all of which went towards eliminating the inherited loss at FTIT – were growing too large. There was nothing illegal about these stock-lending revenues, but our legal advice was that their scale jeopardised our precious trust tax status. This was promptly reported to the FTIT Board on 26 February, and afterwards I issued instructions that LBI should 'immediately cease new stock-lending' and should rapidly recall the existing lending from First Tokyo. (It was all recalled by 11 April.)

But on 8 March 1991 our tax counsel additionally reported that the lending itself was being conducted by the finance department of LBI, under Trachtenberg's control, in an unconventional way. It was not being done as authorised by the FTIT Board in 1989, but was a much more risky and novel kind of lending, about which the board and I had not been informed: this lending was done direct to Maxwell business associates without, as normal in City stock-lending, an intermediary broker taking the capital risk. The independent Chairman of FTIT, Alan McInroy, and the two independent directors, Tony Cassidy and Ian MacDonald, supported by myself and George Willett, immediately insisted on an independent enquiry into the lending. I had originally insisted that we should have an independent chairman and directors at the time we took over the Trust in 1989. This had led to my first row with Robert Maxwell, who angrily queried the need for them. I said that we needed them for public credibility and I told Maxwell that I would not serve on the Trust board without them. He conceded grumpily. From now on the three Scots demonstrated their worth and their independent spirit, as did George Willett, who was a Maxwell appointee to the board but supported the independents throughout.

The background to this mini-crisis was complex. Conventional stock-lending, via a broking intermediary which normally takes the capital risk, was and is common and proper in the City of London. Stock-lending is a standard form of fee revenue for investment and pension portfolios. The Treasury has periodically, as in November 1995, given specific tax incentives 'to boost London's role as the centre of international share lending.' This was the conventional form of stock-lending which was first advocated by Smith via Trachtenberg to the board of First Tokyo in 1989 and was then approved by the board. The board, including myself, was assured by Trachtenberg, the LBI Finance Director, that all our stock-lending was of the conventional kind 'with Morgan Stanley as the intermediary' taking all the risk (as duly recorded in the board minutes). Similar assurances were provided by him during 1990 and again in early 1991.

I had become aware by early 1991 that the stock-lending had recently begun to be conducted with a Maxwell associate, the Mirror Group. But this raised no fiduciary worries providing that there was an intermediary broker (assumed to be still Morgan Stanley International) continuing to take the risk, leaving the portfolio not exposed to default. The Mirror Group was a well-rated borrower. However, I decided to question and check that this remained the case. On 8 January 1991 I wrote a memorandum to our Compliance Officer and Company Secretary, who had the reassuring pedigree of being previously employed by the City's own regulatory authority LAUTRO, and specifically asked for confirmation that the FTIT stock-lending was still being conducted correctly and as authorised. He replied that same day setting out in a long memorandum the terms of our stock-lending and confirming that it 'must be conducted through Morgan Stanley International as intermediaries' (i.e. that it was the conventional and authorised form of lending). He added for further comfort that the Board of FTIT would be notified if the triple AAA risk-rating of Morgan Stanley (our risk taker) changed, and also that 'the ultimate borrower' (implying the existence of an intermediary) of FTIT stock must lodge either a letter of credit or collateral as security. So as late as 8 January 1991 the stock-lending programme was described to me by the relevant compliance executive who had drafted the stock-lending contracts in exactly the same conventional terms as was originally presented to myself and the board in 1989. Hence I was reassured that there was nothing to worry about – and certainly nothing about which I should 'blow whistles' or report to the regulatory authorities, as some commentators later suggested. I was further reassured when I enquired of our Coopers and Lybrand auditor about the financial security or collateral on the lending and was told by him that it was 'all in the safe' and that he had just 'held it in my hand'.

However, these reassurances were unfounded. It emerged that there was, in fact, in operation a different type of stock-lending – that done by LBI *directly* to its own Maxwell associate and *without* use of an intermediary broker taking the capital risk – which leaves the portfolio owner (e.g. FTIT) exposed to loss should the borrower default. This was the highly risky type of new variant stock-lending invented or adapted by Maxwell's associates (because it provided them with ready and cheap finance collateral). At some point in 1989 it was implemented on the

First Tokyo portfolio, replacing the original conventional stock-lending without informing the board.

It should be stressed that this new risky variant was not illegal, nor contrary to any regulatory rules (i.e. those of IMRO). But it was certainly not best practice – and in my view quite unacceptable because, theoretically, it risked the portfolio's and hence the shareholders' assets, and also because, in our case, it was not authorised or even reported to the Board of FTIT (nor to Mark Tapley, nor myself at LBI). The respective LBI executives, based on the finance department, had executed this risky form of unauthorised stock-lending while, as the board minutes clearly demonstrate, continuing to inform the board that they were practising the original kind of conventional and authorised risk-free lending. This deception within LBI was made easier by the 'dualism' within the company, which often cut off Tapley and myself from what was happening on the financial side. The unauthorised lending was easy to conduct without my personal knowledge because I anyway had no hands-on responsibilities in the finance department where stock-lending was administered. Under LBI's management structure the Finance Director was not required to report to me.

At the First Tokyo board meeting in March 1991, and again in subsequent meetings, the three independent directors (all from Scotland), supported where legally possible (provided there were no conflicts of interest) by George Willett and myself from the Maxwell side, took urgent action to rectify the position on stock-lending. Two independent enquiries were set up to report on the affair, one under the First Tokyo lawyers and another under outside accountants. These revealed nothing illegal or contrary to any regulatory rules. The offence which was exposed was that LBI had not obtained the authorisation of the First Tokyo board for its risky – but not illegal – stock-lending method. That dereliction by LBI was a matter for the FTIT board; and the board took prompt remedial action with my full support. There was no reason or basis on which to report anything to the police or the regulatory authorities. The boards of FTIT and of LBI consulted all the relevant professional advisers and all reported back that no actual rules had been broken apart from the failure to inform and obtain the authority of the board for stock-lending direct to associates without an intermediary taking the risk (which permission would certainly not have been given).

The regulatory body IMRO was immediately consulted by LBI and it responded that there had been no breach of the rules. IMRO's Chief Executive John Morgan later told the House of Commons Social Security Committee in 1992 that 'there are no rules against self-investment by pension funds and it is not illegal'. He concluded that 'there had been no risk to the shareholders then concerned, the FTIT shareholders'.

LBI consulted its top City lawyers, who responded that there had been no breach of the management agreement. We consulted our auditors, Coopers and Lybrand, who concluded that the stock-lending had been conducted properly at arm's length, with proper documentation, and that the financial collateral was securely in place. So there was no basis for directors to report to the police. It was clear that the stock-lending was not illegal, nor in breach of contract, nor improperly conducted, nor at that stage uncollateralised. The regulatory authority saw no breach of regulations. Neither of our independent enquiries, nor any of the other City firms and professional advisers involved, saw any wrongdoing on which public 'whistles' should have been blown. The offence was against the FTIT board and that offence was promptly rectified by the board. To historians of Maxwell this episode might be seen as an interesting early trailer for much bigger financial misdemeanours later. But that is only with hindsight.

The FTIT directors (including myself) moved quickly into action. At first they considered dismissing LBI as fund managers for not securing authorisation for this dubious stock-lending – and I, although myself an LBI director, immediately responded by suggesting that LBI should anyway offer to resign. But the proposal of dismissal was retracted when FTIT's brokers reported that the huge costs of terminating the LBI contract would deplete the Trust's assets and strongly advised against as not being in the shareholders' interest.

I separately confronted Robert Maxwell with the need to make full reparations to First Tokyo from the LBI side. On 25 April I sent him a memorandum setting out the eight measures of rectification which I believed should be implemented by LBI, and here quote that memo in full:

To: Robert Maxwell
From: Lord Donoughue
Date: 25 April 1991
Re: FTIT, LBH and LBI

Following my conversation with Alan McInroy [Chairman of FTIT] this morning and with yourself, I set out below the measures of co-operation which I believe should be offered to him today and which I understood from him would make the basis of an amicable resolution and joint statement which promises the least damage possible to the parties concerned and meets our fiduciary duty to our client's shareholders.

1 LBI offers resignation as managers, today 25 April 1991, while an independent inquiry proceeds, but offers to provide indexation advice until appointment of a new manager.

2   We suggest independent accounting inquiry, terms of reference to be set by FTIT's independent directors and their advisers.

3   Full compensation for underpayment of stock-lending fees to be paid into escrow account pending outcome of accounting inquiry.

4   A sum agreeable to FTIT to be paid into escrow against any future liability should the rate of 1.75 per cent be demonstrated to be inadequate.

5   Letter to Morgan Stanley on stock-lending rates to be re-submitted with McInroy's textual agreement.

6   Confirmation of scrip and cash dividend credits to be conveyed as soon as Morgan Stanley reports.

7   Subject to above, we shall attempt to agree an amicable public statement with FTIT.

8   Apologies to FTIT from LBI that stock-lending began in February 1989 before Board approval, and confirmation that executives concerned have been suspended from active duties until satisfactory outcome of enquiry.

Addendum:

For internal consideration that Trachtenberg and Smith should be suspended from day-to-day involvement without prejudice, from LBI plc, LBH plc, and any other relevant companies. This will require of course the proper company procedures.

Maxwell responded verbally to my memorandum with abusive anger, but he was in no position to reject its broad thrust.

The following four months, from April until July 1991, were absorbed in intensive negotiations to establish the terms of compensation for the First Tokyo shareholders because its assets had been put at greater risk than reported to the board and because the stock-lending fees should have been higher to reflect this risk.

This was possibly the most tense and unpleasant time of my life, even worse than during the crisis at *The Times* in 1982 because this lasted much longer. We were involved in endless meetings with fellow directors, with lawyers, account-ants and stockbrokers, and with the irate Maxwells. There were several major rows with Robert Maxwell and the Scottish independent directors showed commendable displays of resilience. I was by now particularly disliked by the Maxwell side for my having supported the independents over compensation and over my insistence that Trachtenberg be suspended from LBI. Their greatest hostility related to my support for publishing the affair in the FTIT Annual Report and also in the takeover offer document, in which Maxwell made a bid for FTIT. He strenuously but unsuccessfully resisted both. On one important FTIT board resolution in April I could not actually vote with the independents against

Maxwell on a motion to ask LBI to resign as manager because my lawyers strongly advised that I had a conflict of interest, being a director on both sides (though I had anyway supported resignation in my earlier memo to Maxwell). So I abstained, and Maxwell was defeated by 4–1 instead of 5–1, so my abstention made no difference.

I felt like 'piggy-in-the-middle', and had several major clashes with Robert Maxwell, who accused me of 'betrayal' for supporting the independent Scottish directors. This hostility reached a climax in June 1991 when he sought to escape from LBI's responsibility for the stock-lending deceit by suddenly alleging that I and fellow FTIT director George Willett had known all along of the new form of risky stock-lending and so technically the FTIT Board of which we were members 'knew' – although this was a complete lie and at no time in the four months since the misdeeds came to light had this ever been suggested from the Maxwell side. This device emerged from his banking advisers at the last moment to try to evade the responsibility of having misled the board, and especially in order to avoid having to refer to the stock-lending affair in the FTIT accounts and in the coming takeover offer document. (Maxwell's lawyers stated the motives behind this desperate manoeuvre in an internal memo which later emerged and a copy of which is in my possession.)

When I confronted Maxwell personally with this nonsense, he shouted that Willett and I must have known and discussed it with one another since 'you were both at Oxford together' – a special Maxwell version of class war.

I explained that we had known only of the conventional stock-lending conveyed to the board, not of the risky new variant kind which was kept from us, but he roared back: 'I cannot see the fucking difference!' – which may have been true, since he once said to me: 'I leave all the details to Kevin.' Anyway, having tried on this shabby manoeuvre, he did not pursue it again.

A radical solution was urgently required to the First Tokyo situation in the interests of the Trust's outside public shareholders. This was found when Maxwell took over FTIT at full net asset value plus a compensation payment. At the AGM in July 1991, the other FTIT directors were re-elected to serve in the following year under Maxwell's full ownership, but I did not stand, not wanting any further association.

At this time Maxwell also took back under his investment management the 10 per cent part of the Bishopsgate Investment Management (BIM) pension funds which LBI had been successfully investing. BIM, which had always retained overall control of the pension funds, had also been stock-lending on its portfolio since at least the beginning of 1991. Mark Tapley and I had indicated to the BIM manager Trevor Cook that we would be happier if stock-lending ceased on our part of the pension fund, as it had by then on FTIT. Maxwell, who was Chairman of BIM, aggressively intervened to refuse our request. At a confrontation with Tapley and myself in early July, he puffed and blew angrily, pointing out (correctly) that it was none of our business but a matter for BIM and the pension trustees, and he concluded that he would certainly have suspended me over my opposition to him on this matter but for the fact that he had anyway already accepted my resignation for the end of that month.

On 31 July, following the AGM of FTIT, I left the Maxwell organisation, was no longer paid and played no further part in the affairs of LBI, LBH or any of Maxwell's companies – and quickly went to our beautiful and peaceful house in Ceret to recuperate from the stresses of the recent months. I had only two further brief meetings with Maxwell, when he sought to renegotiate or even renege on the contractual terms of my termination of employment, previously agreed in March 1991. During these exchanges I was reminded of the comment by one of his senior employees: that for Maxwell the signing of a contract was only the start of serious negotiations. At these meetings Maxwell again expressed angry resentment about my opposition to him on the various issues described above. He referred with particular hostility to my written and verbal support 'for the fucking directors of First Tokyo'; he specified our demanding full compensation for FTIT shareholders and my insistence that Trachtenberg, whom he strongly defended, be suspended from LBI.

When angry, Robert Maxwell could be very impressive. He seemed to grow even larger, like an inflating bullfrog, as he shouted at me, his chest and great stomach heaving and his fat jowls wobbling. He sweated and his black hair looked dyed. I sensed that he might be capable of physical murder, and recalled the story he once told me of how, in early 1945, he had lined up and personally shot from close range the German soldiers who had opened fire on his platoon after first waving a white flag of surrender. He rose from his chair opposite me and shouted that because of my 'betrayals', he could 'not stomach' (an impressive image in his case) honouring the existing resignation agreement we had reached earlier in March of that year. He held that document in front of him as if it were dirty, dramatically tore it up and threw its shreds into the nearby waste-paper basket, then rasped: 'You deserve nothing!' When I explained that my action was not meant to be 'treachery' to him but was because I saw it as 'my fiduciary duty' as a director of FTIT to support the independent directors when they were defending the legitimate rights of the First Tokyo shareholders, he exploded, with a roar that I felt conveyed his deepest principles and beliefs, shouting 'fuck fiduciary duty!' Perhaps that quotation should have been on the headstone of his grave.

After that meeting, I did not mind whether Maxwell paid me my contractual compensation or not. I felt lucky to have got out of Maxwell House alive, and was relieved simply to be away from his organisation and heading for a quieter and more satisfying life in the House of Lords. But one evening in mid October 1991, the telephone rang at our country house in Berkshire where we were eating supper. It was the unmistakable gravelly boom of Robert Maxwell. He sounded remarkably benign, as if without a care in the world. He said: 'My Lord, it is about time that you had your money. Come in as soon as you can to collect.' Then he said 'Goodbye', and was gone. My compensation settlement was, in fact, significantly less than my legal contractual rights and less than half what had been agreed in March. But since I had come to expect nothing, I did not complain. Of course I had no idea of the financial storm which was shortly to hit and demolish the Maxwell empire. Nor do I know why he chose to pay me then, when he was under no real pressure from me to do so and was under greater pressure from elsewhere on his resources. His was a most complex personality with a dark sense of humour.

Robert Maxwell drowned in November 1991, four months after I left LBI. The subsequent bankruptcies of his public and private companies, and the resulting DTI Report, have been well publicised. It emerged that LBI was used as one of the many agents in the network of financial irregularities which Maxwell – or those acting on his behalf – adopted while desperately trying to shore up his crumbling empire. Fortunately his plundering of pension funds was alleviated by Lord Cuckney's tireless efforts to recover money from City institutions.

The Maxwell scandal rumbled on during the rest of the 1990s, fired by the long trial in which Kevin Maxwell, Larry Trachtenberg and two other executives of the Maxwell empire were found not guilty of fraudulent practices. This recurrent publicity proved distinctly unpleasant for me since, especially when I became a Labour minister, there were periodic attempts by a few tabloid journalists on Tory newspapers to suggest that I had 'knowledge' of Maxwell's malpractices which I should have revealed at the time.

Other Labour political figures, such as Joe Haines, Helen Liddell and Charles (Lord) Williams, suffered from similar 'guilt by association' smears. I reported articles by Tom Bower in the *Daily Mail* and the *Evening Standard* to the Press Complaints Commission, specifying a dozen allegations and providing thirty-five pages of evidence documenting their inaccuracy. In response to my submission, Bower produced no factual evidence to support his allegations, seeming to work on the basis that it was fair game to allege anything against someone who worked for Maxwell (and, of course, that it was safe to do so against a minister who could not sue without first resigning from office).

The newspapers published my letters of correction, but in this episode I learned that the business of the Press Complaints Commission was then often conducted to protect the newspapers from their victims rather than the other way round.

The general innuendo in some of the press was that I and many others working in the Maxwell empire must have had knowledge of his wrongdoing simply because we were there when it was going on. This assumption reveals a total failure to understand how Maxwell operated. Many of his senior staff subsequently gave witness to the Commons Social Security Committee and at the Maxwell trial of how difficult it was for any but his closest advisers to know what was really going on at the heart of the organisation. His financial tactics were usually devised at early morning meetings with his inner core of executives. I never attended those meetings, and indeed for long was unaware of their existence. Exclusion from knowledge was one of the reasons why I originally decided to resign from LBI in 1990. I was not one of the 120 or so witnesses who were called to give evidence at the Maxwell trial.

It is also often suggested that Maxwell's misdeeds should have been apparent to all those who worked for him because of his transparently 'bad character', as confirmed by the 1971 DTI Report. As for that report, it should be noted that the Tory Trade Minister who actually received and published the report, Peter (Lord) Walker, clearly thought that it was no longer relevant twenty years later in 1991 when he agreed to join Maxwell as his Vice-Chairman of Maxwell Communications Corporation only months before the entrepreneur's death and MCC's collapse. Furthermore, the implication that misbehaviour committed decades earlier (with no criminal record) should forever be held against an individual runs quite contrary to many of the principles underlying our moral, social, religious and legal codes. Of course, bad track records such as Maxwell's should induce prudence – and, with hindsight, more prudence than I personally showed. But I simply cannot conduct my life on the basis that 'the leopard never changes its spots'. It is only with the gift of foresight or the evidence of hindsight that we learn to distinguish the recidivists from the redeemed. The people who saw the perennial recidivist in Maxwell were proven right. I and others were proved wrong. The many distinguished professional people who by the late 1980s gave Maxwell the benefit of the doubt were naive and imprudent, but they were not all accomplices in his crimes.

My personal conclusions on how Maxwell, or those acting for him, conducted his frauds without others knowing could apply to other similar corporate situa-

tions. I believe that in any commercial situation where a resourceful and dominating man is both owner and chairman of a company or companies, and
especially if assisted by a core of pliable and centrally placed executives, then it is
not difficult for him, at least for a considerable period of time, to commit financial
malpractice and deliberately keep it hidden from other senior executives who he
suspects would oppose and expose him.

I gave evidence for a couple of hours to the second DTI Enquiry into Maxwell
set up in 1992 by the Tory Trade Minister Michael Heseltine (whose own son had
recently worked for Maxwell, so presumably he did not think he was a crook) – a
'lawyers' bonanza' which extended throughout the decade and into the following
century. The two inspectors were courteous. The accountant remained fairly
silent except for when he offered the spicy view that Maxwell's auditors, Coopers
and Lybrand, would 'not enjoy the comments of their professional disciplinary
body'.

Their report, published in March 2001, set out the whole complex panorama
of Maxwell's financial manipulations, virtually all of which was news to me. It
was an ugly story of deceit covering a long period of time, not just the final year
of his collapse. An extensive list of City bankers, brokers, lawyers and account-
ants, as well as Maxwell directors, were taken to task for their failures. But it was
really *Hamlet* without the Prince, since the inspectors could not interview
Maxwell himself, who was the centre of the web.

From my own standpoint the report was reasonably benign. I could not expect
not to be in it, since I was a Maxwell director, but its conclusions about me were
mild. In its conclusions it first named the primary category of individuals who
bore 'the responsibility for carrying out the decisions made by Robert Maxwell'
– that was Kevin (mainly) and Ian Maxwell and, from other directors, Andrew
Smith, Larry Trachtenberg, Robert Bunn and Trevor Cook. The second category
of main blame lists those who bear 'a measure of responsibility for the fact that
these abuses were not brought to light and stopped.' These were the Company
Secretary Alan Stephens and especially the auditors Coopers and Lybrand (who
had misled me by assuring me that all the collateral was in place). I was not in
either of those lists of main responsibility. I was mentioned in a subsidiary list,
including the IMRO Regulator, of those with 'more limited responsibility for
failing in their respective positions to ascertain what was in fact happening.'
There was also another list of directors who failed to perform their directorial
duties, including Lord Williams and my friend Joe Haines (who had been put on
the Maxwell board simply as the journalists' representative with no financial
responsibilities, which is a warning to 'workers' representatives' to think twice
before accepting any such appointments).

So I was mildly in the frame, but well down the hit list with only 'limited responsibility' for not asking more questions – though it acknowledged that I did ask questions and was given 'reassuring answers' by the auditors. There was no suggestion that I took part in or knew of any wrongdoings. The six lines about me read:

> Although Lord Donoughue (1) asked questions about the funds lent and the collateral and received reassuring answers; (2) understood that the auditors were satisfied with the arrangements; and (3) was unwell between May and October 1990, he ought as a director of LBI and LBH, to have ascertained sufficient information about the security being used for loans obtained by LBI and about the lending of funds to the private side in the years 1988–90. Had he done so he might have identified the abuse by RM of the funds managed by LBI and, in respect of FTIT, acted sooner than he did.

It was especially important to me that they used the word 'might' about discovering Maxwell's abuses, and that they referred only to the years 1988–90 and had no blame for the key crisis year of 1991 when I confronted him about First Tokyo and we secured the restitution of the shareholders' funds. Even the 'might' was in my view purely hypothetical and loaded with hindsight. The likelihood that had I put even more questions, I would have received other than more reassuring answers is remote and fanciful. The idea that Maxwell, a master of concealment and deception, would have suddenly responded with 'fair cop, Bernard, I have been nicking the funds', is ludicrous. The reality is that those involved in the malpractices did not wish me, nor any other executive outside of the inner Maxwell core, to have any knowledge of their questionable transactions. The inspectors begged the basic question of how does one obtain technical information, of whose very existence one is unaware, from people who have no intention of providing it? Apart from that, I accept their conclusion in my case to have been fair.

The story soon blew away. At last I was able to get on with my life without that shadow in the background.

The demonisation of Robert Maxwell which has occurred in the British media since his death in November 1991 has left many contemporary readers with an unbalanced picture of him. I do not propose to try to provide a contrary apologia. I did not know him well and towards the end of my employment with him I had come strongly to dislike him – which he reciprocated vocally. He must have seen me as a minor irritating obstacle while he grappled with the bigger problems of his crumbling empire. I came to see him, when at his worst, as a bullying monster.

Yet despite my growing dislike for him then, I can now see that he was certainly a remarkable man – and not just a monster, though he was certainly that. His career has been described often elsewhere: starting with a Jewish boyhood in Central Europe, he escaped from the Nazis (though many of his family were killed in the Holocaust) to France and then to Britain, and fought in our army in the war, becoming an officer and winning a Military Cross for bravery. After the war he made his fortune through publishing and also for a few years became a Labour Member of Parliament. His corporate activities often aroused justifiable concern, and he was criticised severely in a Department of Trade Report in 1971. By the 1980s he seemed to have resuscitated his business reputation, buying the *Daily Mirror* and building the Maxwell Communications Corporation into a global publishing and media empire. His death by drowning while cruising on his yacht has never been convincingly explained and may have been related to the impending financial crash of his companies. The latter collapse exposed a complex web of financial irregularities, with dubious cross-financing between his public and his private companies, with borrowings which were improperly collateralised, and the unforgivable misuse of company pension funds. Many of these worst misdeeds appear to have occurred in the autumn of 1991 when he was desperately trying to avoid bankruptcy, but the improper techniques and habits had been learned and often exercised earlier.

There were many dark, negative, even gross strands in Maxwell's character. But before his final collapse, many of his acquaintances were also aware of some positive sides to him which have since been airbrushed out of the picture. It is worth recalling how he was earlier perceived by some important people.

When Maxwell died in 1991, the Conservative Foreign Secretary, Douglas (now Lord) Hurd, said that Britain had been 'robbed of one of our most colourful and energetic figures … He wanted to get things done. He was truly larger than life and the world will be poorer for his absence.' Former Tory Prime Minister Margaret Thatcher praised the Maxwells for being 'great supporters of charity' and added that 'he had wide contacts throughout Eastern Europe and kept me informed about what was happening in those countries and what their leaders were thinking.' Sir Edward Heath, who was the Tory Prime Minister at the time of the 1971 DTI Report into Maxwell's business affairs, now stated that Maxwell was 'a charismatic figure' and 'a tower of strength' in his support for the European Community. As noted above, Peter (now Lord) Walker, who set up that enquiry, later, in 1991, agreed to become Vice-Chairman of Maxwell

Communications Corporation (though he withdrew shortly before taking over). Former Tory Cabinet Minister Geoffrey (Lord) Rippon was Maxwell's long-time friend and business partner. Tory Lord Chancellor Lord Havers worked for him immediately after leaving the Woolsack.

And these were all from the Conservative political party which Maxwell opposed. On the Labour side he had many friends and supporters, including two Labour leaders in Neil Kinnock and John Smith. Labour's former Lord Chancellor, Elwyn Jones; its former Attorney General, Sam Silkin; and its Deputy Leader in the Lords, Lord Williams, all worked on his payroll.

Maxwell was an honoured guest at the White House under United States Presidents Reagan and Bush (who appointed him to the U.S. Commission on the Media). He was frequently invited to the Elysée by President Mitterand of France and to Bonn by German Foreign Ministers: these were for serious political discussions as well as to promote his continental media interests or for social celebration. Maxwell himself hosted grand banquets for his friends and acquaintances at Headington Hall, Oxford. A vast parade of the British establishment attended them – I was invited to only one, but I usually saw copies of the glittering lists.

Finally, Israel gave him a full state funeral on the Mount of Olives in recognition of his great political and charitable support for that fledgling democracy. That presumably was not something they would have risked if their famed intelligence service MOSSAD had the least idea that Maxwell had been involved in a web of financial crimes. The roll-call of honour attending that funeral service, covered by the world's television, with the British state formally represented and the Archbishop of Canterbury there to mourn the death of Jewish Robert Maxwell, needs to be recalled in order to appreciate how the present view of Maxwell was not universally shared at the time. Several dozen journalists from the *Daily Mirror* asked to be allowed to travel to Israel personally to mourn their late beloved boss – though they withdrew their applications when told that they would have to pay their own travel expenses.

I cite this selection of his distinguished supporters and mourners only to emphasise that the subsequent suggestions that Maxwell was transparently and self-evidently *only* a crook (though he was definitely that as well) does not stand up to serious scrutiny. It also totally underestimates the complexity of the man. Many very experienced public figures were attached to this larger-than-life figure. I recall that when Maxwell was interviewing City candidates to float the Mirror Group in the winter of 1990–1, I was approached by Charles (later Lord) Hambro, a senior member of the founding family of one of the City's blue-blood, blue-chip merchant banks and a senior officer in the Tory party. He told me that he had been a friend and financier of Maxwell for some thirty years. He stated emphatically: 'Let me tell you that you can trust Bob. He always stands by his word.' I was naturally impressed by this experienced establishment view. In his time, Maxwell impressed men of consequence, on all sides, in Britain and abroad.

I had met Maxwell only a few times, and briefly, before joining LBI in 1988. So I was puzzled, though I suppose not entirely surprised, to read later in newspapers that he was 'a close friend' of mine (not a view either of us shared), that he had been a 'regular visitor' to me in 10 Downing Street (I had never even met him then), and, even more incredibly, that we were at Oxford University together. Actually, while at LBI I had many more dealings with Kevin Maxwell than with his father, since the son was the active link between the family controlling share-holding and LBI. Kevin, educated at Balliol, is highly intelligent, works incredibly hard, and seemed to me to be very highly strung, like a violin string. He also then appeared overawed by – or even frightened of – his domineering father.

Kevin's grasp of modern financial markets and the diverse techniques associated with them was far better than mine or his father's. Indeed, during the final years, he, rather than his father, seemed to be running much of the financial side of the business empire. I never felt at all close to Kevin, partly because he was in turn so close to my fellow directors Trachtenberg and Smith. I felt much more at ease with his brother Ian, who had more obviously human qualities and frailties, though he did not appear to be closely involved in the details of the business, preferring to enjoy himself socially. I find it difficult to believe that Ian initiated any financial malpractices.

Robert Maxwell was a huge bull of a man, with fierce dark eyes and a rich shock of black hair on a strong head. He had been very tall and handsome when younger, but by my time was grotesquely overweight, no doubt related to his gross eating habits. His health had deteriorated and he suffered serious insomnia at night and in consequence sometimes fell asleep in afternoon meetings. He could be charming and ebullient, especially when speaking with world leaders or when wanting something, but his urge to bully was ever close to the surface. His driving energy enabled him to engage in more activity than many another dozen people. He had a consuming appetite for action, whether acquiring businesses, launching newspapers, telephoning executives to demand initiatives, or endlessly travelling the globe. It was as if action, of whatever kind, and motion, to wherever, were to him in themselves good and, anyway, always better than inaction or reflection. His mind had never been conventionally educated, but was powerful and probing. His grasp of many European languages gave him access to developments and ideas across continents. He had a voracious interest in what was happening in many worlds, in politics, in publishing and the media, in business and in science. Politically, he had a commitment to the future development of a prosperous and peaceful European Union. He also never lost his fascination with the affairs of the British Labour Party. With me, he would suddenly switch from berating me for my betrayal of him over First Tokyo to asking my views on Neil Kinnock as party leader or on Labour's dubious economic policies. He could also be very emotional, moving swiftly from towering rages to sentimentality. At times he could demonstrate cruel meanness, but at others show great generosity as he aided charities which touched his loyalties or his self-interest.

Stories abounded of his cheek and his alleged bravery (he did win a Military Cross). In Central Africa he went on a safari and a rhinoceros is said to have approached him. The teller of the story ran behind a tree and watched terrified as the huge and fierce animal stared at the huge man and he stared back. The rhino slowly turned away and retreated. He told me of one wartime occasion in France when some of his platoon were trapped under heavy fire with some wounded. His 'posh' commanding officer said that whoever volunteered to go forward would get his recommendation for the Victoria Cross if he succeeded in rescuing their wounded comrades. Maxwell claimed to have done it and rescued them, but never heard any more about the medal, thus apparently confirming his view that even with the British establishment their word was not their bond. There were many such stories, some no doubt invented, some embellished, but the point was that with Maxwell they were plausible.

His negative characteristics were immediately obvious. His ego was offensively boundless, and he enjoyed bullying and inconveniencing people (unless he wished to flatter them). On one occasion he summoned me back from the airport where I was leaving for a family holiday, but when I reached him he could not remember what it was about. The greater the inconvenience inflicted, the more his ego enjoyed a sense of power over others. His vulgarity could be very impressive, using foul language or gobbling huge amounts of food and spilling it over his gaudy suits and ties. One afternoon I sat at a table of smart City advisers while he shovelled down his throat spoonfuls from a large tin of caviar.

I saw him stand by his helicopter on the roof of Maxwell House and urinate in the full view of the vehicle's occupants, some female, splashing himself in the draught from the rotators. One time, he unusually invited me over when he entertained a group of humourless German bankers. Shortly after the beginning of the meeting, which Maxwell conducted in fluent German, he slowly removed his shoes and socks and planted his bare and sweaty feet, toes pointing upwards, on a low table between them. It was a hot day and his feet smelled and steamed visibly. Afterwards, as I was leaving the room following the Germans, he beckoned me back in and said: 'I hope you appreciated my feet. That was for those German bastards. They burned my family.' I had no apparent role at this meeting other than to witness the ceremony of his insult.

My only visit abroad with Maxwell revealed to me several aspects of his character and perhaps conveys some impression of life working with him.

In 1990, he took me with his entourage to Bulgaria to visit President Zhivkov, that poor country's tyrant Communist ruler, when he was promoting some media or financial business in Eastern Europe. I missed joining Maxwell's private plane in Paris, sitting separately reading a novel in the lounge and failing to see his party suddenly dash after their leader to his jet, so I switched to a Bulgarian state airline flight in the evening.

I was the only passenger in the separate first-class compartment at the front of the plane, where, possibly following socialist democratic principles, the seats were identically and uncomfortably the same as in the tourist section, with canvas coverings on metal frames. The food was disgusting and the wine undrinkable. Pushing away my glass and my plate of uneatable food, I said with a touch of brave sarcasm to the strapping comrade stewardess, that I had heard that Bulgaria did have much better wines than this. Her broad face remained blank as she disappeared into the pilot's area. She emerged carrying a bottle and two fresh glasses. She sat with me and poured out the red wine. It was rich and what the experts might call 'full of character'. We quickly finished the bottle, with her seriously outdrinking me.

She explained to me how Communism suited the Bulgarians because it disciplined their basically bad characters; and that the privatisations then being discussed would not be popular with the managements because they could now cheat more from the nationalised industries than they would ever make in profit if privatised. She explained that on the airline the staff kept the best wines in the pilots' cabin for themselves. She went back into the cabin and returned with a half bottle of raw local brandy which we – mainly she – quickly consumed, finishing it as we began to descend into Sofia. She offered her home telephone number to me on a piece of paper and said that if I wanted to stay the night at her flat I only needed to ring ahead – and that if she was away flying somewhere then her flatmate would certainly be happy to entertain me. Then she staggered to her large feet and slurred over the loudspeakers in Bulgarian, German and English that we should fasten our seatbelts ...

As we came to a stop on the runway, the pilot announced that everybody must stay in their seats, except 'Lord Donohump' who was 'please to leave the plane immediately'. I rose unsteadily towards the nearby exit, where two bulky policemen with wide padded shoulders and high peaked caps escorted me off. I wondered of what offence against the People's Republic of Bulgaria I might be accused – corrupting a large stewardess, etc? I was hurried into one of those long Russian official cars and we dashed very fast across sad Sofia, and I soon realised that all the traffic lights were green in my direction, with motorcycle policemen holding the traffic at every junction to let me through. I was being given the Maxwell treatment in Eastern Europe of which I had previously heard.

We drove into a kind of walled compound, with armed guards lurking everywhere around the grounds. I was ushered to the villa occupied by Maxwell and found him, for no apparent reason, standing on his bed dressed only in his voluminous underpants, with his huge stomach hanging in folds over the elastic band. 'You missed the plane!' he roared as his opening greeting. And then added triumphantly with a great belly laugh, 'Maxwell waits for no man. Not even for a Lord.' After subsiding, he said: 'I hope they brought you through fast. I arranged that.' Then, still standing half-naked on his groaning bed, he gave me an informed and fascinating briefing on the history and politics of modern Bulgaria, pointing out that 'they are closest to the fucking Russians because the only alternative is the fucking Turks on the other side, who are even worse.' Of the President, whom he first described as 'my old friend', he finally observed: 'Zhivkov is a complete shit. But he is the shit we have to deal with here.'

Our London team – in which Maxwell's blonde personal secretary appeared then as so often to occupy an especially favoured and influential place – had lunch next day at the President's residence, which was totally characterless in that particular Communist East European way. For most of the meal Maxwell conversed with the President in one of his many Central European languages.

Afterwards we flew to a dowdy Black Sea resort where we attended a dull and empty casino, apparently reserved for the gambling pleasures of party apparatchiks. Maxwell, who carried no money with him (presumably like our royals), borrowed £50 off me to lose at the tables. It was never paid back. Next day we went to a departure airfield, but were kept on the runway awaiting permission to take off. The increasingly impatient Maxwell shouted from his seat to his pilot: 'Tell them it is Maxwell here and I must leave immediately!'

There was no response from the control tower to this imperious call. So Maxwell strode angrily to the front cabin, took over the intercom from his pilot, and I heard him shout: 'This is Robert Maxwell. I have been to visit your President. I now have important business with the President of Poland. I am late and we must take off now!' Turning to his pilot he rasped: 'Go! Now!' And off we flew, without clearance, to Warsaw, where he did indeed visit the military President. I saw on this trip how Maxwell had remarkable access to the leaders of the old Communist empire in Eastern Europe. Whether this access added up to anything substantial in terms of real political influence – or whether he was actually a double agent spy in the Cold War – I have no idea. Certainly Mrs Thatcher valued his knowledge of, and access to, that then crucial part of the world. And when Boris Yeltsin was besieged in the attempted Moscow coup against President Gorbachev, his private secretary chose Maxwell as his contact to convey Yeltsin's message for the West. So to dismiss Maxwell as just 'a fraudster' – though he was that as well – is to miss the scale of the man for good and ill. Certainly, as his Jewish parents might have said, he had 'chutzpah'.

In retrospect I realise that Maxwell's ultimate and decisively negative characteristic was his blatant lack of attachment to the truth. He seemed to me to view truth or non-truth as equal tactical options. He did not operate on the basis that truth was in itself morally superior to, and preferable to, a lie. In fact, I felt that at his centre was a complete moral vacuum. Perhaps the key to Robert Maxwell – and probably to that inner moral vacuum which I sensed – was undoubtedly his young life as an impoverished Jew in central Europe, where his family and most of that society were massacred and pillaged in turn by the Nazi and the Soviet Communist beasts. He survived that barbarianism only through his own physical energy, determination and ingenuity, forcing and deceiving his way to France and to England and then transforming himself into a decorated English army officer with a Scottish name. The result was a complex mixture: partly a remarkably impressive man, partly a chameleon, partly scoundrel, partly a monster, though occasionally touchingly human, partly an actor always seeking the spotlight of the big stage.

None of this excuses him and his crimes, but I believe it may explain him. To Maxwell himself, the main lessons he learned from his earlier terrible experiences were clear: to rely on himself alone; that others, apart from his closest family, were all potential enemies, at best seen as pawns in the great chess game of life-survival, all seeking their own self-interest as he had learned to seek only his. To the end, part of him remained the central European Wandering Jew, always the outsider, living off his hopefully superior wits and viewing the society around him as potentially enemy country. As an outsider, he seemed to view the rules and conventions of British business, social and personal life as having been constructed by the British financial, social and political establishments (as he often claimed) for their own self-interest – and against his. He saw regulations as irritating obstacles which had to be negotiated according to the practical interest of current circumstances: to be obeyed if that was advantageous to him, but ignored if he could get away with it. He enjoyed playing with the City establishment, especially the way that some (definitely not all) of them fawned over him when seeking to share his money or his social parties. But privately, he never deceived himself that he was part of them. He would not have been in the least surprised when after his death and the exposure of his misdeeds so many of them suffered a collective amnesia about their previous associations with him.

The revelation after his death of his financial malpractices showed Robert Maxwell to have been a fraudster on a grand scale. I believe that nothing can forgive that. Even so, it would be misleading, taking a broader perspective, to see him as *only* as a fraudster. In fact, he was a very big and complex man in all respects: big in his ambitions and achievements and lies and crimes; big in his physique, intellect, temper, vulgarity and selfish greed; big in his generosity and in his mendacity; big in his vision, in his ego and finally in his fraudulent deceptions.

I did not greatly enjoy knowing him in the small part of his and my life that we were in bruising contact. But he at least left me with another remarkable portrait in my memory.

Eighteen

QUIETER TIMES AGAIN

It was a great pleasure for me to escape with Sarah from the Maxwell jungle to Ceret, where I was able to recuperate in its beautiful calm. By now, under Sarah's skillful direction, we had good bathrooms and a pool, the latter carefully positioned to allow us to look at the peaks of the Pyrenees as we swam. Each day I walked to the village to buy fresh bread and newspapers, gazing eastwards to the Mediterranean as I strolled down to Ceret in the plain below. I read all of Evelyn Waugh and Graham Greene (uncle of my close friend, the publisher of the same name) under the precious mulberry tree which shades the terrace.

Tipped off by Robin Butler, I began a literary love affair with Patrick O'Brien's wonderful sea novels woven around the characters of bluff Jack Aubrey and subtle Stephen Maturin. We discovered that Patrick lived locally in nearby Collioure, and met him there by the sea, at home in Ceret, and in London. I found him fascinating, obsessively secretive and apparently rewriting his own personal past in fictional mystery. He hinted to me at his Irish background, at wartime attachments to our Secret Service, and youthful sailing in distant oceans, but he rejected all further probes, remarking sharply that 'private lives are private'. Subsequently, newspapers alleged that much of this claimed background was invented, that he had no Irish origins and his name was actually not Patrick O'Brien. This merely increased his fascination to me and in my view took nothing away from his great talent nor from the pleasure that his books gave to millions of readers. He understandably fell for Sarah, flattering her with genteel courtesy. At our final meeting he came to Coll de Bousseils for supper with friends. He was in great form, sitting beaming on the terrace and sipping lots of local white wine, when a vicious Catalan wasp stung his bottom lip. It became grossly swollen, but he refused to bother with the pain and throughout dinner continued chatting vivaciously in his antique verbal style. He told me that he was looking forward to a winter's residence at Trinity College, Dublin, hoping to break a writing block then afflicting him, and no doubt also to reinforce his questionable Irish background. It was in Dublin that he suddenly died. Selfishly, it was a particularly sad blow to me, since I had always lacked cultured friends in the Ceret area. Now I had finally found one, he quickly left us.

I enjoyed Ceret most when our closest family and friends came to stay and share its beauty – our six children, or Sarah's brother and wonderful father with his young new wife, or such friends as Graham Greene, Nori and Phillip Graham, Celia and Tom Reed or Michael and Deborah Bedford. While there I took to walking high in the Pyrennees, especially up 5,000 or 6,000 feet around Llo and pretty Valcebollere above that magical high plateau with its crystal air and stupendous views. I also walked in Cornwall, in Madeira with Margaret Jay, husband Mike and the Reeds (once alone and terrifyingly lost for ten miles splashing along the narrow water channels with precipitous cliffs on one side), and most often in the Swiss Alps on our annual winter holidays to pretty Gstaad. Sarah had been to school there and still has many friends from that time. I usually walked or cross-country-skied between eight and twelve miles a day to the neighbouring villages, which created a great appetite for our evening dinner parties at various friends' chalets. (Most stunning of all was the annual Vivien Duffield bash, attended by much of Gstaad and the international jet set.)

One travelling high point for me was my cricket tour of South Africa in 1995, playing with the Houses of Parliament XI. I was fascinated to see the new black African state and especially to meet its charismatic leader, Nelson Mandela, who struck me as saintly and fragile. I was by now sixty-one and too creaky for my schooldays pace bowling so, encouraged by our talented captain, Graham Allen, (later an undervalued whip in Tony Blair's first administration), I belatedly took up leg-break bowling, and claimed a few wickets for quite a lot of runs. More puzzling was my bottom-order batting, where I survived the tour unbeaten. On returning to England I was proud to play on 5 June 1996 for the Lords against the Commons at the historic Surrey Oval test ground. It was awe-inspiring for me to field on that hallowed boundary and gaze at those gasometers made famous by John Arlott's amusing commentaries. I was promoted to bat at number ten, and with an hour to go we were nine wickets down and our only hope was to fight to survive for a draw. I was joined at the wicket by my portly Indian colleague from the LSE, Lord Desai, his grey locks flowing to shoulder length. We defended our stumps like castles under siege, and batted out the final hour, with me scoring nine not out, certainly my highest total since 1953. Having reached that career peak at the Oval I decided to retire from cricket at nearly sixty-two, just as I had from soccer aged fifty after playing at Tottenham's White Hart Lane in 1984. Harold Wilson often said to me that it is best to go out at the top – as he almost did.

My life style through the early and mid 1990s was comfortable and busy without being too exhausting. For the first time I did not have a regular paid job and I certainly did not miss the office treadmill. I kept close to my four children, watching them pass through unsatisfactory educations, and finally all of them secured jobs suited to their distinctly different temperaments. Their good relations with Sarah pleased me. My daughters Rachel and Kate married impecunious but supportive young men and by the end of the decade brought me the delightful pleasure of grandchildren.

But death also culled its unbearable toll from my too small family and friends, including dear Gerry Fowler and my younger brother Clem (and more recently my loyal friends Henry Carnarvon and Peter Parker).

Clem was always bonded close to me by our searing childhood together. A gentle person of good taste, treated harshly by life and blighted by deafness, he died of vicious cancer in his early fifties. I was with him in his Suffolk cottage shortly before he died. Suddenly waking from a long sleep, he pointed an emaciated finger towards the corner of the room and whispered to me: 'He is there.' Who did he see, I wonder? Some morphine-induced fantasy? Perhaps, though I instinctively felt it was our Dad. When I heard from Agnes the news of his final passing, I suffered a terrible internal pain, as if something integral to me had been physically wrenched away.

My long-lost sisters, Molly and Sheila, came to the funeral, so at least Clem's death brought my fractured sibling family together for the first time in nearly fifty years. Agnes arranged a moving Catholic service in Northampton and burial beside Dad in Roade cemetery.

Clem's death nudged me into the final stage of my long emerging resolve fully to join the Roman Catholic Church. On the advice of my friend Polly Feversham I consulted a leading liberal priest, who assured me that my many sins and dissents from Vatican orthodoxy were not a final obstacle to entry. He described membership of the Church as a personal and private matter between oneself and one's maker – which impressed me as an almost sixteenth-century Protestant approach. For some years past I had attended the local Catholic churches in nearby Twyford and Wargrave, just sitting at the back and thinking about it. We have a wonderful Irish priest, Father Vincent Flanagan, full of affection and humour and tolerance, reflecting none of the less attractive rigid side of the Church. His brief sermons are very amusing, with no sanctimonious lecturing, usually devoted to encouraging us to enjoy our lives and to love our families, friends and neighbours. When the Old Testament reading is dark, about needing to punish ourselves or cut off our offending arms and legs, he comments: 'I don't know what that did for you, but it sure didn't do much for me.'

In one sermon he supported marriage for priests (adding: 'And if I am not here next week, you will know why') and made it clear that he welcomed all sinners in his church, including the divorced. 'Some parishes raise obstacles to faith,' he added: 'We don't have any obstacles here.' He told amusing stories from his times in Africa, California and the west of Ireland. (A ninety-year-old parishioner in Mayo told him that she expected Heaven for her would be 'just like Mayo, but without all the sex'.) Loving horse racing, he announced a dispensation from Lenten self-sacrifice for the Cheltenham Festival in March. After one long absence at what was clearly an uproarious Irish wedding, he returned to report seeing 'one wise sign over a pub door. It said: "Life is too short to bother with cheap wine" – and that is my thought for you in the week ahead.'

His two churches, only a mile apart, are often packed, with children chattering happily and crawling in the aisles. He gives religion a very human face and was a major factor in my taking the final step into the Church in May 1996. Sarah came to the ceremony and it was a most moving and important moment for me. I felt that somehow I had come back home, and that all kinds of loose ends from Father Galvin in my childhood onwards were then tied up. My father was born and buried a Catholic. My brother was buried one and I shall be the same. I did not have a second Christian name so Father Flanagan gave me Patrick after his favourite saint.

My life at this time followed a regular and satisfying pattern. During the week if Parliament was sitting I stayed in London at my cosy and quiet mews house in Belgravia, walking distance from the Lords. I spent long weekends and recesses in the country with Sarah (we set up home together in 1990) at her pretty house overlooking the flat fields of east Berkshire, which I see as my main home. There I read, wrote, listened to music, played tennis with her and primitive golf with her delightful son George.

Sarah, whose husband, Anthony Berry MP, was callously murdered by the IRA at the Brighton Grand Hotel in 1984, is quite different from me: slim, elegant, lively, positive, chirpy, meticulous in her concern for detail, forgiving, full of fun, socially very aware, not intellectual but sharply bright, having been totally uneducated in some important areas by the best private schooling which money could buy in the 1940s and 1950s. She is vaguely Tory while I am independently (but rootedly) Labour. Our differences seem to make a fine loving match and, given my faults, I am very lucky to have her. I also adored her father, the leading solicitor Raymond Clifford-Turner, as I do her charming brother Charles and her sister Susan, who all readily embraced me into their close family. Raymond was very special, a warm and wise friend who even in his late eighties was still interested in every facet of life.

With Sarah, my private life became pre-eminent and, interestingly, I lost most of my public ambition – which I recommend as one formula for personal happiness. Many of those I have observed driven by ambition in politics and public life seemed to have unsatisfactory private lives – though I am not sure which is cause and which effect.

I now had more time to go racing and grew to know the fascinating horse world. My greatest racing love is National Hunt racing and the Cheltenham Festival meeting is my peak enjoyment of each year. Towcester racecourse, close to where I lived as a boy in Northamptonshire, invited me to be a director, which I enjoyed immensely. I had attended my very first race meeting there soon after the war, climbing in at the Shutlanger end. In my view, Towcester is the most attractive racecourse in England, traditional meetings with genuine country people and none of the flash vulgarity which blemishes some of our leading Flat racecourses. I love going racing there, with views over several local village churches, lunching in the tiny wooden stewards' room with Kisty Hesketh and Mike and Angie Buswell, and wandering around the paddock hearing the familiar Northamptonshire accents from my childhood. I was required to resign from the Towcester board when I became a minister at the Department of Agriculture, and I am still not convinced that it was worth the great sacrifice.

My working life was now focussed on the House of Lords. I had been elevated in 1985 as a 'working' peer and felt an obligation to contribute to business there, so from 1991 I attended most weekday afternoons and many evenings – sometimes held there under heavy whips until 2 or 3 a.m. and occasionally all night. The modern House of Lords works harder and longer hours as a legislative chamber than the Commons. I enjoy my life there enormously and count myself lucky to have been given the privilege of membership. The beautiful Pugin-designed Lords Chamber has a remarkable atmosphere and I felt full of awe for many years after I first sat on the benches there. I especially enjoyed looking around and seeing the famous old political warriors there – ex-Prime Ministers Macmillan, Home, Wilson, Callaghan and Thatcher; the Old Testament figure of Lord Longford, a survivor from Attlee's 1945 government; and a whole tribe of distinguished former cabinet ministers from all sides, together with commercial and trade union barons. At times it seemed like a living museum of the relics of past British political history, which I as an occasional historian greatly appreciated.

The Lords also contained many old personal friends from my earlier days in Downing Street – not all Labour, since I have never assessed friendship according to political persuasion. This is much easier in the tolerant atmosphere of the Upper House than in the Commons, where members even eat at partisan tables. But some of the more antique customs of the Lords, while never bothering me because not seeming important, did irritate the new professional generation of Labour peers and provoked a thrust towards modernisation after Labour took office in 1997, led by the determined Margaret Jay. The ancient but by now democratically indefensible right of all hereditary peers to sit in the nation's legislature was removed. I supported this change in principle but regretted the departure of several good hereditary friends.

Harold Wilson joined the Lords in 1983, though he participated rarely in proceedings in the chamber. He only occasionally acknowledged me, possibly afraid that Marcia would learn of it and punish him, but more probably because of his deepening dementia, which was tragic to observe for those who had known him in his prime. On one occasion, he came up to me in the lovely Lords library overlooking the Thames and said: 'Bernard, I have to give a speech on unemployment. I would be grateful if you would look up the figures for the past ten years and analyse them for me. Send me one of your green papers.' (At his suggestion in 1974 in Number 10, I used green paper for Policy Unit briefs so that he could find them quickly in his Prime Minister's red box.) I was touched to be working with him again, however marginally. I quickly completed the simple work on the unemployment figures and a few days later I gave him the typed paper he had requested. He thanked me courteously, but looked vague and puzzled. As I walked away, I heard him say to a nearby peer: 'Who is that? Didn't he work for Mrs Thatcher?' I did not see him again before his death in 1995.

Jim Callaghan also came to the Lords and we regularly chatted and sometimes had tea together. He always drew a full Lords audience and made an impact on his carefully selected interventions in the Chamber. It was good to see him sitting proudly on the Privy Councillors' front bench when his daughter Margaret took over our leadership there a year into the Blair government. The opposition and some of the press suggested this was 'nepotism'. In fact, her great ability and tough character would have taken her to the top of most professions regardless of who was her father – though Jim's genes did clearly give her a particular stamp of political skill, authority, and possibly more than just a touch of steely impatience.

I was keen to contribute more personally in the Lords and was soon appointed in November 1991 to Labour's front bench as official Opposition Spokesman on Treasury Affairs. Then I quickly switched to the Energy portfolio where I did a crash course of homework in that specialist and highly technical area. When the Tories closed most of the coal industry, inflicting savage revenge on Arthur Scargill's foolishly militant leadership of the mineworkers' union, I won a big vote of censure on the government in the Lords. I did not believe that coalmining should necessarily be preserved as an occupation but I did not want the miners turned onto the streets, since in my view they represented the best values and community spirit of the old working classes.

But my most active interests now lay much more in the cultural areas of arts, media and sports, and I switched in 1992 to be spokesman for those areas, which now came under the aegis of the recently formed Heritage Department. I was also a founding member of the London Arts Board, which confronted me with the fast-spreading virus of political correctness currently infecting our society – our worst recent import from across the Atlantic. The arts world is particularly prone to this blight. One example which irritated me was when LAB and the overstaffed Arts Council produced a thick document on multi-cultural and ethnic arts which was riddled with politically correct language and propaganda. Always liking to have at least some statistical basis for generalisations, I fought to include the basic figures on the proportion of the British population which came from ethnic minorities – then still well down into single figures, though much higher in London. But the racial thought police at the Arts Council obstinately refused to print those low numbers. Obstructed on that approach, I then attempted to make the ethnic figures more meaningful by arguing that they should include the percentage of our population which was Irish (at that time as many as all the other ethnics put together), since the Irish make a great contribution to London's cultural life and really should have some grant support. This was resisted equally fiercely by the Arts Council bureaucracy. I was privately informed that these politically correct Stalinists believed that the Irish did not qualify as part of the 'multi-culture' since they were 'white Europeans'. It was reverse racism. It is clear that what I call 'PCC' – Politically Correct Claptrap – has replaced Marxism as the ideological language and substitute-for-thought among the fashionable left and is being imposed on our society, and especially our education system, by a similar process of propaganda, indoctrination and intimidation.

Although I have always supported equality of race and gender, I believe that the distortions of political correctness will have malign social effects. Certainly, like Marxism, it provides a ready excuse and mechanism for busybodies to impose their prejudices and agenda on society and to interfere in other people's lives. I dislike zealotry of all kinds – Fascist, Communist, religious, football hooligan, politically correct claptrap, etc. Some are extreme dogmatist and have led to the deaths of tens of millions of innocent people in my lifetime. Some zealotry is just fashionable claptrap which causes irritation to our lives – politically correct claptrap falls into that category, though the accumulation of its effects can diminish our society.

The Heritage appointment gave me the opportunity to work closely with three future cabinet ministers who successively led the Heritage team in Opposition at that time. (In my time at Energy I had never met my fellow Commons spokesman, Robin Cook, who was perhaps not a great team man.) First was Marjorie 'Mo' Mowlam, a good team leader, warm, open and friendly, though not too sharp on the detail, sometimes a little chaotic, and even verbally crude by some tastes. When Mo moved on to shock the puritanical Protestants in Northern Ireland, she was replaced by Chris Smith, a much more private and elegant personality with a deep appreciation of the arts, who slowly became a good friend. Chris was in turn soon replaced by Jack Cunningham, an authentic north-easterner who was in many ways the best political boss with whom I worked. His sound political judgement and his long experience showed favourably compared with some of the young boys and girls in New Labour. With Jack, Lewis Mooney, Mark Fisher and my old footballing team-mate Tom Pendry, we were a very happy group, and I found the work satisfying as we led up to the election.

A peak parliamentary moment for me was when I led from Labour's front bench on the Tories' 1995 Broadcasting Bill. I fought particularly hard against the government's willingness to allow Murdoch's satellite television to take a monopoly of all major sports broadcasting, leaving the BBC and ITV – then watched by over 80 per cent of ordinary sports fans – with the crumbs of minor sports. Together with my old friend Denis Howell I proposed an amendment to protect the list of eight major sporting 'jewels' for free terrestrial broadcasting. Otherwise most Britons would have been excluded from watching the Cup Final, the Derby, rugby internationals, etc. – or be forced to pay Murdoch's high subscription fees. On 6 February 1996 we passed our amendment protecting the 'jewels' for free broadcasting by a massive majority of 117 – apparently the biggest defeat inflicted on a Tory Government in nearly a century. I was jubilant, tasting some sweet revenge for Murdoch's nasty treatment of me in 1982 when he sacked me from *The Times* with Harry Evans and meanly tried to evade paying my contractual redundancy compensation.

The election of Tony Blair to the Labour leadership in 1994 had initiated a great revolution in the party. Neil Kinnock, Labour leader after the disastrous defeat of 1983, had, together with Tom Sawyer, a good Party Secretary, done a tremendous job in diminishing the influence of the party's left wing whose lunatic activities had rendered Labour unelectable in the 1980s, and by the 1992 election he had virtually closed the huge electoral lead opened up by Margaret Thatcher in 1983 and 1987. But Neil had lost two successive general elections and somehow never quite looked to be a Prime Minister to the British people at large.

Politics is an unforgiving trade, giving no prizes to brave losers, so John Smith, an old friend of mine from the Callaghan government, took over the leadership. Although conservative in temperament and unlikely to give the Labour Party the necessary shaking to propel it fully into modernity, John was a straight Edinburgh lawyer, bringing authority and honest dignity to the party and looking every inch a future Prime Minister, and within a couple of years he had taken Labour into a comfortable lead in the polls. He and his successor were helped by a long string of 'sleaze' allegations blighting Tory ministers, many of which were ludicrous exaggerations of minor personal peccadilloes of no relevance whatsoever to the conduct of national government. 'Sleaze' is often just a convenient excuse for cheap headlines to sell shoddy newspapers, and a convenient stick with which to beat political opponents. If it had been applied so harshly to Britain's historic past, few famous statesmen and military heroes – from Marlborough and Nelson through Disraeli, Palmerston and Gladstone, to Lloyd George, Churchill, Gaitskell, Macmillan and, in the USA, John F. Kennedy – would have survived to achieve their different claims to greatness. The hounding style and Witches of Salem techniques of our modern media do not produce healthy societies, nor even more moral ones. I was sorry that Labour joined in the hounding so enthusiastically.

Sadly John Smith – the fifth Labour leader for or with whom I had until then worked – suddenly died of a heart attack in May 1994. I spoke with him the night before his death as he left a party dinner at a Piccadilly hotel: he seemed full of humour and life and clearly still had much to give. When the next morning at the House of Lords I learnt of his death, I quietly wept in the chamber. With John's departure went the last dominance of the 'old' Labour with which I had worked from the 1960s until 1994. A new generation now swept into power in the party, unattached to the traditional links with the trade unions or to the unquestioning values of welfare and public ownership embedded in Clause 4 of our 1918 constitution. Tony Blair, Gordon Brown and Peter Mandelson now abandoned the historic party luggage of 'old Labour' and created a 'New Labour' Party which was more electable.

Some of that creative process involved just the magic of better presentation, on which they placed great emphasis, packaging their political product using all the skills and techniques of modern advertising. But the overall result of their work also contained benefits of substance.

New Labour was particularly attractive to me because, since the days of the Campaign for Democratic Socialism in the 1960s, I had held the same desire to modernise the Labour Party. To me, the party had long been too conservative, with an outdated constitution. Its antique Marxist ideology and language was supported by only a minority of activists, but until the 1990s they had disproportionate influence, especially over the party machine. Labour was too attached to its working-class roots when the working class was actually shrinking under social change, and to its trade union roots when the unions were a declining force and very unpopular with the electorate. The party remained fixed for too long in its old style, aims and philosophies. Its prime commitments remained to welfare;

to a mixed economy and 'producer socialism'; to large and inefficient nationalised industries and public services; and to government intervention in all possible directions. These outdated aspects had shackled and constrained progress for over forty years and were one reason why Labour had lost eight of the last thirteen general elections since 1951. In three of its five victories it had barely scraped a lead with sufficient majority to control Parliament in support of its programme. By the 1980s it was clear that Labour either had to modernise or it would die – as it nearly did under left wing control in 1980–7. By 1992 Neil Kinnock had recovered much ground, especially modernising the party machine, but in terms of changing Labour's policies and philosophies little was secured under either Neil or his successor John Smith. The party remained basically 'old' Labour with a more efficient machine and a more acceptable presentational face.

It was only under Tony Blair after 1994 that the necessary radical modernisation dramatically occurred. Marxist ideology and language was now rejected explicitly. Clause 4 of the constitution was rewritten, abandoning the sacred commitment to mass public ownership, and Blair's version was supported 3:1 on a ballot of party members – the new one-man-one-vote procedure, which the left had always opposed knowing the majority was against them, was beginning to produce results. Emphasis moved from ideology to 'values', such as 'community' and 'fairness', while 'responsibilities' were promoted as well as 'rights'. 'Market values' were accepted for the commercial and social economies and 'work values' were elevated above welfare. Great emphasis was placed on style and presentation, with words such as 'open', 'inclusive', 'modernisation', and 'middle ground' thick on the airwaves. In terms of policies, old Labour's 'tax and spend' was rejected and the emphasis put on 'financial prudence', on creating work opportunities rather than welfare dependencies, on higher standards in education and the National Health Service, and on toughness in dealing with crime. An alternative and very efficient electoral machine was established in Millbank under the skilful direction of Peter Mandelson, who answered directly to the leader and not to the party bureaucracy. This was a world away from the organisational incompetence I had experienced in the 1974 and 1979 elections.

Some of this Blairite modernisation was very superficial, containing too much flan and political meringue. But it was a shrewd mélange of populist Thatcherite and SDP policies and attitudes, with touches of President Clinton for colour. The apparent priority of presentation over substance was what most irritated old Labour stalwarts, including sometimes myself. But overall, I was enthusiastically behind New Labour in 1994–7. I supported it because it demolished the old left and because it cleverly appealed to a wider electorate. Blair had quickly achieved the revisionist agenda which we Gaitskellites and Jenkinsites had long sought, emphatically defeating the left from within the party and then creating what was basically a new social democratic party. He established and occupied a 'big tent' in the political middle ground from which he could attract soft votes from both the Tories and Liberal Democrats. It remains to be seen how well the tent stands up to the strong winds of inevitable future unpopularity or economic recession, but from that position he was able in the short term to prepare the way for electoral victory in 1997.

I contributed personally in a very small way to Blair's preparations for government. In the autumn of 1996, with the election due by May 1997, Jonathan Powell, the future Chief of Staff at Number 10, asked me to submit to Tony Blair my thoughts about taking power. On 19 November I sent a nine-page document entitled 'Occupying and Operating Number 10', which contained all the relevant lessons I believed I had learned during five years in Downing Street, updated for the new circumstances of the late 1990s. In my covering letter to Tony Blair I stated that my 'overall purpose is to provide a more powerful Downing Street operation able to serve a more powerful Prime Minister which is appropriate to political and media pressures now far greater than when we were last in power. We will have to control the centre and master events. My aim is to get the benefits of a Prime Minister's Department without suffering the bureaucratic and hierarchical disadvantages of formally establishing one.'

The document itself stated that the Prime Minister's central team

> must have speedy access to him; and ... ready access to all papers and committees relating to his policy and political interests. Access, information and mutual trust are the ingredients of team success in Downing Street ... It is important that the team hit the ground running on day one; otherwise crucial decisions may be taken without proper political consideration and prove to be irrevocable ... The Press, Political and Policy Heads should have identified their staff assistants before going in; there is little time for thinking about recruitment once on the battlefield. The Prime Minister will need to authorise these essential steps and formally to secure the access of his senior staff to papers, committees and possibly rooms. It won't happen automatically ...
>
> Direct access to the Prime Minister himself physically, not just on paper, is the most important access; without that senior staff might just as well stay at home. The Prime Minister should make clear to the Private Office civil servants that the Press Secretary, Head of the Policy Unit, Political Head and Chief of Staff have access to him, without appointment, whenever relevant and necessary ... The Press Secretary will need access at all times. If the Prime Minister cannot trust senior staff with most information and access to most meetings, he should not employ them ...

On the Policy Unit, which I had originally set up, I stated that the Prime Minister

> should set up a branch of the Policy Unit in the Cabinet Office to concentrate on longer term issues ... Inevitably the Policy Unit gets almost wholly absorbed in short term issues ... but somebody must monitor the long term priorities. [Blair effectively did that with his new Performance and Innovation Unit] ...
>
> The above suggestions taken together would represent a significant strengthening of the Prime Minister's capability at the centre of government ... without clogging bureaucracy.

The paper then went on to suggest that Blair should focus on

> a small list of key policy priorities ... (perhaps Education and the Health Service) ... and should set up powerful *ad hoc* committees [task forces?] to concentrate on these policy priority areas ... Taken together with the suggestions for strengthening the operations of the personal team at Number 10, these mechanics for monitoring and achieving his policy priorities would enable him better to control his political destiny.

I do not know how far Tony Blair and his team specifically followed my advice, though much of what I suggested did, in fact, happen after Blair became Prime Minister in May 1997. Certainly Tony Blair has impressively strengthened the central capability of British government, effectively creating a Prime Minister's Department without the bother and bureaucracy of naming and formally establishing it as such. Anyway, I was flattered to be again involved in the affairs of Number 10, however marginally.

The May 1997 election proved to be the landslide victory which the polls predicted but none of us dared to expect. There was an unprecedented swing of 10 per cent to New Labour, producing 419 Labour MPs, the highest number ever, and a Commons majority of 179 – twenty-six more even than in 1945 and more than the entire total of Conservative MPs elected. (They lost 177 seats.) Labour finally went back into government and I looked forward relaxedly, hoping to become an arts minister in the Lords to close my political career in territory I would enjoy. However, there were, as always in politics, still some surprises ahead.

Nineteen

INTO GOVERNMENT AGAIN: MINISTER OF FARMING AND FOOD

The 1997 general election returned Labour to power after eighteen often bitter years in the political wilderness. I watched the early televised victories in my Ebury Mews house with Sarah, Graham Greene and our friend Camilla Panufnik. When they retired after midnight, I took a taxi to the Festival Hall and joined friends at the great celebration party there. The atmosphere was euphoric, with waves of mainly young people singing, dancing and cheering each successive victory in hitherto safe Tory seats. The gathering had the air of a revivalist meeting and I had never experienced such political electricity. It certainly contrasted with my experience in the general elections of 1974, when even in victory Harold Wilson met crowds who were quiet, even sullen, and the party workers were more elderly and subdued.

I toured the Festival Hall meeting familiar old Labour faces along with others who had clearly timed their recent conversions to the winning party shrewdly. But my main impression was of a new generation coming to power, and I sensed how quickly the political generations pass. Around 5 a.m. we all poured out onto the South Bank waiting for Tony Blair to arrive from his constituency in the North East. The adrenaline of success eliminated from me all sense of tiredness. As our young leader spoke through the thunderous cheers, the sun began to rise across the Thames beyond St Paul's and we had a tingling sense of a new political dawn. Such naive feelings rarely last long, so I greatly enjoyed them while they did. I then slipped away as it grew light, walking across Westminster Bridge and home. Several cars going to early City offices hooted their horns when they saw my big red rosette – that certainly would not have happened in the 1970s and 1980s.

After breakfast I went to the BBC television studios to watch Blair's triumphally staged entry into Number 10 and to comment on how this election compared with earlier ones in which I had more centrally participated. It was certainly different, almost like a Roman carnival to crown an emperor, and I could imagine neither Wilson nor Callaghan comfortably filling the leading role.

The following weekend I went to sunny Fox's Walk – our Berkshire house – and followed with interest the developing political scenario. The cabinet appointments slowly emerged, with Chris Smith going to the heritage ministry (now renamed 'Culture') and, to my immediate concern, Jack Cunningham switched to Agriculture. Chris phoned me on Sunday to say that he hoped I would be his minister in the House of Lords, but he had not discussed junior ministerial appointments with Blair. By Monday 5 May, I had still heard nothing of any job for myself and most vacancies were filled. I was quite relaxed about that, never having been quite sure that I wanted to sacrifice my comfortable private pleasures for the overrated ministerial treadmill.

On Monday morning – May Bank Holiday – I drove to a meeting of the board of Towcester racecourse and afterwards sped to Kempton Park to watch the racing with Sarah's sister, Susan, and brother-in-law Colin Ingleby-Mackenzie. I was with them in the paddock before the big race when my mobile telephone rang, and the Number 10 operator said briskly: 'The Prime Minister wishes to speak to you.' But then it emerged he was not quite ready yet. I hurried away to the distant car park, not wishing the Prime Minister's voice to be drowned out by the race commentary and the shouts of betting odds – and also fearing his reportedly puritan instincts might be offended by the noisy evidence of my cavalier racing hobby.

There was further delay as the PM was mistakenly put through to my namesake Brian Donohoe from the Commons, and it took him time to retreat from that unintended appointment. Finally, Tony Blair came on the line to say: 'I want you to have a position in my government.' I was delighted and thanked him. Then he added: 'I want you to go to Agriculture. It is a very important area in the Lords, especially with BSE. It needs someone who is experienced at handling the Lords.' My heart sank. I had grown up in and loved the countryside but had never followed with any interest the arcane technicalities of the Common Agricultural Policy. I was also aware that the then Ministry of Agriculture, Fisheries and Food was bottom of the pile in terms of Whitehall reputation and of political seniority. Blair chatted modestly about my knowing more than him about government and then he wished me goodbye and good luck. I drove back down the M3 to Fox's Walk feeling very down. All my years of working in the Lords on arts and broadcasting seemed wasted.

Later, Jack told me that he had especially asked Blair for me to join him at MAFF. I was of course honoured and happy to work with him, personally and politically, but I was not entranced by thoughts of that notorious ministry, from which no minister in recent history had emerged undamaged. However, by the time I was greeted by Sarah, I was more cheerful. I wrote that evening: 'Either turn the job down or be positive about it. No point in taking it but whinging ... Am certainly pleased to be a minister. It seems to complete my career. But I cannot imagine I will be there more than eighteen months. Either up or out.'

In the event it was to be twenty-seven months, and then 'out' at my own choice. But I quickly came to appreciate that I was actually lucky to be in the government at all. The final list of Lords ministers revealed there had been a massacre of the previous front bench veterans, and I was very sorry to see my old friends Frank Judd and Maurice Peston excluded. Apart from our leader Ivor Richard and ex-cabinet minister Stanley Clinton-Davis, both of whom were dropped after the first year, I was the only opposition frontbencher from my over-sixty generation to be given a job – and after surviving the 1998 reshuffle I then became the third oldest minister in the government. Suddenly there had been a generation shift and Tony Blair had put most of my parliamentary contemporaries out to grass. I was fortunate to be reprieved.

On 6 May 1997, at the age of sixty-three, I entered the Ministry of Agriculture, Fisheries and Food for the first time as a minister in Her Majesty's Government. My specific title, chosen by Jack to indicate my main areas of policy responsibility, was Minister for Farming and Food. My clever Private Secretary, Peter Grimley, ushered me through the dreary building in Whitehall Place, once the original site of Scotland Yard. Many political bodies and reputations had been buried there since. My room was small and drab, its walls covered in dirty old yellow paint and its main window looking out onto a dank concrete well between dark high walls. On the desk were trays piled high with documents and a thick file with the formal 'Briefing for New Ministers'. I was introduced to ranks of senior officials from the main policy divisions (meat, grain, milk, trade, the CAP, etc.), some of whom struck me as subdued and almost demoralised by the terrible BSE crisis which had engulfed MAFF in the past decade. I wrote in my notebook that 'I know how Churchill felt exactly 57 years ago when he took over the bunch of generals fleeing towards Dunkirk.' Not that I was a Churchill, nor really in charge.

I plunged straight into an exhausting crash course on the intricacies of the Common Agricultural Policy, where Jack had given me specific responsibility for implementing our commitment to reform. I was not always fascinated with every detail of grain support prices, animal diseases, or of milk quotas, but the broad problems of an important industry in crisis were fascinating.

I quickly realised that today being a junior minister in any Whitehall department feels very insignificant, and certainly much more inconsequential than when I was previously in the government in the 1970s. My ministerial pay was paltry – 131 officials in MAFF earned more than me in 1997 and often I chaired large meetings of officials where I was – and they all knew I was – the lowest paid person in the room. My official car was a grotty four-year-old Vauxhall Vectra with no air conditioning which leaked exhaust fumes into the interior, threatening the life of my wonderful Yorkshire driver, Maggie. One status change I noticed since 1974 was that then the official ministerial 'limo' was usually much classier than most ministers' private cars; but by 1997, this was reversed, and most ministers had to forsake their own smart private car for down-the-range Rovers, Fords and Vauxhalls. My personal Toyota Supra was, by 1997, twelve years old, but was much better than what Maggie called my 'MAFF trashcan'. This shabby vehicle, worth barely £4,000, was actually charged to MAFF by the appalling Government Car Service at around £65,000 a year (including some £20,000 for the driver).

Neither the pay nor the car worried me at all personally, since I needed neither. But they do matter democratically in a general sense because they are part of the growing media-driven lack of respect for all those who work in public life. Respect for public life (not deference, nor even respect for ministers as individuals, which are different and unnecessary features) is essential to achieve democratic consent and preserve respect for the continuity of the democratic state. Without it, democracy weakens and can be replaced, as in Europe in the 1930s, by nastier political forces.

My sense of ministerial inconsequence was heightened in MAFF because so few policy decisions there were actually open to ministerial discretion: 80 per cent of agricultural policy issues with financial implications are decided in Brussels, while on questions of animal health – as with BSE or foot and mouth – prudent ministers are bound to follow the advice of scientific advisers. So there was not great scope for ministerial judgement. Hence, to MAFF, the 1997 Labour landslide made no difference, since its policies, controlled either by permanent officials or in Brussels, remained the same. But I will return to that later.

Despite these constraints, I quickly came to enjoy much of my job at MAFF, enlivened by a constant stream of crises, especially in the area of food safety. I particularly came to enjoy the parliamentary handling of agriculture, and I loved official trips to the regions, where I had specific ministerial responsibility. Visits to the bucolic county agricultural shows in the south west and to the annual Royal Show at Stoneleigh were my peak points. Our Jack Russell terrier Honey also adored coming with me on these trips – especially to game fairs, where she could smell and observe potential prey. On her first such venture she showed her terrier blood by attacking a stuffed fox belonging to the Countryside Alliance.

Overseas visits were another pleasure. I especially enjoyed my first ever trip to St Petersburg with its beautiful low and wide perspectives along its great river. I arrived there at a time of crisis in September 1998 when the Russian currency was collapsing and there were fears of food shortages over the coming winter. I had meetings with the Governor and executives of the province, who requested British food aid. I faxed MAFF for guidance but received no clear response. I had a wonderfully enjoyable visit to the west of Ireland, including Listowel races, with Joe Walsh, the Irish Minister of Agriculture. I also toured Poland, Hungary, Estonia, Slovenia and the Czech Republic discussing their prospective entries to the CAP under European Union enlargement. They were all desperate to join the EU as a statement of their Western democratic non-Communist credentials, and they viewed the CAP as potentially an endless source of financial subsidy (somewhat threatening to the Euro budget since there are more farmers in Poland alone than in any present member of the EU). My visits reinforced my belief in enlargement of the Union, since these countries are genuinely part of our wider European political and cultural history and need our support for their still fragile democracies. I was also attracted to enlargement by the realisation that absorption of their primitive agricultures would helpfully undermine the whole nonsensical edifice of the Common Agricultural Policy.

Further away, I went to Japan and Indonesia promoting British speciality foods. But overall I was never quite clear, apart from my great personal pleasure, what was achieved by such ministerial visits. Unless there are detailed follow-ups to exploit any trade opportunities identified, too often such visits contain just warm waffle and, after the minister's departure, the waters close again and no footprints remain.

In the office my working life in my first year was busy and interesting. I had endless meetings with officials and visiting delegations, as well as always attending Jack Cunningham's weekly 'prayers' meeting with officials and his junior ministers on Wednesday mornings, which had first priority in all our diaries. I was well supported by the three officials in my Private Office – once I had reorganised it, replacing the lady sitting with little to do at an old typewriter with a second policy administrator, Simon Stannard, who brought support and humour to my ministerial life.

I was very comfortable with Jack Cunningham as my boss. He is tall, handsome, straight, open, inclusive, supportive and an authentic north easterner. He never played political games with colleagues and I felt I always knew where I stood with him. His long experience and good political judgement showed to advantage and he carried authority in the cabinet and in the Commons. Several European ministers at the Agricultural Council told me that he was the best British farming minister in their time there. It was an astonishing stroke of misjudgement by Tony Blair in 2000 to drop him from the cabinet, at least half of whose members were not yet fit to shine Jack's political boots.

I was at first much less confident of the two other ministerial appointments at MAFF: Elliot Morley (Animal Welfare and Fishing), with whom I had earlier clashed sharply over his illiberal passion to ban hunting, and Jeff Rooker on the crucial Animal Health side, whose guerrilla tactics under the Wilson and Callaghan Governments had led me to question if he was an irresponsible 'lefty'. I was wrong about both of them. Elliot proved to be a knowledgeable minister who deserved promotion above his lowly position as Parliamentary Secretary, while Jeff was a wonderfully loyal colleague who became a warm friend. Jeff is a true 'Brummy' of gritty integrity and experienced political judgement – quick, energetic, brave, funny and as sharp as a tin-tack. He often reminded me of a little Jack Russell, ferreting out information and snapping at the heels of every recalcitrant problem. He certainly should have been in the cabinet, where few others matched his qualities – another misjudgement by Number 10 and under-use of a great political asset. (I was later proud to be chosen by Jeff in June 2001 to introduce him into the House of Lords, where he became an impressive Home Office minister.)

Jack involved the three of us 'juniors' in everything, his door open to his fellow ministers at all times, and we soon became a happy, united and dedicated political team. I enjoyed that first year with them enormously.

From the beginning we decided that it was necessary to have a new agricultural strategy and to try to modernise the outdated Ministry of Agriculture in order to pursue that strategy. 'Old MAFF', as we usually described it, had been wholly focussed on intensive farm production and on the CAP subsidies which underpin it. The department was basically run to that end and in fact appeared to be a wholly-owned subsidiary of the National Farmers' Union, which had hitherto summoned Tory ministers regularly to their headquarters to receive instructions. It was a subsidy-driven industry and department: in our first year the taxpayer shelled out £4 billion to farmers (making a total of £24 billion between 1990 and 1998). The average British working family with two children contributed £14 per week towards direct farm subsidy and food price support in 1997–8 (by 2002 it was £16 a week), although most such families were poorer than many of the farmers they supported. MAFF's own figures for 1998 showed that twenty-five arable farmers received over a half a million pounds each in direct subsidy payments, with 325 getting between £200,000 and £500,000 each, over 5,000 getting £50,000 to £200,000, and another 40,000 getting up to £50,000 each a year. The beef subsidy was then nearly £4 billion a year. The NFU – a very impressive trade union whose officers I came to respect – visited our department most weeks to explain why farmers should have even more subsidy. When sterling strengthened or food prices weakened, they demanded immediate compensation. But when prices moved the other way in the farmers' favour, there was no clawback for the poor taxpayer. It was a one-way benefit system. More support went to farming, which was less than 1 per cent of the British economy, than to the whole of manufacturing, which was then 20 per cent.

We British ministers could do little in the short run about this financial nonsense which derived from the Common Agricultural Policy, though we were committed to reform it in the longer term. But we aimed from the beginning to broaden MAFF's focus wider than farming and towards the many economic and social groups consti-tuting the diverse modern British countryside. Against much official opposition, we insisted on consumers and other interested parties being included on the depart-ment's key scientific advisory groups. I abolished the Regional Panels, which under the Tories had contained only farmers and the NFU and excluded farm workers. Instead I quickly set up Rural Liaison Groups containing representatives of the people who actually live and work in Britain's modern rural economy – consumers, teachers, environmentalists, food retailers and processors, rural bank managers, hoteliers and caterers in tourism, as well as farmers and farm workers.

Following this line of thinking, I proposed in a memo to Jack on 9 January 1998 that MAFF be transformed into a new Department of Rural Affairs which would relate to the broader rural community and not just mainly to agriculture – though farming would of course always be at the heart of it. I suggested incorporating some of the countryside divisions of the newly enlarged Department of the Environment, Transport and the Regions (e.g. the Wildlife and Countryside Directorate and/or the countryside and rural development divisions which include the Rural Development Council and the Countryside Commission). Jack asked me to refine the memo politically to send to the Prime Minister. So to Tony Blair I stressed that

> we need to provide a new Labour vision for rural Britain. The countryside has changed dramatically since the post-war agricultural regimes were established to concentrate on maximising farm production. The Tories still appeal to the old regimes and to the Old Countryside. We must not abdicate the voice of the coun-tryside to them. We must speak for the continuity of the old values and the new. Announcing the creation of a new Department for Food and Rural Affairs would give a clear signal that the Government is ready to address rural issues and announce new solutions for a sustainable living countryside.

This memo was sent to the Prime Minister in early 1998 and first reactions from Number 10 were encouraging. But then I learned that the plan for a new ministry had hit the heavyweight opposition of Environment Minister John Prescott, who was not enthusiastic about losing part of his ministerial empire. So for a while nothing happened. But when I resigned in July 1999 I again raised it with the Prime Minister, who replied: 'I am still working on it', indicating he was facing opposition in Whitehall. (He abolished MAFF following his victory in the general election on 7 June 2001 and a new Department of Food and Rural Affairs was created: it basically merged the same agriculture and environmental divisions which I had suggested and was placed in the cool and experienced hands of Margaret Beckett.)

The aim of our new strategy was to restructure the farming industry, where too many lived at the unviable margins or used farming as a hobby at the taxpayers' expense. We made only modest progress towards what we called 'New MAFF' in our first year under Jack Cunningham – and no progress at all under his successor Nick Brown, when the department reverted to 'Old MAFF' with a great official sigh of relief.

We did prod officials into more 'openness'. Greater emphasis was placed on environmental factors, and we rewrote MAFF's 'Mission Statement' (though few in the ministry read it) and shook up the deeply inert Information Department, whose prime aim seemed to be not to provide information. One Information Officer explained to me that he did not issue press releases about my regional visits because that 'might draw attention to them' – which may have been a realistic appraisal of my personal impact, but was worrying as a reflection of the division's general approach.

Most visibly, we moved our headquarters to a more attractive part of MAFF's estate in Smith Square, discovered by Jeff Rooker's alert terrier nose. I was told that over the decades officials had acquired virtually all the best rooms in the Ministry's office blocks while junior ministers had been relegated to cubbyholes like mine. We enjoyed reversing that process. I found a spacious room in the old ICI building where the lovely ornate ceiling had been philistinely obscured with plastic cladding and its once gilded walls were covered in chalk, dirt and old graphs and posters. Sarah used her interior decorating skills to beautify it and it contributed both to ministerial morale and to the Whitehall built heritage. But in 2002 a visitor reported to me that the civil servants had recovered Jeff's elegant room for their own use – so presumably the junior ministers were again being banished to lesser accommodation.

Our most serious policy change was to adopt a much more positive approach to the European Union. Recent Tory predecessors had 'waged war' on Brussels, lecturing and hectoring our European partners on their shortcomings and ensuring that Britain received few of the benefits and none of the goodwill from our membership. We set out to improve relations with continental colleagues, especially during our imminent six months of Presidency. We were particularly committed to securing rapid lifting of the ban on British beef exports (imposed on John Major because of the BSE scandal) and over the longer term to reforming the Common Agricultural Policy.

Persuading our partners to lift the beef ban was not easy, not least because several of them, especially the French, benefited commercially from excluding our competition. Britain also was unquestionably responsible for the recent BSE plague which we had irresponsibly exported to the continent (even continuing to send infected feed there after it was banned as unsafe in the UK). Jack Cunningham worked hard to restore confidence in our beef, especially charming the Italians and the Spaniards and winning the trust of the Agriculture Commissioner Fischler. It was because of the need to get the beef export embargo lifted that in December 1997, at the start of our Presidency, we decided to ban domestic sales of beef on the bone. In reality, the scientific risk of catching the fatal CJD disease from this source was mathematically not great. But risk there apparently was.

Once the relevant scientific advisory committee SEAC and the Chief Medical Officer formally advised of this risk, then as ministers we had little short-term choice. To have ignored that advice would have given our European opponents all the ammunition they needed to continue the beef export ban for a long time. The tabloid media showed no understanding of the dynamics of the bone ban and waged malicious campaigns against Jack (though had we ignored the scientific risk they would have waged similar campaigns against our 'irresponsibility' in risking the public's health). In fact the opinion polls showed that less than 3 per cent (including me) of the population ever ate beef on the bone and less than 1 per cent cared about our ban, though from the press it appeared that the whole population was in revolt.

The temporary ban on beef on the bone was in the circumstances the correct policy even if it inconvenienced Sunday lunch for me and a few privileged editors. We were rewarded when the European embargo was lifted from our beef exports eight months later. But the coverage of the ban damaged Jack Cunningham politically because Labour's inner circle was – and still is – excessively influenced by media hostility. By the time the export ban was lifted, Jack had been quite unfairly moved from MAFF where he had been a first-class minister.

Involvement in the beef issue led me to make two intriguing discoveries about my department. The first was the astonishing revelation that the famous EU ban on exports of British beef had never legally been implemented in the UK.

Although the ban had been agreed and imposed at the highest level by the European Heads of Government in 1996, was signed up to by the Tory Prime Minister John Major and was a leading issue in the 1997 election campaign, with all parties promising to get it lifted, MAFF never, in fact, implemented it in British law. So in reality there was no ban to lift. This emerged when some villains were caught exporting British beef to the continent. We ministers immediately demanded their prosecution as a demonstration that we were tough on breaches of the export ban and were committed to safe beef, and at that point the officials said sheepishly that we could not prosecute because the famous ban did not legally exist. MAFF under the Tories had deliberately not implemented it because of fear of difficulties with Tory Eurosceptics in the Commons – and we new ministers were not alerted by officials of this scandalous dereliction. Had our European partners learned of this, they would have had confirmation never to trust perfidious Albion. Jack moved to remedy the defect and laid before Parliament the orders to introduce the export ban which we were all long pledged to lift. It gave us all pleasure that no journalist was sufficiently awake after lunch to question the nature of this beef ban we were now belatedly introducing.

My second amusing discovery related to MAFF's campaign to try to assist British beef farmers suffering from exclusion from the European export markets by seeking to find additional consumers at home. We ministers and the media expressed great indignation with our armed forces for not eating British beef or lamb. I met with John Spellar, an old friend who was a minister at Defence, and he did a great job in swinging the military round to eating British beef. Then it suddenly occurred to me to ask our officials what meat MAFF itself served at its own headquarters and establishments across the country. I received no reply for several weeks, so I knew I was on to something. Then Jeff Rooker intervened and made MAFF, 'the farmers' friend', admit that it actually served foreign not British meat, especially Argentinian beef. I understood the pressures on departments to purchase at 'best value' but this, with its mixture of bad political positioning and attempted cover-up, somehow typified much of my experience with MAFF.

The United Kingdom assumed the Presidency of the European Union for the first half of 1998 and I was very proud when Jack nominated me as our ministerial representative to the Agricultural Council. It was in many ways my most fascinating task at MAFF, demonstrating the occasional satisfactions and many frustrations of membership of the Union (of which I have always been an unenthusiastic supporter). I travelled to Brussels or Luxembourg for monthly meetings and was accompanied by the best of MAFF's otherwise sometimes moderate officials. The then Permanent Secretary, Richard Packer, also came to Brussels and was on these issues at his well informed and ultrasceptical best when picking apart what he saw as the baser continental motives, while Jack Cunningham was authoritative and skilful in the chair. Our meetings in boring Brussels and pretty Luxembourg were held in huge characterless office blocks, with ministers sitting around very long tables backed by official teams. I often exchanged racing tips with the impressive Irish minister Joe Walsh. (Joe left the March 1998 Council meeting early in order to attend the crucial first day of the Cheltenham National Hunt Festival. When I commented that the British press would not allow me to get away with that, his Permanent Secretary replied: 'Any Irish journalist who criticised Joe for going to Cheltenham would be lynched by the Irish public.') The Irish are superior to us in so many ways.

Although the meetings were often rambling and tedious, I was fascinated to observe the EU at work, with the shifting alliances manoeuvring under the dominant Franco–German axis. The UK was clearly an odd man out, with its global outlook, strong national identity and attachment to liberal market economics, and this was particularly brought out in our discussions on CAP reform and the agricultural budget. On the budget, in April 1998 I strongly opposed the CAP subsidy of nearly a billion pounds to EU tobacco growers, which is more per acre than to any other product. European tobacco is poor in quality and a toxic threat to health. I received the support only of the Swedes. The Germans actually pressed for an increase in subsidy to tobacco growers in Austria, Belgium and, of course, Germany, arguing that these northern countries had the extra problem that 'they produce under such difficult climatic conditions'. There seemed no recognition that this might be a market reason not for more subsidy, but why they should not grow tobacco at all. I commented that an incipient African Congo ski industry might argue for subsidy on the same basis. The subsidy culture infected too much of the Council's thinking.

The reality is that there are distinct differences of political mentality and philosophy between the British and a majority of other EU member colleagues, particularly relating to attitudes to free and competitive markets, to the role of public subsidies and trade protection, and to the relative interests of producer groups as against those of consumers and taxpayers. The Thatcher–Reagan model of market economics, which had by then been accepted in refined forms by all main political parties in Britain, is still not accepted everywhere in continental Europe. There, many still prefer the 'Rhone' model, with its emphasis on state direction, social expenditure and social responsibility – rather 'Old Labour' in fact. They point to their superior social welfare and especially their better transport infrastructures in justification. This philosophical divide has special relevance to agriculture, since the CAP, with its intense central regulation, massive subsidies, minimal competition or concern with commercial efficiency and little interest in consumer preference, is a ripe product of the traditional European *dirigiste* approach. To our continental partners, with smaller farms, more rural votes and greater respect for rural culture (which I share), the CAP is a desirable part of the rural welfare system – especially as it is mainly paid for by the British and the Germans. Reform of the EU's *Alice in Wonderland* agricultural system will take time but it will ultimately happen, not least because it is not financially sustainable in its present form.

I launched the UK's drive for CAP reform at the Agricultural Council in Brussels on 31 March 1998, broadly supporting the Agenda 2000 plan from Commissioner Fischler, who was absolutely first class in his handling of the Council. But Agenda 2000 was denounced by virtually everyone there except us and the Swedes. It might have been thought that Fischler was proposing a radical revolution, whereas, in fact, Agenda 2000 contained only relatively mild adjustments to the existing regime. Many of Fischler's critics wanted not just to preserve but to extend every penny of subsidy in their farmers' pockets. I sympathise with support for small family farmers and especially to needy hill farmers, but cannot see why it should apply to the rich grain barons of East Anglia, pocketing many times more subsidy than the average British worker earns in a year – and the latter pay for it.

Our modest CAP reform package was approved at 3 a.m. at my final Council meeting in June 1998, reflecting Jack's diplomatic skill and stamina in the chair. But the French President typically vetoed the package at the next Heads of Government meeting in Berlin. After this I lost sight of the CAP situation since Jack left MAFF and his successor Nick Brown excluded me from all meetings and papers on the subject.

Domestically, I launched a number of minor policy initiatives which made some progress. As food minister, I was a fan of British speciality foods, whose fine quality is underestimated by native consumers, and I particularly sought to encourage British regional cheeses and bacon. Our cheeses currently have an inexplicable trade deficit of over half a billion pounds a year despite being often equal and even superior in quality to the immense flow of French imports, and British bacon is much tastier than its bland but all-conquering Danish competition. Our supermarkets are much to blame here for not supporting our fine regional foods, but the main reason is the typical British weakness in marketing.

Moreover, MAFF, stuck in its post-war mindset, had not taken its food responsibilities as seriously as it did farming – despite the fact that the food industry
accounts for 14 per cent of our GDP (and 10 per cent of our exports), whereas
agriculture is barely 0.6 per cent of our economy.

Personally, I greatly enjoyed the food side of my job and pressed for more
administrative support for our food exports. On foreign visits I pursued opportunities for fish processing in Indonesia, for consumer foods and drink exports to
Japan, grain to China and technology transfer to Central and Eastern Europe.
But this was not the way MAFF thought. In the departmental budget for 1998–9,
officials proposed halving the already minute expenditure on food export
promotion. The French back their food exporters much more impressively. I
concluded there is a strong case for transferring responsibility for these exports
from MAFF (and now from DEFRA) to the DTI, which handles the rest of our
exports and thinks in a slightly more commercial way.

In the farming area, I launched a drive to control 'gangmasters', the shabby
system whereby much harvesting of our horticulture and fruit is conducted by
foreign workers (often illegal immigrants), who are usually exploited by their
contractors with low pay and poor living conditions. I was also particularly
concerned at the number of accidents on British farms and launched a campaign
to improve farm safety. In 1997 alone there were 255 deaths, including children
– this was the equivalent of ten major train crashes like that at Hatfield, but it
received little media attention, possibly because farm accidents rarely provide
good photo opportunities.

A number of my other attempts at ministerial policy initiatives ran into the
sands of MAFF's lack of interest or positive hostility. My first major Lords
debate, in June 1997, was on the contentious issue of organophosphates (OPs),
used in many pesticides and sheep dips. The Countess of Marr, a doughty fighter
in the Lords whom I greatly respected, believed that OPs were seriously
damaging to farmers' nervous systems and for long had waged a campaign to
have them banned, believing that MAFF's reluctance to take more control was
partly because it was officially too close to the big agrochemical producers. I tried
to investigate some of the critics' fears, but my officials stated bluntly that there
was no danger in OPs unless foolishly used and that MAFF's policy line of
inaction was perfect, and implied that any illnesses resulting from the use of OPs
were the fault of the farmers themselves. I rejected their draft speech for the
debate on 24 June and wrote my own speech in the chamber, explicitly committing us to look more closely at the Countess's concerns and to take a more
precautionary approach to OPs. Afterwards, each week I asked for a response
from officials on the changes I had promised to Parliament. There was never any

response. Their line continued to be that since there was not 100 per cent scientific proof of a link between OPs and illnesses among farmers, then there was no proof at all and so there was no problem.

The same had happened over BSE. Officials retreated to their bureaucratic rabbit holes and hoped that the problem – and the minister – would go away. (They were right about the latter assumption but not the former.) When I faced another Lords question on OPs from the redoubtable Lord Peyton, I was astonished to find that the list of eighty-three suggested answers presented to me by officials both ignored his basic question about current OP research and also made no reference to the recent findings on OP health risk. After Questions, peppery Peyton, whom I had learned to like and respect, approached my officials in the corridor and rasped at them: 'As a Conservative minister I observed your department destroying the political reputations of my ministerial colleagues at MAFF – don't do the same to him.' But I made no serious progress on this important issue.

Some other initiatives proved equally fruitless. Jack and I believed that organic food offered farmers a rare profitable market opportunity. Consumer demand was rising at 20 per cent per annum, profit margins were high and 70 per cent of our organic consumption was imported. Jack made an early speech advocating organics, but immediately afterwards, without consultation, officials proposed to eliminate altogether the existing small subsidy to organic farming. We intervened to rescue that and introduced a new scheme with more money and the number of participants rose from 500 in 1998 to 3,000 in 1999. But when I asked the department to arrange for me to visit an organic farm in the summer of 1997 my request was ignored and a year later still nothing had happened. Organics was not part of 'Old MAFF'.

I had similar negative reactions to my attempts to encourage exports of the transfer of British agricultural technology to central and eastern Europe. I discussed the encouraging prospects with the Russian ambassador and also met British consultants who were interested in helping. But my requests to promote a pilot scheme went unanswered. I had a similar experience with my attempts to promote marketing co-operatives to assist the British farming and food industries. I asked repeatedly for an official meeting but nothing happened for almost a year. I was told that MAFF opposed 'co-operatives' because they had a left-wing aura (Mr Benn again!), so I approached the NFU, which launched an excellent regional campaign advocating 'collaborative marketing' – its imaginative verbal solution to the 'co-operatives' semantic problem.

My position as minister for the South West region led me into a number of small policy initiatives there – notably that we managed to preserve from the attack of the Brussels bureaucracy the distinct name of Cornish Clotted Cream.

I was particularly attracted by a scheme proposed to me by Jacob Rothschild to cleanse the rivers of Devon and Cornwall. Jacob was chairman of the Lottery Heritage Fund and was ready to allocate serious money to this magnificent project, which would have put the south west in the lead in terms of water environment and ecology. In return he understandably required some commitment of support from MAFF. I was very excited and submitted memoranda to officials stressing the urgency, since Jacob was due to retire soon and the lottery money could not wait for ever. But nothing happened and the opportunity was lost.

Abattoirs and matters of animal health and food hygiene came directly under Jeff Rooker, but I was also involved because I had to answer frequent questions and heated debates on these issues in the Lords. I was particularly concerned with two aspects: the availability of abattoirs in remote areas and the inadequate supply of vets to supervise them. We need small abattoirs in remote areas so that small farmers do not have to take their few animals on costly long journeys to distant slaughterhouses, which, apart from the ruinous cost, also lowers the quality of the meat. MAFF's policy was to encourage closure of small abattoirs and encourage a few large ones which were easier for its Meat Hygiene Service to administer – and the MHS is statutorily required to recover its growing administration costs through charges, so it is incentivised to maximise these. I tried to help the small abattoirs, since I believe that a living countryside requires small enterprises of all kinds – family farms, small cheese producers, village shops and post offices, local breweries and pubs, etc. That approach may run against the tide of larger commercial scale and it is difficult to reconcile with the CAP, which inhibits directional aid to particular areas of need. But I believe our rural strategy should encourage such small businesses as part of its thinking.

The necessary increased supervision of meat hygiene following the BSE crisis exposed the serious shortage and high costs of British veterinary services. Consequently MAFF had to search abroad and by 1998 some 25 per cent of its full-time and 50 per cent of its part-time vets were foreign, mainly Spanish. These imports might not speak English too well but they had the attraction of often charging only a third as much as British vets. The shortage and high cost of domestic vets derives from our veterinary profession's monopoly control of supply through our outdated system of veterinary education, which keeps down numbers and insists that everyone has an expensive seven-year college training. I believed that what we needed at MAFF was to add to the existing highly qualified vets a supplementary supply of more quickly trained 'para-vets' who could do the basic work of supervising meat hygiene.

I raised this with our then Higher Education minister, Tessa Blackstone, who agreed that the existing vet training was out of date and too expensive. I also discussed the issue with the British Veterinary Association, who left me in no doubt that I was treading on sacred and privileged ground and that it was no business of the government (which did actually pay the training costs). When I finally raised the matter at a ministerial meeting in late 1997, the Permanent Secretary Richard Packer looked agitated and intervened to say: 'I will handle that.' We never heard of it again. Vets had more power than ministers in MAFF. It was later no surprise to me that one of the features of the terrible foot and mouth plague in 2001 was the serious shortage of vets to supervise the dubious policy of mass slaughter.

Towards the end of my time as minister, I attempted two final minor policy initiatives.

The first involved trying to control the growing plague of grey squirrels, which drive out the native red squirrels and do great damage to our broadleaf trees. I asked for a policy meeting and there was an unusually quick response. The purpose of the meeting was to impress on me that 'nothing can be done'. I meekly yielded to the officials' greater experience, simply asking at the end if there could at least be more systematic coordination of the relevant bodies to try to contain the grey plague. I never heard another word – though two years later there were signs that at least the Royal Parks were taking some action.

My final initiative concerned a subject very close to my heart: the horse. As early as June 1997 I had secured Jack Cunningham's support for my proposal that MAFF should become the formal Ministry for the Horse. Apart from my own personal strong interest in racing, the logic was clear. Our 'horsey-culture' is large and growing and has become the third largest rural industry (after farming and tourism), employing directly or indirectly over 100,000 people. Yet no Whitehall department was then responsible for the horse – it was apparently the only major industry without a sponsoring ministry. Since it is basically a rural industry, MAFF seemed the logical home. I minuted Number 10 on this and received an encouraging response. I also asked MAFF officials for a paper on how to handle this issue but received no response at all.

So the following year I raised the issue again with Jack's support. There was no reply until after Jack had been moved. In August 1998 while I was on holiday in France, the Permanent Secretary wrote to the new minister Nick Brown rejecting my proposal, which Brown apparently accepted, though I was never directly informed. I decided to operate more personally and called the various horse interests to meet together in my room in January 1999 to create a single umbrella organisation to represent their common horse interests. I made it clear that I was acting personally and that, regrettably, MAFF would offer no help.

Shortly after, the Permanent Secretary circulated a minute explicitly criti-cising me for holding the meeting and specifically for providing MAFF coffee, stating that I did 'not have the permission of the minister to hold this meeting.' I ignored this petty attack and held a final meeting, again supplying five cups of departmental coffee regardless of public expense. Then the distinguished group formed the British Horse Industry Confederation, which has continued constructively ever since. Once the BHIC was successfully established the department changed tack and took a more positive view. After I retired, my admirable MAFF successor, Helene Hayman, was designated Minister of the Horse by Number 10 and gave the industry great assistance. In 2002 the department finally assigned officials specifically to liaise with the horse industry, a move I greatly welcomed.

My occasional early difficulties in prodding the department into a more positive mode had grown dramatically more acute after Jack Cunningham was moved from MAFF to the Cabinet Office at the end of July 1998 and was succeeded by Nick Brown. Junior ministers only carry any clout with officials or outside if they are seen to have their cabinet minister's active backing, and the reshuffle removed that backing from me. It also gave me, as a past political scientist, the opportunity rarely available to academics to observe directly how a new minister taking charge of a department can make a difference to everyone closely involved. It certainly made a clear difference to Jeff, Elliot and to myself.

Nick Brown is a shrewd and affable party politician, an effective Commons performer and a deft handler of the media on the occasions when he chooses to face them. Although a homosexual from the south, he impressively established himself in the tough and 'laddish' Labour network in the north east of England, where he holds a safe seat. He also enjoys the powerful personal protection of his friend Gordon Brown. Not being very interested in detailed policies as such, he had in 1997 seemed well suited to his first cabinet job as Chief Whip. But Tony Blair was said not to like him, so in the first reshuffle he was demoted to lowly MAFF. Somewhat dumpy and porcine in appearance, he soon attracted a favourable response from British farmers. But when I briefly saw him on his first day in Smith Square he confessed to being 'shell-shocked' by his demotion. He was also at that moment agitated by his urgent need for some private reason to clean the records off his computer disks and telephones in the Whips' Office before his successor Ann Taylor arrived there. (He damaged a computer in the process, involving MAFF in cross-departmental compensation.) I was that first day feeling sad to lose Jack Cunningham as a ministerial boss, but I definitely looked forward to working supportively with Nick, and in that frame of mind I set off to Ceret with Sarah for our usual August idyll.

September, with no meeting of Parliament, is a month for ministers to visit the regions and abroad. So after returning from France it took me a little while to focus on the new situation in the department. Then I began to notice a quite different atmosphere and routine. One morning my perceptive Private Secretary Peter Grimley informed me that 'the Permanent Secretary has taken advantage of the long summer break to capture the minister and has now built a complete wall around him.' Jeff's and Elliot's Private Secretaries reported a similar situation, that they were being completely shut out from involvement in policy matters by the minster's and the Permanent Secretary's private offices. Jeff, with whom I now had a warm working relationship, telephoned me on 9 October 1998 to report that in his own vital policy area of animal and food health meetings were being held and decisions taken without the knowledge of himself or his officials. Most worrying, we learned that Jeff, quite the outstanding member of our team, was being excluded from meetings at which the minister and Permanent Secretary were apparently plotting to subvert Labour's manifesto commitment to set up an independent Food Standards Agency outside the control of MAFF. They sought to keep this vital element of consumer protection within MAFF's producer-driven hands.

I suffered the same exclusion in farming and food. We quickly noticed that Nick's circulated ministerial diary actually contained no details of any appointments at all (whereas Jack had circulated his full diary so that we could attend any meetings we wished). When Elliot tried to gain access through his MAFF computer to check Nick's whereabouts, up on the screen came the words 'E Morley Access Denied'. Our previous routine of Wednesday morning 'prayer' meetings, at which we monitored current MAFF issues and prepared for imminent crises, was abolished. After we protested, such meetings were occasionally held, though with no agenda or minutes, and often without the presence of the Permanent Secretary, so no decisions were ever taken or recorded there. Jack had also held frequent meetings with just us ministers present, to discuss politically sensitive issues, but these were also abolished by Nick and never resumed. We three junior ministers never in my time held a single collective meeting alone with Nick. In fact, my only personal policy meeting with my minister during that whole year was briefly in November 1998 when I insisted on a discussion of how to handle a difficult Lords question on the Government's plans for the new Food Standards Agency, where I knew that the private plans of Nick and his controlling Permanent Secretary differed from the Prime Minister's public commitment. Nick arranged the meeting with me in a crowded parliamentary bar, possibly not wishing his officials to see him reprehensibly consorting with his ministerial colleague, and he gave no indication of his thinking.

On another occasion I needed to contact Nick urgently when he was at home and so I asked his Private Office for his address and telephone number. His

Private Secretary reacted as if I was proposing to burgle him, refused to give me the information and told me to 'try the Number 10 switchboard'. So I obtained the information from his driver. When as Minister of Farming I attended his early meeting with the National Farmers' Union, he humiliatingly asked me to leave the room and when I later returned he pointed to the distant end of the long table, making clear my demotion. Soon I no longer knew of nor attended these meetings. He also quickly removed me from the Honours Committee, to which Jack had appointed me to try to change the department's habit of giving patronage only to South of England Tories.

I had been particularly committed in my role as minister for the regions to try to help the impoverished south west, but I quickly ceased to receive relevant papers, and only one meeting was arranged in that region during 1999. The excellent regional official with whom I had worked closely in the south west informed me that 'the Minister has eased you out' (as was his right, but it would have been nice to have been told by him directly). Nick also quickly abolished the independent group of outside policy experts who had been advising Jack and me (with particular ministerial responsibility) on reform of the CAP and I was myself never subsequently involved in MAFF's policies for reform, rarely seeing copies of the relevant papers.

After I had successfully negotiated that the army should resume eating British beef, my office arranged that I should go to celebrate at the first regimental lunch. But when I turned up I was sent away by officials who explained that Nick had decided to celebrate my victory instead. I did not mind missing the lunch nor the very minor glory, but felt that Nick himself might have mentioned it to me. It was the same when he and the Permanent Secretary moved unannounced to transfer Jeff's and Elliot's Private Secretaries to their own offices.

Most of these incidents were of only trivial consequence, and usually we junior ministers just shrugged our shoulders and chuckled. After all, different politicians have different political styles and it is not compulsory, though it helps, to run departmental ministers as a team. But it was odd that on none of these nor other similar occasions did Nick have the courtesy to discuss his actions with his ministerial colleagues, two of whom were senior and had served with him in the Commons for more than a decade.

His non-communicative style reached the point of apparent physical disappearance when the potent issue of genetically modified foods blew up into media hysteria in early 1999. Jeff and I had handled this politically sensitive matter so far in committee, though without any collective discussion of all ministers to establish our policy strategy. We tried to restrain the department's gung-ho instinct to rush ahead into immediate mass production of GMs. At the start of our first meeting the senior GM official advised us that we should 'not discuss the ethical or political issues involved, but only the production-efficiency aspects of GMs.' I resisted, saying this was akin to discussing 'only the urban-clearance aspects of nuclear weapons.' We made some progress, insisting on a Code of Practice for the producers of GMs. But when the hysterical tabloid scare campaigns began with a flood of questions in the Lords and Commons and numerous requests for TV appearances, we ministers now needed a clear departmental policy to which Jeff and I could adhere in public. But we were unable to establish such a departmental view since our Minister Nick had apparently disappeared from sight. We were told he shrewdly felt that GMs constituted a tricky no-win situation, and the Permanent Secretary's weekly memorandum reported that his Minister had decided it was best 'not to get involved'. Jeff and I had no alternative to getting involved in Parliament, however tricky. Jeff handled the media brilliantly and impressed Number 10.

Perhaps the most important policy issue from which we junior ministers were formally excluded was the construction of MAFF's new strategy for 'The Future of Farming in Britain', which might have been thought to be close to my interests as Minister for Farming. In early 1999 Nick organised a big conference costing £80,000 on this proposed new strategy, and the list of those invited included virtually everyone remotely connected with farming in Britain – except Jeff, Elliot and me as Farming Minister. We were not consulted, invited or even informed. I only heard of it through office gossip, receiving no papers on it. Jeff and I wandered into the MAFF conference hall in the middle of its proceedings, and noted that Permanent Secretary Packer was in the chair on stage and Nick was sitting in the audience. Presumably it was as well to establish publicly who now ran the place.

At the time of that farming conference, we junior ministers concluded that we should ourselves meet regularly as a team under Jeff's chairmanship to monitor departmental issues of collective ministerial importance. I particularly needed this collective overview in order to answer my frequent questions and debates in the Lords. We were quite open about our proposal, informing all Private Offices and inviting Nick. Just before our first meeting, a message was brought to Jeff from Nick saying that we were 'forbidden from holding any meetings together'. Jeff received this ludicrous instruction with a roar of laughter and asked to have it 'on paper for my memoirs'. Elliot asked: 'What if we share a taxi together – can we talk?' We treated it as an aberration and gathered in Jeff's room. In the middle of our deliberations, a Private Secretary came in and said with embarrassment: 'The Minister's office has been on the phone and the Minister now gives you his permission to hold your meeting.' Jeff grinned and said gently, 'Tell him thanks, but we are already holding our meeting and you have just interrupted it.'

Typically, the official machine quickly and professionally adjusted to our subsequent weekly gatherings and began to submit papers and suggestions for consideration at what they called our 'progress meetings' (maybe termed in contrast to Nick's). These gathering cheered me up immensely over my final months in MAFF.

Nick Brown's ministerial style was certainly a distinct one and I could see a logic in it. Nick apparently felt that he best understood all the politics, so he took control of that. He knew nothing of agricultural or food policy, so he left that entirely in the hands of the Permanent Secretary and his officials (which had the added advantage that when things went wrong he would not be attacked and briefed against by some of his own civil servants, as Jack Cunningham had been). By announcing that his basic policy was 'to listen sympathetically' to farmers' complaints (a full time job in itself) and reverting to the 'Old MAFF' style of being under the thumb of the NFU, Nick cleverly ensured that he received the plaudits of the farming community and its press, and so he helpfully took some of the 'countryside' pressure off the Prime Minister.

As such, his approach was definitely shrewd and in the short run successful. But it did contain some downsides. For a start, it left little role for his junior ministers, though that need be of concern to nobody but them. More importantly, it also meant that our original thrust to modernise MAFF – to make it more representative of the 'new' diverse rural economy and responsive to the consumer, was effectively abandoned. 'New MAFF' quickly reverted to 'Old MAFF', to the clear relief of most officials and farmers. Presumably the overt exclusion of Jeff, Elliot and myself from many of the affairs of the department was, whatever the political and psychological motives behind it, also part of the reassurance to farming that the recent aberration of 'New MAFF' was ended and that from now on nothing would change.

For me personally, it meant that my job drastically changed. Effectively, I had no ministerial role, no longer being seriously involved in farming issues, nor in CAP reform, nor in our regional policy, and only marginally in food (where anyway few others seemed interested). In my final year under Nick I only rarely went into my handsome ministry office since I had few meetings to attend and few policies to administer. I spent my time busily in the House of Lords answering a multitude of questions at the dispatch box and speaking in frequent tense debates on agricultural policy issues which I no longer had a role in formulating. I was also kept in the Lords constantly voting on our perpetual three-line whips, which often continued exhaustingly into the early hours. During the session of 1998–9 I voted in 91 per cent of our votes, the missed ones being when I was abroad. Frequently I read and slept in the Lords library till one, two and three o'clock in the morning. In those two sessions of 1997–9 we passed seventy-six Bills through the Upper Chamber, involving 270 divisions, for most of which I was present. The Government was defeated seventy times – on one in four of the votes – reflecting the continuing Tory majority over Labour, even after we eliminated some 650 hereditary peers.

I greatly enjoyed this active parliamentary life, especially since my front bench colleagues were of great ability and personally delightful. We have been blessed with a phalanx of feminine politicians who are attractive and brilliant performers without that strident edge which blights some Labour women. Margaret Jay, Tessa Blackstone, Liz Symons, Patricia Scotland and Patricia Hollis could match professionally and personally any previous generation of Labour ladies. Flanked by Gareth Williams, Andrew McIntosh, Ivor Richard, Derry Irvine, Larry Whitty, Denis Carter and Bruce Grocott, they have constituted the most impressive front bench of either party that I have seen – and at least match Tony Blair's Commons team. I particularly enjoyed the warm friendship of our outstanding party leader in the House, Margaret Jay, who pursued the reform of the Lords with steely determination against a barrage of chauvinist hostility from some of the press.

For my agricultural business in the Lords, I had from the beginning realised that there was little farming knowledge on my Labour side, whereas there was massive agricultural expertise on the Tory benches opposite. If I had attempted to conduct agricultural issues on a partisan basis, I would have been slaughtered at the dispatch box. So I approached my Lords business consensually, being as open as possible to the Tory benches – where, anyway, a number of good personal friends sat. I also decided to incorporate some of the Tory expertise into my thinking. Using Elisabeth Carnegie as a helpful intermediary, I invited the Lords Stanley, Soulsby, Middleton, Monk Bretton, Brookeborough and the formidably knowledgeable Selbourne to discuss agricultural issues over regular teas. This may have helped them feel involved in policy thinking and perhaps drew some of the Opposition sting. I was certainly educated by it and benefited most from the dialogue – which was more easily possible in the Lords than the more partisan Commons.

It would be wrong to conclude from the occasional negative outcomes of some of my minor policy initiatives, or indeed from my experience of the Brown–Packer 'ministerial exclusion zone' tactics, that my life at MAFF was mainly unhappy, as

I enjoyed much of my time there. It was anyway probably a mistake in MAFF to attempt as a minister to influence policy at all. Perhaps I should have listened more to my knowledgeable Private Secretary who, when I had grumpily complained yet again that my requests for meetings or papers had been ignored, pointed out to me that 'the department is not accustomed to ministers interfering, and doesn't really like it'. He hinted that our Tory ministerial predecessors had been much cleverer and happier in spending the week visiting farms and county shows and leaving the policies to the officials who knew best. Given the then character of MAFF, that was certainly wise advice, and Nick Brown seemed instinctively to follow that prudent political line. My problem was that for my first and only ministry, I did not see the point of not at least trying to accomplish something in policy terms that might help the rural way of life.

The crucial question of the character and culture of MAFF fascinated me – not just as a minister within that department, but also as a past and future academic who has often lectured on the workings of Whitehall departments. I will now try to describe and analyse MAFF's predominant 'culture': its collective personality, style and attitudes as I witnessed them.

MAFF seemed to me at that time to have seven main cultural characteristics. It was sincerely dedicated to its agricultural constituency. It was dominated by its farming and agrochemical clients. It exuded a mentality of welfare subsidy and protectionism. It was not concerned with management efficiency and seemed incapable of speedy reaction (hence the foot and mouth shambles was entirely predictable). It was basically negative and hostile to new policy approaches. It was deeply secretive, being inclined to 'cover up' rather than face difficult issues openly. And it was isolated from the rest of Whitehall, showing a 'bunker' and often hostile attitude to other departments. (There was little belief in 'joined-up government' in MAFF.)

The last two of those characteristics (none of which of course applies to absolutely every official in the department, some of whom were excellent, but they were the predominant attitudes) were certainly linked to the institutional demoralisation which followed the awful BSE disaster. This dominant culture particularly affected MAFF's distinctive attitude to ministers as a breed. The latter were often viewed as an intrusion; to be controlled if possible; failing that, to be excluded from the policy process where possible; or finally to be obstructed if obstinate ministers insisted on getting involved. Certainly the traditional principle taught in many college textbooks – that 'officials advise, ministers decide' – did not seem to have percolated through to MAFF. There it was more often demonstrated that 'officials advise and decide – ministers merely approve, but take the blame if the decision goes wrong'. This approach to ministers often manifested itself in what are sometimes called 'Whitehall games' – tactics to control, exclude or frustrate 'interfering' ministers. These games were played not just with me but with all ministers in MAFF – though less so with Nick Brown, who appeared willing to be controlled at the first stage and so there was no need for officials to resort to other tactical games of frustration. I recall and have notes of many examples of these games, and will recount just a few lest any reader suspect they are mere fiction. Some of the games gave me great amusement as an old Whitehall hand; but too many were tediously irritating to me as a minister.

I encountered major games in relation to one of my main policy priorities on entering MAFF, which was to reform Britain's antiquated quarantine laws against rabies. These laws had been introduced under Edward VII and required incoming animals to be locked up in miserable kennels for six months, taking no account of the advances in animal medicine over the past hundred years. On 2 June 1997 I sent Jack Cunningham a memo pressing for action on reform – not only because I strongly believed in reform but also because my Sarah, a life-long Conservative, had promised to vote Labour at the next election if we changed this barbaric law. When we ministers met on 1 July, Jeff Rooker was not at first convinced, fearing the political risks if a rabid dog was found loose on the streets of his beloved Birmingham. But Elliot Morley supported me from the beginning. Jack, as a scientist, soon came round to the need to take account of the past century's medical progress. We were warned that many MAFF vets were opposed to change, as were the outside private vets who made a good living supervising the eighty or so designated quarantine kennels. But we pressed ahead, and in late November 1997 Jack announced the appointment of a scientific committee under the distinguished Professor Kennedy to advise the department on possible changes to the law on quarantine.

We immediately met our first MAFF 'game'. Only one vet had been appointed to the committee, on the specific recommendation of the department. Despite a long list of his qualifications provided to us by officials, his file did not contain any mention that this vet was believed to be an implacable opponent of reform. As the sole vet he would have great influence on the committee – presumably not positively towards reform. The official 'game' was clearly to fix the committee from the start to try to undermine the ministerial policy of reform. When the Kennedy Committee was announced, I was quickly told by friendly outside vets: 'You have been stitched up.' I communicated urgently with Jack and, against some departmental hostility, he insisted on appointing two extra distinguished vets without known bias. (One of them was Andrew Higgins, who became a good friend of mine and helped to form the British Horse Industry Confederation.) The Kennedy Committee produced an excellent report setting out the scientific and low-risk path to reform, and its recommendations were agreed by the cabinet and welcomed by Parliament, with 96 per cent support in a public consultation.

We moved ahead to prepare the reforms with strong personal encouragement from the Prime Minister. But after Jack left the department we ran into another very serious 'game'. In June 1999 there suddenly emerged a paper from a senior MAFF vet stating bluntly that we must reverse the whole reform process and reconvene the Kennedy Committee 'with a different chairman' – implying one less sympathetic to reform. This official counter-attack continued with a paper from the senior quarantine official asserting that 'the whole policy is now being reviewed ... preparations for reform are now on hold' and adding that the author was already writing a new paper with suggestions 'for a new policy'. The Permanent Secretary also intervened, sending a note to Nick Brown informing him that quarantine policy was now being changed – but Nick either failed to read it or to see its significance. This reversal of policy was without any consultation with MAFF ministers and had been effected regardless of the fact that the reforms had been approved by the Prime Minister and cabinet and had been announced to the approval of Parliament.

I immediately wrote a memo to Nick opposing the change of policy. I also communicated with Liz Lloyd, the clever agriculture adviser in the Number 10 Policy Unit, informing her that MAFF officials had unilaterally overthrown a policy which was personally and strongly supported by the PM. She was astonished, saying that Nick had held a meeting with Blair only a few days earlier and had assured him that our quarantine reforms were still on course, and Number 10 quickly instructed Brown not to allow any backtracking. When we ministers finally met to overrule the officials, Nick reassured us that he had already written to the Prime Minister stating that we were 'sticking to existing policies'. But when we examined a copy of his letter to Blair, we found that officials had excluded that key sentence about sticking to existing policies from the final draft without telling him and he had signed without noticing. We were clearly deep into Sir Humphrey's *Yes Minister* territory.

With quarantine reform presumably back on course, we were faced in June 1999 with 'game' number three to minimise and delay its impact. Officials now suggested that the proposed pilot trial in the following year should be 'only for dogs which are staying in Britain more that two months'. I discovered that this would apply to only 5 per cent of dogs travelling, leaving 95 per cent excluded from the trials. This would render the pilot trial valueless, leaving many quarantine questions unanswered. The ferry companies also stated they would not provide special facilities for just 5 per cent of the dogs. We demolished that game by pointing out that there was no way of knowing if dogs would actually stay for more than two months or of preventing them from leaving sooner. It was really just an obstructionist tactic. After I left the Ministry, our ministers commendably saw through a few further stages of the quarantine modernisation; but reform had been achieved despite the worst efforts of MAFF 'games' to torpedo it.

MAFF's culture involved an intriguing general attitude to ministers. Officials saw themselves (not without some cause) as having most experience and wisdom and they viewed ministers as mere transients, to be controlled if willing and excluded if resisting control. An early example of this was in October 1997 when the department produced its budget for the Comprehensive Spending Review, setting our strategic policy priorities for the following two years. No minister had been consulted on its contents and allocations and Jack Cunningham was shown the key document late one afternoon only a few hours before it was due to be submitted to the Treasury. Jack showed the paper to me and on a cursory look I noticed that it contained little relationship to our ministerial priorities. Jack refused to approve the document and insisted on a meeting at which ministers could at least discuss their own budgets. The Permanent Secretary opened that meeting by saying (and I took a note): 'These are decisions which were previously taken by officials' – and he was referring to the financing of our key policy priorities over the next two years. The budget before us took no account of the Labour Government's priorities or public statements by us MAFF ministers. It basically repeated the policy priorities of our Tory predecessors (though probably they had no role in their budget's construction either).

After we had been in government a couple of years, the Prime Minister grew concerned at what he understandably saw as poor line management and failures of executive delivery in Whitehall. The energetic Cabinet Secretary, Richard Wilson, pursued this issue, and in July 1999 his Cabinet Office circulated to junior ministers a questionnaire on it, with particular reference to our relations with our departmental officials. I looked forward to pointing out that my relations with my Private Secretaries – with clever Peter Grimley, supportive Simon Stannard and the lovely Teresa Hart – and with first-class divisional officials like Graham Cory, Kate Timms, Richard Carden, Robert Lowson and Andy Lebrecht were excellent, though there were problems elsewhere, especially at the very top. But predictably – and hilariously – the Permanent Secretary retained my copy of the questionnaire for several weeks and sent it to me only after the final deadline for completion and return to the Cabinet Office was well past. Sir Humphrey Appleby would have been proud of that.

Of course, I well understand from long observation in Whitehall that relations between ministers and their civil servants are inevitably complex. They each have different backgrounds, agenda, priorities and time-scales. Ministers are usually temporary in the department, officials have the strength of permanence. As Michael Heseltine, a very experienced departmental minister, said to me at dinner in May 2001: 'Ministers should appreciate that civil servants are not on their side. And they are not on the Opposition's side. They are on their own side.'

The relationship between the two sides is bound to be sometimes uneasy. Civil servants are expected on the surface to be 'civil', arranging travel tickets and expressing a courteous 'Yes minister' many times a day. Yet they may resent this servility, being often brighter and more knowledgeable about the relevant policy details than their temporary political bosses. Ideally – and this does sometimes happen, especially where the ministerial and official quality is high – the combination of the minister's political judgement and the official's policy experience does produce a reasonable outcome acceptable to both, and usually in the general public interest. Sadly, this balance was not always achievable in MAFF in my time due to the department's institutional resistance to any ministerial input. This general problem for all ministers in MAFF was well summed up to me in 1999 by former Tory Chancellor of the Exchequer Nigel Lawson: 'You must remember that Whitehall is a string of departmental villages. Officials are the village residents. Ministers are just transient tourists passing through. The only difference among them is that some villages welcome ministerial tourists and some are hostile to them. The Treasury welcomes them. MAFF is notoriously hostile.'

MAFF's negative and bunker mentality was in my time partly set in style from the top. The Permanent Secretary was Richard Packer, who had been 'fast-track' promoted under Mrs Thatcher to try to inject some East End grit into the stuffy 'old-boy' Whitehall network. Packer, who looked like a balding former bantamweight boxer, struck me as sharply intelligent and very streetwise about departmental politics. I appreciated his directness, courage, detailed knowledge and rough humour, though not his street-corner manners. Above all, he was too arrogantly dismissive of anyone who questioned how MAFF operated. By the time we came into office in 1997 he had offended so many fellow senior mandarins from other departments that MAFF, which he held in a vice-like grip, was isolated in Whitehall.

I naturally resented his open contempt for all his ministers. Once he dismissed a policy decision by Jack Cunningham with: 'Ministers like you come and go.' (He was of course right on the fact.) Elliot Morley told me that some farmers told him that at a dinner with Packer, they asked him how he found the new Labour ministers and he snapped back: 'They make no difference. I run the department' – again usually factually correct. When I took my charming Tory predecessor Tim Boswell to lunch in June 1997, he commented on Packer that 'it is OK to *think* that all ministers are idiots, but there is no need to push this into their faces all the time'.

Under Jack Cunningham, we ministers quickly realised that we would never modernise and remotivate MAFF while Packer was in charge, and this opinion was conveyed to the Prime Minister and the Cabinet Secretary. But ministers quite rightly do not control official appointments. So we were stuck with him, and most of our modernisation plans ran into a brick wall. As a streetfighter Packer was a formidable adversary – one who saw off Jack Cunningham, Jeff Rooker and myself, and possibly many Tory ministers before us – and I always felt respect for his guts and knowledge, if not his style and attitude. He was retired early by the Prime Minister in 2000 – although, as I was told by the Cabinet Secretary, defended to the end by Nick Brown (himself demoted from the department after the 2001 general election).

So the Ministry of Agriculture was quite an experience and an education for me. It did at times test my sense of humour, but I would not have been without it for the world. Now that it has been rightly abolished by Tony Blair, perhaps no future minister will taste that special flavour of working there. However, most recent experience suggests that its agriculture divisions may be reasserting their undoubted skills at Whitehall office games to reimpose their old culture on the new department, DEFRA – the Department for Environment, Food and Rural Affairs. If so, that would be ominous for the future of our rural community.

Twenty

TONY BLAIR *ET AL.*, HUNTING AND PRIVATE PLEASURES

Not all of my time in the 1997 Labour Government was devoted to the arcane pleasures of MAFF. I maintained my interest in Northern Ireland and financial affairs and through these involvements came in contact with Number 10 and other parts of the government. I already knew many cabinet ministers and quickly got to know other ministers through attendance at cabinet committees. Some ministers, even in cabinet, were of only modest ability with limited political and no previous governmental experience and certainly would not have featured in the higher echelons of Harold Wilson's star-studded administration. But Gordon Brown and David Blunkett are clearly up with the best, while Charles Clarke, Helen Liddell and Jack Straw impressed me with their experienced judgement. (Charles would make a future party leader.) Gordon Brown is the most substantial political heavyweight in the Government and in Parliament as well as being our outstanding post-war Chancellor of the Exchequer – though sometimes he does show a dark side to his strong personality.

In cabinet committee I met the intriguing figure of Peter Mandelson and came greatly to enjoy his company. As co-author of the official biography of his grandfather Herbert Morrison, I was of course aware of Peter and his remarkable achievements in modernising the Labour Party (demonstrating again, as in racehorse breeding, that genes do matter). I was intrigued to observe that in cabinet committee Peter spent most of his time writing notes and only once intervened verbally – on the matter of the European Union, where he made an impassioned plea for a more positive British attitude. His style is prim, with balletic body language, carefully measured though often waspish words and penetrating observation. He is witty, highly intelligent, very clear and the best political strategist in the Labour Party since his grandfather. I can see why Tony Blair depended on him for political guidance and I was sorry when he was unfairly forced out of government.

My continuing interest in Northern Ireland kept me in contact with Blair's Number 10. An able Ulsterman, David Montgomery, former editor of the *Daily*

Mirror and *News of the World*, drew me into very oblique contact with the Unionist leader David Trimble, who had been bravely trying to drag the Orange neanderthals into the twentieth century. On 14 January 1997, a few months before Labour took office, I forwarded Trimble's basic terms for a radical settlement in Northern Ireland to Tony Blair. It proposed a devolved power-sharing government to run Ulster affairs, except for defence and foreign policy. The suggested assembly would be elected by PR and the key committee chairs allocated among parties according to votes cast. The most radical and constructive suggestions were that nationalist Sinn Fein should participate and that there should be a consultative role for Dublin in a joint body. For the first time the Unionists agreed to work with nationalists on cross-border policies.

This proposed 'settlement' represented a major step towards the middle ground by the usually intransigent Unionists, and I supported it to Blair as the most specific outline of the Unionist demands so far, pointing out that without their majority support he could achieve little in Ulster (something often ignored by Labour's instinctive pro-Republicans). I also warned him that the Northern Irish situation, with which he had not so far engaged, was unstable and could crumble into disorder after the election due in May – and this trouble could divert him from central British economic and social issues, as had happened when I was with Harold Wilson in 1974.

At a post-election party for new junior ministers at Number 10 on 13 May 1997, Jonathan Powell, the Prime Minister's Chief of Staff, indicated that I should continue my oblique involvement in Northern Irish matters. I advised Jonathan to press Blair to make rapid preparations for a new peace initiative and settlement in Northern Ireland. During May and June, while still finding my feet at MAFF, I was also busily occupied, together with David Montgomery, in helping to revise the draft of the Trimble Plan for a new elected assembly. I rewrote about one third of it, making it more attractive to Blair's instincts, cutting out several unnecessarily adversarial paragraphs and adding a suggestion for a Council of the British Isles. In its conclusion I wrote that

> a bold initiative to increase democratic participation in the government of Northern Ireland, thus marginalizing extremists of all kinds, would be welcomed by most people in the UK. It would offer a positive framework within which constitutional loyalists and constitutional nationalists could work together ... It should provide the basis for progress towards a lasting peace settlement.

I pointed out in my covering letter to the Prime Minister that if the plan were implemented it would detach the constitutional nationalists from the hardline

Republican extremists and – what I had long strongly felt – that 'the restoration of some governmental activity in Ulster would focus local constitutional politicians on the practical bread-and-butter issues which concern their constituents and fill some of the current political vacuum in which violence and hopelessness breeds. That would make peace more possible.'

In a separate memo to Jonathan Powell, I urged that Blair should quickly pursue peace in Northern Ireland:

> Tony could really make historic progress there, providing he is brave but discreet in the early stages. For the first time in my lifetime I believe that the people there are ready for a settlement ... It must be based on the consent of the majority and the restoration of some representative institutions there. The biggest problem is not the IRA but whether the Protestant side has leaders of the calibre to deliver. Tony could lead them to a settlement.

Tony Blair did launch such an initiative in January of the following year, basing his peace bid on an elected assembly, on Sinn Fein involvement, cross-border activities, and a Council for the Isles, much in common with Trimble's final proposal. By then David Trimble, a seemingly impenetrable loner who rose rapidly from provincial politician to a courageous statesman on this issue, was a regular visitor to Number 10 and no longer needed a marginal agriculture minister as intermediary. But I had greatly enjoyed my Irish involvement. Not every practising Roman Catholic has the chance to play any role, however small, in the counsels of the Ulster Unionists – and this participation was only possible because it was secret from them.

Following these early policy contacts, I observed Tony Blair's Prime Ministership as closely as possible from my remote agricultural eyrie in Smith Square, trying to compare his qualities and the way he ran the Government with those of Harold Wilson and James Callaghan, with whom I had worked much closer. Of course Blair's political situation has been so far quite different, having a huge majority in the Commons and therefore usually no difficulty in controlling Parliament, and (so far) enjoying a healthy economy without the awful 1970s problems of high inflation, rising unemployment and a periodically collapsing sterling.

Blair is also very different from his Labour predecessors in style, in interests, and in his non-interests – in fact he is almost unique among modern Prime Ministers in that he appears not very interested in the economy (Anthony Eden was an earlier example of that deficiency), nor in Parliament, nor indeed in his Labour Party. He does little to encourage his natural constituency of party MPs in the Commons. He does not, as Wilson and Callaghan assiduously did, regularly visit the Commons tearooms or lunch with Labour backbenchers. Few of his chosen aides in Number 10 have much real knowledge of the Labour movement. In fact he personally appears not very interested in the nitty-gritty of party politics. Sometimes he appears positively to dissociate himself from it – and certainly (to my relief) from any old-style socialist dogma. But he is a man of high moral principles, unusual in modern politics.

Tony Blair is the product of his modern times which are very different from those in which Wilson and Callaghan operated decades earlier. His approach is more 'presidential', using the media to build an umbrella of support beyond party confines. Whereas Wilson was usually submerged in day-to-day political detail, Blair is always focussing on 'the big picture', seeking to knit Labour's 'soundbite' messages into a coherent picture which can be successfully sold at the next general election. Therefore presentation matters as much (though not more) than substance.

The media are central to his operational style because he accepted from the beginning that the media, however shabby some of them may be, have become central players in the British political game. Whereas Wilson and Callaghan when in Number 10 loathed most journalists and avoided them wherever possible, Blair seeks out the media to try to influence them for his own political purpose: a *Times* journalist told me in 1998 how that year he personally had been given four long private interviews with the Prime Minister on politics and policies. Few of Blair's own cabinet colleagues except perhaps Gordon Brown enjoyed that privileged access through the whole 1997–2001 Government – and Wilson in his 1974–6 administration did not give four interviews to all journalists in total.

Blair and the generation of New Labour politicians recognise that the modern media, while even more unaccountable and irresponsible than ever before, is now the most dominant political institution in the land with great destructive power. Seeing how the media had effectively destroyed Neil Kinnock's electoral chances and gravely damaged John Major's actually quite successful Conservative Government, Blair, Mandelson, Brown and their aides have sought positively to take on the media and to outmanoeuvre them through media management and 'spin'. As one proponent explained to me: 'We work on the basis that most journalists are idle or even drunk. So if we provide them with a story helpful to us, they would use that rather than make the effort of writing something less helpful.' It worked for a while and, partly through such a professional approach, Blair enjoyed one of the longest Prime Ministerial honeymoons in recent British history. But it always ran the risk of becoming counterproductive. Journalists, who long practised 'spinning' stories on their readership, were bound to protest violently when politicians adopted the same device in relation to the media.

The Prime Minister's main adviser in media management has been Alastair

Campbell, the former *Daily Mirror* lobby correspondent. As with Joe Haines under Harold Wilson, the Press Secretary in Number 10 inevitably becomes the most important aide working with the Prime Minister, because media coverage is today what matters most to any politician. On my observation Alastair Campbell is remarkably professional at his job. He has faced a much more powerful media than in my time in Downing Street, insisting on twenty-four hours' service, and he is an interesting mixture of being very tough on the surface, with practical political judgement about Labour politics, while underneath having strong emotions and sensitivities which make him more vulnerable than many in that hard trade. He has been a major political figure in recent political history, and Tony Blair has been lucky to have him at his side to fend off the relentless media barrage of triviality and negativism.

I myself do not like the slickness of New Labour, nor the lack of concern with old-fashioned substance on which my political generation was bred. But Tony Blair's achievements in radically reforming the Labour Party and winning two massive election victories were not fortuitous. He is a formidable political leader in the modern style and certainly a man of his time. But a feature of this present time is the impermanence of its values. What lasting imprints Tony Blair leaves on British government and society remain to be seen. That mainly depends on whether his administration manages actually to deliver and implement its promised reforms in its main policy areas. So far, education looks promising and the economy has been well managed. But transport is a continuing disaster and the plans to improve public sector management seem to have run into the sand. Labour's heroic efforts to preserve and improve the sponge-like National Health Service by throwing huge money at it may be frustrated by that huge bureaucracy – achieving more managers than beds or than nurses in 2002 was not to me impressive – and may leave the taxpayer with the pain of paying while the sick enjoy few benefits.

Britain's future role in Europe is a major issue which rumbles on, causing a rift across all parties. As the dominant Franco–German axis steamrollers further towards federal union (which I as a lifelong 'European' would vote against), then Britain has some tough decisions to take – and Tony Blair, as in the Iraq crisis (where I supported him), may find himself bravely but damagingly in a minority position which puts his leadership at risk (which Harold Wilson would never have done). His political 'umbrella' may be difficult to sustain over the longer term. Failing to control immigration – an issue which the liberal chattering classes for politically correct reasons refuse to confront but which deeply concerns ordinary voters – could also prove a damaging wild card. If Blair does not succeed in these main policy areas, then the rest is talk and air – or 'piss and wind' as the lads in Roade would say. Then the political and electoral future will depend on whether the Conservative and Liberal Democrat opposition can become sufficiently professional to exploit these failures.

I wrote to the Prime Minister on 27 January 1999 expressing my wish to retire from his government at any time convenient to him, giving the usual general reasons about wanting to spend more time on my private life, including horse racing, and not specifying my basic dissatisfaction with my recent ministerial life at MAFF – though this had been conveyed to friends in Number 10 on more than one occasion. He wrote back a very friendly letter saying: 'You have contributed enormously to the work of the Party and this Government as well as previous Labour Governments. I am very sorry that you will be leaving and quite understand your desire to pursue your other interests.' In his own hand he had added: 'Thank you for all you helped us to do. Yours ever, Tony.'

After that exchange, I continued as farming minister for another six months as I waited for the reshuffle, and I read again William Empson's poem 'Waiting for the End Boys, Waiting for the End'. As rumours of the reshuffle grew feverish in July 1999, Margaret Jay came to see me on the 20th, kindly saying that she hoped I would change my mind and stay in the Government and that this had also been expressed to her in Number 10. She enquired if I would be interested in Defence, where John Gilbert would be retiring. My spirits briefly quickened. I had always been interested in defence matters, adored military history and instinctively took to military men for their honesty and directness. Had I gone there in 1997, I would now have been happy to stay on. But I was already mentally and psychologically out of government. I loved Margaret and would do most things for her, but I shook my head.

The reshuffle was repeatedly delayed through endless media speculation. (Reshuffles should be executed unexpectedly.) But on the evening of 28 July I was summoned to the Prime Minister's room behind the Speaker's Chair in the Commons. It was an emotional time for me since I knew that my serious political career was now ending at this moment. The Prime Minister's then influential secretary, Anji Hunter, came out to give me a big hug and say she was sorry that I was going. (I recalled instantly that her predecessor Marcia Falkender had taken a different approach towards me.) His PPS Bruce Grocott – the best Labour holder of that office I saw – took me to sit in a small room belonging to the Lord Chancellor. Finally, I was called in. Alastair Campbell and Jonathan Powell exchanged friendly greetings and then withdrew to leave me alone with the Prime Minister, sitting on opposite sofas.

Tony Blair looked very tired and said that he did not enjoy reshuffles, but 'at least in your case it is not a sacking.' He kindly thanked me and generously said

'You have done a terrific job there', adding with a puzzled look: 'You seem to be very popular in the Lords and in the countryside.' We had a brief discussion on my earlier proposal to replace MAFF with a Ministry of Rural Affairs – 'we are working on that,' he said. (It was pledged in Labour's 2001 election manifesto and carried out after that election.) I rose and said 'You have much more important people to deal with than me', then we shook hands and I left. I walked back down the corridor to the Lords with a spring in my step.

Next morning, my first day of freedom, I went racing in the scorching sunshine of Glorious Goodwood. The following morning I set off to France with Sarah for our annual summer delights in Ceret. Not for one moment did I, then or since, regret my decision to leave. For the first time when 'out', I have not hankered to be back 'in' – perhaps reflecting a late developing maturity. Being a government minister had been in some ways fascinating and I was fortunate to have enjoyed that privilege, but I knew it was now time to move back into the deeper and more satisfying pleasures of private life.

Since resigning from MAFF in 1999 I have happily exercised the privilege of devoting my time to whatever interests me, making it one of the most enjoyable periods of my life. But I have in no sense retired from public life, continuing regularly to attend the House of Lords. I secured a valuable amendment to the 'Right to Roam' legislation, protecting racehorse trainers from dangerous encroachment by ramblers on their gallops (the only amendment which the Government accepted to that huge bill). But I speak only on issues where I feel I can contribute – not so far on agriculture, since my ministerial successors have problems enough there without my adding to them.

One question of particular interest to me has been the proposal to ban hunting with dogs, a sectarian measure deriving from Labour's massive, urban and under-occupied majority in the Commons. I have myself never hunted nor wish to do so. Only a minority of the public support the pursuit and only a minority strongly oppose it. The majority probably don't care much either way. But it is a traditional country sport and in my view, on libertarian grounds, those who want to pursue it should be left free to do so providing there is no avoidable cruelty involved. Opponents who passionately – and sometimes violently – seek to ban it seem to me to be often motivated more by class hatred of those who hunt rather than by any real concern with cruelty to animals. In fact, independent enquiries, such as the respected Burns Report, have shown that alternative forms of necessary fox control, such as shooting, trapping or poisoning, involve as much and usually more pain to the animals than hunting with dogs.

To try to meet legitimate concerns about animal suffering, I introduced to the Lords in 2001 and again in 2002–3 Private Bills amending the 1996 Wild Mammals (Protection) Act to stop deliberate and avoidable cruelty to animals and to eliminate the exemptions for hunting with dogs. It secured widespread support in the Lords where it was seen a sensible alternative to the Hunting Bill, without the latter's social divisiveness. Ironically, some 'banners' spoke against this reform, suggesting they cared more about the dogma of a ban than actually alleviating cruelty to animals. Sadly, some Labour Ministers seemed to reflect that dogmatic approach. I also took an active part during 2001–3 in devising the 'middle way' compromise of allowing hunting but only under licence, with monitoring of behaviour by hunts. I worked on this with three splendid MPs: Peter Luff from the Conservatives, Lembit Öpik from the Liberal Democrats and my old Labour friend Llin Golding. But it was to prove an uphill task facing the Labour 'chips-on-the-shoulder' brigade in full cry against the 'toffs' in scarlet jackets (in fact many working-class men follow the hunts, especially in upland regions).

The Labour manifesto at the 1997 election had promised to offer Parliament the opportunity to express its views on hunting, and this pledge was met in March 2001, shortly before the general election that May. The Commons and the Lords were offered a vote on a choice between three resolutions: to ban hunting outright, to leave the *status quo*, or to introduce our new 'middle way' compromise, which retained hunting but under strict licensing which would eliminate any unnecessary cruelty. In the Commons the huge Labour majority voted overwhelmingly for a ban. But in the Lords, actively encouraged by our Whips' office, I worked to raise support for our 'middle-way' compromise and wrote explaining it in the press. I also established contacts with Number 10, keeping them informed, and they in no way discouraged me. It seemed to me as an old Downing Street hand that our compromise offered the Prime Minister a New Labour way through, introducing a genuine reform and regulation of hunting while resisting the worst class hatred instincts of some of our Old Labour colleagues in the Commons. Tony Blair may have shared this view. At this time in March 2001, when I was also pushing my Wild Mammals Bill, I received a friendly letter from him saying: 'I do appreciate what you are trying to achieve ... I am most grateful for the constructive approach you have adopted.' It did not guarantee that he would have fought strongly for our middle way but it certainly showed that he might have appreciated a compromise to get him off the hook of a divisive ban which is not his style.

In the Lords debate on 26 March 2001, we were successful in weaning many Labour colleagues away from the ban option, which was defeated by 249 votes.

But to my dismay and anger the Tories, still today the largest party in the Lords despite all the media nonsense about 'Tony's Cronies' taking over the House, voted against the 'middle way' option and for the *status quo*. This was silly because the *status quo* had no hope of surviving under a Labour Government, and the only chance to preserve hunting was our proposal to put it under licence.

Even more inexplicably, the Countryside Alliance, established to preserve hunting, encouraged the Tories to vote against the middle way, resisting the common sense arguments of my Conservative friends William Astor and David Willoughby de Broke that they should take the only hope of preserving hunting in reality on offer. I could not believe my eyes when I saw senior Tories in the Chamber physically dissuading their fellow peers from moving to vote for the 'middle way'. The Tories were jubilant when the *status quo* option triumphed by 249 votes to 108 and the middle way lost by 202 to 122.

One Tory peer explained rather patronisingly to me that I might not understand how their tactic was 'very politically clever' and established a 'strong negotiating position' from which in future they might be prepared to compromise a little towards the middle way. I angrily responded to them and to the Countryside Alliance leaders that they now had no negotiating position; they had established nothing except an appearance of myopic intransigence; that the only hope (and it was only a hope, not a certainty) of protecting hunting from the zealots in the Commons was the middle way, because Number 10 just might be attracted to it as a way through in the coming election; and that the possibility of compromise had been on the table and they had rejected it. I shouted that they had 'betrayed the hunting community' – to which many of them, but not I, belonged. It seemed bizarre that I was fighting this cause of which I was not a part, when they, the hunters, through stupidity not ill will, were betraying it. Anyway, the vote left the apparent choice only between a ban or the *status quo* – and with a predicted landslide victory for Labour in the coming general election that was a one-way choice. I sensed that the hunting cause had suffered a serious and possibly fatal self-inflicted wound.

The new Labour Government overwhelming re-elected in May 2001 was committed to take the opinion of Parliament on banning hunting, and to implement that decision. Again the two Houses were presented with the three options of a ban, the *status quo*, or the middle way. The Commons again voted massively for a ban, virtually all that vote coming from the Labour ranks. Before the Lords debate on 19 March 2002 I networked vigorously with the Tories to change their foolish attachment to the *status quo*. Their influential hunting back-bencher Marcus Kimble admitted to me that their previous vote had been 'a great mistake' and he moved to switch the Tory position, as did Benjie Mancroft and David Willoughby de Broke. The Countryside Alliance also finally saw sense.

In the debate I was given the opening slot from the back benches to present the middle way option to a packed Lords chamber. Aware of my Labour colleagues' sensitivities on animal welfare, I stressed to them the well documented arguments that hunting with dogs is no more – and probably less – cruel than the alternative forms of fox control. To both Labour and Liberals I asserted that the proposed ban (coming mainly from urban politicians) was a breach of the liberties of country people. (Some Labour supporters are loudly in favour of 'minorities', but very selective on which minorities they care about.)

I turned to speak directly to the massed Tory benches and said straight that the political reality was that their preferred *status quo* was not actually on offer. The middle way was the only way to protect hunting. A large majority of the speakers from all sides, many with much greater knowledge and experience than me, supported this position. The small minority of Labour peers who spoke for a ban never engaged with our arguments on cruelty or country liberties. They simply and repetitively asserted that hunting is offensive to them, and of course, I accept that. But they have the right and freedom not to practise nor watch it, as we exclude ourselves from other traditional practices which we personally may find offensive. Personal distaste is not a good reason for legislation. To me this issue represented the familiar old battle in the Labour Party between cavaliers and puritan roundheads, and I have always been on the cavalier side. I am not actually pro-hunting; I am against a ban – and sometimes feel that the only fresh ban we need is a ban on bans.

This issue has also sadly shown the party in the Commons – since 1997 in a massive majority and often with little to occupy its time – reverting to its earlier instincts, based on class prejudice and deeply ingrained resentments. Whatever one's views on the particular question of hunting, it is politically crazy that a Labour Government with a massive future legislative programme of modernising Britain's social services, its law and order and its transport infrastructure, should waste valuable political energy on such a marginal and divisive issue. It would be sad if Tony Blair, who has done so much to lead New Labour away from its old 'politics of prejudice' towards a more tolerant and classless approach, should allow this breach of liberties to be imposed on the countryside by the puritan zealots – especially when public support for a ban has dropped by over 20 per cent to well below 50 per cent since we took office in 1997.

Peers from all sides voted with massive majorities of 257 against a ban and 307 for our middle way compromise. The latter majority was one of the biggest in the long history of the House of Lords (the figure on Gladstone's Ireland Home Rule Bill in 1893 was greater) – and this is Blair's reformed Lords of the new meritocracy, not the old House of the (now banished) hereditary landowners. Taking the two votes in the Lords and Commons together there was cumulatively a clear parliamentary majority for our middle way and against a ban. But so far there is no such convention of computing the overall majority in Parliament to establish its majority voice and will. Furthermore, all the relevant ministers in the new Department for Environment, Food and Rural Affairs, led by Alun Michael, personally had long track records of strong antipathies to hunting and were committed to a ban. Despite our great victory in the Lords, I knew the Commons was intractable and the future looked bleak on this issue.

After intensive consultations, Alun Michael – not an impressive minister – in late 2002 produced a Bill which was not the dogmatic total ban which zealots in the Commons wanted, but by its sole guiding principles of 'utility' and 'cruelty' – with no recognition of traditional country pursuits (putting fishing and shooting also under threat) – it suggested that hunting would be confined to upland areas. I welcomed that the Bill was not as extreme as we had feared, but regretted that it would lead to a serious diminution of traditional country life. The ultimate danger – manifesting at the time of writing – is that the Commons will amend it to a complete ban and the Government outrageously use the Parliament Act to enforce that sectarian view on the House of Lords. I would certainly vote against my Government on that.

Apart from these sporadic diversions into the political field, I now devote a great deal of happy time to the private interests and pleasures in my life: to Sarah, to my children, to old friends, and to Honey our beloved Jack Russell; to reading; to various charities, especially protecting maltreated horses; to watching football, rugby, cricket and horse racing. I took a major share (with David Lipsey, my son Stephen, Sarah's brother Charles and others) in a fine racehorse named Robber Baron, by the same sire as the dual Cheltenham Gold Cup winner Best Mate and trained like him by the adorable Henrietta Knight. After a decisive victory early in the 2002–3 season Robber Baron seemed to be well on on the way to following in the hoofprints of his famous relative, but sadly was then injured in a race at Cheltenham and removed from the fray for a long period of enforced rest. If nothing else, the experience proved to me that racing, like politics, is a highly risky business.

I continue to enjoy some lasting pleasures. One is listening to an ever-widening range of music on my wonderful new hi-fi systems – vinyl LPs with Linn and Brinkmann turntables, French Kora valves and German Brinkmann solid state amps, through French Reynaud and Swiss Piega speakers (audiophile lunatics like me will want the details). In racing, I chaired a committee of the British Horseracing Board which successfully lobbied to preserve exemption from VAT for racing expenses. I also returned to teaching, as a Visiting Professor at the

London School of Economics, once again enjoying the excitement of exposure to fresh young minds – half of my students foreign, reflecting the dramatic internationalisation of the LSE since I last lectured there. The School is more vibrant, dynamic and successful than ever.

Looking back along the wriggly path which I have travelled from the distant deprivations of Northamptonshire to the comforts of my present life in Berkshire and Belgravia, through the sunshine and shadows, I draw no portentous conclusions about life. I have certainly been very lucky in many ways, especially, unlike too many politicians, in having a precious and satisfying private hinterland apart from politics. I have enjoyed dabbling in so many exciting activities which were of interest and consequence, as were the distinguished people whom I worked alongside. My main recollections are of good people, including the many who helped and befriended me along the way. I shall continue to treasure their memories. There has also been for me occasional pain and a few, just a very few, seriously nasty individuals. But they can be happily forgotten. As Father Flanagan said: 'Life is too short to bother with cheap wine.'

Index

1945 general election, 42–43
1997 general election, 335, 336
1992 general election, 331
1974 general elections, 103–117, 145–146, 336
1974–1976 Wilson Government, 147–177, 341
1974 Wilson Government, 126–146
    leading figures in, 126–128
    reasons for failure, 128
1979 general election, 273, 274
1976 leadership election, 188
1964 Labour Government, 94, 95
1963 Dining Club, 95
1963 leadership election, 93–94

Abbado, Claudio, 298
Abbott, Manny, 39
Adams, Walter, 86
'Agreement to Differ', 151
Aherne, Bertie, 253
Aitken, Jonathan, 227
Albert, Michel, 47
Alderton, 4
Aldridge, Alan, 90
Alexander, Andrew, 111
Alexander, Laidon, 64, 67
Alexander, Stella, 66, 67
Allen, Douglas, 186
Allen, Graham, 325
Amis, Martin, 62
Anderson, Eric, 54
Andrews, Granny, 2, 6, 23, 27
Andrews, Maude, (Molly) (mother of BD), 3, 4,
    6–7, 9, 10, 11, 15, 18, 21, 22, 23–28, 30, 31, 32,
    34, 35,36, 46
Archer, Jeffrey, 227
Ardiles, Osvaldo, 62
Arlott, John, 325
Armstrong, Paddy, 217
Armstrong, Robert, 120, 121, 122, 124, 133, 134,
    137, 141, 146, 147, 148, 149, 152, 160, 202, 206,
    217, 222
    describes Harold Wilson's behaviour as
        'utterly contemptible', 148
    Marcia Williams wants sacked, 120, 122

Armstrong, Serena, 217, 218
Arnott, Elizabeth, 130, 240, 241
Arts Council, 330
Arwyn, Lord, 194, 203, 208, 213, 226
Ashby, Bucky, 39
Ashby, Walt, 21
Ashley, Jack, 142, 239
Ashton, 3, 4, 7, 8, 13, 14, 15, 19, 20, 23, 40, 121
Astaire, Jarvis, 197
Astor, William, 371
Attlee, Clement, 43, 88, 107, 126, 146, 190, 330
Auden, W. H., 58
    visit to Oxford, 58

Bacon, David, 89
Baldwin, Stanley, 146, 189, 230, 285
Balfour, Nancy, 77, 78
Balogh, Thomas, 131, 180
Bannister, Roger, 62, 89
Barber, Anthony, 103, 107
Barclay, Clifford, 89, 90, 91
Barclay, Stephen, 90
Barnes, John, 84
Barnett, Joel, 262
Barry, John, 288
Beatles, The, 85, 90, 297
Beattie, Alan, 84
Beaumont, Michael, 297
Beckett, Margaret, 343
Bedford, Deborah, 325
Bedford, Michael, 297, 302, 325
Bedser, Alec, 40
Behan, Brendan, 58, 65
Benn, Tony, 95, 102, 126, 127–28, 130, 131, 139,
    140, 141, 150, 151, 154, 161, 170, 176, 177, 186,
    238, 244, 247, 267, 269, 299
    attacks Policy Unit, 158
    'Bennery', 140, 142
    Denis Healey on, 141
    problem of, 141, 157–160
Berry, Anthony, 327
Berry, George, 327
Berry, Sarah (partner of BD), 78, 225, 300, 324,
    325, 326, 327, 336, 337, 343, 352, 359, 374

Best, George, 89
Bevan, Nye, 43, 88
Bevin, Ernest, 43
Biffen, John, 249, 284, 288
Binchy, Maeve, 57
Bingham Report, 253–254
Bishopsgate Investment Management (BIM), 303, 310, 311
Black, Jack, 293
Blackstone, Tessa, 83, 262, 350, 357
Blair, Lionel, 50
Blair, Tony, 92, 93, 103, 122, 123, 136, 234, 241, 243, 252, 275, 299, 325, 329, 331, 332, 333, 334, 335, 336, 337, 338, 340, 342, 352, 357, 360, 363, 364, 365, 366, 369, 371, 373
    BD's view of Premiership, 366–368
Blincow, Freddie, 40
Blisworth, 13, 39, 40
Blunkett, David, 364
Bohm, Ann, 83
Booth, Albert, 239, 240, 247, 262, 266
Boothroyd, Betty, 239
Booty, Jill (girlfriend of BD), 48–51, 53, 60, 61, 63, 64, 105, 300
Boston, Terry, 108, 112, 145, 147
Boswell, Tim, 362
Bower, Tom, 312
Boyd, Andrew, 77
Bradley, Tom, 92
Bragg, Melvyn, 62
Brasher, Chris, 62
Brayley, Lord, 181
    finances Political Office, 181
    resignation of, 181
Brew, John, 297
British Horse Industry Confederation, 352, 359
British Politics and the American War of Independence, 84
Brittan, Samuel, 249
Broadcasting Bill, 331
Brookeborough, Lord, 357
Brookes, Denis, 41
Broughton, Dr, 272, 273
Brown, Freddie, 41
Brown, George, 93
Brown, Gordon, 332, 352, 364, 367
Brown, Nick, 343, 347, 351, 352–357, 358, 359, 360, 363
    BD working with, 352–357
Brown, Ron, 91
Brown, Tina, 210, 293
Brownjohn, Alan, 57
BSE, 337, 338, 339, 344, 349, 350, 358
Burgess, Mrs, 56
Burnett, Alastair, 77, 293

Burrows, John, 91
Busby, Matt, 89
Bush, George, 317
Buswell, Angie, 328
Buswell, Mike, 328
Butler, David, 76, 77, 94
Butler, Rab, 33
Butler, Robin, 133, 164, 167, 168, 169, 202, 218, 324

Cabinet Office, 131, 132, 133, 141, 147, 148, 149, 167, 189, 221, 361
Callaghan, Audrey, 192, 234, 236, 248, 272, 274
Callaghan, James, 12, 59, 96, 116, 117, 118, 119, 126, 127, 128, 130, 140, 141, 148, 152, 153, 154, 155, 157, 158, 164, 168, 169, 175, 176, 177, 182, 183, 186, 188, 189, 191, 214, 222, 225, 226, 232, 233–250, 251–257, 258–281, 282, 296, 300, 336, 366, 367
    appointment of Government, 237–240
    appoints BD personal representative to
        Roman Catholic Church hierarchy in
        Britain, 253
    behaviour in 1979, 270–271
    BD makes ministerial suggestions to,
        239–240, 262
    character, 234–235, 261
    comment about Marcia Williams, 256
    decision on election timing, 257, 258–261
    dominates Margaret Thatcher in House of
        Commons, 236
    effect of 'crisis? what crisis?' headline, 266
    feelings on defeat, 279
    finding feet in Downing Street, 233
    future role of, 279
    Government of, 233–250, 251–253, 254–281,
        331, 341
        reasons for defeat of, 269
    in House of Lords, 328, 329
    in no-confidence debate, 272–273
    International Monetary Fund, 243–250
    lead over Margaret Thatcher in opinion
        polls, 257, 260, 276
    partnership with Harold Wilson, 127
    political abilities, 244–245
    political style, 235–236
    prime ministerial style, 235–236
    Ruskin speech, 234, 240–243
    speech writing, 258, 275–276
    view of Cabinet ministers, 248, 262, 268
    view of civil service, 270
    view of Policy Unit, 237
Callaghan, Michael, 274
Campaign for Democratic Socialism (CDS), 76,
    91–94, 95, 172, 263
    BD Secretaryship of, 92, 94

Campbell, Alastair, 367, 368, 369
Campbell Square School, 33–34, 39
Camp, Will, 197
Cannell, Lewis, 41
Carden, Richard, 361
Carey, Tommy, 42
Caritg, Dikkie, 244
Caritg, Josef, 244
Carlton, Ann, 174
Carmichael, Kay, 131
Carnegie, Elisabeth, 357
Carrier, John, 62, 82, 254
Carroll, Roger, 258, 275
Carter, Denis, 357
Carter, Sam, 39
Cassen, Robert, 83
Cassidy, Tony, 305
Castle, Barbara, 126, 127, 142, 154, 155, 159, 161,
    176, 177, 182, 186, 237, 239
Caunt, George, 218
Chamberlain, Neville, 16
Chapple, Frank, 266–267
Chataway, Chris, 62
Chequers, 132, 147, 149, 150, 152, 155, 162–163,
    178, 179, 180, 181, 190, 195, 200, 210, 217, 244
Chester, Norman, 76, 87, 89
Churchill, Winston, 8, 16, 43, 87, 88, 121, 178,
    186, 332, 338
City, The, 83, 90–91, 126, 140, 251, 282, 296–301
Clark, Peter, 297
Clarke, Charles, 364
Clarke, Percy, 103, 109, 275
Cleave, Maureen, 65
Clifford-Turner, Raymond, 327
Clinton, Bill, 333
Clinton-Davis, Stanley, 196, 338
    Marcia Williams approaches, 196
Coles, John, 21, 39
Common Agricultural Policy, 151, 337, 338, 340,
    341, 342, 344, 346–347, 350, 354, 356
Common Market, 107, 110, 118, 126, 128, 136,
    150–157, 213, 263, 278
    'Agreement to Differ', 151
    Cabinet meeting, 154–155
    Common Agricultural Policy, 151
    Dublin Summit, 153–154
    Harold Wilson's view of, 155–157
    renegotiations, 150–155, 213, 279
    referendum, 150, 151, 152, 155–157, 179,
        230
    Paris Summit, 152–153, 213
    see also European Union
Confederation of British Industry (CBI), 147
Connolly, Mike, 39
Cook, Robin, 330, 364

Cook, Trevor, 310, 314
Cooper, Jack, 80, 96
Cordle, John, 228
Corr, Jim, 130, 240, 278
Cosgrave, Liam, 205
Courteenhall, 20
Couzens, Ken, 167, 168
Cox, David, 82
Cox, Michael, 273
Crathorne, Lord, 198
Crick, Bernard, 84
Cripps, Cyril, 14, 15, 20, 40, 46, 53
Cripps, Stafford, 107
Crosland, Susan, 188
Crosland, Tony, 91, 92, 95, 126, 127, 131, 141,
    161, 172–173, 174, 175, 179, 186, 188, 189, 221,
    239, 240, 247
Crossman, Richard, 130
Cruikshank, Don, 283
Cudlipp, Michael, 78
Cunningham, Jack, 192, 331, 337, 338, 340–341,
    342, 343, 344, 345, 346, 347, 349, 351, 352, 353,
    354, 356, 359, 360, 361, 362, 363
    BD working with, 338, 340–341, 363
Curtis, Don, 39
Curtis, Tony, 39

Daily Express, 77, 110, 203, 204, 205
Daily Herald, 8, 9, 16, 42
Daily Mail, 77, 110, 112, 116, 203, 204, 209, 266,
    312
Daily Mirror, 114, 206, 258, 259, 301, 302, 316,
    317, 364, 367
Daily Telegraph, 110, 114, 211
Dainty, Miss, 19–20, 21, 24
Dalton, Hugh, 92
Davies, Gavyn, 130, 141, 160, 182, 184, 240, 246,
    247, 248, 250, 263, 267, 270, 276, 278
Davies, Hayden, 41
Davies, Percy, 41
Davies, Peter, 101, 103, 141, 144
Davison, Judy, 69
Day-Lewis, Cecil, 58
Dean, Annette, 63
Dean, Dixie, 63
de Gaulle, General, 156
Delfont, Bernard, 182, 194
Dell, Edmund, 170, 171, 174, 239
Denton, Tarpy, 8, 18
Departure,
    BD co-editor of, 57
Desai, Meghnad, 83, 325
devolution, 131, 175, 261, 270, 271, 272
Diamond, Jack, 95
Disraeli, Benjamin, 332

Docherty, Tommy, 187

Donnison, David, 83

Donohoe, Brian, 337

Donoughue, Agnes, (sister-in-law of BD), 264, 326

Donoughue, Bernard (BD), 3–375
    advisory role on Yes Minister and Yes Prime
        Minister, 131
    and Harold Wilson (HW), 101–125,
        126–146, 147–173, 174–192, 193–232
        BD first meeting with, 101
        BD offers to resign, 219–222
        BD's evaluation of, 229–232
        joins HW, 101–125
        offers BD headship of 'kitchen
            cabinet', 149
        opinion-polling, 101–104, 111, 112,
            115, 125
        role in Roy Jenkins's appointment to
            Home Office, 118–119
    and James Callaghan (JC), 233–250,
        251–257, 258–281
    appointed JC' s personal representative to
        Roman Catholic Church hierarchy in
    Britain, 253
    BD's ministerial suggestions to, 239–240,
        262
    and Joe Haines, 133, 147–149
    and Marcia Williams (MW), 111, 145, 147,
        148, 150, 202, 213, 214, 215, 216, 219–225
        attempts to get BD excluded from
            incomes policy development, 223
        BD confronts, 222–223
        BD suspected of leaking HW's resigna-
            tion, 183
        BD sympathy for, 203, 207
        has BD excluded from overseas visits,
            221–223
        obsession with BD, 224
        wants BD sacked, 147, 149, 211, 220
    and Margaret Thatcher,
        BD's first sight of, 94
        BD has tea with, 94
        waves at BD, 281
    and Robert Maxwell, 302–323
        departure from, 311
        First Tokyo Index Investment Trust
            (FTIT), 303, 304, 305–311, 319
            crisis in, 304–311
        London and Bishopsgate International
            (LBI), 302, 303, 304, 305, 306, 307,
            308, 309, 310, 311, 312, 313, 318
        proposed resignation from, 304–305
        role with, 303
        working for, 302–323

article in New Statesman, 74
at Economic Intelligence Unit, 283, 285
    Development Director of, 283
at Harvard, 68–70, 74
at London School of Economics (LSE),
    81–88
    resignation from, 282
at Oxford, 54–66
    co-editor of Departure, 57
    doctorate, 80
        publication of, 84–85
    finals, 66, 67
    literary editor of *Isis*, 56
    literary set, 56–59
    Lincoln College, 52, 53, 54, 55, 56, 59,
        61, 62, 66, 67, 68, 75, 297
    Nuffield College, 75, 76, 87, 91, 291
    presidency of Oxford Poetry Society, 57
    presidency of Writers' Club, 57
    vacations, 62–66
at Political and Economic Planning, 79–80
at *The Times*, 283–296
    advise Harry Evans against editorship,
        285
    Assistant Editor, 283–296
    departure from, 293–296
    first encounter with Rupert Murdoch,
        285
    on Harry Evans's resignation, 292–293
early years, 3–22, 23–28, 29–36, 37–54
    birth, 3
    break-up of family, 23–28
    childhood, 3–22
    cousins, 11, 12
    development of political views, 6, 15,
        17, 22, 42–43, 60–61
    formative influences, 3–22, 26, 27–28
    friends, 39–40, 46–47
    teenage years, 37–53
    town life, 29–36
        Upper Priory Street, 29, 32, 35, 53
    Waverley, 7, 8, 10, 11, 12, 13, 17, 19,
        24, 25, 27, 36, 37, 39, 43, 44, 46, 53,
        81, 88, 172, 264
education, 19–22, 33–34, 39, 44–53, 54–66
    Campbell Square School, 33–34, 39
    Northampton Grammar School, 39,
        44–46, 52–53
    Roade School, 16, 19–22, 33, 53
in Downing Street, 126–146, 147–173,
    193–232, 233–250, 251–257, 258–281
    arrival, 121–125
    dispute with *Private Eye*, 210–211
    on last weeks at Downing Street, 271
    on leaving Downing Street, 279–281

on 1979 election result, 278
on no-confidence debate, 273
Policy Unit, The, 117, 123, 124,
129–135, 147, 148–150, 158, 160,
170, 178, 183, 185, 186, 188, 189,
200, 203, 207, 216, 219, 220, 221,
222, 223, 224, 251, 260, 261–262,
263, 267, 270, 271, 274, 275 276,
278, 281, 329, 335
    acceptance by Whitehall, 131–135
    attacked by Tony Benn, 258
    Common Market renegotiations,
        150–155, 156
    'Concordat', 132, 133, 134
    economic policy, 138–141,
        243–250
    European Monetary System, 263
    farewell party for Harold Wilson,
        187–188, 197
    Handbook of Policies, 274
    Harold Wilson's view of, 117–118,
        129
    James Callaghan's view of, 237
    incomes policy, 160–169, 179,
        180, 223–224
    industrial policy, 252
    International Monetary Fund,
        245–247
    housing, 172–175
    'Little Things Mean a Lot', 135,
        143
    memos to Harold Wilson, 135, 50
    memos to James Callaghan, 240
    MISC 91, 163, 164, 166, 167
    MW attempts to have moved from
        Downing Street, 147–150, 221
    Northern Ireland, 135–138
    offer of post with, 117
    recruitment of staff, 129–131
    role of Treasury, 162–169
    Ruskin speech, 240–243
    sale of council houses, 173–175
    social policy, 142, 251–252
    staff shock at Harold Wilson's
        resignation, 183–184
    suite of rooms, 123–124
    'Themes and Initiatives', 233, 262
in Government, 336–363
    at Ministry of Agriculture, Fisheries
        and Food (MAFF), 337–364, 369
    departure from, 368–370
    proposes Department of Rural Affairs,
        342–343
    quarantine laws, 359–361
    working with Jack Cunningham, 338,

340–341
    working with Nick Brown, 352–357
in the City, 296–301, 302–323
    Grieveson Grant, 90, 140, 296, 297,
        300, 301, 302
    Kleinwort Benson, 297, 301, 302
    working for Robert Maxwell, 302–323
in the House of Lords, 328–331, 356–357
    energy portfolio, 329
    heritage portfolio, 329–331
    treasury portfolio, 329
interests,
    poetry, 57
    racing, 41–42, 328, 351, 369, 370, 374
    sport, 15, 40–42, 46–47, 61–62, 88–89,
        248, 253, 256, 325
London Arts Board, 320
London Symphony Orchestra, 298
lunch with Harold Macmillan, 84–85
'Occupying and Operating Number 10',
    334–335
on country pubs, 4
on Desert Island Discs, 297–298
on hunting, 12, 370–374
on left-wing of the Labour Party, 91
on political correctness, 330
on railways, 3, 8
on right-wing of the Labour Party, 91
on Tony Blair's Premiership, 366–368
peerage, 300
political activity, 101–375
    Campaign for Democratic Socialism
        (CDS), 76, 91–94, 95, 172, 263
        BD Secretaryship of, 92, 94
    campaigns for John F. Kennedy, 72–73
    declines parliamentary seat, 80, 96, 97
    involvement in Labour politics, 91–97,
        299–300
    role in February 1974 election, 104–117
    role in 1979 election, 274–279
    support for New Labour, 332–335
private life, 3–97, 254–257, 280, 300–301,
    324–328, 374–375
    aunt of, 25
    brother of, 4, 6, 7, 24–25, 26, , 34–35,
        36, 38, 39, 46, 48, 56, 96, 142, 172,
        264, 326, 327
        death of, 25, 326
    children of, 49, 81, 97, 255–256, 278,
        300, 326
    father of, 3–6, 8, 9, 14–15, 17, 21, 22,
        23–28, 29, 31, 32, 34, 35, 36, 37, 38,
        39, 42, 43, 46, 47, 48, 51, 52, 53, 62,
        63, 66, 96, 210, 326, 327
        death of, 96

father-in-law of, 96
girlfriend of, 48–51, 53, 60, 61, 63, 64,
   105, 300
grandmother of, 2, 6, 23, 27
house in Berkshire, 312, 327, 337, 374
house in France, 142, 244, 255, 257,
   258, 280, 311, 324–325, 352, 370
house in Suffolk, 97, 137, 255, 264,
   275, 280
mother of, 3, 4, 6–7, 9, 10, 11, 15, 18,
   21, 22, 23–28, 30, 31, 32, 34–36, 46
Parliament Hill Fields, 81, 82, 97
partner of, 78, 225, 300, 324, 325, 326,
   327, 336, 337, 343, 352, 359, 374
sisters of, 7, 10, 15, 23, 24, 35, 38, 39,
   326
uncle of, 4, 25
wife of, 59, 70, 71, 75, 78, 80, 81, 82,
   96, 124, 184, 214, 254, 275, 278, 300,
   301
   divorce, 300–301
publications,
   *British Politics and the American War of
      Independence*, 84
   *Herbert Morrison: Portrait of a
      Politician*, 85, 87, 88, 101, 194, 364
   Prime Minister, 177, 298
   The People into Parliament, 85
religion, 5–6, 326–327
Sports Council, 89, 90
   Committee of Enquiry into Football,
      89–90
travels abroad, 47, 67–80, 153–154, 256,
   320–322, 339–340
   year in the United States, 67–80
unemployment, 282–283
visit to Buckingham Palace, 120–121
Donoughue, Carol, (wife of BD), 59, 70, 71, 75,
   78, 80, 81, 82, 96, 124, 184, 214, 254, 275, 278,
   300, 301
   divorce, 300–301
Donoughue, Clem (brother of BD), 4, 6, 7, 24–25,
   26, 34–35, 36, 38, 39, 46, 48, 56, 96, 142, 172,
   264, 326, 327
   death of, 25, 326
Donoughue, John (Jack) (uncle of BD), 4, 25
Donoughue, Kate (daughter of BD), 81, 97, 255,
   300, 326
Donoughue, Lotte (aunt of BD), 25
'Donoughue luck', 5, 59
Donoughue, Molly, (sister of BD), 7, 15, 23, 24,
   35, 38, 39, 326
Donoughue, Paul (son of BD), 81, 97, 255
Donoughue, Rachel (daughter of BD), 49, 97,
   255, 278, 300, 326

Donoughue, Sheila, (sister of BD), 10, 23, 24, 35,
   38, 39, 326
Donoughue, Stephen, (son of BD), 81, 97,
   255–256, 278
Donoughue, Thomas Joseph (father of BD), 3–6,
   8, 9, 14–15, 17, 21, 22, 23–28, 29, 31, 32, 34,
   35, 36, 37, 38, 39, 42, 43, 46, 47, 48, 51, 52, 53,
   62, 63, 66, 96, 210, 326, 327
   death of, 96
Dooley, Mrs, 3
Douglas-Home, Alec, 290, 328
Douglas-Home, Charles, 287, 288, 289, 290, 291,
   293, 294, 295
Downing, George Sir, 122
Downing Street, 12, 48, 55, 82, 96, 97, 101–125,
   126–146, 147–173, 193–232, 233–250, 251–257,
   258–281, 295, 328, 329, 334, 335, 342, 351, 352,
   353, 355, 364, 365, 366, 367, 368, 369, 371, 372
   geography of, 122–125
   Political Office, 149, 181, 187, 191, 193, 194,
      195, 197, 213, 215, 218, 219, 227
   financiers of, 181
   Private Office, 133, 134, 155, 188, 190, 198,
      218, 222, 233, 251, 259, 270, 272, 276,
      277, 278
      Press Office, 190, 213, 220, 221
   under Harold Wilson, 101–125, 126–146,
      147–173, 193–232
   under James Callaghan, 233–250, 251–253,
      254–281
Downing Street in Perspective, 179
Duffy, Terry, 266
Dulay, Benson, 3
Dunkirk, 8, 19, 63

Economist, The, 77, 78, 283, 285
Economic Intelligence Unit, 283, 285
   BD Development Director of, 283
Eden, Anthony, 178, 366
Edward VII, 359
Eliet, Francoise, 57
Elliot, Alistair, 57
Ellis, Peter, 297
Emery, Fred, 286, 288
Empson, William, 57, 272, 369
Ennals, David, 239, 240, 251, 262, 266, 268
European Union, 339,340, 343–345, 345–347
   Common Agricultural Policy, 337, 338, 340,
      341, 342, 344, 346–347, 350, 354, 356
   lifting of beef ban, 343–345
   see also Common Market
evacuees, 10, 18–21
Evans, Harry, 82, 131, 183, 210–211, 283, 284,
   285, 286, 287, 288, 289, 290, 291, 292, 293, 294,
   331

Evans, Moss, 266, 268
Evening Standard, 207, 209, 312

Falkender, Marcia
  see Williams, Marcia
Faulkner, Brian, 137
Feversham, Polly, 326
Fiddling, Ken, 41
Field, Peggy, 185, 190, 206, 226
Field, Tony,
  see Arwyn, Lord
Financial Times, 110, 249, 301
Finer, Maurice, 142
First Tokyo Index Investment Trust (FTIT), 303,
  304, 305–311, 319
  crisis in, 304–311
First World War, 5, 8, 49, 142
Fischer, Annie, 69
Fischer, Ed, 69
Fisher, Alan, 266, 268, 269, 277
Fisher, Lord, 181, 228
Fisher, Mark, 331
Fitt, Gerry, 272, 273
Flanagan, Vincent, 326, 375
Fleet Street, 83, 25f4
Follows, David, 89
Foot, Michael, 88, 117, 124, 126, 128, 150, 154,
  159, 165, 166, 176, 177, 186, 189, 238, 247, 254,
  258, 261, 262, 273
Ford, Gerald, 255
Fowler, Gerry, 46–48, 56, 57, 59, 60, 66, 68, 105,
  death of, 48
Fowler, Lorna, 48
Fowles, John, 164
Freund, Otto Kahn, 83
Frost, David, 197, 199
Frost, Robert, 72

Gaitskell, Hugh, 76, 91, 92, 93, 95, 101, 332
  BD view of, 92
  death of, 92, 93
Galvin, Father, 6, 327
Gay Hussar, 76, 254, 295
George V, 154
George I, 123
Giddings, Donald, 40
Gilbert, John, 369
Gillinson, Clive, 298
Gilmour, Ian, 73
Giscard, President, 153, 212, 222, 238
Gladstone, William E., 332
Goldie, Grace Wyndham, 77
Golding, Llin, 371
Goldsmith, James, 181, 194, 195, 196, 197–199
  and Marcia Williams, 195

Goodman, Carol
  see Donoughue, Carol
Goodman, Geoffrey, 258
Goodman, 'Goodie' (father-in-law of BD), 96
Goodman, Lord, 182, 195, 199, 201, 202, 204,
  208, 209, 212, 220, 221, 227, 228
  described by Marcia Williams as 'evil', 202
  describes Marcia William's influence as
  'poisonous', 202
Gorbachev, Mikhail, 322
Gosling, Donald, 197, 228
Gould, Julius, 81
Gower, Jim, 83
Gowland, David, 130, 240
Grade, Lew, 182, 194
Graham, Andrew, 130, 138, 139, 141, 160, 162,
  167, 240, 250
Graham, Nori, 71, 325
Graham, Philip, 82, 325
Graham, Richard, 130, 141
Grant, Bruce, 71, 72
Grant, John, 293, 294
Grantham, Roy, 266
Greene, Graham, 254, 302, 325, 326
Greene, Vivian, 54, 55
Greenfield, Jean, 10
Greenfield, Mr, 10
Greenfield, Mrs, 10, 11
Gregor, Mr, 45
Grieveson Grant, 90, 140, 296, 297, 300, 301, 302
Griffin, Jim, 69
Grimley, Peter, 338, 353, 361
Grocott, Bruce, 357, 369
Gross, John, 57, 71
Guadeloupe trip, 265–266
Guardian, 283

Hahn, Frank, 83
Haines, Joe (JH), 101, 105, 106, 107, 111, 112,
  114, 117, 120, 121, 123, 124, 133, 134, 35, 136,
  137, 143, 144, 145, 146, 147, 148, 149, 152, 153,
  154, 155, 159, 161, 164, 165, 166, 167, 174, 179,
  180, 181, 184, 190, 191, 192, 193, 195, 197, 198,
  200, 202, 205, 206, 207, 208, 209, 210, 211,
  212, 213, 215, 217, 218, 219, 220, 221, 223, 224,
  225, 226, 240, 254, 259, 302, 312, 314, 367
  and Marcia Williams (MW),
  anger at MW's behaviour, 145
  attempts to have JH removed as speech
    writer, 143–144
  JH describe MW as 'our Lucretia
    Borgia', 112
  MW not authorise JH's hotel expenses,
    143–144
  MW's view of JH's influence, 101

at Buckingham Palace, 120
at Guildhall lunch, 181
belief in sale of council houses, 174
character, 105, 108
refuses peerage, 190, 193
Resignation honours list, 197
support for BD, 133, 147–149
The Politics of Power, 256
Halberstam, David, 69, 74
Hale, John, 51, 55
Hall, Stuart, 60
Halls, Michael, 212, 218
Hambro, Charles, 317
Hamilton, Jim, 297
Hampton, Lionel, 50
Hanberry, Lorraine, 71
Handler, Ariah, 181
Hanslope, 4, 15, 63
Hanson, James, 194, 197, 199
Harewood, George, 72
Harriman, Averell, 153
Harrington, Illtyd, 197
    and Marcia Williams, 197
Harris, John, 119, 120, 182
Harris, Ralph, 140
Harrison, Walter, 159, 273
Hart, Judith, 159
Hart, Teresa, 361
Hartwell, 4, 13, 19, 20
Harvard, 68–70, 74
Hattersley, Roy, 155, 239, 240, 254, 262, 265, 267,
    268, 269, 273
Havers, Lord, 317
Hayden, Robin, 124
Hayman, Helene, 82, 352
Hayward, Ron, 102, 109, 275
Healey, Denis, 116, 118, 126, 127, 138–139, 140,
    141, 148, 160, 161, 162, 163, 164, 166, 167, 169,
    170, 179, 180, 183, 186, 188–89, 239, 240, 244,
    245, 246, 247, 248, 249, 258, 262, 267, 268, 273,
    299, 300
    on Tony Benn, 141
Heath, Edward, 103, 104, 106, 107, 110, 111, 112,
    115, 116, 117, 118, 121, 122, 124, 136, 138, 143,
    144, 147, 150, 156, 157, 160, 165, 184, 198, 277,
    316
Herbert Morrison: Portrait of a Politician, 85, 87,
    88, 101, 194, 364
Henderson, David, 54, 55
Heseltine, Michael, 60, 278, 314, 362
    view of civil service, 362
Hesketh, Lord, 42, 328
Hewlett-Davies, Janet, 179, 181, 188, 190, 197,
    212, 213, 224
Heyworth, Lord, 80

Hickey, Owen, 286, 292
Hickling, Donald, 45, 52
Higgins, Andrew, 359
Himmelweit, Hilde, 83
Hindell, Keith, 79
Hobbs, Mrs, 20, 21
Holden, Anthony, 286, 288, 289, 291
Hollis, Patricia, 357
Holloway, Mr, 45
Horton, Brian, 288, 289
Hoskyns, Catherine, 58
Housden, Bill, 120, 147, 148, 149, 179, 181, 183,
    191, 193, 196, 202, 210, 211, 212, 213, 214, 218,
    219, 220, 221, 222, 223, 226, 228, 244, 256
    and Marcia Williams, 202, 212, 218–219,
    228
Howard, Anthony, 60
Howard, Jim, 13, 39
Howe, Geoffrey, 80, 249, 289
Howell, Denis, 88–89, 92, 95, 262, 300, 331
Hughes, Cledwyn, 300
Hughes, Spike, 51
Hume, Basil, 253
Hunt, Arthur, 29, 30, 31, 32, 35
Hunt, John, 131–132, 133, 148, 176, 180, 186
Hunt, Pee Wee, 51
Hunter, Anji, 369
Hurd, Douglas, 316
Husbands, Norman, 6
Hussein, Saddam, 128

Ingleby-Mackenzie, Colin, 337
Ingleby-Mackenzie, Susan, 337
Inside Number 10, 146
Institute of Economic Affairs (IEA), 140
International Monetary Fund (IMF), 170,
    243–250, 251, 252
Ireland, 11, 64–65
Irish Republic Army (IRA), 136, 137
Irvine, Derry, 83, 357
Irving, Sydney, 273
Isaacs, Jeremy, 60
Isis, 56, 60
    BD literary editor of, 56

Jay, Anthony, 131, 297
Jay, Margaret, 279, 325, 328, 329, 357, 369
Jay, Peter, 249
Jenkins, Clive, 91
Jenkins, Peter, 194
Jenkins, Roy, 92, 95, 116, 117, 118, 119, 120, 124,
    126, 127, 128, 150, 151, 152, 154, 157, 159, 176,
    177, 179, 182, 185, 186, 188, 189, 230, 232, 238,
    239, 249, 300
Jennings, Elizabeth, 57

Jimenez, Juan Ramon, 50
Johnson, Derek, 62
Johnson, Frank, 286
Johnson, Harry, 83, 249
Johnson, Luke, 296
Johnson, Lyndon, 141
Johnson, Richard, 39
Jones, Elwyn, 124, 176, 317
Jones, George, 84, 85, 86, 87, 92, 220, 221
Jones, Jack, 166
Joseph, Keith, 249
journalism, 74, 75, 77–79, 80, 282–296
Jowell, Tessa, 254, 262
Judd, Frank, 338

Kagan, Joe, 181, 193, 197, 198, 202, 215, 228
    and Marcia Williams 194
    finances Political Office, 194
    imprisonment of, 181, 194
Kaufman, Gerald, 120, 170, 180, 181, 220, 299
Kedourie, Elie, 84
Kemsley, Viscount, 78
Kennedy, Jackie, 72
Kennedy, John F., 72–73, 118, 298, 332
    BD campaigns for, 72–73
Keys, Bill, 295
Kiely, Benedict, 64
Kimble, Marcus, 372
King, Anthony, 92, 94
Kinnock, Neil, 8, 239, 275, 300, 317, 319, 331,
    333, 367
Kissin, Harry, 101, 194, 201, 220, 221, 228
    view of Marcia William's influence, 101
Kissinger, Henry, 223
kitchen cabinet, 104–105, 106, 119, 134, 149, 231
    BD offered headship of, 149
Kleinwort Benson, 297, 301, 302
Knight, Andrew, 285, 287
Knight, Henrietta, 374
Knight, Laura, 82
Knight, Maggie, 49, 53, 64
Knight, Nell, 49, 53, 64
Knox, Brian, 184, 297
Konstant, Bishop, 253
Kuehl, Jerry, 69

Labour Party, 42, 43, 61, 62, 76, 86, 88, 102, 156
    developments in, 331–335
    left-wing of, 102
    National Executive Committee, 114, 154,
        179, 180, 255
    splits, 95
    Transport House, 102, 107, 108, 109, 111,
        114, 116, 143, 192, 273, 274, 275, 277
    inefficiencies of, 108–109

Laing, Bill, 10, 19
Laing, Linda, 10, 19
Lamb, Editha, 24
Lambton, Lord, 204
Lamont, Norman, 316
Lancaster, Terry, 206
land deals scandal, 202–208, 211, 212
Langford, Paul, 54
Larkin, Philip, 57
Laski, Harold, 83
Lawson, Nigel, 80, 362
    view of civil service, 362
Lebrecht, Andy, 361
Lee, Peggy, 51
Lees, Mr, 45
Leger, Eliane, 47, 244
Leger, Jean-Francois, 47, 244
Lester, Anthony, 68
Letter of Intent, 247–248
Letwin, Oliver, 84
Lever, Diane, 96
Lever, Harold, 95, 141, 148, 171, 173, 182, 183,
    191, 194, 201, 208, 220, 221, 223, 232, 247,
    258, 261, 263, 300
Levi, Peter, 57
Lewis, John L., 74
Lib-Lab pact, 251, 253, 258
Liddell, Helen, 312
Lincoln College, 52, 53, 54, 55, 56, 59, 61, 62, 66,
    67, 68, 75, 297
Lindstrom, Mrs, 56
Lipsey, David, 131, 174, 240, 275, 276, 374
'Little Things Mean a Lot', 135, 143
Livingstone, Jock, 41
Lloyd, Liz, 360
Lloyd George, David, 332
Logue, Christopher, 60
London and Bishopsgate International (LBI), 302,
    303, 304, 305, 306, 307, 308, 309, 310, 311, 312,
    313, 318
London School of Economics (LSE), 68, 80,
    81–88, 91, 96, 101, 108, 128, 175, 178, 184,
    249, 254, 282, 297, 374
    BD at, 81–88
    BD resignation from, 282
Long, Gerald, 286
Long Buckby, 46, 78
Longford, Lord, 328
Lonsdale, Roger, 56, 66
Lorca, Garcia, 50
Lord North Street, 106, 107, 108, 110, 112, 113,
    117, 123, 124, 143, 182, 183, 196
Lowson, Robert, 361
Luff, Peter, 371
Lynn, Jonathan, 131, 297

Lynn, Vera, 16
Lyons, Denis, 143, 144

Macarthur, Brian, 286
McCaffrey, Tom, 192, 258, 259, 266, 270
MacBeth, George, 57
MacDonald, Ian, 305
Macintyre, Donald, 293, 294
Mackay, Dave, 187
Maclachlan, Donald, 80
Macmillan, Harold, 42, 76, 79, 84–85, 328, 332
    BD has lunch with, 84–85
Maddox, Bronwen, 296
Major, John, 42, 136, 177, 344, 345, 367
Mancroft, Benjie, 372
Mandela, Nelson, 325
Mandelson, Peter, 88, 275, 332, 333, 364, 367
Manningham-Butler, Reginald, 42
Mar, Countess of, 348
Marlborough, Duke of, 332
Marquand, David, 92, 95
Marshall, Jim, 273
Martin, Kingsley, 74
Mason, Roy, 170, 176, 253, 273
Maxwell, Ian, 314, 318
Maxwell, Joe, 20, 21, 22, 52, 53
Maxwell, Kevin, 301, 303, 304, 312, 314, 318
Maxwell, Robert, 283, 301, 302–323
    access to Eastern European leaders, 321–322
    BD working with Robert Maxwell, 302–323
    BD's departure from, 311
    BD's proposed resignation from, 304–305
    BD's role with, 303
    character, 311–312, 315–323
    death of, 312
Mayne, John, 255
McCartney, Paul, 90
McElhone, Frank, 109
McGrath, John, 57
McInroy, Alan, 304, 305
McIntosh, Andrew, 357
McNally, Tom, 192, 222, 234, 258, 259, 261, 266, 268, 270, 272
Mellish, Bob, 142, 159
Michael, Alun, 373, 374
Middleton, Lord, 357
Middleton, Peter, 169
Midgely, John, 77
Miliband, Ralph, 84
Millan, Bruce, 171, 172, 239, 240, 262
Miller, Eric, 181, 188, 195, 196, 199, 215, 228
    finances Political Office, 191
    relationship with Marcia Williams, 188, 195–196
    suicide of, 181, 196

Miller, Keith, 41
Miller, Mrs, 196
Millhench, Ronald, 203, 207
ministerial memoirs, 176–177
Ministry of Agriculture, Fisheries and Food (MAFF),
    BD at, 337–363
    cultural characteristics, 358–363
Minogue, Kenneth, 84
Mirror Group, 303, 306
Mitchell, Adrian, 57, 59
Mitterand, Francois, 317
Monk, Thelonius, 74
Monk Bretton, Lord, 357
Montgomery, David, 365
Mooney, Lewis, 331
Morgan, John, 307
MORI, 103, 125
Morishima, Michio, 83
Morley, Elliot, 341, 352, 353, 354, 355, 356, 359, 362
Morley, Mr, 33
Morris, Alf, 142, 239
Morris, John, 239, 262
Morrison, Herbert, 43, 85, 87, 88, 101, 120, 158, 297
    BD joint biography of, 85, 87, 88, 105, 194, 364
Moser, Claus, 83, 283, 297
Mowlam, Mo, 330–331
Mulley, Fred, 239, 240, 241, 262
Murdoch, Iris, 58
Murdoch, Rupert, 79, 283, 284, 285, 286, 287, 288, 289, 291, 292, 294, 295, 296, 331
Murphy, Pat, 79
Murray, Albert, 104, 108, 112, 113, 114, 120, 121, 134, 143, 145, 148, 149, 155, 179, 180, 181, 182, 190, 193, 195, 196, 197, 202, 204, 205, 206, 207, 208, 210, 212, 213, 214, 215, 216, 218, 219, 222, 223, 226, 227, 267
    and Marcia Williams (MW), 145, 202, 207, 215, 218, 219
        excluded from lunch by MW, 218
        pay cheque withheld by MW, 218
    death of, 104
Murray, Anne, 214, 218
Murray, Keith, 54

Nash, Paul, 82
Naylor, Connie, 32
Nelson, Horathio, 332
Nettleton, Joan, 46
Nettleton, Martin, 44, 45, 46, 48, 52, 53, 54, 66
New Labour, 93, 109, 234, 331, 332, 373
    BD support for, 332–335

New Left Review, 60
News of the World, 209, 212, 364
Nickinson, Heald, 293
no-confidence motion, 272–274
Northampton, 4, 5, 6, 10, 11, 13, 15, 16, 17, 19, 22, 24, 27, 28, 29–36, 37, 39, 44, 49, 61
Northampton Grammar School, 39, 44–46, 52–53
Northern Ireland, 135–138, 175, 175, 211–212, 230, 253, 364–365
Nuffield College, 75, 76, 87, 91, 291
Nutter, Albert, 41

Oakeshott, Michael, 83–84
Oakeshott, Walter, 54
O'Brien, Patrick, 324–325
O'Kennedy, Michael, 253
Oldfield, Norman, 41
Öpik, Lembit, 371
Orme, Stan, 239, 247
Orr, Robert, 84
Orwell, George, 293
Osborne, Tom, 50
O'Toole, Peter, 67
Ovington, Mrs, 20
Owen, David, 95, 128, 239, 240, 258, 262, 267, 268, 275, 300
Owen, John, 55, 66, 75
Oxford, 12, 30, 36, 45, 46, 48, 51, 52, 53, 54–66, 67, 68, 69, 75
    finals, 66, 67
    Lincoln College, 52, 53, 54, 55, 56, 59, 61, 62, 66, 67, 68, 75, 297
    literary set, 56–59
    Nuffield College, 75, 76, 87, 91, 291
    Oxford Poetry Society, 57, 78
        BD Presidency of, 57
    Writers' Club, 57, 58
        BD Presidency of, 57
    vacations, 62–66

Packer, Richard, 346, 351, 355, 357, 362–363
    contempt for ministers, 362
Paget, Dorothy, 42
Palmerston, Viscount, 332
Panufnik, Camilla, 336
Pardoe, John, 94, 117
Parkinson, Michael, 297
Parliament Hill Fields, 81, 82, 97
Parry, Glenys, 8
Pearson, Garry, 60
Peart, Fred, 154, 262
Pechet, Maurice, 69, 70
Pendry, Tom, 187, 331
Perkins, Eliot, 70, 74
Perkins, Mrs, 70

Peston, Maurice, 83, 338
Peyton, Lord, 349
Philip, Prince, 187
Piachaud, David, 83, 130, 161
Pickles, Bill, 84
Pickstock, Frank, 92
Pickthorne, Kenneth, 52
Pliatzky, Leo, 173, 245
Plowden, William, 77, 84
Plurenden, Lord, 181, 194, 208, 215, 228
    described as 'a double agent to the Russians', 181
    finances Political Office, 181
Policy Unit, The, 117, 123, 124, 129–135, 147, 148–150, 158, 160, 170, 178, 183, 185, 186, 188, 189, 200, 203, 207, 216, 219, 220, 221, 222, 223, 224, 251, 260, 261–262, 263, 267, 270, 271, 274, 275–276, 278, 281, 329, 335
    acceptance by Whitehall, 131–135
    attacked by Tony Benn, 258
    Common Market renegotiations, 150–155, 156
    'Concordat', 132, 133, 134
    economic policy, 138–141, 243–250
    European Monetary System, 263
    farewell party for Harold Wilson, 187–188, 197
    Handbook of Policies, 274
    Harold Wilson's view of, 117–119, 129
    James Callaghan's view of, 237
    incomes policy, 160–169, 179, 180, 223–224
    industrial policy, 252
    International Monetary Fund, 245–247
    housing, 172–175
    'Little Things Mean a Lot', 135, 143
    memos to Harold Wilson, 135, 50
    memos to James Callaghan, 240
    MISC 91, 163, 164, 166, 167
    Northern Ireland, 135–138
    offer of post with, 117
    recruitment of staff, 129–131
    role of Treasury, 162–169
    Ruskin speech, 240–243
    sale of council houses, 173–175
    social policy, 142, 251–252
    staff shock at Harold Wilson's resignation, 183–184
    suite of rooms, 123–124
    'Themes and Initiatives', 233, 262
Political and Economic Planning, 79–80
Political Honours Scrutiny Committee, 198
Political Office, 149, 181, 187, 191, 193, 194, 195, 197, 213, 215, 218, 219, 227
    financiers of, 181
Pollard, Mrs, 193, 219

Pomonti, Jacques, 47
Popper, Karl, 83
Porchester, Lord, 89, 221
Poscotis, Harry, 38
Powell, Enoch, 111, 112, 128, 157
Powell, Jonathan, 334, 365, 366, 369
Prentice, Reg, 154, 159, 241
Prescott, John, 343
Press Complaints Commission, 312–313
Press Office, 190, 213, 220, 221
Prime Minister, 177, 298
privacy law, 205
Private Eye, 183, 197, 210–211
Protestant Workers' Strike, 137
Public Enterprise Committee, 140
Putnam, Clarence, 39
Puttnam, David, 228

Queen, Her Majesty The, 72, 118, 120, 180, 186, 187, 190, 192, 221

Radcliffe, Lord, 176
Radd, Donald, 50
Rayne, Max, 199
Reagan, Ronald, 317, 346
Reed, Celia, 82, 325
Reed, Tom, 82, 325
Rees, Merlyn, 258, 261, 273
Rees, Peter, 154
Rees-Mogg, William, 284, 287, 290
Riccardo, Boss, 171
Richard, Ivor, 338, 357
Richardson, Gordon, 160, 163, 164
Richardson, Ray, 96
Richman, Alf, 145, 147
Ridley, Nicholas, 249
Rippon, Geoffrey, 317
Roade, 4, 6, 7, 8, 11, 12–14, 16, 17, 18, 19, 23, 24, 25, 26, 27, 29, 31, 33, 35, 36, 37, 39, 44, 48, 49, 51, 52, 56, 62, 63, 64, 82, 96, 121, 172, 326, 368
Roade School, 16, 19–22, 33, 53
Robbins, Lionel, 87, 297
Robens, Lord, 291
Roberts, Ben, 80, 86
Rockefeller, Nelson, 223
Rodgers, Bill, 85, 92, 93, 95, 128, 239, 240, 262, 267, 268, 300
Rooker, Jeff, 199, 341, 343, 345, 350, 352, 353, 354, 355, 356, 359, 363
Rose, Carol, 74
Rose, Michael, 74
Ross, Willie, 171, 172, 174, 237, 239
Rothschild, Jacob, 350
Routledge, Paul, 294
Royal Commission on Legal Services, 176

Royal Commission on the Press, 209
Russell, Alan, 68, 82
Ryder, Richard, 276

Sadat, President, 256
Sainsbury, David, 164
sale of council houses, 173–175, 230, 278, 299
Samuels, Ralph, 60
Sarbanes, Paul, 69, 153
Scanlon, Hugh, 166
Scarborough Conference, 92
Scargill, Arthur, 294, 329
Schapiro, Leonard, 84
Schlesinger, Arthur, 118
Schmidt, Helmut, 152, 153, 154, 213
Schon, Frank, 194, 208, 215, 228
Scotland, Patricia, 357
Scott, Derek, 270
Scottish Nationalists, 261, 272
Searby, Richard, 291
Second World War, 16–19, 88
Self, Peter, 84
Sen, Amartya, 83
Shawcross, Hartley, 292
Shepherd, Malcolm, 154
Sherman, Alfred, 80
Shock, Maurice, 54
Shore, Peter, 119, 124, 150, 154, 155, 175, 183, 221, 247, 262, 268
Short, Ted, 183, 237
Silkin, John, 198, 223, 238, 240, 247, 262
Silkin, Sam, 317
Sinatra, Frank, 216
Slater, James, 195
Smethurst, Richard, 130, 240
Smith, Andrew, 303, 304, 306, 314, 318
Smith, Godfrey, 78, 79, 295
Smith, John, 239, 240, 262, 273, 288, 317, 331–332, 333
Smith, Mathew, 82
Smurthwaite, Geoffrey, 19, 31
Smurthwaite, Mrs, 19, 31
Snell, Gordon, 57, 64, 65, 67
social contract, 107, 110, 115, 144
Social Democratic Party (SDP), 92, 286, 299, 300, 333
Soulsby, Lord, 357
South Africa sanctions, 253
Spectator, 73, 220, 221
Spellar, John, 345
Spender, Stephen, 58
Sports Council, 89, 90
      Committee of Enquiry into Football, 89–90
Stanley, Lord, 357
Stannard, Simon, 340, 361

Stebbing, Mr, 45
Steel, David, 261
Stephens, Alan, 314
Stevens, Caroline, 276
St John Stevas, Norman, 77
Stoke Bruerne, 4, 15, 63
Stone, Joe, 180, 210, 213, 214, 222
Stony Stratford, 7, 13, 15, 24, 36
Stothard, Peter, 286
Stott, Roger, 272
Stowe, Kenneth, 133, 165, 166, 167, 176, 183, 184, 186, 187, 190, 197, 198, 223, 224, 233, 236, 253, 267, 276, 277, 279, 281
Straw, Jack, 364
Stuart, Nick, 184
student protests, 85–87
Sumac, Yma, 51
Summerbee, Mike, 187
Sun, 258, 275, 285
Sunday Telegraph, 80
Sunday Times, 78–79, 82, 183, 198, 199, 210, 238, 283, 284, 286, 287, 295, 298
Sunningdale Agreement, 136
Swain, Tom, 273
Symons, Liz, 357

Tapley, Mark, 304, 307, 310, 311
Tarry, Mr, 10
Taverne, Dick, 92, 95
Taylor, A. J. P., 55
Taylor, Ann, 273, 352
Taylor, Mr, 37
Terry, John, 197
Terry, Walter, 205
Thatcher, Denis, 94
Thatcher, Margaret, 77, 80, 83, 94–95, 115, 144, 158, 168, 175, 177, 179, 184, 191, 233, 241, 243, 245, 257, 249, 250, 252, 257, 259, 260, 262, 263, 264, 268, 269, 272, 273, 275, 275, 277, 281, 284, 285, 286, 288, 296, 299, 300, 316, 322, 329, 331, 346, 362
    BD has tea with, 94
    BD's first sight of, 94
    James Callaghan dominates in House of Commons, 236
    James Callaghan's lead over in opinion polls, 257, 260, 276
    in House of Lords, 328
    waves at BD, 281
The People into Parliament, 85
The Politics of Power, 256
Thomas, Dylan, 58
Thomson, Lord, 283
Thorpe, Jeremy, 117, 181, 185, 204
Thwaite, Anthony, 57

Times, The, 82, 131, 199, 212, 249, 253, 283–296, 331, 367
    BD at, 283–296
Timms, Kate, 361
Tindemans, Leo, 164
Titmuss, Richard, 83, 130
Tongue, Mr, 45
Trachtenberg, Larry, 303, 304, 305, 306, 309, 311, 312, 314, 318
trade union movement, 79, 260, 263–271
Trades Union Congress (TUC), 124, 143, 144, 147, 167, 238, 258, 259, 264, 295
Transport House, 102, 107, 108, 109, 111, 114, 116, 143, 192, 273, 274, 275, 277
    inefficiencies of, 108–109
Treasury, 162–169
Trend, Burke, 54, 186
Trevor-Roper, Hugh, 55
Trimble, David, 365, 366
Turnball, Andrew, 169
Tusa, John, 293
Tyerman, Donald, 77, 78
Tyson, Frank, 41

Ulmann, Dick, 69
Ulster Unionists, 136, 253, 261, 272, 273
Upper Priory Street, 29, 32, 35, 53

Vaizey, John, 182, 194, 197
    and Marcia Williams, 194
Varley, Eric, 155, 159, 170, 171, 239, 262
Vickers, Alfred, 82
Victor, Mr, 254, 295

Walden, Brian, 92, 95
Walker, David, 286
Walker, Peter, 313, 316
Walpole, Robert, 123, 162
Walsh, Joe, 346
Walters, Alan, 83, 249
Warner, Bill, 32–33
Warren, Freddie, 198
Watson, Mrs, 20
Waugh, Auberon, 210
Waugh, Evelyn, 324
Waverley, 7, 8, 10, 11, 12, 13, 17, 19, 24, 25, 27, 36, 37, 39, 43, 44, 46, 53, 81, 88, 172, 264
Webster, Bernard, 39
Wedderburn, Bill, 83
Weidenfeld, George, 177, 182, 187, 194, 197, 220
    and Marcia Williams, 194
    BD at party of, 194
Weighell, Sid, 266–267
welfare state, 43, 52, 271–272
Welsh nationalists, 261

welfare state, 43, 52, 271–272
Welsh nationalists, 261
West, Don, 39
West, Trevor, 253
Westminster, 76, 83, 127, 198
White, Don, 41
White, Sean, 64
Whitehall, 12, 55, 76, 83, 122, 123, 127, 129, 130, 131, 132, 133, 134, 136, 140, 141, 142, 157, 162, 163, 167, 168, 169, 175, 176, 184, 185, 198, 211, 219, 220–222, 227, 235, 241, 243, 245, 246, 265, 269, 270, 281, 339, 343, 351, 358, 359, 361, 362
Whitehead, Phillip, 239
Whitty, Larry, 357
Wickes, Nigel, 133, 169
Wigg, George, 123, 205, 211, 212
Willett, George, 305, 307, 310
Williams, Charles, 312, 314, 317
Williams, Gareth, 357
Williams, Marcia, 48, 101, 105, 106, 108, 109, 111, 112, 113, 114, 116, 117, 119, 120, 121, 122, 123, 134, 143, 144, 145, 146, 147, 148, 149, 152, 155, 156, 157, 178, 179, 180, 181, 182, 183, 185, 186, 187, 190, 191, 192, 193–232, 256, 329, 369
    abilities, 201–202
    and Albert Murray (AM), 145, 202, 207, 215, 218, 219
        AM excluded from lunch, 218
        AM's pay cheque withheld, 218
    and Bernard Donoughue (BD), 111, 145, 147, 148, 150, 202, 213, 214, 215, 216, 219–225
        attempts to get BD excluded from incomes policy development, 223
        BD confronts, 222–223
        BD suspected of leaking HW's resignation, 183
        BD sympathy for, 203, 207
        has BD excluded from overseas visits, 221–223
        obsession with BD, 224
        wants BD sacked, 147, 149, 211, 220
    and Bill Housden, 202, 212, 218–219, 228
    and civil service, 120, 122, 133, 146, 213–214, 215
    and Frank Sinatra, 216
    and Harold Wilson (HW), 193–232
        attempts to delay HW's resignation, 178, 179, 180, 181, 212
        behaviour at Harold Wilson's final lunch as Prime Minister, 190
        controls access to HW, 201
        describes HW as 'King Rat', 207
        diverts HW, 112, 147–150, 202–208, 209–219, 225

        explanations for influence over HW, 226–229
        influence over HW, 105, 106, 145, 152, 200–201
        insists HW not lunch with staff, 144, 216–217
        HW fearful of, 199, 200, 203, 227
        HW hides from, 200
        HW wonders if 'going round the bend', 217
        HW's desire to placate, 152
        MW alleges affair with, 226
        squabbles with HW, 147, 196, 197, 214, 215, 220
        threatens to destroy HW, 203, 207, 212, 227
        treatment of HW, 146, 190, 199–200, 203, 205, 206, 207, 212–213, 214, 216, 217
    and Illtyd Harrington, 197
    and James Goldsmith, 195
    and Joe Haines (JH), 145, 146, 147, 207, 219
        anger at MW's behaviour, 145
        attempts to have JH removed as speech writer, 143–144
        JH describe MW as 'our Lucretia Borgia', 112
        not authorise JH's hotel expenses, 143–144
        on JH's influence, 101
    and Lord Kagan, 194
    and Lord Vaizey, 194
    and Lord Weidenfeld, 194
    attempts to have Policy Unit moved from Downing Street, 147–150, 221
    approaches Stanley Clinton-Davies, 196
    believes of royal descent, 187, 221
    behaviour at Trooping the Colour 1975, 214–215
    black period of, 212, 221, 222
    character, 105, 106, 108, 112, 134, 150
    children of, 203, 204, 205
    demands dismissal of Downing Street cook, 217
    describes Lord Goodman as 'evil', 202
    Downing Street in Perspective, 178
    elevation to the peerage, 211
    fears press smears, 111–112
    formation of 1974 Government, 124–125
    Harry Kissin's view of influence, 101
    in House of Lords, 199
    Inside Number 10, 146
    land deals scandal, 202–208, 211, 212
    obsession with press, 203, 208, 209–210
    on Common Market, 152, 155 157

on February 1974 general election, 111, 112
political judgement, 228
relationship with Eric Miller, 188, 195–196
Resignation Honours List, 193–198
treatment by press, 203–206
wants Robert Armstrong sacked, 120, 122
Wyndham Mews, 194, 195, 204, 205, 206, 207, 211, 213, 218, 220, 227
Williams, Philip, 76, 91
Williams, Shirley, 140, 154, 243, 263, 267, 300
Willoughy de Broke, David, 371, 372
Wilson, Albert, 4
Wilson, Derek, 57, 64
Wilson, Harold (HW), 48, 93, 94, 95, 96, 101–125, 126–146, 147–173, 174–192, 193–232, 233, 234, 235, 236, 237, 238, 239, 240, 241, 248, 250, 253, 254, 255, 266, 275, 276, 278, 279, 282, 296, 300, 325, 336, 264, 365, 366, 367
   and Bernard Donoughue (BD), 101–125, 126–146, 147–173, 174–192, 193–232
      BD first meeting with, 101
      BD offers to resign, 219–222
      BD's evaluation of, 229–232
      joins HW, 101–125
      offers BD headship of 'kitchen cabinet', 149
      opinion-polling, 101–104, 111, 112, 115, 125
      role in Roy Jenkins's appointment to Home Office, 118–119
   and Marcia Williams (MW),
      attempts to delay HW's resignation, 178, 179, 180, 181, 212
      behaviour at Harold Wilson's final lunch as Prime Minister, 190
      controls access to HW, 201
      described by MW as 'King Rat', 207
      diverts HW, 112, 147–150, 202–208, 209–219, 225
      explanation for influence over HW, 226–229
      influence over HW, 105, 106, 145, 152, 200–201
      insists HW not lunch with staff, 144, 216–217
      HW fearful of, 199, 200, 203, 227
      HW hides from, 200
      HW wonders if 'going round the bend', 217
      HW's desire to placate, 152
      MW alleges affair with, 226
      squabbles with HW, 147, 196, 197, 214, 215, 220
      threatens to destroy HW, 203, 207, 212, 227

      treatment of HW, 146, 190, 199–200, 203, 205, 206, 207, 212–213, 214, 216, 217
   behaviour described as 'utterly contemptible' by Robert Armstrong, 148
   believes Downing Street study bugged, 185
   'Black Sunday', 213
   boredom, 178, 179
   character, 101, 102, 105, 106–107, 112, 114, 115–116, 119, 134, 142, 144, 156–157, 185, 190–191, 204, 203, 224, 227, 229–232, 234, 235, 280
   Common Market, 150–157
      role in referendum, 155–157
      view of, 155–157
   demotes Tony Benn, 158
   dinner with The Queen, 186–187
   dislike of National Executive Committee, 179, 180
   dislike of Prime Minister's Question Time, 236
   drinking, 112, 148, 179, 181, 188, 200, 202, 210, 212, 221
   erosion of authority, 159
   final dinner with Cabinet, 186
   freedom of City of London, 180–181
   health, 178, 180, 191, 213, 214
   incomes policy crisis, 160–169, 190
   in House of Lords, 328, 329
   in retirement, 191, 256–257
   interest in Irish question, 136
   kitchen cabinet, 104–105, 106, 119, 134, 149, 231
      offers BD headship of 'kitchen cabinet', 149
   land deals scandal, 202–208, 211, 212
   last Government of, 147–177, 341
   leadership style, 115–116, 118–119, 150–152, 154, 157, 159
   Lord North Street, 106, 107, 108, 110, 112, 113, 117, 123, 124, 143, 182, 183, 196
   lunch at the Guildhall, 181
   meetings in lavatories, 153, 170, 180, 185
   mishandles ministerial reshuffle, 158–160
   1974 general elections, 103–117, 145–146, 336
      assumes loss of February 1974, 113, 114
      contribution to February victory, 115–116
      plans to leave Huyton after election count, 112–113, 114
      pleasure at October result, 146
   1974 Government of, 126–146
      leading figures in, 126–128

reasons for failure, 128
northern roots, 114
obsession with press, 112, 113, 114, 182 183, 203–211, 232
on South Africa, 253
paranoia, 148, 185–186
partnership with James Callaghan, 127
prediction of 1976 leadership election result, 189
resignation, 118, 119, 128–129, 150, 159, 170, 174, 175, 178–192
    Cabinet shock at, 183
    indecision about date of, 179, 180, 181
    Marcia Williams tries to persuade to postpone, 178, 179, 180, 181, 212
    Policy Unit staff shock at, 183–184
Resignation Honours List, 190, 193–199
    and Marcia Williams, 193–198
    claims not to know half of the people on Resignation Honours List, 197
speeches, 108–110, 137, 143–144, 155
support for sale of council houses, 174–175
suspension of collective responsibility, 151
view of Cabinet ministers, 154–155, 179
view of Education Department, 241
view of February 1974 election, 111, 113
view of Policy Unit's role, 117–118, 129
view of the law, 176

view of Tony Benn, 140, 141
Wilson, June, 24
Wilson, Mary, 106, 107, 112, 117, 120, 164, 180, 182, 190, 191, 226
Wilson, Richard, 361
Winterbottom, Walter, 89
winter of discontent, 115, 169, 236, 237, 245, 258–281
Wolfenden, Jeremy, 60
Worcester, Robert, 103, 104, 112, 115, 145
Worsthorne, Peregrine, 80
Wright, Patrick, 133, 190, 208, 212, 215
Wright, Vincent, 84
Writers' Club, 57, 58
    BD Presidency of, 57
Wyatt, Woodrow, 284
Wyndham Mews, 194, 195, 204, 205, 206, 207, 211, 213, 218, 220, 227

Yamey, Basil, 83
Yeats, W. B., 57, 64, 65, 298
Yeltsin, Boris, 322
Yes Minister, 131, 270, 297, 360
Yes Prime Minister, 131, 297
Young, Mr, 45

Zander, Michael, 68, 83
Zhivkov, President, 320, 321